A Second Identity

The author in 1967

A Second Identity

Essays on France and French History

RICHARD COBB

London
OXFORD UNIVERSITY PRESS
NEW YORK   TORONTO
1969

Oxford University Press, Ely House, London W. 1

GLASGOW NEW YORK TORONTO MELBOURNE WELLINGTON
CAPE TOWN SALISBURY IBADAN NAIROBI LUSAKA ADDIS ABABA
BOMBAY CALCUTTA MADRAS KARACHI LAHORE DACCA
KUALA LUMPUR SINGAPORE HONG KONG TOKYO

Printed in Great Britain
by W & J Mackay & Co Ltd, Chatham

To my friend
Louis Chevalier
historian of Paris
and of the Parisians

Prefatory Note

If there is any central theme running through this
collection of articles, essays, and reviews, it is one
that has been imposed by experience. The writing of
history is a form of involvement; in the Introduction
I have not attempted to inflict on my readers an incursion
into autobiography. My purpose has been to explain
my approach to French history in the light of my experiences
in France, as, in my case at least, the two experiences
are inseparable.

Contents

Illustrations

. . . là où sont les gens, les boutiques, les lumières, la vie, là se trouve le centre. Il disparaît là où tout s'éteint, où les façades se ferment ou se spécialisent, là où il n'y a plus rien à faire et à voir, là où on s'ennuie . . .

Qu'il s'agisse de la Saint-Louis des rois ou du 14 juillet des Républiques, l'amour est la manière parisienne de se réjouir collectivement . . .

Louis Chevalier, *Les Parisiens*

Introduction:
Experiences of an Anglo-French Historian

Many cases of specialization are no doubt the result of accident rather than of choice. The late Professor Willie Rose became a specialist in Polish history because, in the late summer of 1914, he was caught, with his wife, in Austrian Galicia, and spent the rest of the War under a liberal system of house arrest with the Polish squirearchical family with whom they had been staying. One of the most distinguished Germanists in Wales went on a return visit to his pen-friend in Kotbus in August 1939; when he reached Dresden, in early September, he discovered that the British Consul-General had already left—a habit of British Consuls in times of international crisis that must have caused many similar vocations; in this instance, as he was still under 15, he was able to attend the local *Gymnasium*, though he was not allowed to accept invitations from his school-mates, and to live with the family of his pen-friend for the next six years. He had to report to the police each morning; and when he was 18, on completing his exams, he was conscripted to work in a paper-mill. He met with much kindness from the start, and by 1945 even the local police sergeant was reminding him of how well he had been treated by himself and his staff. Later that year, after spending a month in Dresden, in search of a British liaison, hauling corpses by wheelbarrow to mass graves, he made his way to Berlin. By that time, he had forgotten much of his English, thought, dreamt, and counted in German. Of Sir Bernard Pares, his son, in a charming essay, writes that, having gone to Russia by chance, he at once became enamoured of the Russian people, and henceforth spent periods of years in the Empire. 'My father was not an English liberal looking at Russia, but a Russian liberal looking at Russia!' His was perhaps the most successful transference, the most complete acquisition of a second nationality, of a second identity, a crossing of the line that is the most important requisite for the English specialist of the history and culture of a foreign society. Perhaps, in all these cases, the need for *la seconde patrie* was already there; but which country it was to be was largely a matter of accident.

In my own case, I was saved from becoming a 'Namierite' by my headmaster and my housemaster. On receiving my telegram from Oxford, in December 1934, with the news that I had been awarded a Postmastership in History, they both wrote, in almost identical terms, to my mother to emphasize that 'Shrewsbury having done all it could for Richard, it would be better for Shrewsbury if Richard were not to return in January'. It could not have been put more politely, but it was clear that I was no longer wanted. They went on to suggest that a year abroad, before going up, might be the best way of filling this suddenly enforced hiatus in my education.

Neither my parents nor I had ever had any such thing in mind. My knowledge of French was poor; moreover, it was a language I much disliked as being identified with *Hernani* (each country has its *pompier national*, and just as ours is Shakespeare, France's National Bore is Hugo), the *Contes choisis* of the lachrymose, self-righteous François Coppée, and with the works of various nineteenth-century poetical bores. English public schools in the 1930s took every possible precaution to prevent any of their pupils from becoming Francophils. My own interests were with the Shropshire gents, the Duke of Newcastle, and the Member for Bridgnorth; apart from a Greek aunt by marriage, my known world made no allowance for any form of exoticism. My aunt displayed a signed photograph of King George of the Hellenes in a silver frame; I was told that he was more or less an Englishman, near enough at least not to make any difference. And my aunt's nephews had been sent to Eton, apparently at the King's expense. I was quite unenthusiastic at the prospect of being 'sent abroad' for nine or ten months.

My parents were equally ill prepared. Germany was ruled out from the start, not because of Hitler, but because some colleague of my father's in Khartoum had told him that German barons were bad and bold and dangerous company for blond young English public school boys. There remained France and Austria, both of which were chosen. My stay in Vienna, however, was brief; after six weeks working for the Quakers, I was arrested, beaten up in a succession of police stations, made to walk very fast through the streets, holding my trousers up, imprisoned for ten days as a Czech student—this went down in the prison register—and, once my identity had been established, accompanied to the Liechtenstein frontier by two men with green velvet tabs on their collars. It appeared that I had been in touch with Otto Bauer and Karl Seitz; my expulsion occurred a little over a year after the assassination of Dollfuss. As a result, I learnt scarcely any German and have retained to this day the strongest dislike for the so-called Austrian *Gemütlichkeit* and for people who dress up in fancy braces and leather shorts and white socks. I was also much flattered by having been taken for a Czech; the Czechoslovak Republic had considerable prestige in my eyes, as a democracy, a friend of the Soviet Union, and an un-neighbourly neighbour of Schuschnigg's and Horthy's unpleasant régimes.

This is to anticipate. My Austrian venture was a disaster. My French was not. Yet at first it showed all the signs of becoming one, for in Tunbridge Wells, as in the novels of Anthony Powell, there was a persistent belief, based entirely on myth but widely shared by the English middle classes, that the best French was spoken in Touraine. The effect of this was that several generations of English boys and girls were likely to be packed off to a *colonelle*, or a *commandante*, in Tours, an Army widow who took in *Le Figaro, La Croix, Ouest-Éclair,* and *Excelsior,* whose other reading was confined to elevating works emanating from Chez Mame,[1] and whose house, shuttered and curtained, draped, pinnacled, *oeil-de-boeuf*-ed, *faux Henri III,* the French school primer house for 12-year-olds— see under *maison* in the Dictionnaire Larousse—smelt of the meanness and stuffiness of the right-wing French provincial bourgeoisie of the west. No surer education for life-long Francophobia could have been contrived, and I have no doubt that it may have recruited many to the generation of Appeasement and to the Germanomania of a section of the English upper middle class between the Wars. For a few days, Tours (a place I had heard about from a friend at Shrewsbury) hung like a damp cloud over Tunbridge Wells Common, the Pantiles, Calverley Park, and the Toad Rock. It was a normal journey from the West Station (the Gateway to the Continent), via Newhaven, Dieppe, Rouen (a change here), and any route that would avoid Paris.

Tours was eliminated by further accident. My mother played bridge several times a week with the widow of an ICS official whose daughter, Philippa, had recently returned from France. She had spent a year with a family in Paris, had learnt excellent French, and

---

[1] The name of a celebrated publisher of religious books.

had come back to all intents and appearances much as she had left. What had been all right for Philippa was all right for me, so it was decided, over the green tables of the Ladies' Bridge Club on Mount Ephraim. I owe much to Ely Culbertson, even more to Philippa.

In January 1935 I was sent to Paris. The family I was to stay with lived in a large fifth-floor flat facing on to the boulevard Bonne-Nouvelle, almost opposite the Rex[1] and a little further on from *Le Matin* and its large blue and red pennant. From the balcony, one could see the Pâtisseries de la Lune, headed by a grinning moon in neon, a huge neon Celt smoking Celtique, with real smoke coming out of his mouth at each puff, the *agent à double barbe*[2] at the Porte Saint-Denis, and the prostitutes in thick clusters at the entries of the hotels in the rue de la Lune, as it climbed steeply inwards. My bedroom faced directly on to the Bains Neptuna, with an oblique shot to the Floréal,[3] on the other side of the boulevard. The flat shook regularly with the rumble of the *Métro*, the smell of which reached up from the near-by mouth of the Bonne-Nouvelle station. At night the ceiling flickered with the neon advertisements, and at week-ends one could hear snatches of *Tout va très bien, Madame la Marquise*, or *Allons les pompoms*, or *Mon frère est poitrinaire*, from the street bands who, with the *baratineurs*,[4] the flame-swallowers, the manacled strong men, then enjoyed *droit de pavé* on the immensely wide pavement just below the flat. One could not have hoped for more Parisian a setting; the press, the theatre, prostitution, particularly in its lower échelons, were within yards, food, pleasure, the *loterie*, the shooting booths within sight, the Halles, the Crédit Lyonnais, the Musée Grévin within ten minutes' walk. This had been the very centre of traditional Paris any time from the eighteenth century to the present day, though since 1914 the centre had tended to move away westwards, towards the Madeleine and the boulevard des Italiens. Below me walked the *badaud*,[5] the *petit bourgeois* from the XIIme, the typists and the shop-girls from the

---

[1] The Rex is a monster cinema constructed in the 1930s.

[2] The double-bearded policeman was one of the monuments of the Paris scene in the 1920s and 1930s.

[3] The name of a café on the boulevard Bonne-Nouvelle.

[4] From *baratin*, Parisian slang for talk. A *baratineur* is a street vendor who uses his eloquence to vaunt the merits of a particular product. The nearest equivalent would be the Brooklyn expression, a 'spieler'.

Hence the Paris saying: 'Pour avoir la fille, qui est si jolie, c'est à la maman qu'il faut faire du baratin.'

[5] An onlooker, the personification of the Paris spirit of inquisitiveness.

eastern and northern suburbs, and at week-ends *les gars de Ménilmontant*, those of Belleville and Aubervilliers. A quarter that seldom slept, that was ceasing to be residential (most of the doors on our staircase bore the plates of *dentistes américains* and of furriers with Polish names). The steppe of the quartier des Invalides and the shuttered silence of the boulevard Malesherbes might have belonged to another continent. I owe to Philippa the fact that, all my life, I have been a *boulevardier*[1]—a term that can only apply to the Right Bank—and that so many of my axes of pleasure and of observation have run from Richelieu-Drouot to Strasbourg Saint-Denis, the home line, especially above ground.

The family consisted of a widow, Madame Thullier, and her two sons, the elder a law student of 21, the younger, at 18, just beginning medicine (P.C.B.). The father had been killed at Gallipoli. The maternal grandfather, M. Feuillas, had been a well-to-do stockbroker and private banker who had invested in house property. Boulevard Bonne-Nouvelle had been his city base, but he had also bought a villa in Saint-Mandé—appartment in the X*me*, villa in the still fashionable western fringe of the Bois de Vincennes: this was very much the pattern of Second Empire and early Third Republic middle-class location; there was also a house by the Seine at Samois, and scattered property in the Seine-et-Marne. Madame Thullier owned the whole block at No. 26. Her sons, though totally indifferent to her attempts to maintain some sort of order at table or to preserve her Chinese screens from knife-throwing, deferred to her in all financial matters; the elder married, in his early 30s, the daughter of a leading family of the Paris *notariat*, after protracted negotiations between his mother and the girl's grandmother, and once he was fully established as a *commissaire-priseur*[2] at the Hôtel Drouot. During my stay, there was a succession of mistresses: Denise, Micheline, Gaby, Janine—mostly typists or *arpètes*,[3] who were received friendlily by Madame Thullier, in the knowledge that her son would not be likely to marry any of them; *en cas d'accident, on s'arrangerait*. There was also the *122* for special occasions. The medical student took out the prostitutes of the Café Harcourt, near the Faculty.

[1] A person who spends his evenings walking along the *grand boulevards*. A member of a declining species.
[2] Auctioneer.
[3] *Arpète:* Parisian slang for a shop-girl.

5

Three days after my arrival, the boys gave a *surprise-party*. It was a surprise to me, for, having dragged me out of bed, they took me to the bathroom, where a nude girl was being cleaned up. They explained to me that she was an admiral's daughter and that her proper element was thus *la flotte*.[1] The fact that an admiral's daughter could end up naked at a party shocked me beyond words, and for a few days I wanted to return to Tunbridge Wells. The feeling did not last, however. Excellent food (eating has, ever since, been one of the greatest joys of my existence, especially when combined with conversation, with reading *Le Monde*, or with eavesdropping) and plentiful wine helped a great deal. For the first time in my life, I found myself listening to French with pleasure, especially during meals, at which there were generally guests, including an amazingly fat barrister, Madame Thullier's brother-in-law. These people enjoyed talking.

The two boys had taken part with gusto in the *6 février* of the previous year, and claimed to have burnt a bus, which seemed in character. But they were not committed politically; what they liked most was a chance to get at the police or the *gardes mobiles*.[2] In 1939, the elder joined the *corps francs*[3] and won the *croix de guerre* in the Forêt de Warndt. In 1940, the younger remained with his hospital to look after the wounded; he was the only doctor to do so. After the War, with the formation of the R.P.F., the auctioneer became a *conseiller municipal* for an elegant western suburb. The doctor, after years in Indo-China and a succession of mistresses that included an Annamite, was eventually induced to settle down; his mother bought him a flat and a practice in the boulevard Malesherbes, and also provided him with a wife, a vague cousin from the Périgord, the 19-year-old daughter of an Inspector of Forests. Madame Thullier explained to me on this occasion that she was *sans le sou et un peu conne, mais elle lui fera des enfants*. She had been worried about the current mistress, an actress, who had been in occupation for several years.

Both sons spent part of the week-end playing football with the Stade Français (they had previously been educated at the École des Roches, the nearest French equivalent to an English public school). Sport would be followed by horse-play of various kinds:

---

[1] The Fleet; also a slang word for water.
[2] The riot police of the 1930s.
[3] French commando units.

6

knives on to silk screens, electric light bulbs down the well of the staircase at 3 a.m., attempting to race the Blue Train on the stretch through Villeneuve-Saint-Georges in their mother's enormous black Panhard-Levassor, throwing fish and salver over the balcony on Fridays to express their anti-clericalism, driving straight at traffic policemen, and fighting with working-class youths from the northern suburbs. They were good-humoured, anarchical, wild, joyful, and resourceful. They enjoyed dressing up and creating a public scandal. They got on very well indeed with girls, especially shop-girls, and they did not boast of their exploits in their mother's presence, nor, indeed, out of it. They had some very nice friends, most of them rich, and as wild as themselves.

My life in France might be divided up into a series of street itineraries, whether in Paris, in Lyon, or in Marseille. My first year in Paris was: boulevard Bonne-Nouvelle, cross, rue d'Aboukir, rue Réaumur, cross, rue du Louvre, place Saint-Germain-l'Auxerrois, quai du Louvre, cross, pont des Arts, quai Conti, Bibliothèque Mazarine (destination), and back, four times a day. My route and my hours were so regular that, for eight months, twice a day always at the same spot, three-quarters of the way down the rue d'Aboukir, I met a sad-faced man coming the other way; we never spoke, but we always nodded. I felt that I fitted into a routine and, by doing so, belonged to a community. From 1936 to 1939, the itinerary was quite different: rue Saint-André-des-Arts, rue Dauphine, Pont-Neuf, the *quais* place de l'Hôtel-de-Ville, under the nose of Étienne Marcel; rue Lobau, rue des Archives (right side), rue des Francs-Bourgeois, Archives Nationales (destination), returning via the pont au Change, the quai aux Fleurs, boulevard du Palais, pont Saint-Michel, place Saint-André-des-Arts. This itinerary is marked with the experience of the Front Populaire, of Weidmann, of *l'Expo*, of the Spanish Civil War, and Munich. After the War, the itinerary went: rue de Tournon, rue de Seine, place Jacques-Callot, rue Guénégaud, with a grateful glance each morning at the charming stone nymph, a smiling fifteen-year-old, eighteenth-century country girl, over the side entrance of the Monnaie, Pont-Neuf, and as before, or with an alternative route quai de l'Horloge, to look at the china. There were, of course, variations to allow for the B.N. (via the Palais-Royal), the A.P.P.,[1] quai des Orfèvres, the

[1] Archives de la Préfecture de Police, in the building of the Police Judiciaire, 36 quai des Orfèvres.

A.D. Seine,[1] via the rue Saint-Louis-en-Ile, Vincennes (by *métro*), and the Bibliothèque Victor-Cousin, over the Sorbonne Library. For several years I took the *métro* at Mabillon at 7.50 a.m. every morning, getting into the middle carriage next to the *Ières*, recognizing the same people—at this hour of the morning, readers of *Le Parisien libéré, L'Aurore*, and *L'Humanité*—and getting out at Duroc, leaving by the exit on the far side of the boulevard des Invalides, near the Enfants-Trouvés, for the avenue de Breteuil and the Centre des Télécommunications. For a brief and unpleasant period I had to take the 7.55 a.m. from the Gare du Nord for Enghien-les-Bains, to teach at the Pensionnat Bigot. In Lyon, place de la Croix-Rousse, a detour by the Gros Caillou (that I had succeeded in climbing, a test that admitted me as a *croix-roussien d'honneur*, after a dozen *pots* of beaujolais), a striding descent down the montée de la Grande Côte, the *mairie du Ier arrondissement* (with steps between two bored black lions looking *louis-philippard*), rue Bouteille, quai Saint-Vincent, passerelle Saint-Vincent, place Saint-Paul, and up and up montée des Carmes Déchaussés, chemin de Montauban, Archives du Rhône (destination). In Marseille: start at the rue des Couteliers, then quai des Belges, the lower end of the Canebière, cross opposite the sentry outside the Marine Nationale, place de la Bourse, rue Saint-Ferréol, place de la Préfecture (monument to Alexander and Barthou), rue Saint-Sébastien, Archives des Bouches-du-Rhône (destination), an itinerary that could be varied by taking the ferry across the Vieux-Port to Endoum.

The rigid adherence to a daily itinerary gave me a sense of purpose, a feeling of security (there could be no great catastrophe, no war, as long as I stuck on course), and, above all, the sensation that I was an element in the hourly heart-beat of a great city, a unit in the flux and re-flux so admirably described in *Le 6 Octobre* and in Louis Chevalier's brilliantly imaginative *Les Parisiens*. I was quick to establish similar itineraries in Rouen, le Havre, Dieppe, Lille, Amiens, or, for that matter, anywhere I spent a few days on local research. It is by following fixed routes, like a bus, that one acquires the feeling of a town, perceives the passage of the hours and of the seasons, the shifting of the light, and the regular movement of the crowds. As long as the *lycées* disgorge their noisy

[1] Archives Départementales de la Seine, quai Henri IV.

hordes, à heure fixe, as long as the cheminots[1] or the employés de la Préfecture pour out at midday, there can be no disaster, no cataclysm, no dreaded lapse back into violence and killing, no corpses left lying in the street. In Lyon, in summer, I swam, from 12.10 p.m. to 1 p.m., at the Club des Nageurs Lyonnais (C.N.L.), below the pont de la Feuillée. Three girls—always the same—were there each day, getting brown on the rafts in the Saône. They smiled at me, but we never spoke.

The work itinerary could be further improved upon by a leisure one, varying day by day, but following a weekly schedule: lunch in the same restaurant with its regular, and therefore reassuring, clientele of painters and stone-masons in their white hats and white smocks, minor civil servants, employés de la mairie, the parfumeuse from across the road. For dinner, a greater variety, and with more time to listen and to watch, while reading the chronique judiciaire of Le Monde or Le Progrès. At week-ends a sense of involvement could be further enhanced by a trip up the Saône, by the Blue Train to L'Ile-Barbe, or by the ficelle[2] to Saint-Just, thence to Vaugneray, in the Monts du Lyonnais, in a Wild West sort of train: both places to which the Lyonnais would flock in great numbers, en famille, in couples, or as solitary fishermen. It was Simenon country, like the riverside guinguettes of the Marne; at least, it was frequented by Simenon-type people, and regularly, for Maigret never seems to have come here. The same people came each week-end, and in this way relations were established.

With two hills—the red and the black—the long peninsular entre Rhône et Saône, two rivers, twenty bridges, a wonderland of passage-ways, three ficelles, a multitude of tiny squares, perched perilously on some diminutive pocket handkerchief of level ground, Lyon is an endless, inexhaustible invitation to exploration, discovery, and wonderment. In the Croix-Rousse, the long blind windows in peeling ochre façades are those of the canuts[3] and of the old prints, images d'Épinal, of the 1830s, with the cotton-wool puffs of the cannons of repression. A sense of joy at just being there, in the amazing up-and-down, stepped city, climbing up and up between high, blank, black walls, huge, dark, closed green doorways, yellowing walls surmounted by Greek pots and greenery. As

[1] Railway workers, employees of the SNCF.
[2] Funicular.
[3] Silk-workers of the Croix-Rousse.

9

Henri Béraud looks down on the Terreaux from the top of the montée de la Grande Côte, down on the pont de la Boucle, on a dull November day, with the gulls swirling, he exclaims: 'La ville bleue! Ma ville!' Mine too, a beloved place, with friendliness and fraternity *Au Pot des Gônes*,[1] near the Caillou, or *Au Club des Grognards de la Boucle*, where they played bowls.

One could also stay put in Paris; rather than spend a few days in Joinville-le-Pont, it was more adventurous to cross the river and spend a fortnight in an hotel on the canal Saint-Martin, or in the Batignolles, or off the Ternes, to create a new routine and to observe unfamiliar groups of *habitués*. The *Métro*, curving towards Bolivar and the Buttes-Chaumont, the *ligne 96*, clambering laboriously up the rue de Ménilmontant and the rue du Télégraphe, the *ligne 75*, heading through the button wholesale depots of the Marais, are the most worthwhile *invitations au voyage*; there is no better observation post of the changing world unrolling backwards, than that of the relaxed, leaning comfort of the *plateforme d'autobus*, squeezed between an *agent* and a large man with a drooping cigarette. It is a good platform too for the sharp, North-Parisian wit of the *receveur*, a calling that produces some of the best conversation to be heard in the XX*me*. There will be little to be heard, nothing to be observed, once the old buses are gone, to be replaced by the closed coffin-like vehicle with automatic doors, with a seated *receveur*, behind glass, like a bureaucrat. If, to emulate Jean Galtier-Boissière, one were to write the recollections of a *vieux Parisien*, or to follow in the steps of Aragon, through the Louis-Philippe arcades of the VIII*me* and the IX*me*, one would be tempted to entitle the book: *Vu d'une plateforme d'autobus*.

In February 1935, sitting at the edge of a concrete-lined lake in the Bois de Vincennes, with *Boule de Suif*, I suddenly realized that for the previous two hours I had been enjoying reading French. It was no longer a burden and had become a pleasure, which, from then onwards, grew and grew, to include *L'Oeuvre* and *Le Canard*, and an increasing range of novels. After about a month in Paris, wandering on the boulevard Montmartre, I met my first French friend, Maurice, at the time an unemployed cinema hairdresser from the Épinay studios. We had both been enjoying an argument that had arisen from an accident, in which the car of Mlle Malvy, the

[1] *Gône*, Lyon slang for child.

Minister's daughter, had been damaged by an ancient Renault driven by a drunken *marchand de bestiaux*, who had both the crowd and numbers on his side; there were four red-faced colleagues with him in the *gambarde*.[1] After the free entertainment, we went to a café. Maurice was a lead-in to the dreaded horrors of military service; he had succeeded in getting himself discharged from the artillery on medical grounds, by distending his stomach on seven litres of lemonade a day—worth it at the price. He lived in a horrible little room behind the Gare de l'Est, possibly the most melancholy quarter of Paris; the floor was covered with back numbers of *Paris-Turf*. He was a change from the Thullier brothers and we found that we had a lot to say to each other. I never ceased to marvel at his total rejection of all authority. After that, we used to meet once or twice a week and I would offer him a meal in a Greek restaurant in the rue de la Harpe.

About the same time—it was the anniversary of the *12 février*[2]— I was sitting in the park of Saint-Cloud when a man in a cap came up to me. 'Lis ça, camarade', he said, and left me with *L'Humanité*. In April I went for a holiday in Rouen by myself. One day on the quai Victor, a small group of dockers, carrying red flags, came past, heading for the Bourse du Travail; I followed them and attended their meeting in the courtyard. 'Le patron ne veut rien faire pour nous', said their leader. A red-faced docker, who had drunk a lot of calvados, held me by the lapel and told me how it was to live, in Sotteville or le Grand-Quévilly, on 100 francs a week with a wife and three children. I returned to the rue Beauvoisine, after having had a row with a taxi-driver; I shouted at him, called him names. I was over the barrier, could think in French.

My first view of the Latin Quarter was a January day, with the long, clipped avenues of the Luxembourg disappearing in a cold fog. Lower down, opposite the medical school, a group of young men wearing floppy berets and carrying walking sticks with sharp, pointed metal ends, were chanting: 'La France aux Français, à bas les métèques.' In the following March, the Austrian dictator, Kurt Schuschnigg, came on an official visit to France; it was rumoured

[1] An old car.

[2] 12 February 1934. This was the republican counter-demonstration that followed the attempted fascist *putsch* of 6 February. Organized by the Radical, Socialist, and Communist parties, by the trade unions and the Ligue des Droits de l'Homme, it might be seen as the origin of Grand Alliance of the Front Populaire of 1936.

that he would arrive at the Gare de l'Est—his carriage was in fact taken off at Noisy-le-Sec—and there was an immense demonstration, the red banners only just visible in the gloom, from the boulevard Magenta to the huge neo-Gothic church. There was a single whistle blast, then the sound of galloping horses, as the dark-blue, black-helmeted *gardes mobiles* rode into the crowd, hitting out with their long batons; the first three waves were followed by fifty or more *paniers à salade*, long dark charabancs of 1920 vintage, into which bleeding demonstrators of all ages and both sexes were literally hurled. After fifteen minutes, the square was quiet and littered with slogans and banners.

It was not difficult to know which side one was on in the France of 1935; and it was easier still in 1936. But I was, above all, appalled by the readiness with which violence was accepted by the Thullier brothers and by most of their friends. They told me that the *passage à tabac*[1] was an old French institution; they did not like the police, but they thought it quite natural that anyone who fell into their hands should have a preliminary beating up. The father of one of their friends horrified me, at the time of Munich, by saying to me, in the most cheerful manner, as if it were a matter of going on a cross-country run: 'Eh bien! Monsieur Cobb, vous allez bientôt prendre votre fusil!' There did not seem much point explaining to him that this was the very last thing that I wanted to do. I was—and still am—completely puzzled by the reckless readiness of the French to get themselves killed, and equally shocked by their apparent readiness to kill. Fortunately there was Maurice, who had no intention of doing either, and I used to console myself with the thought that there were probably many more like him. In the summer of 1940, he deserted from his unit with a like-minded Parisian, held up a farm to obtain civilian clothes, hitched a lift from a German civilian driving a Darmstadt furniture van; together, they drove eastwards, avoiding the main roads, stopping in village and *bourg*, loading up the contents of deserted houses: furniture, bedding, books, food, silver, wine, typewriters, tyres, *allez oup! et en route!* parting, near Reims: *Gute Reise! Bon voyage et bon retour!* Maurice headed for Paris, serving for a time as a guide to *Wehrmacht* N.C.O.s: *Viele Schweinerei.*

In the Bibliothèque Mazarine, seated facing outwards, on to the

[1] A preliminary beating-up.

back of Condorcet, I discovered first Mathiez, then Jaurès. What appealed to me most in the former was his utter intransigence, his polemical vigour, his capacity to deride, his insistence on taking sides. Mathiez was exciting, because he was quite unlike any other historian I had previously read, he was always uncovering plots, using the Archives like a detective. Robespierre was pure, uncompromising, he loved the common people. By the summer of 1935, I was a convinced *robespierriste*; I was not, however, a Unitarian, for I took in Saint-Just and Couthon as well. My excuse was that I was not yet 18. I shed most of Robespierre on resuming research in the mid-40s; there is no historical personage I now find more repellent, save possibly Saint-Just.

Jaurès had a different and, I like to think, more lasting appeal. I was fired by his rolling eloquence, moved by his immense compassion and generosity. Jaurès was a popular historian, with a wide range of forgiveness; he did not condemn the counter-revolutionary out of hand, but tried to understand him, he did not mock the priesthood, nor denounce deluded women for their 'superstition', he did not think that any of the revolutionary leaders held a monopoly of virtue. He was a warm man with a good heart; he understood poverty.

In 1937, I visited Georges Lefebvre, at his home in Boulogne (avenue Jean-Jaurès) and attended his lectures on the Revolutionary Government in an overcrowded and wildly enthusiastic Sorbonne. There was a total sense of identity between the stiff, red-faced Northerner, extraordinarily effective in his rendering of Marat or of Saint-Just, and an audience that was predominantly Front Populaire. The same year, I was received, Hôtel Saint-James & Albany, by General Herlaut, who had commanded a tank division at Versailles at the time of the 6 *février* and was then in command of the Rouen military division; with his *képi à feuilles de chêne*[1] and a pair of white gloves on a marble table beside him, he called me 'jeune homme', and, after a long tirade against Mussolini and Hitler, ended our interview with the words: 'Vous verrez, jeune homme, tout cela finira dans la boue et dans le sang.' I needed no convincing of that, living as I did with fear, every day, almost every hour.

On going down in June 1938, I returned to Paris and began what is now a 30 years' friendship with the Archives Nationales, one of the most beautiful buildings in Europe and a secure refuge from

[1] A French general's rank is indicated by the oak leaves that fringe his cap.

fear. Violence, one felt, could never lap into that elegant, semi-oblong courtyard. War and revolution must stay outside. The A.N. remained open from 1939 to 1944; and, after 1940, was regularly attended by a commission of *Wehrmacht* officers classifying the documents concerning the confiscated estates of French Huguenots who, in virtue of the Edict of Potsdam, had entered the Prussian service; nearly all the officers concerned had French names. Theirs must have been the most agreeable War job enjoyed by any Army.

Georges Lefebvre had suggested that I choose as a research subject one of the *hébertiste*[1] leaders, François-Nicolas Vincent, the general secretary of the Ministry of War in the year II. General Herlaut and Georges Javogues gave me invaluable advice as to documentary material. I made one or two interesting discoveries, and espoused, with passion, the strident quarrels of my subject, one of the most violent, most foolish, most sanguinary, and most hysterical of the revolutionary leaders. On returning to England, at the outbreak of war, I wrote up my research. The result was a disaster; I fell into all the usual traps awaiting the biographer, re-writing the whole history of the Revolution around a man who was at best a secondary figure, and bringing down the curtain with his rather well-deserved death. I made claims for his participation in most of the *journées* on the flimsiest of evidence, throwing at my examiners all my material, much of it trifling or irrelevant, subjecting them furthermore to a language barely recognizable as English. When I returned to research in October 1946, I decided to start afresh. Twenty years later, at the end of a lecture that I had been giving at the University of Chicago, I was approached by an elderly lady who handed me a packet containing my abortive excursion into the history of *hébertisme*, which I had sent to Louis Gottschalk in 1940.

When I had finally readjusted to civilian life, I decided to return to research. It was not that I felt any great enthusiasm at the time for academic work (the Army had offered me a varied range of employments, nearly all of which I had enjoyed); but I needed an excuse in my own mind to stay permanently in Paris, and I could not think of a better one. I had seen Georges Lefebvre again in 1944 and 1945, during leaves in Paris, and in 1946 met Pierre Caron. I decided to research on *hébertisme*. In 1947, I was introduced to Albert Soboul, who was then similarly engaged. After a few months

[1] One of the political groups of the year II.

working parallel and following each other, not without some mistrust, through the same boxes, we both independently came to the conclusion that *hébertisme* was a non-starter. But, while in its pursuit, we had each stumbled on something else: Soboul, on the Sections[1] and the *sectionnaires*,[2] myself on the Paris Revolutionary Army, and thence to some fifty others, and the *problème des subsistances*.[3] In both instances, our eventual choice of subjects had been largely dictated to us by the nature of our documentary material; Soboul had gone to the *fonds sectionnaires* in search of *hébertisme* as a popular party, and he had discovered an independent popular movement that owed little or nothing to *hébertisme*. I had been after *hébertistes* rather than after *hébertisme*—a line of division that has no doubt always distinguished me from Soboul; I had found few, but I had in the process stumbled on hundreds of *révolutionnaires*,[4] ultras of a less exalted, less self-conscious, more spontaneous kind.

Once he had found his subject, Soboul worked with speed and determination, to a careful plan and with a vigorous refusal to allow himself to be led down any side channels. My own method—this is perhaps not the right word—was very different. I was in no hurry—I was not aiming at any particular career in England; more and more I enjoyed the excitement of research and the acquisition of material, often on quite peripheral subjects, as ends in themselves. I allowed myself to be deflected down unexpected channels, by the chance discovery of a bulky *dossier*—it might be the love letters of a *guillotiné*, or intercepted correspondence from London, or the account-books and samples of a commercial traveller in cotton, or the fate of the English colony in Paris, or eyewitness accounts of the September Massacres or of one of the *journées*. I paused here and there, to write an article, to publish a *glane*, on this or that. And as my research took me to about forty Departments, and especially to Norman ones, the Nord, the Seine-et-Oise, the Oise, the Seine-et-Marne, and the Rhône (there was plenty of material in all these for me, but I also liked being there, so I kept

---

[1] Paris was divided into forty-eight Sections. Originally electoral wards, in 1793 they became the principal unit of popular militancy and remained an effective force until the spring of 1794.

[2] Members of the Sections, hence *sans-culottes*.

[3] This word is difficult to translate; it means mainly the problem of provisioning of the urban markets.

[4] I use this word in the particular sense of 'member of a revolutionary army'.

on returning for more) I likewise multiplied excursions into provincial history. It was hard to put down resolutely the register of a municipality at a date in 1794; I wanted to know what followed; inevitably I dribbled over into 1795—this was first out of curiosity, but later, when I realized what a gold mine the year III could be on the year II, I did so systematically. Nor was this a stopping point. Much of my material came from individual *dossiers* of officers, in the Archives administratives de la Guerre; but these did not stop in 1794, some went on to 1820, to 1830, a few to 1840, and with them I went on too. I was interested in individuals rather than groups; and when I could pin down one of them, I naturally wanted to follow him through, to pension and grave, to letters from his widow or children, as the paper, the words on the top, and the handwriting changed, as well as the names and titles of Ministers of War. I was lucky, in this respect, to have had to spend so much time on Army personnel, for soldiers, in France, leave more traces than civilians, and their widows have to be paid. They also tend to live longer; or so it appeared to me.

I researched and wrote for my own enjoyment, taking a particular pleasure in spreading my merchandise over as many provinces as possible. I liked *Annales de Normandie, La Revue du Nord*, and *Cahiers d'Histoire* best, because I was happy in Rouen, le Havre and Dieppe, Lille and Lyon; but it gave me particular satisfaction to publish in small reviews like *Présence Ardennaise*; and I preferred *Mémoires: Paris et Île-de-France* to a national review, because they represented the history of Paris and the Paris region. And the great strength of French historical research has always been the survival of local reviews. I would have been shocked if anyone had suggested that I should be paid for doing what I enjoyed doing. Nor would I have enjoyed doing it so much, if I had been paid for it. Research was a luxury in which I was able to indulge, by earning money by teaching English to telecommunications engineers, Agro[1] students, and Air France hostesses (this was enjoyable too). I bought my time at the Archives and so valued it more. My brief marriage to a French girl employed by the SNCF facilitated research in local records by the yearly issue of a free ticket, *Ière classe*, usable anywhere on the French internal network. And, if the worst came to the worst, my mother would advance me the odd £50. My approach to historical research was that of a

[1] Institut National Agronomique.

dilettante. I have never understood history other than in terms of human relationships; and I have attempted to judge individuals in their own terms and from what they say about themselves, in their own language.

Most interesting of all, to me, is the individual unrelated to any group, the man, the girl, or the old woman alone in the city, the person who eats alone, though in company, who lives in a furnished room, who receives no mail, who has no visible occupation, and who spends much time wandering the streets. For, apart from the everlasting problem of violence, the principal one that faces a historian like myself is that of loneliness, especially loneliness in the urban context. Hence my inveterate taste for the *chronique judiciaire* of *Le Monde* and, in its day, of *Libération* (the realm of the marvellous, the generous Madeleine Jacob, the warmest of popular historians, the most at home of any in *la correctionelle*). Gaby, from Pézenas has committed suicide in a *chambre de bonne* in the XVme; the body of Micheline, scantily clad in black underwear, her throat slit, has been discovered in the bedroom of an *hôtel de passe*, rue des Acacias. Madeleine, a Lyonnaise, in Paris only for the previous three months, has been shot dead, coming out of a Cours Pigier. Marcelle has been found stabbed to death, in the Bois de Boulogne; she was from la Ferté-Bernard. And so on. The *concierge*, plied by reporters, can only say: 'Ce fut une jeune fille tranquille, une vraie jeune fille, je ne lui connaissais aucune liaison, elle ne recevait point de visites'. The parents, back home, are bewildered. Sooner or later, the *dossier* is closed. But not for the historian. What road, thus terminating in violence, has been followed by the daughter of a *cheminot* from Saint-Germain-des-Fossés? Into what fearful trap has the lonely provincial girl stumbled? For many years, my favourite historians have been the late Pierre Bénard and Madeleine Jacob (to whom I am further indebted for much information concerning Marie Besnard (see pp. 287–95, below), all of whose trials she attended).

For myself, history has never been an intellectual debate. This may be due in part to my own insufficiencies, for I am no debater; but also I have never felt the need of it. For historians should not 'intellectualize' about people often less sophisticated than themselves, and about societies less complicated than those in which we live. In history, intellectual debate can so often be a cover for over-simplification, lack of experience, insufficient culture, lack of involvement and of sympathy, and the impetus to compare and to generalize in cases where comparisons and generalizations are either irrelevant or positively misleading. Why, one wonders, when reading certain sections of *Past and Present*, why do historians spend so much time arguing, imposing definitions, proposing 'models', when they could be getting on with their research?

I have, then, worked on French history because I like being in France and have now reached the second generation of my French friends. To live in France is to live double, every moment counts, the light of the sky of the Île-de-France is unique and a source of joy, there is joy too in a small rectangle of sunshine at the top of a tall, greying, leprous building, the colour of Utrillo, and in the smell of chestnuts that brings the promise of autumn, *la Rentrée*, and the beloved repetition of the Paris year. There is joy in speaking French, and in listening to women, children, Louis Jouvet, and Michel Simon speaking it. Paris is the abode of love, as well as of violence; if, as Louis Chevalier reminds us, the Paris street *sent le poudre*, it is only sometimes, whereas love is there all the time, in a cat arching its back in the sun, and in the eyes of *la belle boulangère* in her white apron. To speak and to write in French is to acquire a second personality and to express oneself not only in another gear, but in a manner other than in one's first. I do not say the same things in French as I do in English, because I am not the same person. For nine years I dispensed with my initial nationality almost entirely, and without any great feeling of deprivation.

My sense of involvement has been further enlarged by the experience of events over a long period, by personal contacts, and by random reading, over the years, of such populist and regionalist novelists as Eugène Dabit (the Paris suburbs), Louis Guilloux (Saint-Brieuc), Maxence van der Meersch (Roubaix), Marc Bernard (Nîmes), Henri Béraud (Lyon), René Fallet (Villeneuve-Saint-Georges), Raymond Queneau[1] (Le Havre, the northern

[1] THE WRITING GAME

Sir,—Your reviewer (May 25), in his excellent article on Raymond Queneau, has illustrated some of the techniques of an author who is often difficult and has suggested some clues to his mathematical and philosophical riddles. But Queneau is not just a writer, who indulged in intellectual gymnastics, and it would not be quite fair to compare him, even in his most intractable moods, either to Valéry or to Sartre. For he is not deliberately perverse, he is never a fraud, he is more than just clever, and he does not write about sick or try to make his readers it.

suburbs of Paris, Paris itself), Hervé Bazin (the Craonnais), René Lefèvre (Paris), Julien Blanc (mostly *maisons de redressement* and prisons), Panaït Istrati, and Blaise Cendrars (especially on the subject of Marseille.) History is a cultural subject that cannot be disassociated from literature and language. And both resist the attempts of syllabus-merchants to impose upon each the iron frame of periodicity. A great deal of Paris eighteenth-century history, of Lyon nineteenth-century history can be walked, seen,

---

Loin de Rueil is quite the funniest novel in the French language; *Exercices de Style* is an encyclopedia of verbal observation. Queneau is as familiar with the 27 as with the 21, with the 24 as with the 28—all his lines begin at Saint-Lazare—and the *plateforme d'autobus*—yet another of those amiable, leisurely, lounging institutions now in the process of suppression by the technocrats—is as good a vantage point as *le zinc*—and better than the *Métro*, too crowded for conversation, too noisy for eavesdropping—for the social novelist; and this is what Queneau is, in the happiest populist tradition. For if his extraordinary verbal inventiveness and his joy in rendering speech owe much to a childhood spent in Le Havre, during the 1914–18 War, listening—on the tram from school he has certainly made the most of the *transports en commun!*—to English soldiers mauling French, and Havrais girls English, his great qualities as a novelist are his joyful humour, his innocence, his compassion and his enjoyment of un-elevated company. Much of his dialogue goes—and has been heard—in the sort of restaurant—*restaurant des chauffeurs*, &c.—in which it was possible, in the 1940s or 1950s, still to get a good *boeuf gros sel*—and which were likely to be found, on small squares, off the rue de Vaugirard, in the XV*me*. They are too *restaurants d'habitués*—with the painters and builders in their white coats and the horse slaughterers in their leather jackets. And the conversation is of a kind enjoyed by those who meet daily and who share their allusive jokes. (This is what is so reassuring about such places.) The creator of *Zazie* is very close to his model; and there are sharp, observant and rather naughty children in many of his novels. Like the sturdy characters who eat in the *restaurant des chauffeurs*, and like Zazie, Queneau shakes with fits of uncontrollable laughter.

Finally, unlike so many French novelists, whose approach to Paris has been via the Gare du Lyon or Austerlitz—the first view of the Promised Land of so many *Normaliens*, including the creator of Jerphanion—his first contact with the Capital was via the Cour de Rome and the rue du Havre. Sartre found le Havre intolerable—the Havrais, no doubt, were just not clever enough, worse, they may even have seemed happy; Queneau writes of the place with the same warmth as Béraud wrote of a childhood in les Terreaux, between Rhône and Saône, or poor Maxence van der Meersch of Roubaix, its mills, its canal and the long, long rue de Lannoy, during the First World War or under the Front Populaire. Many of his characters too trail the Seine Maritime behind them, when in Paris or *banlieue Saint-Lazare*. He has come in the best way. Queneau, even in the heart of N.R.F., is still a provincial, like Louis Guilloux or Hervé Bazin. This too is part of his appeal, especially to the English, for nothing could be more reassuring than Le Havre.   RICHARD COBB
                                                                      Balliol College, Oxford.

[Published in the *Times Literary Supplement*, 1 June 1967.]

and above all heard, in small restaurants, on the platform at the back of a bus, in cafés, or on the park bench. I have at times been so much aware of this that, in order to improve my chances as an investigator of the past and to cast deeper roots in France, I have been tempted to apply for naturalization. Fortunately, I have been deterred on each occasion by the slowly grinding mills of French bureaucracy, as well as by the thought that I would no more belong in a French institutional framework than in an English one. I have tried to have it both ways: to increase my sense of involvement, and to preserve my status of Lone Wolf. It has not always worked very well. But after the *13 mai*, French naturalization lost all its attraction.

Research in revolutionary, or in any other, history, can never be a full-time occupation; nor, indeed, should it be. Even the Archives are not entirely a safe refuge, and the historian, however much he may try, cannot entirely escape from the present. Time and place will affect him, and their influence will inevitably increase with the years, as experience and memory add further layers to the sense of involvement. 1935, however it looks now, was dominated at the time by the constant harping back to the *6* and *12 février*, while the *affaire Stavisky* was given a further lease of death by the endless speculation regarding the disappearance of the *conseiller* Prince, whose body had been found along the railway line near Dijon, at a spot evocatively called *la combe aux fées*. 1935 was then as much *l'année Prince*, as it was that of M. Flandin or of *Madame la Marquise*. It was impossible, at the age of 19 and living alone in a furnished room in the rue Saint-André-des-Arts, not to partake of *la Grand Espérance* of 1936, of the Front Populaire, *les grèves sur le tas*,[1] Léo Lagrange, the first Minister of Sports and Leisure (killed, along with so many other hopes, in 1940), *congés payés* which, for the first time, brought Ménilmontant and Belleville to the Mediterranean and the tandems of athletic campers to the inner recesses of *la Bretagne bretonnante*. In the 14 July procession of that year, one marched hand in hand with Fraternity and Hope. It was impossible too not to feel the utmost revulsion for those Frenchmen—few, but rich, sanguinary, fanatical, and dominated by fear and egoism— who looked on Franco as they had looked on Mussolini, as the potential saviour of *la bourgeoisie française*. Madrid seemed very

[1] Strikes accompanied by the occupation of factories.

close to Paris, the Gare d'Austerlitz so often resounded with the incantation: *des avions pour l'Espagne!*

1937 was above all *l'année Expo*. And the *Expo* brought to Paris Weidmann, the young German mass-murderer, who, after killing the American dancer, Joan de Koven, a commercial traveller, a taxi-driver, and various others he had met, generally by chance, stored their effects, including food and clothing, in a villa that he had leased at la Celle-Saint-Cloud (villas were cheap in those days), *banlieue* Saint-Lazare; one can imagine the sort of thing: *faux manoir normand*, with enormous projecting eaves. He was the last man to be guillotined in public, on the place d'Armes in Versailles, an occasion attended by *le Tout-Paris* with champagne suppers, while awaiting the dawn that would see the erection of the death machine. There was something particularly weird about the Weidmann trial, the herald of the violence to come. But something of the spirit of the Front Populaire survived; in 1937 Jean Zay opened the *Lycée Claude-Bernard*, a monument to the elaborate, copper-covered bad taste of the mid-thirties. It could be classed with *la Normandie* and the current banknotes (with a nude Republic not unlike those on the murals of the Sphinx).[1]

Few can appreciate the deeper, more secret wells of Appeasement if they have not experienced the dreadful, naked panic of the summer of 1938 in Paris: queues outside the banks (and the wealthier the quarter, the longer the queue; as usual, in times of fear, *la bourgeoisie française* was taking out its gold, prior to running west), the green buses filled to the roof with stretchers, pitiful pails of sand in the wells of staircases, fast-moving military ambulances, the semi-civilian, semi-military, drunken chaos of the Gare de l'Est, choked with *réservistes* in *képis* and civilian trousers, large cars loaded with mattresses, the readers of the B.N. rushing out into the courtyard in the late August 1938, at the sound of a low-flying plane, the evening succession of screamed *Édition Spéciale!* The relief at the news of Munich was physical and visible in the faces of passers-by; no wonder Daladier was welcomed like a conquering hero. People could sleep undisturbed that night, whatever the future. And, in Paris in 1938, one did not make too big claims on

---

[1] The Sphinx, the property of the Sarraut brothers, was one of the most celebrated of the *maisons closes* of the inter-war years. Situated behind the Gare du Montparnasse, it was closed in 1945 and has since served as a students' hostel.

the future, one was grateful for a few more weeks, or a few more months, it was all time gained. I too was physically and morally a *munichois*; even so, if disaster were to come, I preferred that it should come to me in France. I had no inclination to leave Paris in August 1938; the French panic had been mine too. 1939 did not seem quite so bad; it is perhaps difficult to go through the whole process of panic twice, at quite such a short interval; Marcel Déat apparently drew little response, *Match* published impressive photographs of the Polish cavalry, *Paris-Soir*, photographs of W.V.S. organizing canteens and the women of the English upper-middle classes 'going to it' with looks of enormous satisfaction (there was a particular luxury in looking at such pictures and in reading of England's warrior mood from the terrace of a Paris café). But this time, things did not work out as I had hoped. The outbreak of war caught me in England, another accident for which I had not planned. On 9 May 1940 I obtained a visa from the French Consulate in London to return to France. For much of the first year following the Fall of France, I attempted to gain permission to join the F.F.L.[1] (not, I hoped, in any very dangerous capacity); but I was eventually placed in the British Army, to be trained as a storeman.

A 'lucky' among other 'luckies', most of them lorry-drivers and mechanics from North London, I was placed in a horse-box which I shared with three others, all of whom boasted of their prison experiences. To their *palmarès* of Brixton, Pentonville, the Scrubs, Strangeways, the Mountjoy, Armley, I could only counter with an obscure prison in Vienna and the cells in Tunbridge Wells magistrate court; it was rather like Sutton Valence or Hurstmonceux competing with Eton and Winchester. They were very decent about it, soon took me in and used their (considerable) influence in the cook-house to get me extra rations and double helpings. After about a fortnight of bantering ('Hoxford, wot wot!'), I was accepted too by the other 'luckies'. My long stay in France had enabled me to acquire a second nationality and to discover fraternity; the Army did me the enormous service of divesting me of class. There was fraternity too in the North, in Scotland, and in South Wales, all places in which I was fortunate enough to be stationed; it was back to the warm kitchen, the tea on the boil. It was quite a new Britain to me. Also, for the first time, I became aware of the infinite guile of

[1] Forces Françaises Libres.

the Londoner when it was a matter of avoiding work or of giving the appearance of work to the reality of almost blissful idleness. A long stretch in 'sanitary', emptying latrine buckets spread over an area of many miles, in beautiful rolling countryside, gave me a valuable grounding in the old Army art of making a little go a long way; one could make four or five buckets last out till 4 or 5 p.m., by which time it was possible to return to camp, filthy and suitably stinking, get cleaned up, and go to the pub. I much preferred *les Servitudes* to *les Grandeurs* of military life; and Jaroslav Hasek and Julian Maclaren-Ross have a much clearer appreciation of the realities of military life, in an unwilling conscript army, than Alfred de Vigny.

The Army, it is well known, 'moves in a mysterious way'. I sought liaison work, still in the hope of gaining access to the F.F.L. From 'sanitary', I was transferred to the Poles, thence to the Czechoslovak Independent Brigade Group. I did not know either language, but I was not alone in this. At least an extended period with both forces added to my awareness of Europe and of national minorities; some of my closest friends among the Poles were Ukrainians from Wołyn, among the Czechs, Ukrainians from Pod-Karpatska-Rus. At a period when I was making a serious attempt to learn Polish, I was almost persuaded by Professor Willie Rose eventually to invest in Polish history.

In 1943 and 1944, I made a number of broadcasts for Jean Oberlé; they were sentimental and mushy. I also wrote in French papers published in London. In the spring of 1944, I succeeded in obtaining a transfer to 21st Army Group. This was the first time that things had really come my way, for in April or May, while in a sealed camp somewhere in East Essex, we were all paid 200 francs —the two notes were quite unfamiliar to me, Henri IV and Sully and the bucolic slogan: 'Labourage et pâturage sont les deux mamelles de la France'; if the Maréchal was sinking more and more into dotage, France, it would appear, was going Back to the Land. On receiving the notes, we all concluded that we must be heading for Norway. The notes were a feint. But, of course, they were not. I always wondered where they had been printed, for they were crisp and new.

The Army is the most unpredictable of travel agencies, and has a much wider range to offer than Dean & Dawson, or Swan and the other merchants of sun, sand, and bronzed torsoes. It took me first to the Bessin, then to the Nord, then to Ixelles, with several leaves in Paris and Marseille, and fortunately only a few weeks in Germany, at First Corps Headquarters at Iserlöhn (a horrid little town situated in a sinister Grimm-like countryside of thick, pagan pine forests and lakes).

I was in or near Bayeux from July to September 1944—long enough to make a number of friends in the town, mostly among the *cheminots*, but including a Belgian shoemaker, M. Ploemakers, who had settled there in 1918; long enough too to write regularly for *La Renaissance du Bessin* (the old *Journal de Bayeux* under a new guise, but under much the same management, which was largely royalist); long enough to spend 14 July at a football match and be arrested by the Provost Corps for distributing a news-sheet in French to the Bayeusains; long enough to witness the arrival of groups of black-marketeers from Rouen, Amiens, and Paris, wearing coloured arm-bands and bearing requisition orders in the name of shadowy authorities. Bayeux was experiencing its *heure de gloire*; the Bayeusains were prone to admit that they could well have done without it (and the farmers felt much the same: 'M. le sergent, on fait la guerre en rase campagne, comme l'Argonne ou la Somme, on ne fait pas la guerre dans un pays à herbages, vous savez ce que ça coûte d'abattre 200 poiriers pour faire un piste d'envol?', etc.). The Hôtel du Lion d'Or was crowded in July by an enthusiastic group of young prefects and sub-prefects, even of one or two *commissaires régionaux*,[1] waiting to take up office once their apportioned territories were liberated; the food there was surprisingly good and my civilian friends supplied me with *tickets de pain*. Calvados was easily obtainable in exchange for cigarettes; and I spent much of my time (as I worked at night, I had most of the day free, going from farm to farm—I had my place at the *grande table* in half a dozen; the farms were full of young men who were not from the Bessin). In Barbeville, where I was stationed, I delivered a small cyclostyled news-sheet in French every morning before going to bed to the local *mairie*, which was also the *école communale*. The sheet was thence sent to the neighbouring villages and even as far as Balleroy. Every day, at twelve, a small girl with

[1] Super-Prefects appointed by the French Provincial Government and entrusted with the task of taking over the administration of liberated territories. Most had very large areas; there was one for Normandy, one for the Nord, one for the Toulouse area, one for the Lyon area, etc. The best known were Yves Farge (Lyon) and Berteaux (Toulouse).

very fair hair and wearing clogs, came to the *mairie*, from Cothun, 7 kilometres away, to pick up a copy. She was sent by the *maire*, an elderly farmer with strong anti-clerical tendencies. To see this small figure as she arrived each day gave me a sense of permanency and the feeling that I had at least one foot in the Bessin. My sheet was widely read, though *M. le curé* regarded it with some alarm and the local *châtelain* with distaste.

Most evenings I also had dinner at the *école* with the *institutrice* who was also *secrétaire de la mairie*—this was how I had met her— a girl so blond that she looked as if she had come down in direct descent from the Vikings. She had taken a liking to me (this was reciprocated) and used to cook me steaks, which we ate out in the vegetable garden, in cream. As I returned to work, in the evening, to the camp, I met long lines of ambulances driving slowly and very gently from the battle area, over the bumpy, unmade, dusty roads. At night one could see the artillery bombardment, but the countryside was dead quiet. I used to think that I was perhaps the luckiest soldier in the B.L.A. Certainly I must have been one of the happiest. A little before my departure, I heard at dusk the faint rumble of a train—the line between Paris and Cherbourg had been re-established and it was the first to reach Bayeux. The *heure de gloire* was at last over; it was the most beautiful, reassuring sound I had heard since 1939. The war was receding from the Cotentin, civilian life once more imposed its priorities; and, for me, the sound hinted demobilization, the resumption of freedom as a civilian in France. I was happy for the Bayeusains, who could return to their sleepy existence, made relatively more prosperous by the presence of three large war cemeteries, a greater tourist draw than the *tapisserie* had ever been. The town, which before the Revolution had lived off the Church, could now live off the Allied dead. When my unit left the Bessin for Brussels, there was a girl in white standing outside the *école*, who waved to me as we passed.

There followed a brief, alien interlude in Malines (or, more horribly, Mechelen), an unpleasant Flemish clerical town. We were stationed in the Caserne des Grenadiers, next door to the prison, so that on Thursdays and Sundays, visiting days, we could see the long queues—many fur coats—of the wealthier Malinois, come to visit their sons, *inciviques*[1] who had militated in the VNV[2] or the Flemish SS Legions. We were treated with marked

---

[1] Belgian for collaborator. [2] Vlaamsch Nasionaal Verbond.

hostility, save by the *cheminots* of the C.F.B.[1] The Malinois were too, judging from the photographs displayed in windows, mostly *léopoldistes*, which was in character. They showed a marked reluctance to speak French, preferring English. In fact there was not much to be said for them at all; their priests put pressure on the girls to prevent them from attending our dances. At least one could enjoy the sight of Flemish farmers queuing up with suitcases outside the banks, at the time of the Guth Decrees withdrawing the old currency; they must have been hard put to it to explain the sources of their enormous earnings since 1940. The news that we were, in December 1944, to be transferred to Roubaix, was received with general satisfaction and, by me, with joy.

We arrived in Roubaix amidst a snowstorm. In the boulevard de Paris, schoolboys stopped to throw snowballs at our lorries and at the passing trams. It was a guarantee of what was to come, for this was not Malines; here the British Army was treated with enormous friendliness, a friendliness which, in many cases, was based on memory and experience. In many small houses in the *corons*,[2] there would be photographs, proudly displayed, of British regiments stationed in the city in 1918; on three occasions members of my unit had the surprise of recognizing their fathers, hanging thus, in a spotless, tiled kitchen in the rue de Lannoy or the rue aux Longues Haies. Neither street was, in fact, very far from Bradford, Halifax, Keighley, or Dewsbury. At Christmas 1944 there was not a member of the Army, in the other ranks, who did not have his feet under the table, in some *coron* or other. Many Roubaisiens had to go away unsatisfied, there were not enough British soldiers to go round.

Christmas and New Year, despite so much kindness, were overshadowed by a gnawing fear, felt alike by the inhabitants and by ourselves. The wildest rumours circulated concerning the progress of the Ardennes Offensive, German commandos were reported in the suburbs, and we were suddenly re-issued with arms—in my case, a sten, which I persisted in leaving in trams, or in civilian houses, to be retrieved the next day ('Monsieur, vous avez laissé chez nous votre parapluie'). The inhabitants were anxious, and became even more so when they witnessed an apparent transforma-

[1] Chemins de Fer Belges.
[2] *Coron*: a back-to-back in brick, characteristic of the Nord and the Pas-de-Calais industrial belt.

The author in 1945

tion from a headquarter unit into what was supposed to pass off as a fighting force. Fortunately this was never put to the test. The sense of relief, early in January 1945, was almost as physical as that of September 1938 in Paris.

Roubaix is well off the tourist circuit, though it is well known to Australian wool salesmen and some of its *patrons* and buyers speak English with an Australian accent. Its football team was coached by a Yorkshireman, and in the whole connurbation of L.R.T. (Lille—Roubaix—Tourcoing), the three great textile towns, there were a few score of veterans from the First World War who had married local girls and many of whom, by the late 1940s, had lost their command of English, spoke with the hard *chtimi*[1] accent and had French grand-children. It was they who had been absorbed by the strong, close-knit family life of the industrial Nord, more akin to Belgium than to France (in both the Nord and the Kingdom, beer and *café au chicoré*—the pot was always to hand and on the boil—predominated; in both, the Saturday night booze-up, on beer or on *genièvre*, gave a noisy, collective, spewy climax to a regular and very laborious week). Indeed, with over thirty frontier posts, and the frontier cutting through a street, sometimes even through a house, so that it was possible to go to an *estaminet* and drink at one bar in the Republic and walk across the room and drink at the other in the Kingdom, it was always rather hard to say where Roubaix ended and Belgium began. The telephone book was full of names under *Van*; many Roubaisiens had brothers or parents over the border, while since 1905 the very pious wool barons had been in the habit of sending their daughters and their sons to schools run by French orders situated often less than a kilometre over the frontier. Some of them had their country houses or their week-end cottages in the Tournésis, and when the *grand patron* thought in terms of pleasure —whether *la table* or *les filles*—it was to Brussels rather than to Paris that he headed. Labour organization, particular among the S.F.I.O.[2] militants, was on the Belgian model; one of the main streets was named after Edgar Anseels, while *Jocisme*[3] had been imported by the Abbé (later Cardinal) Cardijn. There was a constant coming and going of the *gendarmerie nationale* and the *gendarmerie royale*, French *douaniers* operated on the tram routes, the early-

---

[1] Paris slang for an inhabitant of the Nord.
[2] Section Française de l'Internationale Ouvrière.
[3] Jeunesses Ouvrières Catholiques.

morning trams brought in tightly packed *frontaliers*, mostly from the Courtrésis, some of whom had cycled ten or fifteen miles through the dark before taking the tram, and who came to work in France as stonemasons and builders' labourers. Along the canal de Roubaix, in Wasquehal, in Hem, in Watrelos, in Lannoy, the children played *douaniers* and *contrebandiers*; few wanted to be the former, it was a role forced upon tearful little brothers or little sisters by the bigger boys and girls, while at working-class level most families could boast a close relative—often a brother—who gave up most of his time to smuggling in tobacco. Belgian cigarettes were more in evidence than those of the Régie;[1] and while the frontier existed for civilians, it did not for the British Army, a fact which was very rapidly put to lucrative use both by civilians and soldiers. There were *estaminets* near the station that specialized in this trade and where Army transporters could be rewarded in cash and in kind—drinks and the *serveuses montantes*. The 21 July was fêted as much as the 14th, and at week-ends there were cock-fights in the neutral zone, where it existed between the two countries. Frontiers have their advantages, as well as their romance, and there is much to be said for living on top of one.

A great industrial sprawl, astride two countries, its tramlines disappearing into the misty murk and sticky *pavés* (this is the real grind for the racing cyclist, so many of whom have come to grief on the terrible *Paris–Roubaix*) of January nights, its endless streets and rectangles of *corons*——so like Manchester back-to-backs—— offered innumerable opportunities for temporary escape into the many and warm recesses of civilian life, and these did not always mean into the welcoming and well-scrubbed arms of *cardeuses* and *fileuses*, though these too were plentiful. The town was widely acclaimed by the troops as a 'cushy billet', and those who did not have girls (our only casualty, an RSM in the Pay Corps, drove himself and his girl into the canal on VE Day, a watery end to an Anglo-Roubaisien understanding) had their families and a meal waiting for them in well-heated kitchens, at 6 p.m. The Northerner especially felt at once at home. The *estaminets* were cheerful and noisy.

I was particularly fortunate in working at night in the Cercle de l'Industrie, just off the Grand'Place. I even wore civilian clothes that had been given to me by M. Roussel, the director of the

[1] The French tobacco monopoly.

establishment, including a jacket, much too big for me, that sported the *ruban rouge*. Most of my days were free, so that I could painlessly move over the gulf—and what a gulf!—that separates the enslaved soldier, the property of a Government, from the free civilian, the envy of every conscript. (I was very careful never to introduce any members of my unit to my French civilian friends.) There was a wide choice of refugees, all of them well out of reach of the Army. At the top were the wool barons, among whom a former acquaintance of undergraduate days, Albert Prouvost, occupied a prominent position. These were the roomy, comfortable, well-heated houses of the boulevard de Paris, the boulevard de Cambrai, and the extravagantly crenellated baronial halls of the Parc Barbieux, the pseudo-châteaux of mid-nineteenth-century family prosperity. There was a regular pattern to such establishments: many children, a sister a nun, a brother a priest, or a monk, the others *dans l'Industrie* or married into it, a large modern statue of the Virgin, in cream against a blue background, in a niche in the main room, *Les Grandes Familles de Roubaix-Tourcoing* displayed in evidence on a table. This was a sort of industrial Debrett in which every possible marriage commutation was declined: Prouvost-Prouvost, Prouvost-Wibaux, Prouvost-Glorieux, Wibaux-Florin, Glorieux-Pierrepont, Motte-Masurel, Motte-Motte, Masurel-Toulemonde, Toulemonde-Toulemonde, Toulemonde-Tiberghien, and so on. Every combination had been thought of, and, for younger sons and daughters, there was little chance of escape from a position between the covers of that family litany. Even in death there was a niche for them in monuments the size of mini-Sainte-Chapelles, double-named to eternity. To be introduced to one family was to be introduced to the lot, all doors would open. All were closely related. Few ever looked far beyond *l'Industrie*, though this might take some to Mazamet, to Paris, to Bradford, to Mulhouse, and to Australia. All were deeply attached to the ugly, sprawling, blackened-brick industrial town, and in their intense regionalism, they differed little from the mass of their workers, whom they often knew by their Christian names. They were no doubt relatively good employers, very paternalistic, much concerned with morals and *crêches*, though somewhat suspicious of worker priests and those, like the local novelist, Maxence van der Meersch, whom they described as *Communistes blancs*. But of Maxence they were also proud, like almost everyone else in the town, because he was a regionalist who had written almost exclusively about Roubaix and who had brought honour to the town by winning the Prix Goncourt. He was, in fact, a clumsy stylist, a Christian-Socialist Zola, who wrote off an accumulated stock of *fiches*; but all his characters were identifiable in local terms, and the *patronat* was tickled by this. This is not to give the impression that the *patronat* was absolutely monolithic, even though entirely included between the hard covers of *Les Grandes Familles de Roubaix-Tourcoing*; there were a few rebels. One had written a novel, under a pseudonym, about a family funeral in one of the big houses off the Parc Barbieux; the daughter of another had broken away, taking her *licence* at the Faculté des Lettres in Lille, instead of going to the Institut Catholique there; she eventually went to live in London.

So much for the *patronat*: ecclesiastical gossip, complaints about Paris and its politicians ('Le Nord, c'est la vache à lait de la France entière'), boasts about economic Resistance, plans for slum clearance, a considerable reticence on the subject of the wool industry, a great willingness to demonstrate new techniques to visitors to their mills, lunch quite often with beer (they drank less wine than the Bruxellois, but when they did drink it, it was Burgundy, as in Brussels), bridge in the evening, a manifestation of anglophilia. They read *La Croix du Nord*, and as, in the conditions of 1944–5, the Right had been temporarily driven out of existence, they financed and voted for the M.R.P.[1] (*Le Sillon* had previously grown deep roots here.)

The *patronat* needed to be savoured in small quantities; it was too invasive, and one had to be too careful, too much on one's best behaviour. I was much more at home in Wasquehal, in Maxence's house by the canal, overlooking the coal barges and the cranes. In the early months of 1945 the barges were frozen hard, and crowds of poor people walked on the ice, pushing prams which they filled up with the captive coal—an episode that would have gone into Maxence's next novel—a study of Roubaix during the Occupation and Liberation periods—but poor Maxence died two years later in 1947.

Maxence, Thérèse, their daughter Sarah, and their little adopted son Valère (the result of a Franco-German liaison), afforded me what is most precious to a soldier: the warmth and security of a family. Maxence took a liking to me, stopped me smoking, made

[1] Mouvement Républicain Populaire.

me cut down on drink, even attempted to get me married off to a Lilloise who was worthy, poor, and pious (recommended, *sous tous les rapports*, by the clergy) and insisted that I take my meals at home: home-made bread, potatoes, and everything else boiled. He was tubercular and had fallen under the influence of a medical eccentric who preached under-nourishment as a cure to tuberculosis; his most recent novel was an attack on orthodox medicine. Many of the afternoons were spent upstairs, while Maxence rested and Sarah sang me little songs: *Le Petit Quin-quin, Mon mari, qu'il était petit*, and so on. It was not only family life, but an introduction into the enclosed, secure world of childhood. Maxence's brother-in-law was a *contrebandier*, and when I took Valère out, the men at the lock and the bargees would greet me.

Maxence had a tremendous range of friends quite outside the *patronat*. They included a semi-gangster from Lille, who had done well out of the black market and financed the local Resistance, a sad businessman with wife trouble, a host of people who came to consult the bearded writer about their personal problems (he did have a law degree too), and a large number of men and women who worked in the mills (Thérèse had herself been a *cardeuse*) and who were active *Jocistes* (I never met, through his agency, any socialists or communists). After a month or so, I was so integrated into the spreading van der Meersch network that I found myself regularly attending weddings, baptisms, and, above all, funerals—including one of an infant—in Hem, Lys-lès-Lannoy, and in the *corons*. He also introduced me to some fringe industrialists—*les tapis boulgomme*,[1] and so on—who, not being in wool, nor marriable into the *GFRT*, were more open-minded, more aware of Paris (Maxence too had the deepest distrust of *la Babylone moderne* and its inhabitants: a godless, irreverent, and lazy lot), and, so Maxence assured me, more *social*. Another sector was that of the textile engineers, a few of whom were even anti-clerical and read *La Voix du Nord*. I even knew two doctors and received free medical attention. At the house by the canal, *bonnes à tout faire* came and went with bewildering rapidity. They were all fallen girls, who, after being rehabilitated by *le Bon Pasteur*[2] in Lille, were taken on by Maxence in the belief that the experience of a genuinely Christian household would

[1] Matting in artificial rubber, manufactured by Pennel Flipo et Cie.
[2] A charitable organization run by nuns for the rehabilitation of delinquent girls.

complete their moral regeneration. In my time, all eight of them went over the wall, on Saturday night, to return, bedraggled, on the Monday morning, after attending the *kermesse* somewhere in northern Roubaix. All were dismissed. One was an enormously fat Pole. Maxence might be kind and generous, but he expected a return on his charity.

The Maxence world, like that of the *patronat*, would have been stifling, had there not been other forms of escape. The way up to Wasquehal was a very long street, crossed by the line to Paris, lined with *estaminets*, in many of which it was possible to spend the night, for a reasonable fee, with the *serveuse montante*, in the room over the *grande salle* (it was reached by a corkscrew staircase from behind the bar), to wake up to the sound of the early-morning trams or to the crow of cocks or the cooing of pigeons in back-yards (the Roubaisiens, even the *cafetiers*, were fanatical *colombo-philes*). This was only a Saturday night indulgence, as I worked every other night; but it was a change from a surfeit of virtue and good works, and preserved my sense of freedom.

This, however, I was doing my best to lose. For I asked at least two girls to marry me; one of them was dark, with blue eyes, flower ear-rings and Croix de Lorraine. Her father was *maire* of Lannoy, her cousin a *cardeur*. The father's house was a strange structure, right on the frontier, an admirable setting for a film about smuggling. I think the house, the setting, the cousin, and yet another tiled kitchen with the coffee pot on the stove attracted me as much as the girl. In the next few years, I asked a number of French girls to marry me; they all, fortunately, refused. They were all very nice about it.

Roubaix had sucked me in. I hardly ever thought about Paris, and when I did, it was with some disapproval; and I only rarely took the *Mongy*[1] to Lille. No, my place was with the warm, solid Roubaisiens! I even contemplated settling in Roubaix, or possibly in Lille, after demobilization. Plenty of other Englishmen had done so. I daily exchanged gossip with the *marchand de journaux* of the rue Foch, a political crackpot who was a devotee of Georges Valois. On VE Day I found myself hand in hand with two mill girls, in a huge, whirling circle dancing on the Grand'Place, the apotheosis of our collective joy, just as much as the week of the

[1] The high-speed trams from Tourcoing and Roubaix to Lille, named after their inventor.

Ardennes offensive had seen us huddled together in common fear. In the late summer, we were ordered to move to Ixelles. It was just in time. Even so, every time I see the long streets of low brick houses, the advertisements *Bières Motte-Cordonnier*, the sticky *pavé*, and *Les Docks du Nord*, I remember the scrubbed kitchens with large stoves, the blond children neat in their *tabliers*, the noisy *estaminets*, the intense, comfortable, protective warmth of regionalism, the frolicking schoolchildren with their burning chestnuts on strings on St Nicholas's Day, and I feel the pull of home. When Maxence died in 1947, I was back in Paris; but I still felt I had lost a close and dear relative.

In Roubaix, my life had been mostly at ground level. In Ixelles, off the Chaussée, the best part of it was at basement level. In Roubaix, Maxence had been the magician who had pulled the front off so many *corons*, to introduce me, *de plein pied*, into the kitchen and the smell of coffee and boiling potatoes. Jean Diederickx, an independent artisan who made toys in his basement flat, which also had a workshop, rue du Couloir, and who only worked at night —the *café au chicoré* was again always on the boil—had a more modest, but in human terms, much closer, more integrated range of friends: Marcel Veau, an unemployed tailor, his mistress Reinette, a big, noisy, gusty nurse from Charleroi (plus accent); Charles, a very drunken, savorously vulgar Ixellois; Georges, a garage mechanic, who, after serving in the SS, had been condemned to death by a *kriegsauditoriaat*, had been reprieved, was silly, wildly anti-semitic, terribly mixed-up and ignorant, very generous and completely reliable; a Cossack officer, who stood outside a Russian night-club, Porte de Namur, with his rig-out on, and who was waiting for a visa to go to Argentina and join his mistress, a Bruxelloise who had a prosperous *pâtisserie* in Buenos Aires; the *patron*, another White Russian, of the café on the corner of the rue du Couloir and the Chaussée, a place much frequented by the NCO's and soldiers of the near-by Red Army liaison. It was here that I met Jean, on a very cold night, while, with the help of a Red Army sergeant, attempting to revive a corporal from the Argyles, whom we had discovered, dead drunk and his face quite blue, in the snow. The Scot was revived, with slaps and brandy; and Jean took the Soviet soldier and myself back to his basement. And there I remained, for the best part of a year, occasionally sleeping at my billet, avenue de la Cascade (later avenue du Géneral de Gaulle, the General coming, with the Regent and the *bourgmestre* of Ixelles, to rename it in person). Jean's wife, Émilie, was a big, blond country girl from Mariembourg, who had come up to Brussels to work at *L'Innovation*. She painted the toys. They had one son called Poum; he rarely went to school, as, like Jean and Émilie, he slept during the day.

Jean was an autodidact, with intellectual pretensions and a dislike of being contradicted, an anarcho-Christian, and a convinced Belgian patriot. Any criticisms of the Kingdom from outside made him very angry, and, like so many Walloons, his attitude to France was strongly conditioned by jealousy. He was a very free man; the family unit only worked seasonally, from October to December, for the St Nicholas and Christmas market, and from January to March, to satisfy Easter demands. They lived mainly off sausage, salami, bread and butter, and coffee; but they had to feed, intermittently, quite a lot of people. They were apolitical, were regularly fined for not voting (in any case, it would have meant getting up in the daytime), and must have been virtually the only Belgians in 1945 not to have any strong views on *la question royale* (on the whole, I think they favoured Prince Charles but only because he was said to have as a mistress a Bruxelloise, the wife of a *garagiste* from the rue Haute). Occasionally, when money was plentiful, in December or in April, they would come above ground and there would follow a round of very heavy drinking, with Charles, Marcel, Georges, and the Cossack, in the neighbouring cafés or in the rue Haute: Export, Stella, and the devastating Gueuse, the most ferocious of all drinks, the most conducive too to the pronouncement of the fatal phase: *espèce d'architecte*, at once followed by the crash of broken glass and the heavy breathing of a first-class brawl.

As a complete contrast to the basement in the rue du Couloir, and in order to remind myself that *léopoldistes* did exist, that there was another side, and that a few people did read *Septembre*, and did not take their cue from *Le Soir*, there was the hôtel d'Oursel, a large, eighteenth-century town house, rue aux Herbes, near Saint-Gudule, the Brussels home of the Prince de Croy. Tea and *sablés*, listening to the eldest of the daughters, a loud-voiced girl in the uniform of the Belgian Red Cross, and who had big bones and liked horses. On my rare visits to this archaic world, I always made sure to display *Septembre* well in evidence. After each visit, a rapid plunge, Chez Bastiaan, a very small café almost under the Palais de Justice, as a means of purging myself of the aristos. Jean and Émilie were entertained by my accounts of visits *chez la Princesse*. They were better to talk about than to do.

In later years, when suffering from an overdose of French political instransigence, the rue du Couloir offered me the most effective therapy. There was a serene harmony in the anarchical existence of the underground household, with its own baroque pattern of work and leisure and its odd assortment of knowledge and prejudice. In the nineteen-forties and fifties, the Diederickx family managed to live almost entirely independent of any institution, their contacts were limited to those who were social outlaws like themselves. They were dependent on *L'Innovation* for their orders, but this was their only concession to capitalism. To the State they paid their regular fines as non-voters, from the *commune* they drew relief, during the long months of unemployment. They received occasional help from various ecclesiastical authorities, and were visited every now and then by *une dame patronnesse* from the area of the Bois de la Cambre; they readily accepted her admonitions and her presents of fruit. But they channelled very little back into the Church in return; in general, they were unable to attend mass as they were asleep at the time. As they were always very short of money, they could very seldom go away. Their year was entirely predictable, the only thing that changed was that Poum got bigger, eventually married, and had twin girls, so that there were three more in the basement. XL remained a harbour of reassurance, to return to, an example too of the Breughelian good humour and joyous vulgarity of the Brussels Saturday night, Chez Jef Denym, the proverbial unwilling soldier, who asked to have inscribed on his grave: *mort contre son gré*.

But Belgium stretched westwards, too, via Hal, to Leuze, Tournai, and the frontier. And there was a stopping-off point at Leuze, at a farm owned by a socialist Senator, a haven of goodwill discovered by a friend of mine who was a dispatch rider. Just outside the small town, on the road to France, there was a small, squat, white café, with a low red roof, Chez Maria, kept by a very dark Flemish woman and her startlingly beautiful daughter, who might have been Spanish. The Leuzois disapproved of the couple, whose clientèle consisted of lorry-drivers and commercial travellers. Both the mother and the daughter were said to be *accueillantes*, the café was cool, very dark, and shone with polished brass. It was good Simenon material: the white café on the edge of the small town, another version of the café by the canal lock.

Paris 1946, the longed-for return to civilian life, were represented by the rediscovery of Maurice, now visibly prosperous, florid, and even rather fat, a jaunty hat perpetually pushed forward over his eyes, surmounting the perpetual cigarette dangling from his lower lip, all of which with his broad shoulders and his rather washed-out, boiled cod blue eyes, gave him the look of an *inspecteur* from the Mondaine.[1] His appearance was, in fact, so convincing that he was received with a mixture of deference and complicity by the ladies who kept hotels in the Quartier des Ternes, when he put his feet on the red staircase carpet, between the potted plants. 'M. Maurice', however uncertain his status, was a well-known figure anywhere from the Étoile to the Porte Champeret. He was one of many, in this area and at that period, who could produce stores of American-printed 100 franc notes—his were printed in Montmartre—US Army red petrol coupons and tyres from Army depots. He was also now well set up in second-hand furniture, and affluent enough to treat me from time to time to an evening out Chez Félix, a blackmarket restaurant kept by a retired boxer. And he was sufficiently well established to be able to pinch any bottoms to be seen bulging over bar stools from the avenue Wagram to his own base in the rue d'Obligado.

Although I was nominally resident at this time in the boulevard Saint-Michel (the most unpleasant street in Paris), most of it was spent either in the Ternes or waking up in the morning in unknown rooms and trying to guess, from the quality of the light and from the sounds of the street, in which quarter I had landed up on the previous evening. Coming out into the street, in the bustle of 11 a.m. or midday, was always a surprise: it might be the rue de la Boule-Rouge, off the rue du Faubourg-Montmartre, or it might be anywhere in the Ternes network. But the hazards of a night out, with or without Maurice, seldom took me beyond the IX*me*, the X*me*, the XVI*me*, the VIII*me*, or the XVII*me*; Pigalle and the Place Blanche were never reached. Nor was the Left Bank, so long as the war gratuities lasted.

[1] La Brigade Mondaine: a section of the French Police Judiciaire dealing with prostitution and procuring.

1947 brought a change of itinerary, as I was now confined to Vanves. I was so reluctant to return there at night that I paused, for hours, in various stopping places on the long, long rue de Vaugirard, to end up, in the early hours of the morning drinking in the various cafés, rue Brançion, opposite the horse slaughter-house, in the company of the slaughterers, big men, clad in long bloody leather aprons, who worked all night. A further itinerary ended in a singularly unattractive street, avenue Verdier, in Montrouge, shadowing the home of a blonde girl called Mauricette, who had gone out with me three successive Sundays, on romantic expeditions to Saint-Nom-la-Bretêche, and who had then suddenly given me the push, *'Pense à moi comme si je n'étais qu'un petit nuage rose'*, was her way of putting it. I did not like the bit about the little pink cloud, and spent hours, every evening, in a dreary little café, watching the entrance to her block of flats.

In 1948, the task of supplying me with an evening meal was taken over by the French Communist Party, Albert Soboul having imposed an eating roster on a selected number of *les copains*. So it was the Party almost every night, soup out of plates through which gradually emerged Picasso's dove, entrée plates bearing Picasso's feminine, doe-eyed, moustached, idyllic Stalin—I found it slightly irreverent thus to eat off the coryphaeus of the Arts and the Sciences—cheese plates with another dove. Behind glass-fronted bookcases stood neat ranks of dolls in regional costume: Hungarian girls from the Puszta, Polish mountaineers, Bulgarian peasants, all the *peuples frères* were there, in full folksy-wolksy gear (but, in the same year, the Dalmatian girls, the be-fezzed Bosnians, the Serbs with fierce moustaches, the wide-sleeved Croats, the Slovene milk-maids disappeared from the shelves).

It was not all easy going. I had to talk for my supper, and sign for it too; I had to make the appropriate orthodox noises and to express appropriate indignation at the wicked designs of the US and UK Governments. Round about cheese, the petitions would start to circulate: *libérez Henri Martin, Ridgeway à la porte*, and so on. I signed them all; it was the least I could do. What was much worse was to be subjected to endless discussions, among these revolutionaries, about plans for the summer holidays, or how to fiddle the Assurances Sociales and obtain a *congé de maladie* in la Bourboule, or inside gossip about salary increases for CNRS[1] researchers.

[1] Centre National de la Recherche Scientifique.

I supped with the Party from Monday to Friday; Saturday was my day off, and I much enjoyed the luxury of a non-political meal by myself, in a restaurant, listening to other people's conversation. Sunday too was non-Party. It was often reserved for the meal ticket of families of the French Reformed Church obedience—a different sort of orthodoxy, but also with its own built-in dangers, for the PCF militants did eat and drink quite well, when they had a hand to spare from signing petitions, while with the Huguenots there was always a danger of water, and I knew one HSP[1] family that was so anglophil that they persisted in serving me *la cuisine anglaise*; it did not seem particularly English, but it was very bad.

I was on the Party roster for the next three or four years—an experience that left me with a lasting distaste for the Believer, particularly for the female version: be-plaited or hair in a bun, exuding political *lapalissades*. Party girl guides and Puritans, utterly boring, self-righteous, and totally humourless. The worst thing of all about these people was their inward-looking chumminess; the word *copain* was like a masonic handshake, it was like living among members of a secret society to which one did not belong. I never felt that my efforts to give the impression that I did belong can have sounded very convincing; it was quite apparent that I did not read my daily *L'Huma*, my weekly *Regards*, my monthly *La Pensée*. It says much for the Party discipline of these good people that, Soboul having said they must feed the English historian, the English historian they fed. I never felt in the least bit grateful; the sponger does not manifest *la reconnaissance du ventre*. Reading Mercier, I could later recognize myself in those *abbés* who had their place at table, their napkin and their napkin ring, in the houses of the *dévôts*, in the Marais. Like the *abbé*, who knew that the greatest threat to his position would be another *abbé*, I was careful above all to preserve my monopoly as the Only Authorized (and Fed) *camarade anglais*. I viewed with extreme alarm the occasional presence of English militants, over in Paris to look up French brethren. And they eyed me with unconcealed loathing.

If, then, I was hardly a convert and was always relieved to escape, with a full stomach, from these houses of virtue, after 1948 I found much in the Party line to recommend it. In the growing awareness of the aggressive intentions of the United States, I became correspondingly sympathetic towards the diplomatic efforts

[1] Haute Société Protestante.

of the Soviet Union, which I saw primarily as the preservation of peace on the basis of the Yalta Settlement. At the time of the Rosenberg murders, George Rudé and I wrote a letter to *Le Monde*, which published it; and in the next few years, from 1951 to 1955, I wrote regularly in the *Tribune libre* of that paper, in support of its campaign against German rearmament. Several of my articles were quoted favourably by *L'Humanité*. When Stalin died, I attended the commemorative meeting at the Vel d'Hiv,[1] and, like most people there, I wept. I was deeply shocked when, on coming out, one of our Japanese friends expressed the intention of going to look for a prostitute, and disappeared down the *Métro* in the direction of Montparnasse.

My eating roster was not my only excursion into a community in which I felt alien and which I did not frequent as a matter of choice. In 1951 I married a colonel's daughter; her uncle was a general. Two of her brothers were colonels (one of them later made a sort of fame for himself as one of the leaders of the OAS), another was a naval officer, one sister had married a *médecin-général* in the medical corps, another worked for a military laboratory in the Val-de-Grâce. The naval officer had been on Admiral Estéva's staff during the Occupation, he and his dog, which he called 'de Gaulle' ('Viens ici, de Gaulle!' 'Ne fais pas caca là, de Gaulle!', and so on) were well-known figures in the port of Tunis. Another of the brothers had served on Dentz's staff in Syria. The whole family—at least among the younger generation—showed an unerring flair for choosing the wrong side, and then serving it with devotion. The naval officer was, of course, stripped in 1944, the army officer was almost shot. (Dentz *was* shot.) They were quite unrepentant, very brave, very generous, completely un-bourgeois, and, although Catholics, they had acquired *les moeurs de garnison*, with a succession of wives and mistresses of various colours. They were very nice indeed to me. My wife was a kind, gentle person, who believed that the French Army was the best in the world and who was one of the least ostentatious social workers that I have ever met. On the only occasion that I stayed with my in-laws, in a broken-down country house situated in a large, weedy park with a lake almost invisible in reeds that contained the remains of a rotting boat, a portrait of Jean Mermoz looked down on me from over the

---

[1] Vélodrome d'Hiver, Javel. Now destroyed. It was used for political meetings and for the celebrated six-day cycle race.

bed, and there were crucifixes in every room. Both were company that made me feel even more uneasy than the Polish dolls. Yet the family had not always been right-wing; in the 1890s, the grandfather had been a Republican Senator for the Sarthe and a great friend of the Caillaux dynasty. While he himself had been an anticlerical, his son became a *dévôt* after going to Saint-Cyr; he was also of the 1914 generation. It was an evolution no doubt typical of many provincial families from the West that gave their sons to the Army and their daughters to Army officers. The break would have come in the 1900s. There was something quite unreal about my presence within such a community; this, too, had been the result of an accident, for Françoise had paid for a meal of mine, at the restaurant at which we both habitually ate, during one of my recurrent periods of *fauche*. Later, she lent me 5,000 francs, later still, had me to supper at her flat. The next day was 1 May and a holiday for employees of the SNCF.

During a very long stay in France, I met with much more kindness than otherwise. In the knowledge that their culture and history are universal, the French are perhaps more sympathetic to foreign scholars than most other peoples, though at times their sympathy might be rather patronizing. At least many of them would be prepared to help materially and with advice.

The only wholly deplorable people that I have met in France are Bordelais, the employees of the Prefecture of Police (especially the sinister-sounding Service de Refoulement), most of them Corsicans, and the females that sit behind the *guichets* in Paris *mairies*, presiding over birth, marriage, and death. France is, after all, the country of *fiches*; and it is impossible even to sleep in an hotel without filling out a condensed autobiography of worthless and uncontrollable information. I was lucky enough not to have been born in France, for I would have given my poor parents endless trouble if I had been. My eldest sons, however, were. I got married in France —a frustrating and formidable process, not unlike a game of Snakes and Ladders. And I hope I do not die in France, for that would be a cruel trick to play on those who had to dispose of my remains. Perhaps the greatest challenge of all is to have someone cremated: *une signature de médecin traitant, une signature de médecin légiste* (a rare bird, not easy to run down at short notice), a document from the deceased, expressing his or her desire to be *incinéré*; I have been

through that one too. France is, I imagine, the most difficult country in the world to be born in, to marry in, to die in, to be cremated
in. Divorce, too, involves a steeple-chase with many runners:
*avocats, avoués, huissiers, notaires, juges de première instance,
greffiers, employés de la mairie*—many visits to Balzacien *études*,
the walls piled high with green boxes: *affaire Bigorneau, affaire
Chastellux*—a cascade of paper in various colours and in archaic
language (*parlant à sa personne physique* . . .); a journey back into
the nineteenth century, confrontation with men wearing celluloid
collars, whose *clercs* write at high stools and whose studies have
padded doors. I did at least avoid the *contrat de mariage*, as neither
party had any possessions to contract about, but I have been inter-
preter for the reading of one of these monuments to French pessimism: everything was listed, including needles and chamber pots.

The Bibliothèque Nationale is the most difficult place in the
world to get a book out of, and its motto has for long been:
dégoûter le lecteur; much thought, ingenuity, rudeness, and persistence have been employed to reach this end. The catalogues are
a cemetery of half-finished schemes and a splendid monument to
French perfectionism; they are so complicated that, in the opinion
of one of my French friends, one needs at least twenty years'
experience to be able to find one's bearings when jumping from
one to another. The management even provides a chart, in different
colours, rather like the tourist plan of an English cathedral—
yellow for Perpendicular, mauve for Decorated—further to confuse
the reader.

The *secrétariat* of the Sorbonne adopts similar tactics. The
administrative process of presenting a thesis for a *doctorat-ès-
lettres* is almost as daunting as that of cremation, and rather more
complicated than that of naturalization, at least in the case of a man.
(Naturalization for a woman is almost impossible, unless she
marries a Frenchman.) After the initial three months of preliminary skirmishing, it so daunted me that I gave up just beyond
the stage at which I had unloaded 150 printed copies of my main
thesis at the *secrétariat des thèses*. I presume that they are still there,
unless they were burnt, in the recent troubles, by the *katangais*.

It is often hard to love a *concierge*—indeed, their function is not
to be loved, but to watch, and to report. And just as the main purpose of the Bibliothèque Nationale is not to provide books, the main
concern of those who sit in the admission sections of Paris hospitals

is to prevent the sick, the dying, and the *accidentés* getting anywhere near the doctors and nurses, and the doctors and nurses anywhere near them. Each patient actually admitted represents a resented and humiliating defeat for these street-level bureaucrats.

France is a very old *pays administré* in which most of the habits of the *ancien régime* and of the First Empire have persisted. The Frenchman, it is true, is nominally a citizen, but his real status is much better described in officialese, he is an *administré*. He must constantly be protected against his own wickedness. It is assumed, for instance, that in the absence of a system by which his true identity can be established, he will assume a false one. Hence a series of paper checks—not just one *carte d'identité*, but a whole pack of them. One can see them bulging in the inside pocket of a jacket, one can catch a sudden flash of transversal colour when an important-looking person flicks his *carte de priorité* as he jumps the queue at a bus stop. Bigamy, so easy in England, is a very rare crime in France, simply because it is so difficult, save in a period of catastrophe, like 1940, when communications break down. Landru was able to operate only in the favourable circumstances of the First World War. He picked his Departments with great care. Dr Petiot likewise benefited from wartime conditions. There was, it is true, a case a few years ago in Versailles, in which a lady dressed as a man managed to marry her girl-friend; they went through two ceremonies, one at the *mairie* and one at the parish church. The 'husband' had borrowed her brother's identity card, on a visit to her home in Strasbourg. The maid at the honeymoon hotel later admitted, when cross-examined, that, on bringing up the breakfast tray, she had thought that 'Monsieur avait la poitrine un peu forte', but she had given the matter no further thought, and 'Monsieur' had told her, in a gruff voice, to put the tray down on the side table. But, in the home of *fiches*, such fantasies are rare.

The habit of mistrust is so engrained that it has seeped down from the State to the citizen; I have been denounced on three occasions while in France. In 1945, the Sûreté in Lille was given a tip-off that I was a German deserter masquerading in British uniform. I was arrested by an impressive array of armed men, while having supper with a wool engineer in the rue Sarrail, in Roubaix. The Sûreté men were horrified to discover that the British soldier's brown book contained neither photograph nor finger prints. How, they asked me, did the Army check on deserters? While staying in a village in the Haute-Saône, I was denounced to the *gendarmerie* as a suspicious character. I had been seen visiting the cottage of a local eccentric, who lived alone in the woods, was known to be a poacher, and was believed to be a magician. And, later, I was denounced by my *concierge* for having spent more than three months in France without a *permis de séjour*. She was unaware that I had spent the previous week-end in Brussels. When the men from the Service de Refoulement walked in on me, very early one morning, I was able to show them the triangular stamp of the Baisieux frontier post. It was so much more simple to take the train to Brussels than to embark on the disagreeable and often dangerous process of obtaining a *permis*.

In *Rue du Havre*, Paul Guimard describes the scene outside Saint-Lazare, between 7.30 and 9.30 a.m., as witnessed by an elderly man, something of a sentimentalist, who lives in a *chambre de bonne* in the XIIme and who, as a war veteran, takes up his daily stand as a lottery ticket salesman, at the street corner. The man, who is utterly lonely, embarks on a series of fantasies in which various regular passers-by in the morning rush are not only identified, but, through the intervention of the stationary witness, introduced to each other, so that their lives are permanently changed. At 7.55 each morning a tall blonde girl—she could be a *bretonne*—her fair hair bobbing in the fast-moving sea of commuters, is carried past the vendor on his raft. At 7.59 there follows a young man, bareheaded, who smokes a pipe. The lottery man becomes attached to the two, looks out for them each day, establishing for them an imaginary itinerary: the girl, he decrees, lives in le Pecq with her widowed mother—or perhaps her grandmother—she takes the train at le Pecq at 7.20, and works for an *agent de change* somewhere near the rue Vivienne. (He has at least been able to ascertain that, on leaving the rue du Havre, she crosses over, left-turns, and disappears behind Le Printemps.) The young man lives in Rueil, taking a direct train from there at 7.30 a.m. He too heads left after Le Printemps; he must be some sort of engineer, working for a big industrial firm. He is unmarried—the old man is sure of this—but does not wish to remain permanently so. The blonde too is thinking eventually in terms of a family, but she has not met the right man. The two can never meet on the same train, and they are never likely to find themselves jostled together in the early-morning ish. Four minutes separate, apparently for ever, the two lives. The witness is powerless, he would like to stop the girl, tell her not to hurry, to wait till she is left in the trough of the wave, to be carried forward in the next swell from the station. He longs for some minor accident: a power failure which would keep her train stuck in le Vésinet or in Chatou for $3\frac{1}{2}$ minutes. There are days when one or other is missing; there is an occasion when the girl is carried along in the 8.12 wave; the old man notices that she is looking pale. And then, after weeks, after months, the miracle happens: both emerge, almost level, at 8.1. The vendor plunges into the crowd, pulls the girl's sleeve, calls to the young man, it is all a matter of seconds, they disappear, talking together, round the left bend. Contact has been established, not only between the girl and the young man, but between what is now the beginnings of a couple and their introducer. All three lives are radically changed, and for a period at least the vendor is pulled out of his loneliness; the young man, who is a *chef de rayon* in Le Printemps—for that is as far as he ever went —secures him a temporary job as Father Christmas in the toy department.

The situation of the old man is similar to that of the historian— or of a certain sort of historian—also a stationary witness, an observer of a swirling collectivity of which he is not a part. He too is lonely, given to fantasy, having to make do with a few scraps of evidence, in an effort to give life to the passing faces. In his passionate desire to know, to establish contacts, there is an element of self-identification; he is both the blonde girl *and* the young man, *and* the red-faced, leather-coated gas man in the peaked cap, *and* the hard-faced woman in her late 40s who looks as if she runs her own small business. He too is attempting to break out of loneliness, even if it is a matter of living with the dead. For, to live with the dead, he must live with the living. Loneliness gives him that extra perception, those qualities of curiosity, imagination, and compassion, that are the necessary tools of his trade. I can only speak from experience; and history is experience. One becomes a certain sort of historian because one is a certain sort of person. I have always been a very lonely person, and like others similarly placed, I have sat in restaurants, picking up fragments of conversation, have headed for the café open late at night. In this perpetual attempt to escape from loneliness, the people that one is most likely to meet are themselves lonely. So many of them, after the third or fourth

44

glass of calvados, will push their hats back and begin to give forth, to reminisce and to complain.

The historian then, as I imagine him, is Guimard's hero. He is also the Commissaire Maigret, his old-fashioned Gladstone bag, hastily but neatly packed by Madame Maigret, in his right hand, as he walks through the *salle des pas perdus*[1] of a provincial station, heading for the place de la Gare: a pause to look at the *planisphère* and map out the town, a few indecisive steps to look through the doors of three or four cafés, before deciding on one for breakfast, over the local paper and with ears attuned. An hour or more walking through the town from end to end—the station at one end, the cathedral at the other, the *sous-préfecture* half-way down—for how many French provincial towns resemble thus the simple plan of Fontenay-le-Comte of *Au bout du rouleau*! Having thus completed the exploration of the backbone of the herring, there is time to look at the side streets, before finally heading, in Maigret's case, for a certain house, for an hotel, in the historian's, for the *mairie*. It is the period at which the Commissaire is content to put his nose to the wind, to establish an ambience and the hour-by-hour clockwork of a small provincial town. Later he will talk to people; but first he must get his bearings, then he can explore assumptions and relationships and find out who is important. It is the most exciting stage of his *enquête*, before anything begins to fall into place, and it is often the most exhilarating stage of research.

There is more too that can be learnt from Maigret, for the Commissaire knows how, with patience, to reconstruct a life, a pattern of work and leisure, even a *vie intime*, from a few scraps of evidence and the inflexion of a voice. He is already loaded with a considerable weight of experience, and he is easily at home with small people. He feels uneasy, on the other hand, with the wealthy, the fashionable, the snob; the only foreigners for whom he feels an affinity are the sort of people Simenon's mother used to lodge in Liège: students from Russia and Eastern Europe, Jewish tailors. Though he shouts loud, has a terrible temper, he is not without compassion. For his older customers, *vieux chevaux de retour*, semi-criminals who have made good, set themselves up in the restaurant business, he has a genuine affection, the sort that is derived from shared experiences in the past and from the recollection of old times. He is rather out of sympathy with the young, does not like

[1] Entrance hall.

change, makes no allowance for revolution, believes that things were better when he was a young man in the career; there were less clever chaps about then. The *commissaire* is an artist in his way who likes seeing things for himself, even if it means staying up most of the night in a café by the canal or opposite the quai des Orfèvres; he does not like paper-work, nor employing assistants. He is an amateur, for he has never been trained in techniques. He does not even use *fiches*. But he knows where to find them, at the top of the PJ.[1]

At 4 o'clock one morning in a *tabac* in the rue du Four, I met a very drunken couple. One was a civilian pilot, who was to fly the next morning, and who had already been threatened with the removal of his licence after a drunken landing. The other was a very well-dressed, rubicund man, with neatly brushed black hair, a hat with a dark band, well-kept hands, and a diamond pin in his tie. He looked professional, and was at first reticent. But by 5 o'clock he was anxious to speak of himself, and gave me a number of hints. 'I am a Belgian; I come to Paris for the summer; I only work here in July, August, and early September; I only work in the XVI*me* and the XVII*me*. My work involves me with Post Offices, female servants, and chauffeurs.' It did not seem very difficult; I told him he was a professional house-breaker. He was delighted, opened a handsome pigskin bag, displaying some hundred instruments on runners. He was a man who enjoyed his work, but he also liked talking about it, and needed an audience.

This is both a personal and an aesthetic view of history. There are, of course, many sorts of history, and the historian makes his choice, which will always be dictated to some extent by his own sense of involvement and by a certain feeling of identification with the period and with the country to which he devotes his research. Indeed, I believe that such a sense of involvement is not only inevitable but even necessary, for the historian is not a cold clinician, he is not dealing with steely concepts *à la Saint-Just*, nor with geological 'social structures', he is concerned primarily with human beings. Olwen Hufton can write with such sympathy of Bayeux because she was partly educated there, of women, because she is a woman, of the nuns, because she was taught by them, and she can understand what poverty means to the mother of a large

[1] The building of the Police Judiciare.

family, because she is aware, from her own experience, of the preponderant place occupied by the Catholic Church in the lives of the female poor. Edward Thompson became the leading historian of a section of the English working class after living for more than fifteen years in Halifax. He also possesses literary gifts which are, unfortunately, rare in an historian.

It is possible to write history that is in no way human. Many economic historians and some diplomatic ones have demonstrated how this can be done. It is no doubt a necessary kind of history, as important as any other. But in the end, history being a cultural subject, one can only judge it by applying to it cultural values. I distrust, when applied to history, such words as 'laboratory', 'workshop', 'group project', just as I distrust those who speak of universities in terms of 'the plant'. Something very alarming occurred in France when, in each university, the old and meaningful title of 'Faculté des Lettres' was given the meaningless and baroque addition of 'et des Sciences Humaines'. For history is not a science, nor should it be written by teams. We can leave that to surgery. The writing of history is one of the fullest and most rewarding expressions of an individual personality.

The historian should, above all, be endlessly inquisitive and prying, constantly attempting to force the privacy of others, and to cross the frontiers of class, nationality, generation, period, and sex. His principal aim is to make the dead live. And, like the American 'mortician', he may allow himself a few artifices of the trade: a touch of rouge here, a pencil-stroke there, a little cotton wool in the cheeks, to make the operation more convincing. Of course, complete understanding is impossible and the historian of the common people, of popular movements, and of individualistic eccentrics can only scratch at the surface of things. He may recapture a mentality; but he cannot probe deeply. He can only make one man witness for many by the selective use of the individual 'case history' as a unit in historical impressionism.

I do not know what history is about, nor what social function it serves. I have never given the matter a thought. There is nothing more boring than books and articles on such themes as 'What is History?', 'The Use of History', 'History and Something Else'. I do, however, find enormous enjoyment in research and in the writing of history. I am happy in it, and that is the main thing. It is always embarrassing and rather impertinent to write at length about

47

oneself. There are the dangers of a jocular whimsicality, or of a studied, pseudo-eighteenth-century reticence, or of false candour, or of endless narration of trifling personal experiences. It is not an easy thing to do. And I can hear the objections: 'too much Cobb', 'historical narcissism', 'indecent exposure', 'il s'écoute parler', or, merely, 'what has all this got to do with a book of essays on French history?' My excuse is that I write history subjectively and often, no doubt, with prejudice and that I do not believe it is possible to divorce history from experience. I have not intended to project myself, like a lean shadow, over all that follows, and in what precedes. I have not meant to write about my French friends and acquaintances in terms of their relations with myself; I have tried to keep myself out of it as much as possible and to use individuals: the Thullier brothers, Maurice, Jean, Maxence, and others to illustrate a period, a place, a social climate, the process of change. The people included here have not been selected on account of their personality so much as to illustrate their assumptions and attitudes to a country and to a society in which they were living. The Thullier brothers, for instance, both married late and belonged to a period before the habit of early marriage changed the character of the French *bourgeoisie* and of French society as a whole, by rendering the young couple the hostage to political and social orthodoxy; the change came under Vichy, the Occupation years being the great divide between my generation and those who were born ten years later. In 1944 I returned to a France which, while in rural terms was still completely recognizable, had, as far as city life was concerned, undergone changes of appalling dimensions as a result of the strengthening of the family unit, with the advent of the married student, the *jeune ingénieur*, *jeune technocrate* couples— avid, ambitious, and conformist, the unpleasing characters of Christiane Rochefort's *Stances à Sophie*—and the consequent disappearance of the bachelor, the *boulevardier*. After 1944, it would no longer have been possible to enjoy pleasure in the lusty, rumbustious manner of Galtier-Boissière's *La Bonne Vie*—a group of male friends on a night out in Paris: *la table, les filles*, the old pleasures. Vichy disappeared, but, unhappily, much of Vichy puritanism has remained, and even Paris is in the process of becoming a dull place. It will be a lifeless one too once *les Halles*— with the joy, the violence, and the lust that accompany *les Halles*— have been expelled from the very heart of the city to Ris-Orangis.

In all that I have written I have tried to use individuals in order to illustrate the attitudes and assumptions of a society at a given period. In France in particular, history is perpetual and self-perpetuating; the French Revolution is still going on, there was another one—the fifth or the sixth (if one is prepared to concede the Front Populaire such an illustrious title; Daniel Guérin has called it, perhaps more accurately, the *révolution manquée*)—as recently as May 1968; it still uses the same labels and the same slogans, speaking still in the voice of the year II, the old conflict between 'possibilists' and 'impossibilists', between Jacobin bureaucrats and ultra-revolutionary 'wild men', has been run through once more, like an old film, at break-neck speed, so that what in 1793–4 had been concentrated into weeks and months now became concentrated into hours and days. It is suitable that the French Communist Party should have made a take-over bid on Robespierre; M. Waldeck-Rochet, in the recent crisis, acted as a Jacobin. And, as in 1795, a failed Revolution, or the failure to concretize a revolutionary situation, resulted in Reaction, just as a revolutionary situation was precipitated originally, as in June–July 1789, by the misuse of the repressive powers of Government (too much repression, or too little: my article on Professor Godechot's book, *The Beginning of the Revolutionary Crisis in Paris* (see pp. 145–58), may have some bearing on the origins of the May Revolution). France is now experiencing yet another of her many Thermidors—the favourite month, just as *homard à la* is the favourite dish, of a selfish and easily-frightened French *bourgeoisie*. Once more, the sheer violence of repression has created an unprecedented and totally unexpected revolutionary opportunity, and yet again, as in the year II and even more in the year III, violence has ultimately proved the most persuasive weapon of a French Government. The police, unfortunately, are always with us, always loathed. It is not only on General de Gaulle that the weight of French history lies heavily. Revolutionary students have looked as much to the *Enragés* as to Che, and much of the discussion *chez Renault* among the young workers echoed the clubs of 1848 and the endless, optimistic *palabres* of the Commune. In 1793–4, the women of the people envisaged equality in a physical and visible form: *à nous maintenant de rouler carosse*. And in May 1968, the cars of the bourgeois were the principal targets of student violence. How Christiane Rochefort must have applauded such an initiative!

With one exception—and that is about a Belgian deeply influenced by Maurras (and van Severen can witness as well for the recrudescent Fascists of today, in his own country, in England, and in France, as for those of the 1930s, for he too was a racialist)— all the articles and reviews that follow are about France. Most were written anonymously (18 out of 23), but my anonymity seems generally to have been poorly guarded, so much have they been conditioned by my own experience and prejudices, and, above all, by my awareness of the endless variety of French provincialism. Most of the articles, like my own life over the last thirty-three years, are so many historical excursions into *le plat pays*, wandering from Quarter to Quarter. My history is not French history, but French provincial history: Lyonnais history, Norman history, Lille history, Paris history. One French historian, fifteen years ago, said that I wrote, spoke, and thought *comme un titi parisien*. It is the greatest compliment that I have ever received.

So I have been unable to separate my own identity from what I have written. My own identity is something that, despite my *fiche*, I find very difficult to establish as I tend to react to environment rather than to impose my personality upon it or dominate it. The Balliol poem could not apply to me. Balliol did *not* make me. But France did; at least it gave me a new identity, into which I slip almost unconsciously as soon as I cross to the other side. Then I cannot even keep my hands still, and when I lecture over there, I turn down the corners of my mouth. So here too I am *fiché*, pinned down, along with other Parisians, Lyonnais, Roubaisiens, Havrais, Dieppois, Ixellois, all company that I like to keep, all towns that I love.

In Search of French History

1 'Au Car de Milly'

If the Simplon-Orient Express, hissing at the platform in the Gare de Lyon, is a physical reminder of the unity of a Europe happily more extensive than 'the Six', the *gares routières* at the Porte Maillot, Place de Stalingrad, Denfert-Rochereau, Porte d'Orléans, and Cours de Vincennes offer direct and discreet access to the hidden places off the *routes nationales*, through the medium of the familiar, brown Citroens, or the more nondescript Renaults, their roofs piled high with bundles, bicycles, and old suitcases tied together with rope. That strange little train, *l'Arpajonnaise*, that used to steam and whistle its way down the middle of the boul'Mich at about midnight, disappeared in 1937: but for the explorer in provincial locomotion, there is still, on the quais near the Bastille, the café with the reassuring, impressionist name *Au Car de Milly*; the terminal for the bus that leaves, once a day, to ply between Paris and Milly-la-Forêt. From Stalingrad and Maillot, from Denfert and the Porte d'Orleans, the roads fan out towards the Grand and the Petit Morins, to Rozay-en-Brie, to Montfort-l'Amaury, to Jouy-en-Josas and Jouy-le-Châtel, to Brie-Comte-Robert, and Cormeilles-en-Parisis, to Pithiviers and Coulommiers: so many *invitations au voyage*, so many reminders that Paris is still a port and a very ancient market town, in the centre of a rich countryside.

Only such improbable activities as historical research or the necessity of tracking down a lost aunt or of teaching English in a *boîte à bachot**1 to the sons and daughters of dolts, or the desire to visit the embittered and destitute survivors of obscure revolutionary movements—the last Machnist, or a companion of Petlioura, or a Maximalist—are likely to take one to the exotically named places on the misty edges of the *Métro* map or to the hidden villages of the Île-de-France and the Pays Briard. For research at least, such journeys offer their own reward, always of an unexpected, often of an altogether charming kind. The *mairie* of Jouy-en-Josas, for

1 Words marked with an asterisk can be found in the glossary.

instance, is a big, solid, rambling, eighteenth-century Île-de-France house, a *maison de maître*, full of cupboards and passages, that once belonged to M. Oberkampf of the *papiers peints*; the walls of the council chamber, that must have once been the dining-room, carry ample evidence of the great man's talent, while the French windows give on to a yard which, at break, suddenly fills with rural children, in their blue or pink *tabliers*. As the researcher, sitting in the spring sun, reading the minutes of the *société populaire* of the year II, attempts half-heartedly to concentrate, his attention is distracted by the reedy voices of the children in the building next door, as they attack the strangely innocent, bitter-sweet *La Claire Fontaine*.

Elsewhere, after seeing *M. le secrétaire-général*, he will be directed to the *salle des mariages*, where he may sit, in dusty splendour, through warm afternoons in the mayor's chair on the rostrum, under the sightless eyes of a white Marianne, or to the *salle du conseil* with its green table, ornate inkpots containing dried purple ink, in the ghostly company of shrouded fake Louis XVI chairs. There are other possibilities: an attic in the *mairie* of Brie-Comte-Robert, with, as sole furniture, fifty-seven volumes of the *Annuaire du Département de Seine-et-Marne*—twenty will make a seat, thirty-seven a table of a sort—or the office of the *secrétaire* himself in that of le Pecq, its windows opening on to the Seine, to the gentle chug-chug of the barges; or the cellars of the town hall of Argenteuil.

There is always the danger that he may suffer the fate of his rather odd companions in these dark of dusty places: at Saint-Denis, an enormous portrait in oils of Jacques Doriot, standing on a barricade of the conventional sort, against a background of red flags, clenched fists and factory chimneys, gazing resolutely towards a future that was to end messily, an unbeautiful reminder of lost principles; or, in the depot of the Archives de la Police, a bust in bronze of Jean Chiappe, who, like Icarus, fell into the sea, and a piece of hangman's rope, including noose, presented to some former Prefect of Police by a colleague from Scotland Yard; or else, in rural attics, the official photographs of former Presidents, the reassuring features of M. Fallières, the deceptive benevolence of the unfortunate Paul Doumer (the revolver that ended his term of presidency is there among the papers in the quai des Orfèvres), the flags and Chinese lanterns of the 14th, and in one place, perhaps

Moret-sur-Loing, a *garde nationale* flag of 1848. The danger, that is, that the researcher too may be forgotten, among these dethroned objects, discarded toys, and find himself locked up in a prison of history, the cell walls lined with those pale-green *cartons* that decorate the studies of provincial *notaires* safe behind their padded doors. The present writer once had to emerge, backwards, from a third floor window, and make a difficult descent to the street, via the letter 'A' in MAIRIE, cornice, flag-stone, and drain-pipe, from a rural depot on a hot Saturday afternoon; on another, he found himself locked away in the Musée de la Police, among the bombs, knitting-needles, sticks, knives, guillotine blades, revolvers (F.N.B. Herstal)—and the spy-hole used by Dr. Petiot—that dispatched the eminent or the notorious.

It is safer to accept a seat at ground level, with the use of a corner of a table, alongside the ladies concerned with the Allocations Familiales: safer, but also more distracting, for it is difficult to give full attention to the minutes of the town council of Rozay-en-Brie in 1794 when one's three neighbours are discussing, with enormous enjoyment and a wealth of salacious detail, the activities among the virgin population of Rozay-en-Brie and surrounding villages, in 1953, of a lecherous and apparently highly successful Polish butcher's apprentice. Where to draw the limits of social history? There are, too, other distracting presences: at Rouen, for instance, for a number of years, that of Boufflers, a Russian Blue cat, who reported for work each day, at 9 and at 2, at the Archives de la Seine-Maritime, in a suitcase punctured with air holes, and who took his exercise—and the attention of the feline-inclined historian or genealogist—in elegant arabesques from planks contrived for his benefit beneath the ceiling, to land with perfect aim and timing on the open registers of the Parlement de Normandie or on the *état-civil* of the parish of Saint-Séver. Boufflers was primarily a decorative figure, to judge from the sieve-like state of many of the documents—nibbled, at the corners and even in the middle, into patterns as complicated as those of a pianola score, by the rats and mice of this ancient city, the rodents of which seem to display a particular penchant for the revolutionary period.

The profession of archivist, so often attractive to people of ancient lineage and impoverished means—the École des Chartes is vintage *vieille France*—is a last refuge, in a Prisunic and *4-chevaux* age, both of charm and eccentricity. Generally, the two are combined to add up to one delightful, civilized, informative, and utterly disinterested person (for few professions can be worse paid). But of course there are cases when this has not been so, and the result then has been eccentricity unchecked by any other consideration. In a certain Department north of Paris the chief archivist, who was a bachelor of crapulous habits and a man so fantastically mean that like Tocqueville's Blanqui he only went out at night, so as to avoid the necessity of wearing a shirt (and the possibility of meeting any of his employees), lived for many years in his own office, sleeping, from 7 a.m. to 6 p.m., on one of those indefinable objects half-way between a stretcher and a camp bed, that the French call a *grabat* (they exist too in Austrian prisons and in the cells of the police station at Tunbridge Wells), doing his cooking in empty tins of Abeille floor polish, and, occasionally, on feast days, hanging out his scanty and revolting washing on a string, from a window that faced on to the *cour d'honneur* of the fine seventeenth-century Préfecture building. The Prefect during the Vichy period—a Darlan appointee, of naval background and tidiness—while merely remonstrating with the keeper of the records when he introduced to his office-bedroom women of absolutely certain reputation, objected strongly to these periodical displays of sordid underwear, so strongly indeed that their owner, a man of the old school of honour, slapped the *igame's* face and was at once suspended, a circumstance which enabled him to be restored, with a certain aura of *résistance* and with full back-pay in 1944.

This particular archivist was not especially interested in the documents entrusted to his care, adding however to their bulk by filling up 325 schoolboy notebooks with minute to minute commentaries on his waking night: '6h. du soir, me suis levé et lavé (sic), 6h. 2 habillé, 6h. 15 café, tartine beurre et chocolat . . . 6h. 25. sorti, croisé, avenue du Mail, M. Bernard, à qui il manquait le quatriéme bouton du gilet', and so on, a *fonds* inherited by his successor and now, no doubt, duly classified. There have, however, been other archivists who have tended to regard the papers in their *dépôts* as their own personal property, to be kept away, above all, from historians. In the eighty-odd Departments of France there are still one or two of these awkward fellows, the archival equivalent of those infuriating *châtelains*—or, more often, plebeian husbands

56

of *châtelaines*—who, having pretensions as amateur historians, listened to with respect by a few mad old ladies, jealously sit over family papers that they are quite incapable of putting to any useful purpose.

Generally, however, these former *chartistes*, primarily concerned, both by inclination and by training, with medieval history, and therefore with the rather rare medieval records that have survived into their charge, are only too willing to give the searcher a completely free hand with the despised documents belonging to the *archives modernes* (1789 onwards), one of them even going so far as to allow the present writer to take away with him boxes of papers, an act of generosity which produced an embarrassing situation when one of these flew open, at rush hour, on the Porte de Versailles line, to scatter the correspondence of the year III under the feet of readers of *France-Soir*.

Documents of the revolutionary period, excellently classified, in virtue of a system that is uniform throughout the French Departments (and, like so many things in France, has been laid down by decree), tend rather to be disparaged by members of a profession who, often believing that the rot set in in 1789, would perhaps be only too willing to erase from their national past all trace of the Great Revolution. Indeed, one middle-aged *archiviste adjointe* proceeded to do just this, by systematically and industriously cutting off the tops of all documents bearing the hated heading 'République Française', a method which, by the time she was taken away, had made a fairly considerable hole in the over-stocked *archives modernes* of that particular *dépôt*.

For nearly a century now France has employed trained archivists, both on the national level (*archives nationales*, and the *fonds* of the lesser-known collections of the Assistance Publique and the Travaux Publics) and on the provincial *archives départementales*. (These include not only the Departments of Metropolitan France and Algeria but also Martinique, Guadeloupe, la Réunion, la Nouvelle-Calédonie, all of which have full-time archivists.) Most of the larger cities—this is the case at least in Rouen, Bordeaux, Nantes, Lyon, and Marseille—have given the care of their records (*archives communales*) to *chartistes* or professionally trained librarians. In smaller towns and in villages, on the other hand, responsibility for the parish registers, for the minutes of the municipality and for the very considerable mass of documents accruing from the revolutionary period falls to a municipal official without any specialized training in archive work, the *secrétaire de la mairie*.

This indeed is only a part, and a comparatively minor part, of his manifold functions; even in his capacity as archivist the *secrétaire* will far more often be called upon to deal with queries concerning contemporary matters—the *cadastre*,* tax returns, the *Journal Officiel*, the decrees and regulations issued monthly by the Prefects, and so on—than with matters of purely historical interest. Once, however, he has recovered from his amazement that anyone should want to look at 'a lot of old papers somewhere in the attic', the secretary will be extremely helpful and, if the searcher is lucky enough to chance upon one of these officials who is also the local schoolmaster and therefore probably historically inclined, he will derive from him guidance amid the enormous complexities of French village life and the deep, persistent, subterranean currents of rural quarrels.

How often one must render thanks to the left-wing, revolutionary tradition of the French *instituteur*! If the secretary is a local man he can again give valuable assistance with regard to family history; sometimes, indeed, the striking continuity of French rural life, through so many régimes and revolutions, is suddenly brought home to the visitor by the fact that the secretary himself bears the name of one of those village families that polarized, in rural communes, the tremendous conflicts that were rending asunder revolutionary France. Thus, in the pretty village of Villeblevin, near the place where Albert Camus was to die a few years later, the writer received advice and hospitality from a secretary whose great-great-grandfather had been the revolutionary mayor of the commune in 1793 and 1794; and rightly proud she was of her vigorous terrorist ancestor! Were it not for the burden of the *Journal Officiel* and of teaching, many of these *instituteurs* would undoubtedly have joined the depleting ranks of that peculiarly French phenomenon, *l'érudit local*.

A word then about the latter. He is likely to be a retired schoolmaster, or the local *curé*, a country doctor, an old-established *notaire*, a *contentieux*, and, in the cities, often an *avoué*, an *agent d'assurances*, an *administrateur des hypothèques*, sometimes even a member of the Bar. Each will have his own particular contribution to make and his own, often closed, sources of information. The *curé* will naturally be mainly concerned with the history of his church and its previous incumbents, with Wars of Religion and wars against religion; but he is liable to be well read in local lore, from municipal history to the reading of Latin *graffiti* and the discovery of fossils. *Notaires* and *avoués* have direct access to family records—and family secrets—that are not to be found in official *dépôts*; and, having bought or inherited their *charge* from a whole dynasty of predecessors, they may also be in possession of estate records and testamentary papers that give a microscopic and accurate picture of the social structure of a community. In the past ten years, two *notaires* at least have taken to writing their own history, and their contributions have been extremely important.

French doctors, both of the urban and rural sort, have for years been afflicted by a veritable historiomania. For many years the practitioners of Lyon have succeeded in running a quarterly, *Les Albums du Crocodile*, devoted to the history of their lovable city and its neighbourhood and publishing detailed monographs on medical history, including the various plagues, pestilences, famines, and dearths that have afflicted man and beast in the ancient town over the centuries. In Paris itself the yearly *Entretiens de Bichat*, published in the form of a review, have drawn attention to such subjects as the history of the Paris hospitals, the use that the economic and social historian can make of their account books, the recruitment into the medical profession under the *ancien régime*, the development of private *maisons de santé*. Doctors all over France show a peculiar interest in the revolutionary period, seeing possibly in Marat the example of a colleague who achieved success and fame in other fields. There is finally another type of *érudit local*—the *châtelain*—but the less said about him the better, for the historian will receive little help—and much hindrance and dissuasion—from him, when he is not actually set on by his dogs.

The great days of the *érudit local* were in the period of the thirty peaceful years that came before the 1914–18 War, years during which the republican tradition developed steadily, bringing with it a revived interest in the local history of the Great Revolution. Printing costs remained low and the rural *pharmacien*, who was also an amateur historian, had the incentive of publication to spur on his researches in the local records. During these years hundreds of reviews were formed not only in every Department but pretty well in every town numbering ten thousand inhabitants or over. There is an immense wealth of erudition to be dug out of these publications, and anyone who has spent some time working in French provincial records must often have had the chastening experience of discovering that what he had thought to be original material has been published—and competently edited—by some long-extinct local journal. Woe betide the Anglo-Saxon scholar who, with the reckless intrepidity of M. Braudel's young Mediterranean *chevaux-légers*,* embarks on the great sea of provincial archives without having first systematically worked through the *Bulletin de la Société Archéologique et Historique* (and maybe *Philosophique* and *Numismatique* as well) *du Saintonge & de l'Aunis*, and the hundred and one similar collections, in the Bibliothèque Nationale.

Those days are now over, and most of these reviews have been killed off since 1918, and even more since 1944, by the high cost of printing. In many places little of a once-active tradition is left but the formal skeleton of semi-extinct *sociétés savantes*, bodies as reactionary, as utterly conservative and as useless as the Académie Française itself, given over entirely to an annual indigestion of speech-making and over-eating and to the production of a *bulletin* that contains little more than the encroaching number of *notices nécrologiques*. Many of these local societies are dying on their feet, often through their own fault, through their refusal to recruit new blood and to allow into their hallowed walls the despised *universitaires*, the professional historian, much less—*horreur!*—the schoolmistress. The present writer, who has the doubtful honour of being a corresponding member of one such venerable institution, one of the few surviving members of which is President Coty,[1] can recall the enormity of his gaffe when, on being asked to read a paper to the half-dozen aged stalwarts who formed this society, he invited three female *professeurs* from the local *lycée* to come and hear him. Not since the society was founded, 130 years ago, he was told by the treasurer, in deeply shocked tones, had a *woman* ever been admitted to one of its *séances*, not even Mme V . . ., the sister of General Koenig and the wife of the presiding member!

[1] This was written in 1962 when President Coty was still alive. The Société Havraise d'Études Diverses (*fondée par Bernardin de Saint-Pierre*) is still in existence.

Nowhere are the advantages of administrative centralization more apparent than in the organization of the French local records. In the early years of the Third Republic, archives both *départementales* and *communales* were provided with a system of classification common to every Department and every commune of the Republic. Once this extremely simple system has been mastered, the researcher will have acquired a master key with which to rifle the secrets of virtually any public *dépôt*. The letters of the alphabet will take on a new significance: 'L' for the Revolution period in the Departments, 'Q' for the 'séquestres', 'D' for the minutes of town councils and village assemblies in the *archives communales*. 'I' for police and public opinion, 'F' for grain and food supply, and so on, from Ain to Yonne, from Lys-lès-Lannoy to Palavas-les-Flots. In many places the inventories of Departmental and local records have been published and it is then enough to quote the index numbers of the boxes or registers required, in order to have them sent up to the Archives Nationales in Paris: a system of one-way centralization that is clearly of endless advantage to the historian established in the capital. The over-all picture, no doubt, is not quite so beautiful; there are both Departments and communes where the *archives modernes* still await classification—in most cases the failure to do so can be traced to royalist, reactionary-minded medievalists—and there are others where they have unaccountably been lost. But on the whole the system works and the visitor can generally be sure of very rapidly tracing down the type of material he is looking for.

Despite five foreign invasions in the period covered by the *archives modernes*, France is still enormously rich in local administrative records from the Revolution onwards. Losses through enemy—or Allied—action have been surprisingly light, and there are few places that can compete with the unhappy fame of Soissons, with its local records destroyed, first in 1814—when the Cossacks accidentally set fire to the *hôtel de ville*—then in 1870, again in 1914, and once more in 1940. Lille, for instance, still possesses immense collections, as does the Nord. In the last war only two Departments lost almost all their *fonds*: the Loiret, when Orleans was bombed in 1940, and the Manche, as a result of the Allied bombardment of Saint-Lô in 1944. Far heavier losses have been caused by rodents, by neglect, by the scant respect shown by many Prefects—especially Vichy ones—for their country's past. (During the Pétain régime the rich *dépôt* of the Seine-Inférieure was expelled from its building, to

61

A SECOND IDENTITY

make way for the police, with the result that in 1944 part of the archives of the Parlement de Normandie were discovered floating in brackish water, in a largely roofless chapel; what has survived is now housed in a disused, but roofed chapel, in a maternity hospital four miles north of Rouen where researchers find themselves outnumbered by pregnant women, walking in sedate crocodile formation in their bulging blue smocks.)[1] The Vichy Government, despite its obsession with *Jehanne* and Péguy and phony regionalism, caused even greater destruction through its paper drives.

If the historian of Paris has a convenient alibi in the widespread destruction of municipal records at the time of the Commune, in the provinces there can be no such excuse for turning one's back on research and for taking refuge in the giddy upper air of comparative history or of the *conjoncture*. Every year there is more, not less, material available, as chambers of commerce, *chambres de notaires*, hospitals and public services, banks and industrial concerns hand over their records to the appropriate archives. In another sense too the field has been made wider as historians take cognizance of the possibilities offered by previously unexploited *fonds*: *hypothèques*, notarial records, hospital accounts, records of educational establishments, bankruptcy suits, local newspapers, and so on.

Nor is the field overcrowded, though since the war more and more French professional historians have been undertaking detailed regional studies of institutions and societies, the conclusions of which, while not being decisive for the understanding of a period of French national history, are of immense local significance. This indeed is the direction that one hopes Anglo-Saxon research historians will also take: the study of local societies and institutions for their own sake and in their own context, and not with a view to making general statements about France as a whole. There are some very welcome signs that this is indeed the trend of things and that larger numbers of students, abandoning the arid, dreary uplands of political history on the government level, are prepared to settle down, maybe for years, to the minute dissection of a commune, to the history of a provincial society. What is required is not yet

[1] Since the time of writing, both the *dépôt* and the records have been moved, the former from the rue de Crosne, the latter from the maternity hospital, Mont-Saint-Aignan, to a modern building on the left bank of the Seine. The Archives de la Seine-Maritime now form the most up-to-date record office in France.

another *History of Modern France*, nor a further reinterpretation of French history, but rather a detailed and sympathetic study of let us say, emigration from the Auvergne during the eighteenth century, or the application of the *loi des suspects* in a given district during the Revolution. In other words the prospect facing the French regular army officer after Indo-China: *le retour à Romorantin.*

The *retour à Romorantin* has much to recommend it on grounds other than historical. Research in French records offers its own pleasures, on its own unpredictable terms. As, after love, experience is the most important quality for the historian of a foreign country, *le chemin de Montauban*, as one puffs up its steep steps to the Archives du Rhône, through the sides of black, blind houses, provides not only *tourisme* at its most *inédit* but also the sense of a time and a place, the feeling of a city, the impression finally of belonging to a community of human beings.

Perhaps it is possible to write French history away from France, and some people have done it without ever going to France at all; it may be good, careful history, too, based on fair judgement, on a perception of the inherent weaknesses of a political system. But it will not be the history of living people.

2 'Les Nuits de Paris'[1]

What is the endless attraction of social history? One explanation would appear to be that, by removing the walls from lodging houses, the roofs from attics, by revealing the secrets of the poor and the humble, secrets which are not, like those of state, secrets at all but rather human and often shameful, it satisfies the prying instincts that keep the research historian steady on his austere course. Anyone who has not experienced the extreme delight of rifling the private correspondence of persons long since dead—it is only by the accidental good fortune of war that we may do the same for that of the living—of undoing the pink ribbons on ancient love letters, of ploughing through the repetitive declarations of pregnancy of country girls seduced by their employers, of reading the hastily written notes of suicides, poor ladies of ancient lineage, left behind in a hateful revolutionary Paris by the tide of emigration that carried away the healthy and the young, cannot appreciate the incentive to go on and to search further.

French history in particular, thanks to one great upheaval that swept into the multitudinous files of the Public Accuser the flotsam of personal papers and even personal objects—the spectacles of a man who died on the guillotine, the wool or cotton samples of an eighteenth-century commercial traveller, the scribbling drawings of the day-dreamer—has much to offer the vicarious historian. He can also fall back on all the minute written evidence of a system of law based ultimately on the *dossier* and on *l'instruction*, as well as on the testimony of humble folk when confronted with the police *commissaire*. The social historian should be thankful for the police state: but his curiosity can also be satisfied in works of fiction and in accounts by contemporary observers.

Restif de la Bretonne, probably best known as a prolific pornographer who had peculiar views about the spelling of French,

---

[1] Review of a re-issue of Restif de la Bretonne, *Les Nuits de Paris* (Paris, 1960).

appears also, in the latest edition of one of his lesser-known works, *Les Nuits de Paris*, as a witness both acute and intimate of the street life of Paris in the years immediately preceding the Revolution, as a masterly observer of the speech, manners, standard of living, behaviour, and leisure habits of the common people. The editors of *Les Nuits de Paris* have revealed a social historian.

'Je marchais légèrement et sans bruit, à l'ombre des maisons, comme le Guet', writes this *spectateur nocturne*, who also makes the claim that: 'de tous nos gens de Lettres, je suis peut-être le seul qui connaisse le peuple en me mêlant à lui. Je veux le peindre; je veux être la sentinelle du bon ordre . . .'. And how admirably he succeeds, at least in his efforts to portray the people, even if as a pillar of order and government he remains rather unconvincing. Perhaps the last phrase is merely a gesture to the formal morality of his times, or perhaps Restif, like other extreme individualists before him, was an upholder of order and discipline provided they were applied to people other than himself. But as an observer of the *fait divers*, of the *chose vue*, Restif is incomparable in his own time.

Little that happened in the chaotic streets of central Paris between 1786 and 1793 seems to have escaped the rather crankish observer, wrapped in his outlandish garb to match the night, which is as much the element of this refugee from the countryside as that of the *boulevardier* of the turn of the century or of the proverbial Grand duke on the treadmill of his grand tour. Here we can see him as he wished us to see him, for he likes to surround himself with an air both of mystery and omniscience and he has all the pride, in his oddly acquired, jumbled, and ill-digested knowledge, of the typical autodidact, night after night on the prowl, going about in search of good deeds, arriving generally just too late to save virtue in peril, but in time at least to get the ruined girl's story from her trembling lips, calling out the *garde* on the least pretext, meddling in other people's affairs—on one occasion he uses the communal lavatory halfway up the stair of an old house so as to crouch within eaves-dropping distance of a family dispute on the storey above—the Friend of Order, reporting back, in the early hours, with his nightly consignment of rescued but tarnished maids, to the salon of the apparently ever-wakeful Marquise, whose dedicated interest in fallen womanhood is never adequately explained.

Yet it is not entirely a flight of fancy that portrays the tiresome *spectateur* hugging the houses of the ill-lit streets or keeping well to the middle of the road in order to avoid the contents of chamber pots, and climbing dark stairways in response to piteous (and feminine) cries for help. Restif is as omniscient as he is peripatetic; his brief sketches reveal him removing the leprous façades from mansions or lodging-houses, to reveal here the fat priest in bed with the thirteen-year-old laundry girl, there a group of counterfeiters crouching in the light of oil lamps over their engravers' plates, or again standing by while the builders' apprentices squander their increased earnings, in a Paris growing every day, in a billiard room in which the bets have been rigged by a secret syndicate. Restif even notes the changes from hour to hour in the clientele of such establishments: idle servants in the afternoon, sharp but conceited hairdressers' assistants in the early evening, and he can identify the small group of semi-criminals, ponces, fish-porters, old-clothes merchants (Restif is perhaps the first of contemporary historians to emphasize the connections between the old-clothes dealer and the fence, between the rag-and-bone man and the *demimonde* of crime and vice) who fix the stakes and lead the unwary to disaster.

On another occasion we see him dining in a cheap restaurant, watching the rhythmically racing jaws as fifty-odd people rush through their meal, to free the tables for those who are waiting: fifteen minutes each for soup, entrée, and dessert, and, above all, *no talking*. This king of gate-crashers is even on the heels of the priest and the choirboy as they bear extreme unction to the virtuous artisan on his death-bed; Restif, a journalist to the last, is there to hear his dying words.

Of course, like Vidocq, he is often an impudent liar; we must not take him too literally, for he could not have witnessed all the things that form the narrative of *Les Nuits*. He cannot *always* have been present when a family of small children was burned to death in the locked attic of a carpenter while the parents were out drinking, or when an innocent girl, fresh from the country, was raped, or a provincial fool, gaping at the fortune-tellers at the fair, was robbed of watch and wallet, or when a pretty child was sold by her nurse to satisfy the complicated lust of the sophisticated. But it does not really matter, for all are *cas témoins*, and Restif knew what he was about.

It was hardly surprising that he often got himself into trouble—indeed one is amazed that someone did not do away early on with this self-appointed auxiliary of the *garde* and of the *exempts**— receiving copious insults in the vivid vocabulary of the common people (there is a passage in the present collection recording an exchange between two washerwomen that would put to shame even Hébert's expletive *Père Duchesne*), or having mud thrown at him by the urchins of the Île Saint-Louis, who probably suspected him of being a *voyeur*.

As a result of his peculiar accoutrement, he is often mistaken for a monk; at times, this may get him out of awkward scrapes, when he is remonstrating with young fops who are attempting to carry off a seamstress, but more often it involves him in further blows, the ordinary people taking out on the night owl some of the violent anti-clericalism it would naturally reserve for the friar and the monk, detested as unproductive and lazy and even more as seducers of the wives and daughters of the poor.

'On sait que, laissant à d'autres les affaires publiques, je m'occupe plus volontiers des affaires particulières.' He knows his own limitations and it is only incidentally, generally through the medium of the various odd causes he takes up—he is a campaigner for better hygiene, a reformed spelling, compulsory swimming—that he becomes involved in affairs of public interest. Occasionally in *Les Nuits* he slips in an account of a great historical event (inevitably, he is present at all the great days of the early period of the Revolution, even receiving vague overtures from one of the ladies of the bedchamber on the eve of the flight to Varennes), but his main purpose is to observe and to chronicle private behaviour, to put on daily record the *fait divers*.

In this he is greatly aided by his intense love and fantastic topographical knowledge of Paris (he is in love with the great city as only an individual deprived of personal affection and devoid of compassion can be; he loves Paris and fears and despises its inhabitants) and by his acute understanding, as a classless eccentric, of the varying social attitudes of the different estates. Being a *déclassé*, a peasant come to the town, which he no longer leaves even to go as far as the deserts of Charenton or Passy, he is able to move at ease between the various conditions of people, passing without transition from a gaming house or a billiard room to the salon of the Marquise. We may be rather sceptical about the salon, for Restif,

67

like most self-educated cranks, is inordinately vain and constantly boasts about his connections among the great ladies; but he is certainly at home in the ill-frequented café, the busy workshop, the steaming laundry, and, when he can get in, the female bathing establishment. And, like anyone who has thus, thanks to origin or perseverance, succeeded in obtaining a passport across the frontiers of class, *le spectateur* is prone to read into his own ubiquity a tribute to his superior wisdom.

He writes with artistry and simplicity of the sprawling, dirty city, noisy with the curses of its three-quarters of a million unruly, disrespectful, and brutal inhabitants; many of his brief sketches are poems to urban delights. There are two Watteau-like scenes when he becomes (as always uninvited) involved in moonlit parties in the Luxembourg Gardens and of the terrace of the Tuileries; at first he is mistaken for a Marshal of France by two *sylphides* dressed in white; at the second he has to hide behind a tree, from which he watches a priest and a young widow making love on the grass. Elsewhere one is reminded of Goya in his happier, Madrid mood: in a narrow street he suddenly comes upon two harlequins and a pierrot amusing themselves by throwing stones at the street lamps. On another occasion a group of revellers in black silk masks overtake a good bourgeois coming home with his wife and two daughters; amidst laughter, they hold the father up to ransom, remove his wallet, and carry off his giggling wife and delighted daughters.

Restif, like the commissioners of police and, later, the members of the revolutionary committees, is constantly complaining of the dangers offered to public order by the prevalence of disguise, and we become familiar with a world of *travestis* and *efféminés* that recalls the young fops of *Jonathan Wild*. In Restif's Paris homosexuality emerges as a vice of all classes, while the *amazone* seems to have been almost as common during the latter years of the *ancien régime* as in that heroic period of the Revolution when the female warrior became an object of patriotic propaganda. No wonder the Lieutenant of Police and the Parlement multiplied ordinances and regulations forbidding the *travestis* and limiting the period of carnival!

He writes of the wonders of the rue Saint-Honoré and the Palais Royal, the centres of European civilization, and he adores the moonlit quays of the Île Saint-Louis, his favourite nocturnal retreat. For the faubourgs and the Île de la Cité ('gothique et barbare') he has little use; there is in the former, particularly in Saint-Antoine, Saint-Marceau, and around Saint-Paul, a complete absence of lavatories (Restif is peculiarly English in his equation between lavatories, civilization, and progress). La Cité is a nest of medieval smelliness. He does not like dirt; the Parisians are dirty, they do not wash enough, or they wash their feet in the Seine, despite the stringent ordinances of the Lieutenant of Police, despite too the presence, alongside the Île, of such establishments as the peculiarly named Bains des Dames Publiques et Particulières.

Our social historian, ostensibly in the cause of hygiene, spends much of his time hanging about outside this and similar establishments, in the hope of picking up snatches of conversation between the *dames publiques* and the *dames particulières* as they soap themselves in the waters of the Seine. His zeal in the interests of segregation enables him to discover the ruse of a young man who had succeeded in entering a ladies' bath, disguised as a girl; for once, Restif does not denounce the culprit to the guard. No doubt he envied him his ability thus to cross the frontiers of sex, for he himself was constantly obsessed by the desire to penetrate into the closed, secret, and cruel world of women together. Like many historians later, he was constantly chafing at the check on knowledge placed by biology; his most constant preoccupation is with the thoughts, desires, motivations, emotions of women, and, above all, of the women of the people.

Not that he had any great love for the common people of either sex; their violence, their lack of respect for authority, their dangerous envy, fill him with horror and alarm. The river-workers ('les horribles tireurs de bois flotté') notorious for their unruliness and their independence, the coal-heavers, the women who work on the Seine barges, the Auvergnats and the Savoyards (in Restif's rendering of Parisian dialogue, a common form of insult is: 'Va-t-en donc, Savoyard, assassin! au voleur!') seem to fill him with particular alarm. For, living in the suburbs and being without personal possessions, they have no interest in the maintenance of order and the defence of property, and will even stand by and laugh while a fire consumes the homes of the wealthy.

He fears, too, the tumblers, mostly gypsies, lewd fellows who corrupt the young and who are in alliance with the fences, and the mysterious armies of pallid-faced ponces, whom he also depicts as taking an important part in the September Massacres, profiting from the occasion to release from prison not only their protégés but a number of aristocratic girls as yet fresh to the profession. At the time of the Parlement riots, in 1787 and 1788, he refers to the lawlessness of the watchmakers' and jewellers' apprentices and of vociferous rowdies of the *basoche**—always the first to defy the Government, in the very centre of the city, and to cry for 'le bon roi Henri'.

J'avoue [he writes, in a sketch a few years before the outbreak of the Revolution] que j'ai tremblé toutes les fois que j'ai vu la portion basse du peuple en émotion . . . parce que je la connais, parce que je sais quelle est sa haine contre tout ce qui est aisé, haine éternelle, violente, qui ne demande qu'une occasion de s'exercer. . . . Si une fois cette bête féroce croyait qu'elle peut oser, elle bouleverserait tout . . .

Elsewhere he has some pertinent things to say about the primitive class jealousies of the women port workers,

ces femmes de bateau, aigries par la peine . . ., qui ont contre l'épicière, mieux habillée, mieux vêtue, la même jalousie qu'une bourgeoise avait contre l'avocate et la conseillière, que celle-ci avait contre la finance et la noblesse . . .

Such jealousies are part and parcel of any feminine society; but Restif proves himself more observant still when he speaks of the 'spirit of insubordination' which he sees spreading from the top downwards to affect every portion of society, as respect for authority decreases. Some of his remarks, indeed, might have come out of Taine, and so alarming is his portrait of 'la bête féroce' that one is reminded of Louis Chevalier's picture of the working class of the same city forty or fifty years later.

There are hints in Restif too of a class racialism, of the fears felt by the bourgeois and by the artisan for the pale men with dark, ill-kempt hair, piercing eyes, and shaggy moustaches; his *canaille* is always dark and glowering; the respectable, the men of property, the virtuous craftsmen are fair and have good complexions; the good girl is rosy-cheeked and blue-eyed, at least until her fall. Restif exclaims on Charlotte Corday's innocence, for she is blonde and Norman. In the 1780s the population of Paris, drawn mainly from

Flanders, Artois, Picardy, Normandy, and the hinterland of the capital, was still predominantly fair; the dark stood out as strangers. In the 1790s royalist pamphleteers, writing from Verona, Hamburg, and London, make much of the fact that the terrorists tended to be dark and from the Mediterranean area; Marat in particular served their purpose in this respect. And so too Restif's *massacreurs* would almost inevitably be depicted as men of the south.

Restif was afraid of the people, but there was in his fear an element of sympathy and understanding that is completely lacking both in the royalist or Thermidorian pamphleteers of the 1795 period, who refer vaguely to the *canaille*, to the *lie du peuple*, and in the nineteenth-century, middle-class historians who were content with reproducing these epithets. Restif was a marvellously accurate observer of social behaviour and he was particularly at home in the analysis of the social structure of the more obscure trades; he was gifted with a social insight more acute and a knowledge of the common people more real than that of any of his contemporaries, and if the author of *Jacques le Fataliste* is without doubt a far better novelist than the clumsy Burgundian, Restif is a more sensitive observer.

Himself an eccentric, as well as something of a sex maniac, Restif is above all at home with the odd, the cranky and with the *demi-monde* of crime. One night he watches a man tearing down one poster after another; he notices that he only removes those that announce events already past. The man tells him that this is his sole livelihood and that he is able to live off this strange trade because he is the only man in Paris to exercise it. Restif observes sagaciously that 'cette singulière vie . . . ne pouvait convenir qu'à un individu', and he goes on to air his knowledge: there are only two or three ink-peddlers in the capital, and only about half a dozen collectors of broken bottles; there is strength in small numbers, and even the rag-and-bone men work only part-time, supplementing their income with other casual employment. Unconsciously perhaps, he touches on the two phenomena most familiar to urban historians of this period, that of the second job and that of the mobility of labour.

On the subject of prostitution Restif is probably the most reliable authority of his century, and in *Les Nuits* he presents a series of case histories of extraordinary interest, describing the recruitment into that ancient profession of country girls, maid-servants, laundry-workers, seamstresses, pastry-cooks, runaway nuns, and gover-nesses. His prostitutes or semi-prostitutes appear to be happy in their work and tell the prying owl that, thanks to their good protectors and their good clientele of gentlemen or nice boys (for they still retain plebeian tastes and cut their prices for the builders' apprentices), they are making a handsome profit; one could not imagine a more convincing picture of contented vice.[1]

But he is equally acute in his analysis of feminine motivations; he can appreciate the consuming desire of the fishwife to lord it in the seats of the rich, but he also understands that it is by working on masculine pride that aristocratic women induce the unwilling nobleman to leave France and lead a life of honourable poverty in Coblence. 'C'étaient les femmes qui faisaient émigrer les hommes', just as it was the women who brought out the men on so many of the revolutionary days (*journées*). Perhaps this is obvious, but it is still worth saying. Restif, as a witness of his time, is constantly stating the obvious, but many of his great truths later became submerged and were lost to historians, so that we now have to return to this contemporary account to find explanations for much that we might have guessed.

A theme that recurs throughout *Les Nuits* is that of violence, both popular and aristocratic. It is as well to be reminded that the butcher's apprentice who is supposed to have cut up the body of Madame de Lamballe had been brought up in a Paris in which extreme brutality was a daily occurrence, the worst possible example being given, of course, by the old ruling class, by the nobility. Restif's night revellers are astonishingly quick on the draw, and *le spectateur* likes to depict himself placing his stick between their naked swords. Gentlemen's servants will cudgel out the brains of an insolent fellow for a misplaced remark, a Savoyard errand-boy is beaten to death by a young man whose fiancée had had her skirt dirtied by a cake of mud thrown by the little imp. The sons of the rich drive their two-wheelers like Jehu, running the crowd down against the walls of houses, and their example is followed by that of

[1] This was written in 1961, before I had read Mercier and had worked in the Archives de la Préfecture de Police for the period 1795–8 on the papers of the *commissaires de police*. I would not now subscribe to such a picture of 'contented vice'. See my *Problems of French Popular History 1789–1820* (Oxford, 1969), Part Three, 'Prostitution'.

cab-drivers, who, according to Restif, take a deliberate pleasure in the sound of crushed bones as the wheels pass over a body. Watching an execution, in the Place de Grève, Restif is horrified by the attitude of a pretty girl, laughing and grinning, on the arm of her young man, clearly taking tremendous pleasure in the spectacle of a man being broken on the wheel; time and again he returns to the inherent cruelty of the people.

With this experience as a witness behind him, he has some very pertinent things to say about the September Massacres, the most terrible manifestation of popular violence. It is true that, like most of the conservative historians of the nineteenth century, he tends to attribute the planning of these massacres to the machinations of wicked and hidden agitators, but his intimacy with popular behaviour enables him to perceive also that they represented a return to the rough justice of the people. 'Dans cette nuit terrible', he writes, 'le peuple faisait le rôle des grands d'autrefois. . . . C'est le peuple qui régnoit cette nuit. . . .' This is merely another way of expressing an idea familiar both to Pierre Caron, in his great book on the Massacres, and to Georges Lefebvre, which he developed in his *Foules Révolutionnaires*, that of popular justice and popular vengeance, the old millennarian dream of the common people resuming the function of justice that goes with sovereignty, and sitting in judgement on their oppressors. Restif very clearly perceives that for the *massacreurs* it was a matter of resuming an ancient right that had fallen into abeyance. Yet before the two great historians of this century no one had attempted to explain the Massacres other than in terms of the brutish instincts of the mob.

On the subject too of the ills and weaknesses of the *ancien régime* Restif is equally perceptive. There is a long passage, written in the early eighties, condemning the evils of the *ferme générale*, while unlike the Physiocrats, who are far removed from the realities of the popular mentality, he understands that free trade in grain is impossible in a country like France; he condemns the export of grain outside the kingdom, and favours the maintenance of the close regulations controlling the distribution of grain and the policing of the markets within the country.

Restif is close to the people and he is able to see what escapes the high-minded, but dogmatic, reformers: what the common people will stand for and where lie the frontiers between good government and public disorder. In his *choses vues* we witness, like Restif, with one eye conveniently closed, the smugglers running across flower-beds, near the Barrière de Chaillot, to bring barrels of wine into the city. This is a daily occurrence which Restif approves, for, he observes, foolish regulations are made only to be broken. He has little sympathy for the Parlement, but he appreciates their influence, and when he wants to get a petition considered in the right place he goes to the wife of a counsellor.

He fully shares the popular hostility to the clergy and later, during the Revolution, even approves the September Massacres in so far as they represented a solution to the problem of the recusant priests. On the subject of the nobility he is less consistent; clearly, during the *ancien régime*, he is something of a hanger-on and prides himself on having his entrées in the Faubourg, even if his Marquise may have been a fabrication of his own fancy. But once emigration starts he follows the public and sheds few tears over the fate of the former oppressors.

Perhaps his most interesting remarks concern the steady breakdown of the machine of government, the spread of disorder, disobedience, and disrespect during the ten years preceding the Revolution. Restif, who is essentially a government man, to the extent even that in 1793 he emerges as a partisan of the Jacobin dictatorship—any government, one feels, has his approval, so long as it is strong and gets itself obeyed—and who has a great admiration for many of the intendants, including the unfortunate Bertier, deplores these daily signs of collapse and frequently predicts a general subversion. For one so given to boasting it is even surprising that, in his sketches for the Revolution period, he does not make more of this and offer himself the luxury of saying 'I told you so'.

Restif's jottings open in fact a new layer of historical evidence and must be of immense value to the social historian. He is the historian of the intimate and the personal rather than of the collective and the general, and his sketches reveal the individual, in bed, in his family, at play, drunk, in the pursuit of vice, eating (sometimes cat's meat or dog's meat, for among Restif's numerous acquaintances we meet a man who makes it his living to sell dead cats and dogs to restaurants), gaming, arguing about wages or reading over the shoulders of those who take coffee in the Café de Chartres. He gives faces, personality, eccentricity, and even a dialogue, in that inimitably ironical and disrespectful language of the Parisis, to Carlyle's King Mob, to Taine's scum of the earth, to Soboul's *Sans-culottes*, to George Rudé's *Crowd in the French Revolution*.

Restif understood the people, even if he could not love them, and his comments on popular life and behaviour represent the most valuable source to come recently on the market for the historian who is concerned more with the governed than the governors, more with the common people than with the power élite. His portraits are as rich as those of Hogarth, without attaining that quality of carica-ture that is the mark of the London artist, and his sketches are in effect prose *cris de Paris*, bearing the authentic voice of the unruly and generous population of the great city. *Les Nuits* is a work of historical imagination, based on observation, on knowledge, and on sympathy, and therefore a contribution to historical knowledge in the same way as the film, *Les Enfants du Paradis*, is an addition to historical perception; the book, like the film, recreates the ambiance of a period and preserves for future generations the moving vitality of the common people.

The publishers are to be congratulated on having rescued this vivacious sketch-book from the semi-obscurity of the *réserve* of the Bibliothèque Nationale and from the other dark and hidden places to which worthy librarians have consigned collectively all the 200-odd works of the productive pornographer. They are to be con-gratulated too on the quality of presentation, the beautiful print (some of which reproduces faithfully Restif's own peculiar experi-ments in his trade), and the many contemporary illustrations, in themselves objects of beauty and a perfect commentary on the text.[1]

[1] This was in fact an abridged edition of a work that normally runs into twelve volumes. The selection is by no means entirely representative of the full range of Restif's observations of the Paris scene.

3 'Nous des *Annales*'[1]

It is hardly surprising that, after nearly forty years of existence—the review was founded in the 1920s—and after twenty years of imperial power, by virtue of the famous Sixième Section of the École Pratique des Hautes Études—the *Annales* school ('Nous des *Annales*', the opening words of so many articles) should have acquired not only the mentality of a dedicated and closed fraternity, but also a language of its own which is almost immediately recognizable and, in the course of years of strenuous self-advertisement, has become so formalized as to be easily parodied. The *Annales*, after conquering the Mediterranean and colonizing the Baltic, have now moved into the French Revolution. The co-authors of the present luxuriously illustrated history of the Revolution, François Furet and Denis Richet, the former a specialist of the eighteenth-century Paris middle-classes, the latter researching on sixteenth-century Paris, are among the most distinguished younger members of the Brotherhood; writing in the language of the faithful, they represent, in an extreme form, both the virtues and the faults of a group of historians who, while extending the areas of historical research, have often been over-exclusive and almost hysterically sensitive to any form of criticism from outside.

The school does not hold any monopoly of new subjects, Ariès, Foucault, and Chevalier all being independent researchers who have felt their way along the dark corridors of the history of the family, of madness, of crime, and popular violence, without ever having been admitted as *frères-ès-conjoncture*. No one would deny that the Masters (Febvre, Bloch, and Braudel) were great pioneers who, even when they were wrong, were wrong intelligently and inspiringly. Their disciples, on the other hand—at least those hardy ones who have stayed the course and remained in the fold—for the French historical world is dotted with ex-apostles, *disgraciés*, and heretics—have tended to be imitative, amplifying and fossilizing the Masters' Voice, and when they have been wrong they have

[1] Review of François Furet and Denis Richet, *La Révolution: des états généraux au 9 thermidor* (Paris, 1965).

76

often been just plain silly. It has not always been a matter of imita-
tion, in the tradition of the Master-Disciple relationship. Every cult
puts a premium on orthodoxy, and orthodoxy can best be expressed
in a language increasingly rigid. So the cult has been formalized,
following each successive purge of the unorthodox, often as an
overriding search merely for novelty. *Annales* must be the first in
every new field. Novelty can often result in vulgarity and preten-
tiousness. M. Furet and M. Richet are two very representative
members of the school.

The most obvious characteristic is the style, very much *style
Annales*. This might be described, at its worst, as the faculty to
restate obscurely and in a French almost Sartrean in its muddiness,
what previous, non-juror historians have stated clearly and simply.
'. . . le pain cher, avec ses effets socialement sélectifs . . .', is the
Furet-Richet way, the *Annales* way, of saying that high bread prices
hit the poor harder than the rich. It is the faculty too of making the
self-evident sound like the discovery of the theory of relativity.
Much play is made of *sacraliser, désacraliser, désacralisation, césaro-
Papiste*; the *sans-culottes* militants of the year II form 'une véritable
micro-élite à l'échelle du quartier'. The basic pessimism of the
idcological assumptions of Robespierre and Saint-Just is tenta-
tively attributed to 'l'idée chrétienne de la chute . . . laïcisée'
(this is an unusually good example, as it illustrates the capacity to
state a silly idea sillily). There is also the constant research for the
striking phrase: 'le peuple est debout pendant que le modérantisme
et la Cour sont couchés', or, better still, 'la mobilisation, c'est
bientôt la guerre'.

We learn, not without surprise, of 'la formation, autour de Barnave
et des Lameth, d'un parti *tory*' (Smith Square, please note). And
what is one to make of this: 'La bourgeoisie française de 1789 sait
beaucoup mieux que les marxistes de 1917 où elle veut aller, où il va.
Au fond des choses elle comprend mieux l'Histoire qu'elle fait. Mais
elle's'est refusée au pronostic sur l'accidentel'? Or of the phrase: 'La
Révolution continue à tourner hors du cycle mis en route par le
siècle'? Chapter V, which deals with the period from 1790 to 1792,
is entitled 'Le dérapage de la Révolution'; no wonder then that the
Revolution, having gone into a long skid, should have left the track
assigned to it by the Grand Prix officials Furet and Richet ('la
Marche de l'Histoire', another much favoured incantation), hit the

bank, and burst into flames. The final chapter, covering the period of the Jacobin dictatorship, is called 'Le temps de la détresse', for what reason one cannot guess, as for the common people of the towns it was the only period in which their distress was to some extent alleviated by effective government and price controls on foodstuffs; perhaps it was just a matter of *not* calling it 'The Revolutionary Government'? Of course, we hear frequently of 'les hasards de la conjoncture', while the mechanism of the cyclical dearths and near-famines occurring in France in the last third of the eighteenth century is described in the phrase: 'Dès lors s'enclenche à nouveau le mécanisme de la convulsion courte'. 'S'enclenche' is very much house style. Of the various factions, the authors write, almost lyrically: 'Aux temps de l'espérance heureuse, les Girondins; aux temps de la douleur et de la mort, les Montagnards; demain, quand reviendront les beaux jours, les silencieux, les prudents, les habiles de la Plaine . . .' (Tune: 'Aux temps des cerises'). Recipe: it does not matter what you say as long as you say it differently. MM. Furet and Richet are historians of the sort who would use 'le mental collectif' for 'la mentalité collective'.

The authors are clever; their cleverness consists mostly of adopting the general theses of recent historians of the Revolution, while giving them a slight push, a sleek New Look. Pierre Caron, Georges Lefebvre, more recently Albert Soboul and George Rudé, have drawn attention to the naïve, almost mystical, attachment of the common people to methods involving the use of force and violence as a panacea to all ills. There is nothing very startling in such primitive reactions, especially at a time when violence, in one form or another—collective or private—was the only means of influencing policies and events available to the *petit peuple*. But this comes out as: 'C'est un des traits les plus permanents du long martyrologe des classes inférieures que cette croyance en la vertu de la contrainte comme instrument de la justice et comme solution quasi-magique des contradictions sociales.' The authors have, however, their own contribution to make in this matter, their own interpretations to propose of certain examples of popular violence and popular pride. Of the September Massacres, they surmise, with their usual gravity:

On n'a pas assez exploré les zones d'ombres que découvrent par moments les formes primitives. *Incontestablement d'origine sexuelle*, les violences faites au corps de la princesse de Lamballe renouent avec les vieux rites symboliques des 'émotions populaires'.

Later, they refer to the almost fanatical attachment displayed by the *sans-culotte* to his pike—the weapon of his rights and of revenge, also the visible symbol of his citizenhood, at a time when each citizen was an armed citizen; this is old hat:

On peut se demander [and they do a great deal of this] si, par-delà ces souvenirs conscients [of the popular days in which pikes had come in quite useful, especially for the triumphant display of severed heads] l'adoration de la sainte-pique ne recouvre pas un très ancien symbolisme d'origine sexuelle . . .

No wonder the book is to be translated.

Throughout the Revolution and well on into the Directory, popular terms of abuse abound, particularly in culinary and cannibalistic expressions; women of the people state 'that they would like to have the head of a bourgeois to eat', 'cuite au pot, avec du persil'—or according to some other recipe, depending on the region, 'tête au lard', 'à l'ail', 'à la crême', and so on. All over the Midi, both ultra-terrorists and ultra-royalists are commonly reported as stating 'qu'ils aimeraient jouer aux boules avec les têtes de leurs ennemis, pour les manger ensuite'—a useful combination of sport and gastronomy. Indeed, these metaphors enjoy such a wide acceptance that, during the Thermidorian period, ex-terrorists are generally branded as 'cannibales', 'anthropophages', 'buveurs de sang' (they are commonly reputed to have stated, during their brief period of power, 'qu'ils aimeraient boire dans les crânes des aristocrates'), 'tigres d'Afrique', 'hyènes', and so on—an anti-revolutionary animalia almost as formal as professional titles in Italian: terrorist = cannibal; shoemaker = African tiger. But even their bitterest opponents among the *jeunesse dorée* and the Thermidorian hack-writers never suggested that there was anything other than the natural verbal exaggeration inherent in revolutionary and counter-revolutionary language; it was generally conceded to the former terrorists that they thought eating people was wrong. Our authors will have none of this; such expressions, as well as the much-invoked guillotine, represent 'le recours magique d'un peuple qui a souffert une faim séculaire', it is all part and parcel of the French tradition of *crises des subsistances*. The authors are

79

singularly fond of distant origins, ancient atavisms; the adjective 'séculaire' recurs on many pages.

Another method is to trundle out a nameless historian (call him 'On'), attribute to him some idiotic over-simplification, then proceed to show what a fool he is (and what clever fellows MM. Furet and Richet are). 'Lorsqu'on songe à la contre-révolution', they write, 'on a tendance à la considérer comme un bloc. En réalité, elle est aussi diverse que la Révolution elle-même. . . .' As every historian of the Counter-Revolution over the last twenty years—Godechot, Vidalenc, Chaumié, Tilly, Hutt, Mitchell, Lewis, Higgs, etc.—has been saying just this, has been insisting on the extreme diversity of the Counter-Revolution, who then is this convenient and silly 'On'? A puppet, invented to give at least one good line to our two ventriloquists. Later they dismiss, with their usual airiness, a whole generation—and a very distinguished one—of historians: 'On a été passionnément pour ou contre Danton, pour ou contre Robespierre', and refer to others, not named, of the present generation: 'On est aujourd'hui pour ou contre Hébert'. Yet with the exception of the late Louis Jacob, it is hard to think of a single recent historian of the French Revolution who has attached sufficient importance to Hébert to take up the cudgels either for or against him. This, of course, does not worry our tandem, determined to see that their colleagues are suitably rock-hewn. There is a final use of the argument: 'Pointe avancée de la révolution bourgeoise, 1793 séduit ou répugne parce qu'on y croit déceler les signes annonciateurs de 1871 ou de 1917. Une telle perspective est terriblement déformante.' Who are these simpletons? As the authors have dispensed both with footnotes and a bibliography, they do not have to answer; they merely insinuate.

Apart from the style, apart from occasional surmises regarding the sexual or cannibalistic undertones of popular violence and the age-old tribalism of the common people of France, the authors have nothing new to offer, no goods to display. They are quite good at historical charades, borrowing the clothes of MM. Caron, Lefebvre, Soboul, Rudé, Chevalier, and even Guérin, and sometimes the coat of one, the shirt of another, the trousers of a third at the same time, and then cutting them *Annales* style. They are non-committal on controversial or uncertain issues ('on peut se demander', 'il y a du reste toute une analyse psychologique de la Terreur qui reste à faire', etc.) and have absorbed—sometimes even gobbled—most recent work on revolutionary anarchy, on popular mentalities, on the minority character of militancy, on dechristianization—on which they take a prudent Mathiezo-Soboulian middle line—on the Germinal crisis. They are, it is true, always hinting at the imminence of some startling new interpretation; with them, the important thing is that new frontiers are about to be pushed back, to reveal stupendous Mont Furet and dread Mont Richet, snow-topped and inaccessible, even if, in fact, the reader is merely being led in a donkey cart around the concrete paths of the Bois de Boulogne. They are masters at Hint History, at About-to-be History. Occasionally they score a bull's-eye, as when they say of Robespierre: 'de ces années d'études . . . il a conservé une sorte de complexe de boursier'—this is excellent and this is why we have all met Robespierres at one stage or another. But the overall impression is of mutton dressed, with some typographical elegance, as lamb.

For historians so severe on their many nameless predecessors or contemporaries, these authors might have had more regard too for accuracy. The Camp de Jalès was not—as they suggest—'easily dispersed'. Couthon was not a deputy of the Cantal, he represented the Puy-de-Dôme. Jacques Roux did not commit suicide 'en plein tribunal révolutionnaire'; it would have been difficult for him to have done so, for he had managed to kill himself, at his second attempt, in prison, on 10 February 1794, before he could be tried. Ronsin did not appoint himself General; he held a commission from the Ministry of War. The *armée révolutionnaire* did not 'go off to reconquer Lyon'—it would never have managed that—Lyon had already been taken before it left Paris. Nor is it true to say that 'Ronsin did not appear in the Revolution until after 10 August'; he was elected Captain of the National Guard in July 1789, while three of his (execrable) plays were performed on the Paris stage in 1790, 1791, and 1792. Far from the militants of the Sections 'being unable to prevent the Commune from placing under its control the *comités révolutionnaires*', they did in fact succeed in just this, with the help of the Committee of General Security—and the point is an important one—nor were they 'unable to prevent the Government from dissolving the women's clubs'; they asked for nothing better, and helped in the process. Robespierre did not write to Danton about the death of his wife in February 1794, for the good reason that she had died in February 1793, which was the date of the letter and the whole point of the story. As the book is likely to be very widely read, these points are worth making.

It will be widely read, even more widely looked at; for it is copiously, intelligently, and very beautifully illustrated (we are indebted to Mlle Simone Houel-Soupault for this, but the authors have shown considerable ingenuity in relating their textual commentary and narrative to the illustrations on the same page). Mlle Houel-Soupault has, of course, drawn principally on the great collections: Bibliothèque Nationale (Estampes), Carnavalet, Louvre, Musée Condé at Chantilly, Musée du Château de Versailles, Musée de la Police, Musée de l'Art Moderne in Brussels; but she has also used the Musée d'Amiens, the Musée Dauphinois—an admirable painting of the *journée des tuiles* in Grenoble—the Musée Lambinet in Versailles, the Musée de Cholet; one could only wish that she had cast her net still further, so as to include the Musée de l'Histoire de France in the Archives Nationales, the Musée de l'Assistance Publique in the quai de la Tournelle, the Musée de la Poste, the Musée des Arts et Métiers and the Musée de la Révolution at Montreuil.

Probably the most astonishing item is a child-like drawing of the Princesse de Lamballe, wearing a huge, beribboned hat, by one of her assassins. There is also a sketch of the forecourt of the Bastille, by an artisan Sunday painter who took part in its storming. Little use has been made of the *imagerie de Chartres* and other sources of popular inconography, with the result that the old *compagnonnages* are scarcely represented. We are shown the common people through the eyes of outside observers, rather than as they liked to portray themselves. Yet such material exists in the collections of the Musée des Arts et Traditions Populaires. Most of the material being contemporary, it is very regrettable that, for the portrayal of the soldiers of the year II, and even of Hébert and of other popular leaders, the authors should have felt the need to fall back on Raffet and Lamy—very second-rate nineteenth-century artists, who were already in the process of transforming the *sans-culottes* and the *défenseurs de la patrie* into the shaggy, hairy, pseudo-soldiers and reassuring *bon-enfant* 'people' fearful to look at but with a heart of gold beating underneath, dewy-eyed at the evocation of Napoleon —the sort of thing, in fact, to afford a comfortable half-hour to a betasselled Second Empire *notaire*, fighting over past battles in his smoking jacket. They look all the odder for being neighbours, on some pages, to the real thing.

Here is at least the public, dramatic, solemn, and brutal face of the Revolution—*journées*, severed heads, battles, burning buildings, dead soldiers, massacres and murders, speeches, solemn occasions, processions, fêtes, Te Deums godly and pagan, recruiting platforms, riots. But there is little to illustrate hope, optimism, candour, generosity, fraternity, enthusiasm, the pride of citizenship, the naïvety of a world repainted in blue, red, and white; the podgy cherubim of revolutionary letter-headings are nowhere to be seen and the eyes and triangle of vigilance have escaped the collector. We look in vain for Old Age Honoured, for Maidenhood Respected, for Motherhood (even unmarried) Rewarded, for Virtue Triumphant, and for Love walking hand-in-hand between straight avenues of ribbon-strewn poplars in the hot summers of revolution. As it is, even the most hardened specialist, who has counted the death certificates and read the tear-stained letters of the condemned, comes away from the spectacle of so many scenes of carnage disturbed by so much savagery and pondering on the sources of popular brutality. Yet the Revolution was not all blood, death, heroism, and vengeance. Magnificent though it is, the present collection is likely to convince the Anglo-Saxon purchaser of this expensive book, if he does not read the accompanying text, that the Revolution was just a bloody shambles; probably many will leave it at that, which would be a pity, for the text, though pretentious and often somewhat spurious, succeeds in giving life to the abundance of illustrations. Like men at the fair who, with their long pointers, spell out the Rise and Fall of a celebrated bandit, the two authors have succeeded in giving to their revolutionary Rake's Progress (the last print in the book bears the title *Ouf!*) a pointed commentary closely related to the series of stills. It is very superior Guignol; and this is probably all that the publishers asked for. What they have added is a sort of Golden Treasury of *style Annales*; it is this which gives their book a particular interest to the historian, for it is admirably representative of a school that has produced some of the best and some of the silliest historical writings in the course of the past twenty years.

[This article was adversely commented upon, shortly after it had appeared, by Dr Eric Hobsbawm and by Professor Pierre Goubert, in letters to the *Times Literary Supplement*. It has also been referred to in a recent article by M. Claude Mazauric in the *Annales Historiques de la Révolution Française* of 1968.]

4 Georges Lefebvre

Anyone so old—Georges Lefebvre was 85 when he died—must necessarily have an appeal to an historian, and even in appearance he was a figure from the past, a living embodiment of republican rectitude, of lay probity, a sort of French Abraham Lincoln, dressed in antiquated clothes. In very hot weather he transformed himself into a French rural postman, or a Victorian explorer, or Tartarin himself, appearing in a many-buttoned tussore outfit, with a high collar and innumerable pockets. At other times, a variety of wingy collars, dark coat, striped trousers, the uniform of the professorial fathers of the Third Republic. On very important occasions, he wore a sort of *jabot*. If his colour—he was quite amazingly red, and became purple at the mention of Marie-Antoinette or Talleyrand—and his very blue eyes denoted his origin as a *Wallon français*, his small white beard was *universitaire*, *laïque*, and *républicaine*. Dressed in a peculiar shiny black mac with a hood in wet weather, he looked like a sectarian Father Christmas. At home or on platforms he sat bolt upright, like Justice at the Feast. The general effect was of great simplicity, unassuming dignity, and benevolence; but he was not always benevolent.

He had one characteristic that owed nothing to the traditions of the Third or any other Republic: his terseness. To telephone him was a terrifying experience, and I know one Italian professor who was so disheartened by it that he never raised the courage to visit him. 'May I come and see you, M. Lefebvre?' Answer: 'Pourquoi?' Hastily prepared explanations. 'Quand?' Time and date suggested. 'D'accord' and silence. His testimonials were equally sparse: 'M. *X* a suivi mes cours et a préparé sous ma direction une thèse de doctorat. Je le considère comme apte à assurer un cours d'enseignement superieur. *Signé*: Georges Lefebvre. *Professseur honoraire à la Sorbonne*'. He refused even to write this much for his nephew, Laurent; it would have been nepotism! If Laurent became a university teacher, it was certainly not due to any help from his incorruptible uncle. In a country where professors are expected to

84

look after their favourite students, Lefebvre was not a good patron to have.

When one went to see him, one was confronted with the Justice-figure. He would point to a chair, resume rolling his *tabac gris* into cigarettes, the incandescent branches of which would start small bonfires on his cotton waistcoat. 'Et alors?' Accusingly, rather than questioningly; then silence, smoke, and firey particles, penetrated by an alarming bright blue stare, while one fumbled guiltily for words to make one's report. He would listen in silence right through, and would then proceed to analyse and criticize, point by point, everything one had said. Conversation would gradually un-freeze, and once he was launched on biology, sex, the class struggle, or his University colleagues, the rest was plain sailing. But the approaches were uninviting and awesome. Charm was not his strong point; I think he associated it with privilege and moral laxity. His economy of manner was, however, a change from the *cher ami cher collègue* style of the French University *cacique*.* Lefebvre was as conscious as any of his professorial status, all the more so because he had reached it only after a long hard struggle. He certainly thought *l'Université* to be the sanctum of *l'esprit civique*—an insti-tution to be spoken of with gravity. But he was a very simple man.

His furniture was as sparse as his party conversation. No carpets (they could hardly have survived anyhow). One broken armchair (for reading *L'Humanité* in the morning, *Le Monde* in the evening). An ugly bust of Robespierre's self-righteous profile. Photographs of Jaurès (whom he described as the greatest single influence on his life), Marc Bloch, and of his younger brother, Théodore Lefebvre, whom he had educated and who, while Professor of Geography at the University of Poitiers, had been arrested by the Vichy police, handed over to the Gestapo, and beheaded in Germany.[1] He gener-ally spoke of the leaders of Vichy France as *MM. les assassins de mon frère*, and he refused an invitation to become a member of the Institut, saying he did not wish to sit next to the accomplices of the murder of Marc Bloch. Upstairs, in his study, a photograph of Flammermont and (I hardly like to mention this) a small bust of Napoleon. The furniture was the nondescript *faux Henri II* of the

---

[1] *A(nnales) H(istoriques) de la R(évolution) F(rançaise)*, xix (1947), pp. 68–70: Obituary Notice on Théodore Lefebvre by Georges Six. Théodore Lefebvre was condemned to death in October 1943 by a section of the *Volksgericht* and was executed by axe on 3 December 1943.

French *petit bourgeois* of the nineties. The only departure from austerity was food and drink: all his life he had been partial to the heavy artillery of the Burgundy reds, the Pommards, and the Chambertins, and I am glad to say he stuck to them to the very end.

Of women he had a poor opinion: historians, he said, should not marry, though he had married twice, both times disastrously. Soboul, who was both fond and afraid of him, did not dare tell him for over two months that he had got married, much to the amusement of Lefebvre, who had been informed by a gossip of the event the day of the wedding. He had two daughters by his first marriage: the death of the elder, in 1954, removed the last vestige he ever had of a family life. 'Je n'ai plus d'amie, il ne me reste que mes papiers', was his comment. He was a very lonely old man, far lonelier, I think, than Mathiez, of whom he wrote, in 1932, that he sought in work an escape from an unhappy and empty life in which there was no place for affection. During the last twenty years of his life he lived with a servant, Jeanne, almost as old as himself, whom he treated as an equal. When he was in a bad temper, he locked himself in his study upstairs; but he always emerged at meal times.

His austerity was not a pose, as it was with Robespierre. He simply did not feel the need for small articles of comfort. Until he was over 80 he never travelled first class by train. He only went abroad once, and then to Oxford, in the mid-thirties, at the invitation of J. M. Thompson and All Souls. He told me he thought so much luxury and high living must have been very bad for the industry of *MM. les professeurs d'Oxford*. The English always puzzled him; he could not understand why J. M. Thompson, after becoming an atheist, should continue to call himself 'the Reverend', and how the descendant of a Governor of Gibraltar, Rudé, educated at Shrewsbury (one of those places at which, according to Lefebvre, the English governing class looked after its own self-perpetuation) should be left-wing in his politics and a specialist of the French Revolution. He was amazed when the British Academy made him a corresponding member: did they realize that he was a socialist? He found the whole thing very puzzling and rather flattering.

Until he was over 50, he was constantly short of money. His father had worked in the office of a Lille cotton mill; his grandfather, half peasant, half *tisserand*, had moved from the country to Roubaix, to work as a carder in the first big mill, Wibaux-Florin, early in the Restoration period: a typical migration, his historian grandson claimed. His great uncle, also a weaver from the Lille area, fought against the army of the Duke of York outside Menin, in the 1793–4 campaign, as a volunteer in a Lille batallion.

Once he had seen his brother through university, he was out of the shadow of want. But he never showed any interest in profit, and was one of the few French university historians never to write *ouvrages de librairie*. His thesis was paid for entirely out of his own pocket, and the royalties from his *Quatre-vingt-neuf*[1] went into various funds for the protection of the *école laïque*. He had a particular horror of borrowing and of any sort of financial carelessness. In his articles, he explained that the qualities he most admired in Robespierre, in whom he saw the personification of the French *petit bourgeois*, were those of probity, economy, and hard work.[2] It is not surprising that the central theme in all his works is social advancement, and that his favourite author should have been Balzac, obsessed by wealth, debt, and bankruptcy.

He was a French Jacobin and a nationalist, and he rather resented foreigners who presumed to work on the history of the French Revolution, even more those who elected to remain in France. An Englishman, he said, should stay in England, and work on English history. From his childhood, he was deeply attached to the republican tradition of one nation one language, and he witnessed with satisfaction the recession of Flemish in his native province, under the impact of the *école communale*. Regionalism, regional dialects, he condemned as stagnant pools in which ignorance, superstition, and clericalism would flower unhealthily. Folk-lore, folk language, dressing up in silly regional costumes he saw as an invention of catholic obscurantism, and he showed little patience with the folksy-woksiness of the Musée des Arts et Traditions Populaires, one of the strongholds of the embroidery and maypole-dancing type of communism in France. He was a Jacobin too in his immense pride in the achievement of France as the country to have established equality before the law. He was more interested in equality than in liberty, more concerned with society than with the individual.

Unlike almost all French historians, he could—and did—read foreign languages. Geyl (whom he greatly admired—and this was

[1] Paris, 1939.
[2] See his preface, in French, to *Maximilien Robespierre 1758–1794, Beiträge zu seinem 200. Geburtstag* (Berlin, 1958).

87

reciprocated; perhaps the only foreign historian who thought as highly of Lefebvre was Henri Pirenne) he read in Dutch, a language familiar to him from his childhood in a bilingual community. He had an immense respect for German scholarship, erudition, and methodology. He thought that every historian should know German, and next to Loutchisky, the most important influence in his choice of a thesis subject was a work by the German historian, Minzes, published in the early nineties, on the sale of the *biens nationaux* in the Paris area (Seine-et-Oise).[1] He had read—and admired—the great English medievalists, and the English historians whom he held in particular esteem were, first of all Maitland, and also Vinogradoff, Tawney, Unwin, Lord Ernle, Christopher Hill, Habakkuk, and Hoskins. He constantly quoted as an example to be followed in France the early English specialization in economic and social history, but until the middle twenties he found himself preaching in the wilderness. His thesis, in 1924, was a major scandal to the political historians and at the time was accepted only by the geographers. Although he did not read Russian, the work of late nineteenth-century Russian historians on French agrarian and economic problems in the eighteenth century had a great influence on him. He acknowledged a particular debt to Ivan Loutchisky, whose first book on the sale of the *biens nationaux* and on the distribution of small-holdings on the eve of the Revolution was published in Russian in 1895 and, in article form, in French, the same year.[2] With the exception of Tarlé, Lefebvre held Soviet historians in rather low esteem; he was particularly critical of their contributions to the history of the Revolution and to peasant studies: they failed to understand, he often said, the complexity of the French land system, and the fluidity of social divisions, did not take into account the existence of large numbers of small-holders (despite the work of their compatriot Loutchisky), and altogether misjudged the profoundly conservative aspirations of the lower ranks of the French rural proletariat in their attempts to preserve

[1] Boris Minzes, *Die Nationalgüterveräusserung während die französischen Revolution mit besonderer Berücksichtigung des Département Seine-et-Oise* (Jena, 1892).

[2] Jean Loutchisky, 'De la petite propriété en France avant la Révolution et la vente des biens nationaux', *Revue historique*, lix (1895), published as an offprint in the same year. Two years later, he published in French *La petite propriété en France avant la Révolution et la vente des biens nationaux* (Paris, 1897), which is his best-known work.

the unity of the village community and the *communaux* and other collective rights; Soviet historians, he thought, tended to confuse eighteenth-century rural France with rural Russia of the nineteenth century and to see the peasantry as a homogeneous rural proletariat, completely isolated from the towns, whereas there was profound inter-penetration, at all levels, between rural and small-town bourgeois, between rural *ouvriers à domicile* and urban artisans. Furthermore, he considered that even historians like Tarlé failed to appreciate the composition of the urban population of eighteenth-century France when they spoke of an industrial proletariat and the toiling masses of the working-class faubourgs. His very admiration for the Soviet Union made him more critical than almost any other French historian since the War of the shortcomings of Soviet research in French history; and, shortly after the war at the Société d'Histoire Moderne, he took some of his Russian colleagues severely to task, accusing them of confusing history and propaganda.[1]

Georges Lefebvre was a nineteenth-century scientific rationalist, devoted to the *école laïque*, to which he owed all his education, and always proclaiming, as a fundamental doctrine of republicanism, the necessity of the complete neutrality of the State in matters religious. He was therefore passionately attached to the 1905 settlement. Militant atheism he opposed, however, as illiberal; and as bourgeois, the activities of the masonic lodges with which Alphonse Aulard was so intimately involved. Despite his deep mistrust of clericalism, he accepted Catholicism as one of the strongest traditional influences in rural France; the peasant of the North, he said, was an *églisier*, attached to the church by habit and social conformism; but he was equally aware of the coexistence of paganism and ancient superstitious practices in this area. Christianity, he liked to claim, was only skin-deep in rural France. He was obsessed also with the problem of explaining how huge areas of Central France had become completely dechristianized, even in the remotest villages, long before the Revolution. He felt an almost affectionate sympathy for the eighteenth-century *curés de campagne*

[1] At this meeting of the Société, Camille Bloch, who had just been on a visit to the Soviet Union as the guest of the Academy of Science, read a series of précis detailing the main points in books and articles published by Soviet historians during the previous decade on French history. In these résumés, considerable claims were made for Soviet reinterpretations of French history, while French historians were criticized.

of his native province, themselves so close to the soil and to the peasantry, the wretchedness and despair of whom many of them recorded in the marginal notes on parish registers. He certainly felt more sympathy for the Catholic clergy than for the great personalities of French free-masonry, but he often regretted as one of France's major historical tragedies, the failure to establish, in the seventeenth century, an Anglican solution to the problem of Church and State.

Owing to the accident of his education, he only learnt Latin and Greek after the age of 17, and this debarred him from entering the École Normale. He had had, on the other hand, excellent grounding in German and English, the natural sciences, and mathematics, and to this he attributed his early concern with economic history. Like everyone else up to the forties, he took the combined *agrégation* (*histoire-géographie*) and much of his best work is that of a geographer. His preoccupation with biological and medical history became almost obsessive in later years. He would have liked to have been able to look forward to a time when the vagaries of human conduct could be explained and predicted by advances in what he hoped would eventually become an exact science—characterology —and all his books teem with references to the physiological condition of his great men: much did he regret not to be able to find a report on the state of Robespierre's liver! Before 1914 he was already much impressed by the early French sociologists, Durkheim, Lebon, Halbwachs, and later he was to contribute to the *Revue de synthèse* of Henri Berr. It was from them that he derived most of the ideas concerning crowd psychology that he was later (1932) to exploit in his work on the *Grande Peur*.[1] His scientific optimism was such that he was always eager—too eager—to accept new techniques, and his desire to enlarge the vision of the historian was probably the beginning of his association with Marc Bloch, Lucien Febvre, and the *Annales*. This led him at times too readily to accept theses that were quite unhistorical but that were attractively dressed up in pseudo-scientific or biological garb. I am thinking in particular of the equation between the class mentality provoked by plague epidemics and the collective desire for vengeance that produced the Terror, an extremely hazardous thesis, the work of Baehrel, one of his Alsatian pupils.[2]

[1] *La Grande Peur de 1789* (Paris, 1932).
[2] René Baehrel, 'Épidémie et terreur: Historie et sociologie', *A.H.R.F.*, xxiii.

But Lefebvre did not share all the views of the Febvre-Braudel group. Like the *Annales*, he was all for taking into the scope of historical research medicine, disease, plague, weather, death, love, arson, and so on. But he never followed them in their condemnation of narrative history, *l'histoire événementielle*, insisting on the contrary on the *récit* as the best form of historical writing.

In short, like Robespierre, he had the limitations, as well as the virtues, of the French *petit bourgeois*, but, unlike Robespierre, whom he criticized for his complete lack of curiosity in matters of science and technology, he was also a nineteenth-century positivist. A Jacobin, he held cosmopolitanism in horror, as artificial, lax, contrary to the *esprit civique* and the sense of community with which every man should be filled. His virulent hatred for that charming and attractive man, Talleyrand, was derived as much from his incapacity even to understand an eighteenth-century nobleman, as from his narrow, rigid, unimaginative, *petit-bourgeois* nationalism. He did not like Voltaire, but responded to Rousseau's uncomfortable and parsimonious romanticism. Perhaps one of the reasons why he was such an imaginative historian of the French Revolution was the fact that he passionately shared the hatred felt by the French middle-class in the late eighteenth century for the nobility: privilege and inequality, especially legal inequality, were abhorrent to him. Furthermore, he mistrusted the nobility as *frondeurs*, as a constant source of disorder, for, like any bourgeois from Louis XIII's reign on, he constantly aspired after ordered government and an *état policé*, whether by parliamentary or autocratic means. There was no element he hated so much in society as the rake and the *bohème*; flippancy infuriated him, and he never forgave me for making fun of the *sans-culottes* and for blaspheming against Robespierre. He thought compromise a fool's game—an invention of English conservatism to keep down the people.

Strangely enough, for a historian of the Revolution, he held Paris and the Parisians in a mixture of contempt and awe; he was immensely proud of the solid qualities of the Roubaisien and Lillois cotton-owner and textile operative and, much to my surprise—for he held capitalism to be as pernicious as it was inevitably and surely damned—he spoke with great affection and admiration of members

---

(1951); 'La haine de classe en temps d'épidémie', *Annales*, vii (1952). See also R. C. Cobb, 'Quelques aspects de la mentalité révolutionnaire' in *Revue d'histoire moderne et contemporaine*, vi (1959), for a criticism of Baehrel's thesis.

of *lainier* families, leaders of the wool barons, with whom he had been at school; these were not idle and frivolous people, nor fickle and mercurial, like the Parisians. In the few comments he has made in print about his career, he takes a deliberate pleasure in pointing out that at no time did he ever owe anything to Paris or to the intellectual life of the capital. The French are always talking of their birthplaces, as though these held some hidden significance, and Lefebvre was extremely proud of his origins as a Lillois and a *Wallon français*.[1] Before his death, he left most of his books to the Lille Public Library.

Ultimately, he was a man of order. He even thought historians had a duty to society, to the community, writing, in 1946, in a brief autobiographical note: 'J'ai travaillé à mon rang dans la communauté'. He had too, like so many of his compatriots, a sneaking admiration for military prowess, military leadership, strategic genius, writing almost affectionately of Napoleon and of Saint-Just.

As an historian, his greatest virtue was his insatiable curiosity. 'J'ai poursuivi des recherches par curiosité d'esprit', he wrote of himself, in his late seventies. At 85, Lefebvre had the curiosity of a boy of 16, and he has described the supreme satisfaction of untying the strings on a bundle of papers in the attic of a village *mairie*. He immensely enjoyed the exploratory period of research, and the accumulation of material took him to several hundred villages in Flanders for the preparation of his thesis. This was probably the happiest time of his life; but, at the age of 79, he set out to explore the records of the *communes* of the Orléanais, travelling by bus or being given lifts by farmers; he described this expedition as his third honeymoon: his second one was the Grand Tour completed in the thirties in search of materials for his *Grande Peur*. He would have liked to have gone on and on accumulating material, for he hated writing. Every sentence cost him a considerable effort.

Yet he wrote wonderfully well. *La Grande Peur de 1789* and *Quatre-vingt-neuf* are admirable in their simplicity and clarity; they carry one forward with the relentless rigour of their logic and the compelling economy of their arrangement. The French is simple; the sentences are short and final; the narrative is clear, and the

[1] For the autobiographical details on Lefebvre see *A.H.R.F.*, xviii (1946), pp. 185–6; ibid., xix (1947), pp. 188–90; and the brief autobiographical note at the beginning of *Études sur la Révolution française* (Paris, 1954).

descriptions of hunger, vagrancy, disease, and the other sores of the French countryside are prose masterpieces of economy and sparseness. A few years ago, an anonymous article in the *Times Literary Supplement* spoke of Lefebvre's style as 'impeccable' but 'drab';[1] Lefebvre asked me what 'drab' meant, and when I told him it was *terne*, he expressed real pleasure. He would not have liked to have been thought flamboyant. His prose at its best is comparable, in its restraint, to Voltaire's admirable *Histoire de Charles XII*.

Lefebvre was a pioneer of economic and social history in France, his first works on price controls and on the maximum dating back to 1913, when he began to write on the grain trade and on the problem of feeding France's over-populated countryside.[2] *Le problème des subsistances* was, at all times from the seventeenth century to the 1820s, the central problem of government, as it affected public order. Lefebvre was certainly the first historian to grasp this and to understand the difficulties in the way of the distribution of grain, and there has been nothing better written on the subject since his long introduction to a collection of documents published on the eve of the First World War. At this time, Mathiez, Aulard, and other specialists were still exclusively concerned with political and religious history.

But I think his greatest originality was in his appreciation of collective mentality. He was probably the first French historian to suggest that what people think has happened (or has not happened) is even more important than what has actually happened. This obviously takes us much beyond the collective panics of rural France and, when applied to the Revolution, in a sense re-invents such incidents as the aristocratic plot and the September Massacres. His *Grande Peur*, the study of the collective panic and rumour that spread through France in the early summer of 1789, might serve as a

[1] Issue of 16 April 1954, p. 249.
[2] His first detailed treatment of the food problem is in his article 'La société populaire de Bourbourg', *Revue du Nord* (1913), published the same year as an offprint (Lille, 1913). On 22 January 1914 he devoted a public lecture to the subject at a meeting in Lille: 'La cherté des vivres dans le département du Nord pendant la Révolution française'. His first important work on the subject was his long introduction to a collection of documents published in 1914 by the Jaurès Commission: *Documents relatifs à l'histoire des subsistances dans le district de Bergues pendant la Révolution (1788-an IV)*, vol. i (Lille, 1914). The proofs of the second volume having been destroyed during the German bombardment of Lille in 1914, it did not appear till 1921. His introduction remains to the present day the most authoritative work on the subject.

model for research on similar episodes in other countries (and he always hoped that English historians would undertake a similar study of the Irish Fear in seventeenth- and eighteenth-century England). The book is by no means exhaustive, and later work on local panics has shown that Lefebvre was sometimes inaccurate in his anxiety to make the *peurs* fit into a fixed chronology, but the basic argument is as sound as it is novel. He is the first of a group of historians of popular myths. Every major event in the Revolution was conditioned by such myths: famine plot, Austrian plot, foreign plot, English guineas, the Duke of Orléans's plot, Protestant plot, prison plot, Pitt and Cobourg, bankers' plots, corruption plots, strangers and spreaders of germs and plague plots, escape plots, peace plots, assassination plots, theological plots; some of course were not myths at all; but their importance depended mainly on the popular interpretations put upon them and on the vagaries of popular suspicion and desire for vengeance. The Queen *may* have plotted with her household troops; but what is important is that 90 per cent of the people in Paris *believed* she had. Lefebvre always insisted on the importance of popular credulity and collective reactions in a period during which the myth-makers and the myth-believers could have a direct influence on events and even reach positions of power.

He could appreciate the workings of the popular mind because he had studied the history of the *ancien régime* and the Revolution from below, and not, as most previous historians (with the exception, of course, of Michelet), from government level, from that of assemblies and committees. When he talked of the *petit peuple*, he knew what he was talking about. Both Lefebvre and Labrousse have been described as historians of *structures sociales*, an expression constantly recurring in their works. Lefebvre's vision of class structures is never static; the limits he draws between one group and another are not frontiers, and he constantly insists on the mobility of rural life, especially from the 1770s onwards; while, at every dearth, thousands of small-holders are reduced to the state of landless vagrants or are depressed to that of day-labourers, there is a movement too in the other direction, and it is impossible even to make a clear division between town and country: the *bourgeois* are everywhere, France is quite unlike Eastern Europe, and no province within France resembles completely any other. His descriptions of social groupings are never purely statistical, and even if he did like to say that 'pour faire de l'histoire, il faut savoir compter', when describing a society, a community, he never forgot that it was composed of human beings, and not just social categories, of human beings who were all the time changing, some on the way up, others on the way out, and that for a variety of reasons, many of which were by no means economic or explicable in graphs. His greatest merit, I think it would be generally agreed, was to have mapped out the intricate pattern of French rural society. His ambition, never realized, was to write a general history of the peasantry during the Revolution; but he was too honest and too cautious to undertake such a synthesis before others had produced regional studies as exhaustive as his own. He was too ambitious for other people; when one looks at the two hundred pages of statistics at the end of his thesis, one can understand why he has had no imitators. He was less informed about urban society, and wrote often rather loosely about the *sans-culottes* as a homogeneous social group, that he at times identified with the Jacobins. But at the time of his death he was working on a social and economic history of Orléans during the Revolution. Furthermore, recent work by others on the urban revolutionaries owes much to his initial encouragement and to his warnings against the dangers of purely statistical and mechanistic descriptions.

Labrousse has called him the historian of class; Lefebvre, who always described himself as a Guesde Marxist—though the influence of the doctrinaire Guesde was offset to some extent by that of Jaurès's parliamentary opportunism and profound humanity—believed, for instance, that a class struggle was a historical reality in the eighteenth century. But he did not make the mistake of Guérin and of so many Soviet historians and lend to eighteenth-century society the class divisions of a later, industrial age. Time and again he allowed his material to modify his views. In 1932 he severely criticized Mathiez for his dependence on flair, on the *document unique*, to prove points about which he had already made up his mind;[1] Mathiez was a barrister, who used the Archives like lawyers' briefs. Lefebvre always made a clear distinction between history and propaganda, was deeply suspicious of idea history (he did not believe men were much influenced by ideas, and wrote the

---

[1] His obituary of Albert Mathiez, first published in the commemorative number of the *A.H.R.F.*, ix (1932), is included in *Études sur la Révolution française*.

most telling criticism of Talmon's much overrated work),[1] and constantly insisted on exhaustive research (*recherche en profondeur*); there could be no short cut: 'sans érudition, point d'histoiré'. The first task of the historian must be to find new material, and up to his last paper, in 1955, on 'Les Archives hypothécaires' (mortgage administration),[2] he was continually recommending new sources: fiscal rolls (*vingtième, impôt foncier*), bankruptcy suits, notarial records (immensely rich in suspicious and litigious France), bank records, etc. He was a wonderful research historian, with a knowledge of records comparable only to the great nineteenth-century French archivists. When reviewing English or American work on the French Revolution his constant criticism was that it was based on secondary material and that however interesting or imaginative, 'il n'apportait rien de neuf'. He suspected that Anglo-Saxon historians did not work slowly enough or hard enough.

Despite his obsession with wealth and with class, he was a complete historian: not merely a political or religious historian, like Aulard and Mathiez. He is best known as the historian of the peasants' revolution, but one of his best books (*Quatre-vingt-neuf*) is on the whole crisis of 1789; he was the first to study the resumption of foreign trade during the Revolution; he has written on currency problems. In political history, he has given a definitive judgement in the controversy about Danton, and, until he was very old, he preserved himself from the excesses of Robespierre-worship. His lectures, published in the *Cours de Sorbonne*, are, in my opinion, far the best introduction to the general history of the Revolution. A pioneer in the study of panic, he was penetrating in his assessment of individuals, even if he relied too much on medical evidence and on the humours. His book on Napoleon and on world history from 1799 to 1815 is considered, in England, to be his most attractive work; certainly his description of French society in 1805 is as wise as it is original, and his account of Napoleon himself is only surpassed by Tolstoy's.[3]

[1] J. L. Talmon, *The Origins of Totalitarian Democracy* (London, 1952), reviewed by Georges Lefebvre in *A.H.R.F.*, xxv (1953), pp. 182–4.

[2] 'Les Archives hypothécaires', paper read at the *Société d'histoire moderne*, 4 December 1955, résumé in *Bulletin de la société d'histoire moderne*, 2nd ser., No. 16 (Nov.–Dec. 1955).

[3] His book on the outbreak of the Revolution, *Quatre-vingt-neuf*, has appeared in translation in English, Italian and Japanese. His articles on foreign trade and his final verdict in the sterile controversy concerning Danton have been republished in *Études sur la Révolution française*. The most remarkable of his lectures are 'La

Ultimately, his interest in the Revolution was two-fold. As an historian, he was mainly concerned with assessing the long-term consequences of a revolution that was social as well as political and that resulted, in France, in an immense change in the distribution of wealth, and, above all, of land, the form of wealth in which the French middle classes, like the nobility, preferred to invest. This was why he went to such immense pains in his thesis: he wanted to know exactly how much land had changed hands, who had acquired it, and for how long. So he was not content with studying the immediate effects of these changes; his thesis he carried to 1799, and he congratulated Nicolle on carrying his study of Vire down to the 1840s.[1] But in the process of calculating the social consequences of the Revolution in the Nord, he came first of all to write a study of rural society under the *ancien régime* in all its complexities—and goodness knows how complicated eighteenth-century France was in everything, from administration and taxation to social *nuances* and legal quibbles; then to give a sweeping account of the impact of the Revolution down to the Directory, in the most populated area outside Paris, including a picture of Austrian and counter-revolutionary occupation which is of particular interest, because it is all we know of what the re-establishment of the old régime would have

---

Fuite à Varennes' and 'La Première Terreur' (*Cours de Sorbonne*, Centre de documentation universitaire); one of his most penetrating biographical studies is his article on Siéyès, republished in *Études*. His *Napoléon* first appeared in 1935 (*Peuples & Civilisations*). His *Grande Peur de 1789*, and his articles 'Les Foules révolutionnaires' and 'Le Meurtre du comte de Dampierre' (both republished in *Études*) are among his best-known contributions to the study of the popular mentality. As well as his thesis *Les Paysans du Nord* (Lille, 1924; republished without notes, Bari, 1959), he devoted a number of studies and articles to agrarian and peasant problems, among them: *Questions agraires au temps de la Terreur* (1st edn., Strasbourg, 1932; 2nd edn., La Roche-sur-Yon, 1954; the first edition was published in Russian in 1936); 'La Vente des biens nationaux' (republished in *Études*). His political studies include *Les Thermidoriens* (Paris, 1937); *Le Directoire* (Paris, 1946); *La Révolution française* (*Peuples & Civilisations*, 2nd edn., Paris, 1951), *Le Directoire* (*Cours de Sorbonne*, Centre de documentation universitaire, s.d.), and several hundred articles and reviews. He also edited the *Recueil de documents relatifs aux séances des États Généraux de 1789* (Paris, 1953). His review of Labrousse's thesis, 'La Mouvement des prix et les origines de la Révolution' (*A.H.R.F.*, xiv (1937), and republished in *Études*) is a valuable contribution to the study of price history. He also wrote a number of articles concerning the history of ideas, and more particularly *babouvisme* (see his preface to the edition of *La Conspiration pour l'Égalité dite de Babeuf* in *Les Classiques du peuple*, Éditions sociales, Paris, 1957). His study of French society in 1805 appears in his *Napoléon*.

[1] Paul Nicolle, *Historie de Vire pendant la Révolution* (Vire, 1932).

97

meant, in practical terms, had the Allied armies defeated revolutionary France.

The other reason for his interest in the Revolution was personal. It was the key to his immense pride in being French (though he had little esteem for the French of his later years). The *chant du départ* and Robespierre's speech denouncing traitors aroused him in violent and generous responses. Certainly he was no worse an historian for having, at all times, taken sides in France's unceasing civil war.

If he was a *maître*, then what of his disciples? There have been several attempts recently to link Lefebvre with a school. Guérin, in 1945, spoke of him as a pupil and continuator of Mathiez, neglecting the fact that master and pupil had been born in the same year and had only met twice. Lefebvre himself was insistent that his development and interests had always been very far from those of the polemical *robespierriste* historian. There was no Mathiez–Lefebvre school.

Professor Saïtta does me the honour of placing me under the protective cupola of a pantheon for four, in an Italian edition of articles by Lefebvre, Soboul, Rudé, and myself;[1] yet this will not do: Soboul and Rudé are Marxists, and I am nothing at all; the only thing we have in common is the type of document we use and a preoccupation with the Revolution and its personnel as seen from below rather than from government level; if this constitutes a school, then Asa Briggs and everyone who is concerned with the history of popular movements belong to the Lefebvre school; but neither Rudé nor Soboul has attempted to follow Lefebvre's lead and work on fiscal records. In fact he had very few disciples: Alun Davies in England, Baehrel, Werner, and his own nephew, Laurent, in France; for these are the only historians who have attempted to follow up the questions he raised concerning peasant history, the distribution of property, and so on. In another field François Crouzet too may be said to owe the subject of his thesis on the British economy and the Continental Blockade to Lefebvre.

His main weakness as an historian was one that he had in common with most French specialists: *le goût de la synthèse*, the search for a plan, for a mysterious Grand Design, the construction of a general argument, in fact the tendency towards intellectualism and universa-

[1] G. Lefebvre, A. Soboul, G. E. Rudé, R. C. Cobb, *Sanculotti et contadini nella Rivoluzione francese*, preface by Armando Saïtta (Bari, 1958).

lism that is the cursed inheritance of every French boy who has followed a *classe de rhétorique*. This is why the French write such admirable textbooks and construct such beautiful lectures. But being a great historian, Lefebvre was able to produce, in the process of the search, admirable pages of analysis, despite his dogmatism and despite his conclusions, and he introduced into French revolutionary history an immense new documentation. And, when all is said and done, his honesty and his common sense stopped him, time and again, on the brink of some sweeping torrent of dogmatism.

His personal limitations were those of his background. He was sometimes unfair in his imputation of motives, especially when dealing with classes or categories of which he was naturally suspicious. There was in him a certain lack of generosity and he was rather heartless. No doubt the Terror can be explained away by the desire of the Government to prevent popular justice taking its own bloody course; no doubt peasant violence and nastiness can be condoned, against the background of aristocratic violence and brutality; but Lefebvre has no word of pity for the victims of the Terror of the year II, though he waxes indignant when referring to the far more horrible White Terror of the royalist murder gangs of the following year. He was a hard man.

His Spartan existence had left him indifferent to many forms of artistic satisfaction. This was serious, for while he rightly insisted on the prior importance of the *document inédit*, he neglected literary sources, including popular literature such as almanacs and broadsheets, at a period in which they were abundant. The extent of his loss will be appreciated by those who have read Louis Chevalier's book on the Paris population in the first half of the nineteenth century. His lack of understanding for the nobility arose partly from his indifference to taste. He did not appreciate *Les Liaisons dangereuses*, and thought of it, much as the *sans-culotte* puritan of the year II would have thought of it, as an immoral book, proving the utter depravity of France's unworthy ruling class and, by implication, the worthiness of the revolutionary *bourgeoisie* that took its place.

He took rather a low view of man, and a still lower one of woman. Man was a creature quivering with fear and lust (his views on love were as crude as those of Napoleon), dominated by want, moved by jealousy and social ambition, but occasionally capable of sudden hot waves of violence, generosity, and mad altruism. No wonder he was as good an historian of the peasantry as Maupassant. I think he would have liked man to be a Cartesian piece of mechanics, articulated by pulleys, levers, springs, and glandular secretions; then history could have become a science. But he knew this could not be so and admitted, though with impatience, the factors of temperament, idealism, and plain idiocy. He was imprudent in his acceptance of many of the claims and jargon of the sociologists; it was as if, once he left the field of history, his caution and common sense left him. On the subject of Robespierre too he became increasingly dogmatic and reverent.[1] He was a very naïve man, who believed in human progress. But he was a very great historian, because no aspect of human activity escaped his attention, because he was enthusiastic, had imagination, and common sense, because he was endlessly curious and always wanted to go on. 'Il faut travailler.' He certainly did.

[1] This is apparent to anyone who cares to compare his extremely fair assessment of the Danton controversy in 1932 with his preface to the Berlin Robespierre volume published in 1958 (p. 87 n. 2).

5 When to Translate[1]

Four works and several articles by the late Georges Lefebvre are now available in English. His *Quatre-vingt-neuf* was translated some years ago, under the title *The Coming of the French Revolution*, by Professor R. R. Palmer; more recently his general textbook on the French Revolution—*La Révolution française*, in *Peuples et Civilisations* (Paris, 1952 edition)—came out in two volumes, both equally badly translated. Last year, three of his articles appeared in a collection edited by Professor J. Kaplow in the New York series *New Dimensions in History*. *The Thermidorians* and *The Directory* are the latest additions.

Thus, several years after Soviet, Japanese, East German, Polish, Czech, Slovak, Hungarian, and Italian specialists and students have been given the opportunity to read his major works in their own languages, the English-speaking public has, at last, access to a fairly wide selection of Lefebvre's more general work. This is certainly a considerable progress on the situation in 1955, when it was pointed out in these columns that none of his books was available in English, and only one in American. It could, however, be objected that the selection now accessible is not sufficiently representative of the enormous range of work produced by one of the last, bearded, *grands maîtres*, especially in the fields of local and social history, which were those to which he made his most original contributions and to which he devoted the most detailed and patient research. Indeed it was in the records of Lille, Hazebrouck, Dunkirk, Saint-Omer, Cambrai, Bourbourg, and Bergues, in those of Cherbourg and Orléans, that he perfected those qualities of numerical precision and balanced judgement that he was much later to apply to more general themes. No selection of his work could be truly representative in the absence of *Les Paysans du Nord*, *La Grande Peur*, and *Études orléanaises*; while perhaps his most brilliant lectures—on Varennes and the First Terror, and on 1848—have never been published at all, even in French.

[1] Review of Georges Lefebvre, *The Thermidorians* and *The Directory*, translated by Robert Baldick (London, 1965).

As it is, the English student who does not read French will have an opportunity of becoming acquainted only with his work as a teacher; and even his best textbook, *Napoléon*—greatly superior to the encyclopedic and exceedingly dry general history of the Revolution—still awaits a translator. If translation is the solution, the choice should have been more selective. Lefebvre is not indispensable as a writer of historical textbooks—we have, in English, a number of such, of excellent quality, most of them based on the work of Lefebvre and of more recent specialists—but he is the author of *Les Paysans du Nord*. Equally, there would be no particular call to translate Albert Soboul's *Précis d'Histoire de la Révolution française* (or of his even shorter history of the Revolution in the *Que sais-je?* series), but we do need something more than an abridged version of his *Sans-culottes parisiens* that represents only a quarter of the text and leaves out most of the narrative section, which is much the most valuable. Probably few people today are likely to read the English version of Mathiez's general history, but there is still no translation of his *La Vie chère*. However, to judge from present trends, these omissions are likely soon to be remedied.

Whether the present tendency to translate at least the more general works of French historians, over the past thirty or forty years, is altogether desirable is another matter. Specialists of French history and university teachers must regard it with mixed feelings. In so far as it makes available to the average student, even to the schoolboy, at least some of the work of Lefebvre, Braudel, Febvre, Bloch, Albert Soboul, Pierre Goubert, and thus offers them a cure from Madelin, Funck-Brentano, Robiquet, Romier, Gaxotte, Bainville (all of whom have long been translated!), such an initiative is wholly desirable. The more good history that becomes available to the more students, the better; and until recently the English reading public, for reasons known only to publishers, were allowed mainly bad history, trivia, or royalist propaganda. There are welcome signs then of a change on the part of publishers. The English, henceforth, are to be allowed to read some good French history.

The translators' case is a pessimistic one. They take a low view of the standard of French teaching at school level, and they are in disagreement with at least the stated policies of most universities that normally make an adequate reading knowledge of French an essential qualification for admission to an honours school. In purely educational terms, it is difficult to see why students should be encouraged to be lazy and unenterprising; the solution is not to translate, right and left, from the French, but to improve the standard of French teaching—as, apparently, it has improved in the past twenty years. Furthermore, the only justification for the teaching of history at the university level is that it is a cultural subject; part of the cultural process involved in taking an honours degree in history is becoming familiar with the history of a foreign society, in its own language and on its own terms. Translation almost always results in amputation, it is always deformative. Historical prose, like any other other prose, is a cultural medium and a means of self-expression; Voltaire wrote history, and French has, for centuries, been the greatest vehicle of international culture (hence the attempt to expel it from the University of Louvain). It would be impossible, in English, to convey the fire, the passion, the intransigence and the unfairness of Mathiez, the eloquence and compassion of Jaurès, or the caustic incisiveness of Lefebvre. History is not written the same way in French as it is in English; it is not even quite the same history.

Of course there are limits to what can be asked of the average honours student; few, on arrival at university, appear to have even a reading knowledge of Italian and Spanish; and it would of course be too much to assume that they could read Dutch or German, or one of the Scandinavian or Slavonic languages. The difficulty is in fact recognized by many of the historians from these countries; the Scandinavians publish a review in English, Dutch historians write much of their work in English or French and, in recent years, some of the proceedings of the Polish Academy have been published in French. Professor Kalman Benda, of Budapest, is the author of a number of articles in a French review. Only the officially bi-lingual Flemish Belgians, out of a spirit of narrow fanaticism and deliberate parochialism, choose, predictably, to turn their backs on the world of scholarship and to publish their research in Flemish rather than in French—an extraordinary case of self-mutilation—with the result that some no doubt excellent work has remained unknown outside Ghent.[1]

[1] This statement resulted in a letter of protest from all the Professors of History in the University of Ghent. In their letter to the *Times Literary Supplement*, they drew attention to the fact that the University of Ghent had published many

Then there is the purely technical difficulty, familiar to editors of volumes of the *New Cambridge Modern History*. The translation of historical works is not simple; if it is not entrusted to professional historians, who are also specialists of the country and the period concerned and who have in addition a wide experience of the national culture of that country, all sorts of mistranslations, errors in emphasis, confusion about definition, and comical howlers are likely to arise. Translation is not enough: the same words do not have quite the same meaning from one country to another and institutions are even more deceptive. The historical translator must then be a very rare being. It is not surprising that much recent translation has been exceedingly bad. This was especially the case of the two volumes based on Lefebvre's general history of the Revolution, both crammed with errors and, in some cases, with literal translations that are totally misleading, when not bewildering.

How much more difficult, then, the task of the translator of specialized work on the Revolution period. If he is English, he has to contend with the most intractable problems. We may draw what satisfaction we choose—surely some?—from the fact that such words as *dénonciateur* and *dénonciatrice* (the commoner rendering) do not exist in English, or, at least, cannot be easily translated (nor does, nor can, the word *concierge*), and that, in the absence of a revolutionary tradition and lacking the experience of revolutionary institutions, specialized in repression and terror, there is no adequate English equivalent for *comité de surveillance*, *société populaire*, *ambulance*, *permanence*, *fraternisation*, *scrutin épuratoire*, *affiliation*. Verbs like *révolutionner*, *électriser*, or verbs in phrases like *se refaire une virginité républicaine*, are difficult to conjugate in English (never, for that matter, having undergone the experience of foreign occupation, we would probably have difficulty with *collaborer horizontalement* and *collaboration horizontale*). The language of Revolution affects euphemism—*glaive de la justice*, *défenseur de la patrie*—and constantly tends to exaggeration: a man who threw a brick at a *représentant*, and missed, is described as an *assassin*, his act as an *attentat contre la répresentation nationale*; a *patriote* who is assailed,

---

works of research in languages other than Flemish.

It is none the less a fact that many valuable works of research have been published in Flemish by historians with an excellent knowledge of French and that this regrettable tendency is likely to increase in the next few years.

in a country lane by a group of royalists armed with sticks, cries out, before he is even hit; *au secours, je suis assassiné*. It is also thickly strewn with death labels—*fayettiste, brissotin, rolandin, fédéraliste, exagéré, ultra-révolutionnaire, philipotin, pourri, hébertiste, dantoniste, chaumettiste, robespierriste, collotiste*—most of them used by those immediately behind in the queue for power about those immediately ahead of them. Almost everyone is someone's bad word, there is no necessary limit to the slanging match, other than total extermination. Equally, the spirit of a regime that can call a child—or a grown man—*Épinard, Haricot, Cèdre, Érable*, that can reduce Lyon to *Commune-affranchie*, demote Marseille to *Ville-sans-nom*, and that attaches a mystical importance to the power of words (how many *actes d'accusation* carry the phrase *avoir mal parlé de*—a hundred things, from the Convention and the *maximum*, to Robespierre and the cockade?) is not easily rendered into the cold light of English. Once translated, such things appear ludicrous or comic, yet at the time words were dangerous, and Fouquier's red pencil runs smoothly beneath phrases of reported speech; words could send the incurably irreverent, the salacious, the doubters, the drunk, to the guillotine. This is in every sense an alien language; and there are limits to what the translator can do.

That this is so is well illustrated in the present case. Dr. Baldick is a skilled and sensitive translator, very much at home with the most complicated literary text. Unfortunately, he is also one of those translators who have made it their golden rule to avoid italics at all costs, with the result that he has attempted to translate everything. This gives 'warders' for *gardiens*—that is, persons put to guard suspects in their own homes; *garde-scellés* (poor wretches occupying a similar function, in this case to keep an eye on the sealed-up property of the suspects and the condemned) are promoted, bizarrely, to 'keepers of the seals'; he will not even allow *sans-culottes*, translated, at one stage, rather lamely, and not at all helpfully as 'poor citizens'; 'revolutionary taxes' is not an adequate translation of *taxes révolutionnaires* (a very specific type of forced loan, often in kind). The English reader must be sufficiently familiar with the *tribunal révolutionnaire* for it not to be necessary to confront him with something called a 'revolutionary court' and 'provostal justice' for *justice prévôtale*, would have only significance as 'court martial' or 'military court'. An *insoumis* is more than an 'absentee' and there is surely no need to inflict upon us the barbarism 'attorney-general-syndic', for *procureur-général-syndic*. If the translator had followed Dr. Gwynne Lewis's example, in his translation of Soboul, and added a glossary of revolutionary institutions and expressions, he could have dispensed with the need to translate everything. As it is, many of Lefebvre's references to specific institutions are lost or thrown out of focus, so that the reader often has the impression that he is missing something, which he often is.

When these two books first came out in the Collection Armand Colin, in 1937, they were designed, as textbooks, to fill one of the most obvious gaps in French historical study, the Thermidorian period having previously been almost completely neglected, while the Directory had been the subject of a single, enormous study, published at the end of the nineteenth century, and of Professor Reinhard's thesis on the Sarthe. But the same need no longer exists today, both periods having been the object of detailed research, locally and on the national level, by recent French, English, Canadian, and Italian historians (some of these are listed in the bibliographies). Both books are out of date, and though *The Directory* is still a useful introductory guide to a period that is quite appallingly confused, with its repetitive tangle of *coups d'état*, new directors, new elections, and will help the student pick his way through the minefield of violent days—18 fructidor, 22 floréal, 30 prairial, 18 brumaire—Professor Godechot's *La Grande Nation* is a much better one (it also has a chronological table, something very much needed in both the present volumes).

This is not Georges Lefebvre at his best. Indeed, in an attempt to give some sort of coherence to a period marked above all by political instability, uncertainty, and confusion, by *un*government or by the coexistence of rival governments, regional pressure groups, and various degrees of federalism, he tends to make far too great a claim for consciously directed class interest, particularly on the part of the *bourgeoisie*—though all the Thermidorians were in fact *bourgeois*, no group could have been less united; they were a very mixed bag indeed, drawn together, for a matter of hours only, by fear and the will to survive—and for highly stylized class conflicts. Equally, his analysis of social composition is often crude and unsophisticated, particularly in the light of the more recent definitions put forward, with extreme caution and many reservations, by

Albert Soboul and George Rudé. He refers, for instance, to the Montagnards as 'coming from the upper middle class' (a number came from the lower), while the terrorist of the year II, as seen in the eyes of the Thermidorians—who seem to have been remarkably well read in their Marx—is described as 'the man who had undertaken to curb social individualism and to bar the way to a nascent capitalism'. The Jacobins were 'partisans of social democracy', while the *sans-culottes* included artisans and shopkeepers 'as well as the proletariat'. The Thermidorian ruling class had no choice but to return to a free economy, because that 'was the necessary condition . . . of capitalist expansion'; its aim was 'to assure the predominance of the *bourgeoisie* whose rise to power [was] prepared by the entire history of France . . .' In the year II the *bourgeoisie* had been deprived of power 'and the Montagnards . . . had put themselves at the head of the *sans-culottes* . . .'. Finally, the 18 brumaire, 'initiated by a few bold *bourgeois* . . . finally established the power of the *bourgeoisie* . . .'. And there is a lot more of this kind of Bad Baron class history.

Statements of this kind are misleading and often quite meaningless: nothing can be gained by lumping together, in a single group of Thermidorians (*la bourgeoisie thermidorienne*), politicians of whom some were open royalists, others ex-terrorists and terrorists-to-be, moderates like Thibaudeau, and frothing fanatics like Isnard or Cadroy. The insistence with which the author returns to this theme in order to ram home his point about class interest, nascent capitalism, and so on (a theme, incidentally, that has been most effectively disposed of by Professor Cobban), may also have something to do with the fact that both books were written in 1936, in the first flush of the Front Populaire. In his post-war works Lefebvre tends to be more flexible.

Another weakness of both works is the narrowness of the platform of local research on which they are based. Apart from Lefebvre's own explorations in the records of the Nord and the Orléanais, his general statements regarding the situation all over France any time between 1794 and 1799 are based on examples drawn from half a dozen Departments only: the Nord, Orléan (for the years III and IV), the Aisne (for a few months of the year III), the Vaucluse and the Var (for the year III), the District de Vire, in the Calvados, and the Sarthe, for the whole period. This is not much to go on. Since 1937, however, detailed local studies have been made of the Thermidorian period and of the Directory in Lyon (Renée Fuoc), in Paris (K. Tønnesson), in Rouen (C. Mazauric), in Toulouse and the Mont-Terrible (J. Suratteau), in Amiens, in Metz (I. Woloch), while a general study of Thermidorian Marseille is at present near completion.[1] At the same time M. Reinhard and a team of young researchers have devoted a series of studies to the demographic crisis of the two-year period of dearth, from Thermidor year II to Thermidor year IV. The general effect of this work has been further to emphasize the extreme variety of conditions prevailing from one area to another during a period that, for long, was regarded as a sort of hiatus in French history—one cannot blame historians for having for so long steered clear of it— and that might be best described in the words used by General de Gaulle for the revolutionary period as a whole: 'ces années troublées'.[2]

They certainly were. Indeed, save during the Wars of Religion, there is probably no more chaotic and violent period in French history. It is only bit by bit, as a result of these local *enquêtes*, that the collective 'pay-off' on the Terror—and on the terrorists—the hideous flowering of public and private vengeance, the full effects of a famine crisis, here severe, elsewhere mild, the breakdown of authority (even the *gendarmerie* turned to crime), the enormous difficulty of recruiting officials, the full complexity, in fact, of the 1795 situation, are being discovered. Nothing could be more confusing historically—a confusion reflected even in the mixture of motives dictating conduct on a personal level—than the liquidation of a revolutionary régime and of a vast bureaucracy of repression. Thermidor was claimed, at the time, as a return to 'normality', to harmony, forgiveness, and the *règne des lois*; as it turned out, it was a jump into unrestrained violence, chaos, and lynch law. The years 1794–7 in particular are jungle years; no wonder, in order to describe their opponents and to define a situation which was giving rise to every possible example of human passion, intransigence, brutality and cruelty, contemporaries should have had to look to

[1] Renée Fuoc, *La Réaction thermidorienne à Lyon* (Lyon, 1955); K. Tønnesson, *La Défaite des sans-culottes* (Oslo, 1960); Jean Suratteau, *Le Département du Mont-Terrible* (Besançon, 1966); Issar Woloch, 'The Jacobin Club in Metz in the Year IV', *American Historical Review* (1966); M. Claude Mazauric is engaged on a study of Rouen throughout the revolutionary period, while M. Martinet is working on a thesis concerning the year III in Marseille.
[2] In a letter to myself dated 9 September 1964.

another continent—*tigres d'Afrique, cannibales, hyènes, la France divisée en deux tribus diamètralement opposées, buveurs de sang*, and so on. In some places, at least during the hot summers of 1795 and 1796, France really was given over to headhunters, hired killers, *détrousseurs de cadavres*, cannibalistic women.

It was natural that, faced with an African scene, some should have looked to Africa; others referred back to the bloody days of the Ligue and of the Chevalier des Adrets, of the *compagnies*, while north of the Loire many recalled Cartouche and Mandrin. The only possible guide, through the maze of *coups d'état*, conspiracies and rigged constitutions, is the varying fortunes of given individuals or groups, as they are buffeted by a rapid succession of table-turning, *règlements de comptes*, denunciation, and counter-denunciation; 1795 (*nonante-cinq*) represents a collective revenge on 1793–4 (but it was not entirely a class revenge, as the terrorists had not belonged to a specific class); 1796 avenges at least some of the (surviving) victims of 1795. Each year—year III, year IV, year V, etc.—stands out in more or less clear contrast to its predecessor; the contrast is perhaps brought out in even starker terms as the years, in the new calendar, close with the harvest and open with the *vendanges*—both favourable occasions for collective rejoicing, thus for collective violence, the pattern of each coming year generally being set by the events of Messidor, Thermidor, and Fructidor, which, in the years II, III, and IV, witnessed the largest number of killings and the greatest mortality from epidemics.

If, even during the high tide of the Revolution in the year II, it might have been possible for a few prudent, wise individuals to have remained uncommitted—they would even then have been running a grave risk, indifference being the worst of crimes during a revolutionary period—in the two years that followed people were given little choice; they were liable to have intransigence forced upon them by the intransigence of others. A degree of militancy might, willy-nilly, be a form of self-preservation, a matter of survival. Individuals saw themselves deprived of their personalities and recruited into one or other of the contending tribes. It might simply be the way they dressed or spoke or the fact that they were thin or dark or had a certain hair-style. 1795 was a terrible year for the poor in town and country, for a myriad of small officials of the previous régime, for the old and for those living on fixed incomes, for mothers of large families; 1796 was rather worse, as well as being physically dangerous for anyone unfortunate enough to find himself in public office. Once in office, there was no means, other than a medical certificate, of getting out of it; one is constantly amazed by the hosts of mayors, *notables*, and so on who suffer from dropsy, consumption, rheumatism, as if the France of the years IV and V had been converted into a vast lazaretto for the sick. In parts of the south, public office during these years was an invitation to lynching; even in the northern Departments it might end abruptly in being thrown through a window—by a crowd of infuriated women.

It is only possible to appreciate the complexities of the two periods in local terms—the only ones that matter at a time when the central authority was often powerless and sometimes non-existent; Thermidor in particular was anything but a centralized régime, power resided above all in departmental *députations*, in local pressure groups; the Thermidorian Convention was something like a Dutch Estates-General, a council of ambassadors, with each *représentant* supreme in his own area—to such an extent that men like Cadroy and Isnard could organize the massacre of republicans with complete impunity, for months at a time. There was not a Thermidorian régime, there were Thermidorian régimes. The Directory saw a limited return to centralization; but this would hardly have been apparent in most of the south-east and right up the Rhône valley, to Lyon, where the local authorities, in complicity with the judiciary, did very much as they liked. One must turn, for such matters, to Renée Fuoc's study of Lyon in the year III, and to Dr. Harvey Mitchell's account of French royalism,[1] to M. Soboul's colloquium on Gilbert Romme—*Gilbert Romme (1750–1795) et son temps* (Publications de l'Institut d'Études du Massif Central, University of Clermont-Ferrand)—to Dr. K. Tønnesson's description of Paris in the year III, and to the second volume of Lefebvre's own *Études orléanaises*. These—and a score of other books and articles—only serve to emphasize the inadequacies of the two books under review. A lot has happened since 1937 and publishers, when considering a list of works to translate, should not allow themselves to be dictated to by a great name simply because it appears gilt-edged.

[1] See pp. 184–91.

6 The Counter-Revolt[1]

The Vendée, though an historical reality, is something of a geographical misnomer, for the revolt in fact included three other Departments and indeed drew its most persistent support from an area that was largely situated in the Maine-et-Loire. It was the bitterest and longest of the civil wars that emphasized and often caricatured the polarizations brought out by the revolutionary period, radicalized the course of the Revolution, and, perhaps even more than the successes of the Allied armies, necessitated—and justified—the implementation of the Terror. It was indeed the immediate cause of the creation of the various institutions of the Terror at national and local levels, and by simplifying the issue into a straight choice for or against the Revolution it brought the Terror into the minds and habits of most adult males in the Republic, and, in the area covered by this frightful civil war, extended the Terror to women and to thirteen and fourteen-year-olds as well.

It began officially in March 1793—though as Dr. Tilly insists, in one of the most important sections of his book, it really began as a series of scattered disorders and as the increasingly widespread defiance of Government authority, in 1790, 1791, and 1792—was crushed in the winter of the same year, reviving endemically in 1795, 1796, 1799, 1815, and 1832. At the time it was seen as the principal threat to the survival of the Republic, the west of France not then being the derelict backwater it has since become (though the history of the Vendée does much to explain why it should have become so). For one thing, it jeopardized the meat supply of the capital, Paris drawing as much on the Bas-Poitou as on the Pays-d'Auge and the Charolais; it was a constant menace to such important towns as Nantes, Saumur, Angers, and even le Mans; it held down a considerable army in the west and as the rebels, at different times, succeeded in controlling strips of the Atlantic coast it was a standing invitation to English interference. As it turned out, the English did not make full use of their opportunities, and their help

[1] Review of Charles Tilly, *The Vendée* (London, 1964).

was not to amount to very much; but this the republican authorities could not have predicted.

Other revolts were in fact probably more serious: that of Lyon, because it seemed to give the Counter-Revolution the chance of splitting the Republic in two and of eventually controlling the French frontiers with the Swiss cantons, Geneva, and Piedmont; that of Toulon, because it made far more effective the British blockade of the French Mediterranean coast; that of the Vivarais, because it offered the potential base for a vast rising in a strongly royalist south-east; but none lasted so long, nor caused so much alarm in Paris.

The Vendée, then, has, very properly, been the subject of a vast historical literature, much of it either deeply hagiographical or bitterly hostile, most of it devoted to the actual course of the rising, to the military campaigns, and to the endless bickering and quarrels of the republican generals. The campaigns of the west have been fought over again and again, generally with as much passion and prejudice as were displayed in the contemporary reports of rival generals, of competing *représentants en mission*, for the Vendée was fought almost as much in Paris, Tours, and le Mans as on the spot; the conduct of the war has a direct bearing on the faction fights of the winter of 1793 and the spring of 1794, both the *hébertistes* and the well-named *philipotins* (for Philipeaux, himself a deputy from the west, was much more the leader of the so-called *dantoniste* group than Danton himself) had their stakes in the war, their pet generals, and their pet policies—whether to burn all before them or, on the contrary, to extend the arm of clemency. There are few political events in Paris during the interminable post-mortem on the Vendée campaign that cannot be related to the revolt and its settlement.

Dr. Tilly very sensibly has not attempted to write yet another history of the rising; he gives to the war itself only the briefest summary. He is concerned with causes and origins: *Why the Vendée?* and, after examining the various accepted hypotheses on the subject, he finds them all wholly or partly unacceptable. Those that the author proposes are far more sophisticated, more intelligent, and based on much more solid research than any previously put forward. His is a serious and an important work which is likely to remain, for many years to come, the definitive analysis of the causes, origins, motives, and composition of France's greatest peasant revolt since the *va-nu-pieds*. It is rather more than this, for Dr. Tilly has much to offer on the subject of rural revolt and of the primitive rebel in a context more general than that of the Vendée. Indeed, one often has the feeling that the Vendée is in fact a pretext for Dr. Tilly to discuss much wider problems and to test out certain theses concerning collective behaviour against a French regional background that he is at pains to compare, at times, with Calabria, or even with certain communities of South America.

Historians, at least, will be grateful to the author primarily for the wealth of evidence that he has brought to bear on the various aspects of his subject: the social structures existing in the areas that he has placed, as he characteristically puts it, 'under the lens', the various types of economy, market organization, social mobility, loyalty polarizations, the élites, property, popular assumptions, patterns of marriage, power. For he has dug deeply into local records—departmental archives, communal archives, notarial records, the *état-civil*; and, for a work so much of the value of which is thus to have presented entirely new material, it is a serious disadvantage that the author should have omitted to list his archival sources in his bibliography, with the result that we have to follow his clues through the text. On the basis of detailed but intelligently selective local research, he has succeeded in describing the collective lives, habits, and assumptions of a series of communities: urban, part-urban, semi-rural, itinerant, wholly rural, outward-looking, or closed in entirely on themselves.

Dr. Tilly's method is to take three of the geographical areas— and he admits, with his usual modesty, that there were others, and that he could, with more time, have greatly extended his territory of search—and then to apply to each a certain number of tests designed to bring out the similarities, and, much more, the contrasts, between them. These are the Val de Loire, the Saumurois, reduced almost from the beginning to the single unit: Val-Saumurois—a method that has the advantage, from the author's point of view, of emphasizing the contrast with the remaining area—Les Mauges, focused throughout as the principal centre of the revolt. Dr. Tilly, of course, knows that throughout the rising, and indeed before it, during the sporadic disorders of 1790–2, and after it, the stronghold of resistance to the Revolution was this region of *bocage*: thickly hedged, with deep-rutted roads, isolated farms, virtually no villages, almost no communications other than the semi-secret tracks cutting through the greenery, a mental isolation, cut off from the rest of France, out of sympathy with the nation, coupled with a deliberate closing inwards, a lost, embittered Green Fastness, comparable perhaps to Hervé Bazin's Craonnais, further east. This is Les Mauges.

The Val and the Saumurois form ideal positives to the negative offered by this grim, fanatical jungle of ignorance and superstition; in the Val-Saumurois urbanization dates back centuries, the countryside is closely and harmoniously linked to the market economy of the towns; the Loire forms an ancient cultural and economic highway, attaching the area to the rest of France; monastic establishments of great wealth are numerous, possessing most of the property of the Church; the countryside is thick with vineyards—and with egalitarian, independent *vignerons*; agriculture is intensive. The country clergy, overshadowed by the wealthy monastic orders, have no stronghold; there is a powerful middle class in the towns, its influence and clientele spreading to *bourg* and village. Religiosity is tepid, churchgoing irregular; during the Revolution the clubs in this area spread quickly and apparently with little prompting from above, reaching down to village level; people often marry beyond the visible limits of their birthplace; mobility is almost as swift as the Loire is sluggish; the refractory clergy are in a minority.

Take then Les Mauges; and what an ideal contrast! Almost too ideal, for, at each successive test—geographical, social, religious, political, professional, agricultural, human—the *bocage* is revealed as the direct contrast of the Val. Time and again, we run up against the same, convenient frontier—the line of the Loire, then of the Layon as it turns north-westwards—almost as immutable as the linguistic frontier dividing vexed Belgium; we can hear Dr. Tilly exclaiming, in semi-surprised triumph: 'Here it is again!' And it is there in 1789, in 1793, and again in 1889. In the 1920s it becomes 'pantheonized', embalmed in Siegfried's famous thesis, *La France de l'Ouest*. And all this is no doubt correct, long-recognized in local antagonisms, hallowed by ancient hostilities. The inhabitant of Les Mauges and that of the Val, like the children of Cain, just do not, cannot, get on, dragging behind them, through generations, a weight of regional atavisms, the burden of the native earth—whether clay or chalk—of which, apparently, they can never divest themselves; it is there to cramp them, their children, and their children's children, almost to the end of time—or at least till the construction of the Chemins de Fer de l'Ouest (later *État*)—and even these neglect Les Mauges—who can blame the railway engineers? —like a sort of Hardian curse. It is all very gloomy, rural, and predestined.

And yet this is not entirely convincing, despite all Dr. Tilly's well-drilled theorems. For, after all, in almost any region one might find similar contrasting conditions existing in close, festering, contemptuous proximity; all over the place there are the opposing polarizations between *le val* and *le bocage*, between *ceux d'en haut* and *ceux d'en bas*; all over France, faced with the test of Revolution, villages with double names become once more truly bifurcated between 'Culmont' and 'Chalindrey', their components (there is an excellent example of this in the present book). Nor do Les Mauges, however peculiar they may appear to the visiting American sociologist, exploring in Deepest France, hold a monopoly of deep, muddy runnels topped with high hedges, of scattered farmsteads; the Whiteboys operated often in similar terrain in Ireland; 21st Army Group fought at Thury-Harcourt and Bény, in another *bocage*, in the summer of 1944. Nor surely are Les Mauges unique in an absence of vineyards, in the persistence of subsistence farming, or in the existence of a growing industry in the few towns alien to the countryside. In other areas, too, weavers tend to marry the daughters of weavers, *journaliers* those of other *journaliers*, and, as one goes higher up the social scale, so mobility in marriage is likely to increase. And there are plenty of other areas in France in which the local priests were the natural leaders of the community, in the absence of the nobles. Sometimes one has the impression that in Les Mauges Dr. Tilly, wide-eyed, has discovered a microcosm of all the ills of a certain, intensely backward, rural France.

We are given every opportunity, in thirteen chapters, exhaustively to contrast Les Mauges and the Val; and we are readily convinced why the latter region, more go-ahead, less isolated, more in sympathy with national life, more urbanized, more 'civilized', should have remained attached to the Revolution; we can see why the revolt never got a firm foothold in the Val, why, too, it had to be Les Mauges. But why had it to be only Les Mauges? For, when all is said and done, the Vendée is unique. Why were there not similar revolts in those other areas that could offer most of the characteristic ills that one meets in Les Mauges? This is a question that the author is unwilling or unable to answer.

Part of the trouble is that, by utterly depersonalizing his rebels, he deprives them of the opportunity of telling *their* story; and these poor peasants, though not trained sociologists, might have had something to say for themselves that would have been of interest, at least to the historian. Being only interested in collectivities, communities, neighbourhoods, Dr. Tilly will not allow the individual to get a word in, and in this whole account not one single personality emerges, even among the élites. His rebels are quite characterless, save as regimented members of definable groups (and let them not dare attempt to step out of their assigned platoon!), and so his approach is the direct opposite to that adopted by Professor John McManners in his admirable study of the clergy of Angers:[1] the result is that while Professor McManners's canons and *curés* are understandably human beings, Dr. Tilly's rebels are merely algebraical symbols; they are even made, at one stage, to fit into a piece of higher mathematics. The author, who has shown such admirable industry in the pursuit of documents illustrating group reactions, has totally left out of account—perhaps because they will not always 'fit'—the multitude of individual *dossiers* and personal case histories that may be found in the papers of the various commissions of summary justice—Commission Militaire d'Angers, Commission de Saumur (Commission Parein-Félix, etc.)—that contain the interrogation of prisoners; yet these papers exist, and the accused, when facing their republican judges, are, like other captured counter-revolutionaries, quite willing to talk at length about why they took up arms against the townsman and the townsman's Republic. It would be useful too to hear the other side; and some of the republican generals, including the rather haywire Rossignol and the ferocious Dutertre, did at least attempt to understand this new, unfamiliar, and alarming enemy, a peasant one minute, a soldier the next, and in their reports to the Minister, they had often much to offer that could usefully have completed the author's evidence concerning groups. Dr. Tilly appears to be unaware of the existence of the Archives de la Guerrre, and though

[1] See pp. 159–67 below, 'The Bells of Anjou'.

he has read Turreau and Choudieu, he makes no mention of such tried specialists in repression as Ronsin and Parein.

Certainly his most valuable point is an historical one—and one that he has discovered as a result of exhaustive local research—and it has, for once, nothing to do with sociological 'models'. This is the persistence of disturbance, violence, riot, and defiance in Les Mauges in 1790 and in the two following years; this would not mean very much in itself, for these were disturbed years in many areas of rural France. But he quite conclusively demonstrates that these disorders were much more severe in Les Mauges than else-where. It is important thus to be reminded that great, sweeping revolts do not spring up overnight, that they are patiently prepared by smouldering grievances, by the emergence of identifiable hate figures who have names and faces, as well as functions or profes-sions—the rebels from Les Mauges chose with care those they sought out for killing, they knew them by sight, knew where they lived, and they often killed their families as well—and, lastly, even by a series of increasingly realistic dress-rehearsals.

In this area, both sides had tasted blood two or three years be-fore the Vendée, had indeed become sides, and could recognize each other as such. As early as 1791, the authorities in Cholet felt themselves to be on the extreme edge of civilization, beyond which stretched an impenetrable woody jungle of violence and brutish ignorance; as early as 1790, village artisans—strangers in a hostile community—might look anxiously to the nearest *bourg* or to the distant town for eventual protection. Both sides had lined up their potential armies long before general fighting broke out; the towns-men, the inhabitants of the *bourgs* and the village artisans—and the other allies of the towns, carters, innkeepers, schoolmasters—had the *garde nationale*. The inhabitants of Les Mauges started with religious processions, pilgrimages to sacred trees and to well-tried, reliable shrines that had shown their mettle in previous times of trouble, that might muster thousands, and soon the pilgrimages became armed assemblies and expressions of open defiance; the sacred banners, battle flags. Already, long before the revolt, the rebels had marched under the emblem of the bleeding heart pierced by a cross. If twenty scattered farmsteads could be got together to hear a non-juror priest preach damnation to the jurors and to their allies among the authorities, sooner or later they would respond to a call to arms coming from the same pulpit. Long before March 1793, some sort of outbreak was accepted as inevitable by both sides; the republican authorities had been calling for troops in 1792.

Dr. Tilly has much else to offer of great historical interest; but we have to wait a long time for his treasures. He is excellent on love and marriage; but then he has to draw a diagram of inter-marriage patterns, and we do not need all this complicated paraphernalia to discover that townsmen command a wider potential marriage market than isolated peasant farmers, nor that pedlars, carters, and bargees, who walk, ride, or float, are more likely to marry outside their own areas than farm-hands, nor that village artisans may sometimes marry the daughters of town artisans. Equally, the town versus country theme—minutely explored in Dr. Tilly's mecano-graph—has recently been investigated, though in a more pragmatic way, by other specialists of this period. Again, while Dr. Tilly is quite right to stress the importance of the 'link men'—the *hommes de liaison* as Professor Godechot has called them—rural artisans, transport workers, pedlars, *vignerons*, wine merchants, innkeepers —all people who, at one time or another would have to take their goods to the town, or get their materials from it—as purveyors of news and as propagandists for the cities, and, in the case of cobblers, smiths, basket-makers, as hostages of the town within the rural community, none of his conclusions is particularly novel. One would expect a *coquetière*, a woman who carries a basket of eggs to an urban market, to be more in touch with things than the wife of a subsistence farmer; and Georges Lefebvre and other historians have stressed the part played by innkeepers, *vignerons*, and village artisans as *apôtres civiques* in the spread of the institutions, habits, and ideas of the Terror. These were the *sans-culottes de village* who, once their brief role had been played out, were to find themselves in such dangerous, often murderous, isolation.

Dr. Tilly, armed with a battery of compasses, field glasses, range-finders, altimeters, so loaded down with apparatus that his prose limps heavily from one demonstration to the next, eventually ends up more or less where other, less prudent, more haphazard travel-lers have preceded him, after crashing impetuously through the bush, or simply following their eyes and noses. With Dr. Tilly, we go the long way round; the author will not even let us start off at all before he has offered us long disquisitions on 'urbanization' in

Kansas City, and minute definitions of such difficult words as 'city', 'neighbourhood', 'commune', 'affiliation', 'parish' (described as 'the portion of a community's social organization built around beliefs and their control . . .'). One can see what Dr. Tilly means when he exclaims, still unwearied, on page 159, at the beginning of Chapter IX: 'So, at last, we arrive at the Revolution'. It has been hard going.

An approach so narrowly methodological may also lead to over-simplification and rigidity. The *bourg*, for instance, as the author insists, is the link between town and country, or rather the tip of the urban arm, outstretched into an alien countryside. But it is not *only* that; the communes on the outskirts of great cities, those just outside the barriers, did not always ally themselves with the cities, with their powerful neighbours; indeed, perhaps more often they marched against them and into them, bringing riot and violence rather than fraternity. Yet we do not understand this from Dr. Tilly, for in his rather exclusive preoccupation with town versus country, he does not perceive that the *bourgs* of the periphery would often be the first—and chief—victims of urban selfishness, having the markets of the city denied them, while not themselves being rural producers. But, in this unhappy position, they might in fact march in either direction—into the city, with their carters, *vignerons*, and laundresses at their head, against urban egoism, or into the country-side, holding up farms—or they might even march against both. Either way, in times of shortage, they would be bound to get the worst of both worlds. So one must not make too much of Dr. Tilly's *bourg*-town alliance, though in Les Mauges it no doubt held good; anyhow, the rebels *thought* it did, seeing in the inhabitants of these large villages the vanguard—or the rearguard, as the case might be, depending on whether the rebel armies were advancing or retreat-ing—of the enemy, so that they would be the first or the last—and often the first *and* last—to bear the brunt of rural savagery and to be subjected to pitchfork justice.

Equally, it would be unwise to take the spread of clubs and *comités de surveillance* as an indication of the degree of attachment to the revolutionary régime of any given area. There were many clubs and *comités* in the Val-Saumurois and scarcely any at all in Les Mauges, a contrast that Dr. Tilly takes as a further confirmation of his theses. But one must also take into account revolutionary conformism and simple prudence; it was easy enough for a local

authority to earn its passage in revolutionary loyalism by setting up
both, and this is, in fact, all that many of them did; having set them
up, they forgot all about them; many *comités* met only once or
twice, at their formation and dissolution, and there were many
clubs that existed only on paper, until perhaps they were hastily
brought to life so as to be found in session, if a *représentant* were
heard to be in the offing. Certainly the lack of clubs is an indication
of how Les Mauges felt about the new régime, but the fact that
they were thick on the ground in the neighbouring area cannot be
taken as a necessary indication of the republicanism of the Val.

There are other dangers in mechanization. For the author is not
even always sure of his mechanics. Why, for instance, classify a
miller as an artisan? An eighteenth-century artisan would certainly
not have thought of him as a brother; he would have been much
more likely to burn down his mill, and the owner with it. How can
a beggar or a schoolboy be classified as an 'artisan'? And why does
the author make no provision for domestics, transport workers, and
those in the food and drink trade, three of the most important
occupational categories in eighteenth-century France? His 'Occupational Classification Scheme', despite its grand title, is often
inadequate, misleading, and anti-historical.

The author can only be applauded when he states—though he is
by no means the first to do so—that the Revolution, at local level,
brought out into the open all sorts of rivalries and jealousies that
had been building up over the years. Or equally when he declares
that class and social structure are not enough, that the ties of family
or neighbourhood have also to be taken into account; at times he
seems almost on the point of discovering human beings. Nor would
anyone disagree when he insists on the aggravation of ancient
vendettas between cities or towns when it came to handing out the
new administrative divisions: for every town that successfully
obtained a position as a *chef-lieu*, there would be two or three
others left in sullen rage. This was not peculiar to the west, every
Department having its quota of such sulky localities. Of course the
Revolution increased the gulf between town and country, of course
neighbourhood disputes became further embittered by the external
political challenges offered by the Terror.

Yet this is a good and welcome book. It could have been so much
better—and shorter—if Dr. Tilly could have been induced to forget

his sociology, abandon his jargon, and show less desire to accommodate everything neatly. Instead of adapting sociological techniques to historical research Dr. Tilly has gone one worse; he has applied the Vendée to sociological techniques. He seems not so much concerned to illuminate the origins of the Revolt as to use the Vendée to prove the validity of his sociological 'models'. It is a pity, because somewhere beneath this armour there is a man of common sense and sympathy; Dr. Tilly is such a natural historian that, even weighed down with his Tables of Laws, even despite his devotion to a Master Sociologist, he still cannot prevent himself entirely from writing good history.

7 The Revolutionary Mentality in France

It may be objected that the title of this article refers to something that has never existed, that there is no such thing as a 'revolutionary mentality' and that in periods of revolution men think and act much as in more normal conditions. This objection may be valid, but is very difficult to put to the test, for if there exists a body of information concerning the behaviour of a certain group of people during the period of the French Revolution, we are much less informed about how they thought and acted in the years before 1789, so that it is not really possible to say how far what we call the revolutionary mentality was a product of the revolutionary situation or how far it was, on the contrary, a continuation of attitudes and prejudices that had already enjoyed a long lease of life during the eighteenth century.

It is possible, on the other hand, to state quite firmly what is *not* meant by this term. The revolutionary mentality is neither a carefully reasoned philosophy of life, nor again a conscious attempt to grapple with all the major problems of the revolutionary period by recourse to a considered body of doctrine. We are concerned here only with the personal attitude of a hypothetical person, called for the sake of convenience the average revolutionary, towards the common events of everyday life in revolutionary France during the high tide of the revolutionary movement, between the summer of 1793 and the late summer of the following year. It is a matter of attitudes, reactions, prejudices, behaviour in the face of given problems and given situations, rather than an ideology derived from any school of thought.

Who is this average revolutionary and how is one to decide on his 'averageness'? Is it not possible that he may in fact be a caricature who, because he makes a great deal of noise and is constantly taking up attitudes, has left some record behind of his activities and utterances, while the voices of his less ambitious or more moderate colleagues fail altogether to reach the historian? In other words, is not the average revolutionary in reality the professional super-revolutionary, the man who quite deliberately goes about making a career for himself in the revolutionary movement by not only always swimming with the prevailing current, but also, whenever possible, a few lengths ahead of it? Or if this is not so, will he not at least be turned in the orthodox mould and constantly looking over his shoulder to make sure that he is still in step? Before attempting to answer these questions, it will be useful first of all to see how others have portrayed what they believed to be the typical revolutionary, and then to discuss what social groups we have in mind in identifying him, and the source material from which our information can be derived.

The most familiar portrait of the revolutionary of the Paris Section or of the small town is that drawn by the enemies of revolutionary France, in the cartoons of Gillray or in the prints issued in Cologne and Verona, representing, let us say, the members of a revolutionary committee at work: empty wine bottles are rolling on the floor, between the legs of scraggy dogs and scrofulous cats, piles of tarnished silver candelabra and gold plate are stacked on chairs or in corners, while the revolutionaries themselves, unshaven, haggard, squinting, or with glazed eyes, sit stupidly, under the disapproving gaze of a bust of Marat, some with ladies, gorgeously decked in stolen finery and wearing hats topped with sagging plumes, draped around them like lifebelts; others sleeping loudly with their heads on the table, while watches, necklaces, and jewelry dribble from their pockets. The drunken, villainous, wall-eyed brigand of the Coblenz and the London prints (who, incidentally, bears a strong family likeness to the cadaverous, lank-haired, priest-ridden Frenchman of Hogarth's *Calais Gate*) is, of course, little more than a creation of counter-revolutionary fancy and propaganda. It is hardly necessary to add that it is a portrait inaccurate in almost every detail.

More respectable than these caricatures is the evidence of those who survived to recount their experiences in revolutionary prisons: in these memoirs emphasis is not so much on the depravity of the minor revolutionary official, as on his ingratitude. The most ardent revolutionaries, one gathers from this source, were former servants, valets, coachmen, cooks, butlers, ladies' maids, *'valetaille et piédetaille'*. The 'ungrateful servant' thesis does not bear a close examination, however, and there are many more examples of former servants who accompanied their masters into emigration, who remained behind in an attempt to save their property from confiscation or took immense risks in sheltering nobles on the run. The careful analysis of the incidence both of the Terror and of the emigration carried out by the American historian, Donald Greer,[1] suggests that there was a high percentage of former servants and of skilled artisans in the luxury trades—barbers, engravers, fanmakers, and the like—among the victims of the Terror. Revolutionary opinion was extremely suspicious—and not without reason—of all those whose living had depended on the favour or the custom of the *ci-devants*.[2] Could such persons be relied upon to serve faithfully a régime that had brought them loss of custom and grave economic hardship? Many revolutionaries did not think so, but at the same time it was natural that many in this group, thrown out of work by the decline of the luxury trades, should have eagerly sought paid employment under the new revolutionary bureaucracy and should also have attempted to assuage suspicions attaching to their former state by making a great show of revolutionary ardour. Any new régime will bring a host of new possibilities of employment, and posts on revolutionary committees and in other branches of the plethoric revolutionary and wartime bureaucracy created many new openings for people who could show a clean card of political orthodoxy; naturally, there was something of a stampede to get the plums. The *valetaille*, however, never obtained a very considerable share in the distribution of favours.

The average revolutionary is then neither the Gillray wretch with his red cap and squint, nor necessarily the ungrateful servant repaying kindness with plebeian callousness. Politically, he is a member of a Paris Section, in which he might hold revolutionary office, or of the *société populaire* of a town or village, in which he might exercise functions in one of the many committees that came under the control of these revolutionary assemblies. The highwater mark of his active existence as a revolutionary would be between the spring of 1793 and the summer of 1794. We are not

[1] Donald Greer, *The Incidence of the Terror during the French Revolution* (Cambridge, Mass., 1935), and *The Incidence of the Emigration during the French Revolution* (Cambridge, Mass., 1951).

[2] On the prejudices attaching to former servants and the like in revolutionary circles, see my article 'Le "complot militaire" de Ventose an II. Note sur les rapports entre Versailles et Paris au temps de la Terreur', in *Mémoires de la Société historique de Paris et de l'Île-de-France* (1956), pp. 221–50.

concerned here with the administrative importance of this group: it is enough to say that, as an active minority, it fell to them above all to execute the innumerable orders and directives of the huge revolutionary bureaucratic machine.

It is here that there arises the problem of source material. Such men, the humble labourers in the vineyard of the Revolution, are not likely to leave personal records of their activities and to keep diaries recording their day-to-day impressions and intimate convictions. Those who have left us personal reminiscences of their experiences during the Revolution were nearly all victims of the new régime, or at least persons who had little sympathy for the revolutionary aims. Possibly some active revolutionaries on the level we are considering may have occasionally recorded their impressions, but if so such records have not come down to the historian. It is only, then, from collective sources (apart from very occasional personal letters) that the historian can draw his material for what must necessarily be a composite and impressionistic portrait of the average urban or rural revolutionary. We can perceive the *sans-culotte révolutionnaire* as part of a group, not as an individual, and we really know nothing of how he behaved in his home on the sixth or seventh floor (in Paris and other big cities social distinctions went not by quarters but by storeys) nor what were his principal thoughts and preoccupations: we can see him mainly in his public and collective capacity, in the midst of those clubs— the *sociétés populaires*—in which the presence of his fellows, as well as of a noisy and censorious public in the galleries, might be expected to impose on him a certain desire to conform at least to the most obvious standards of revolutionary orthodoxy. Source material of this kind will inevitably focus attention not so much on the average revolutionary, for that would imply some possibility of comparison, as on the orthodox *sans-culotte*. As there is a considerable range of collective evidence of this kind, it is quite possible to distinguish between the politically orthodox, the *parfaits sans-culottes révolutionnaires* as they would no doubt have preferred to define themselves, and the genuine rebels, a minority within a minority, most of whom were to suffer the fate reserved for ultra-revolutionaries who, according to official revolutionary logic, were but the other face of the Janus-figure of counter-revolution. But sources of this kind, however widely spread, have very obvious limitations, and the minutes of collective assemblies like the *sociétés populaires*, and even of smaller and more intimate institutions, such as the *comités de surveillance*, give a premium to orthodoxy rather than to sincerity, offering the place of honour to the most vociferous and the most eager revolutionaries, rather than to the average. The picture thus obtained of the collective revolutionary, if not so much of a caricature as the Gillray prints, is nevertheless an over-simplification as well as an exaggeration of certain common traits. In this type of open forum of orthodoxy, pride of place would almost always go to those who slightly overdid the prevailing tendencies. In the choice of material, therefore, I have not deliberately rejected the commonplace in favour of the curious or the fantastic, but have attempted rather to concentrate on those manifestations of revolutionary attitudes that recur the most frequently.

So much for the limitations of a source material that clearly does not allow for precise, mathematical, sociological treatment. What then do we mean by an average revolutionary, one who would have described himself, and been recognized by others as a *bon sans-culotte révolutionnaire*? The *sans-culottes* do not constitute a class but they do represent an identifiable group. They are not drawn from the workers (*ouvriers*), and the lower grades of eighteenth-century wage-earner (*manoeuvre, gagne-denier, commissionnaire,* etc.) were seldom admitted as full members to the *sociétés populaires*. They are not necessarily poor, by any standards. Revolutionary terminology is particularly deceptive in this respect for a certain inverted snobbery caused many people to 'democratize' their occupations. Some of those who call themselves artisans, carpenters, joiners, are revealed, when one examines their tax returns, as affluent contractors, employing up to sixty or a hundred labourers, or as comfortable *rentiers* with places in the country bought from confiscated lands.[1] Furthermore, eighteenth-century terminology generally makes no distinction between master and journeyman, between *maître* and *garçon*. From what we do know—thanks primarily to the writings of Soboul, Rudé, Brinton, and others—it can be asserted that the backbone of the *sans-culotte* movement was supplied by master-craftsmen, small employers of labour

[1] The case of Jean-Baptiste-Antoine Lefranc, *'charpentier'*, commander of the *canonniers* of the Section des Tuileries, in reality a prosperous building-contractor employing at one time over 200 workmen, is an example of this type of verbal deflation. See my *L'Armée révolutionnaire à Lyon* (Lyon, 1952), Appendix H, pp. 117–19.

(in eighteenth-century Paris the average size of a workshop was from four to fourteen *garçons*), small shopkeepers, publicans and *marchands de vin*, the 'better sort of clerks', particularly former *clercs de procureur*, together with a thin sprinkling of professional men—schoolmasters, public letter-writers, *maîtres-d'armes*, and, in the countryside, ex-priests and monks and former pastors of the R.P.R., as well as a few survivors of the luxury trades. Doctors, apothecaries, and barbers are rather rare, popular prejudice against them still being strong; lawyers and notaries rarer still save in the smaller towns; in many places there were even efforts to exclude them *en bloc* from office-holding, along with former priests (though a great many of these got in by the back-door as *greffiers*, secretaries, officials of one kind or another, thanks to their superior education), noblemen, and personal servants, as having been the instruments, in one form or another, of the *ancien régime*.[1]

The revolutionary might also be a professional soldier. Indeed it would be hard to overestimate the contribution made by the regular soldier, especially the non-commissioned officer of the *ancien régime*, to the revolutionary movement during this period. The Revolution gave these men a brilliant prospect of promotion in the semi-civilian *garde nationale*, in the new armies, or in civilian revolutionary institutions. The part played by this group in the development of a standard, conformist, revolutionary pattern of behaviour was all the more effective in that the ex-soldiers, unlike their artisan and shopkeeper counterparts, were less parochial in attitude, had fewer local attachments, and, if they were still serving in the Army, or in one of the innumerable organizations that offered posts on the fringes of military life, formed the principal link between the revolutionary movement in Paris or the other big cities and the provinces, and, later, between revolutionary France and the conquered territories. It was people of this type who penetrated the army of Italy and made it into a republican stronghold in which many ardent revolutionaries found a refuge after Thermidor, helping the Italian republicans with their knowledge and experience. Constantly on the move, in many cases a

---

[1] See for instance *Arch. nat.* D III 78 (470). Comité de Législation, Chartres: comité de surveillance de Chartres à la Convention (18 germinal an II) 'Ne souffrez pas de ces palfreniers de chambre qui croyent avoir beaucoup travaillé quand ils ont épongé ceux qu'ils appellent leurs maîtres, forcez-les de devenir libres, en décrêtant que, hors l'agriculture, il ne pourra y avoir de valets mâles.'

Parisian among provincials, the soldier or semi-civilian played a leading part in the proceedings of provincial *sociétés*.

The average revolutionary is of course, as I have said, in a sense an abstraction. However, the particular group of people with whom we are concerned did think of themselves, as a unit distinct and identifiable, under the expression *sans-culottes*, while their general attitude to life constituted *sans-culottisme*. Both words were used quite consciously and deliberately in 1793 and 1794 to designate the élite of the revolutionary movement. A self-imposed label during the Terror, it became in 1795, in the language of its enemies, a synonym for the *bas peuple*,[1] which, of course, it never was. The sense in which the term was used during the earlier period may be gathered from a few examples. At Auch, a member of the Jacobin Club explains that *sans-culottisme* does not consist in the smallness of one's personal income, but in the sincere cult of equality,[2] that is, it is not an economic, but a moral category. Another definition, from the Lozère, states that 'true *sans-culottes* [are] men who have no other resources on which to live than the work of their hands',[3] which may seem at first to imply an economic definition, if one that was seldom attained, for many of the most ardent revolutionaries would not fit into such a category. More correctly, it reflects the moral preoccupation of the average revolutionary, an article of whose creed was the sanctity of work, particularly of useful manual work. For this reason he had little use for artists, scholars, and other useless people, branded as *oisifs* along with the aristocracy.

Vingtergnier, a revolutionary professional soldier who ended up by being deported to the Seychelles, similarly stresses the moral factor.

The *sans-culotte* [he writes] is a man who always goes on foot and who lives simply, with his wife and children . . . on the fourth or fifth storey. The *sans-culotte* is useful. He knows how to plough a field, how to hammer and saw, how to cover a roof, make a pair of shoes. And since he works, you are sure not to find him at the Café de Chartres . . .[4] In the evening, he goes to the meeting of his Section, not powdered, not scented, nor booted in the hope of being noticed by all the citizenesses in

[1] e.g. *Arch. Nièvre*. Registre du comité de Corbigny (frimaire an III).
[2] *Arch. Gers*. L. 694. Société d'Auch (26 ventôse an II).
[3] *Arch. Lozère*. L. 532. Société de Mende (9 pluviôse an II).
[4] The Café de Chartres, in the galleries of the Palais-Royal, was a favourite meeting place of literary men. In 1793 it was reputed to be a rendezvous for Orleanist agents.

the galleries,[1] but in order to support to the utmost the right sort of resolutions.[2]

An austere, homely man, in fact, for a bachelor cannot be a good revolutionary, it is the duty of a good citizen to raise up children, future '*défenseurs de la patrie*', and bachelorhood is a manifestation of selfish individualism and of a lack of civic sense. The orthodox revolutionary opinion on this subject was no doubt influenced also by current economic theories relating a nation's strength and wealth to the size of its population, and there are plenty of indications that the revolutionaries, citizens of the most populated country in Europe at the time, were conscious of France's demographic strength. Social and moral objections to celibacy are well brought out in a petition, typical of many others, presented to the Convention in the summer of 1794 by the revolutionary society of Sens, in favour of a decree penalizing the bachelor,

that hideous monster who engenders nothing [and who] is born of luxury. . . . Virtue will never exist in society so long as there are men who scorn the laws of nature, carrying scandal into society and shame and despair into families; he who does not marry, although normally constituted, cannot in general be virtuous, because, organized like anyone else, he seeks victims everywhere . . . he introduces into society the germs of the passions which sooner or later must subvert it.[3]

Sans-culottisme can be defined, then, not so much in terms of wealth as of moral and civic utility. Indeed, in some places the local revolutionaries denounce those who seek to make invidious distinctions between rich and poor and who use the word in a purely economic sense. A member of the society of the small town of Brie-Comte-Robert, on the highroad from Paris to the Brie cornlands, insists on the necessity of

avoiding those diatribes, those ridiculous attacks against the rich, that base flattery of the poor in speaking of the *sans-culottes*. . . . I cannot see in this town any rich man [adds the speaker, a prosperous farmer]. I see *some* citizens who are better off than others . . . and we should hope that their numbers increase as much as possible. . . . Let us not flatter

[1] For a similar condemnation of 'foppery', see *Arch. nat.* D III 306 (31). Comité de Législation, Yonne, pétition de Héry, Ier pluviôse an III.
[2] Quoted by A. Soboul in 'Problèmes du travail en l'an II', *Journal de Psychologie* (1955), pp. 39–58.
[3] *Arch. nat.* D III 307 (33). Comité de Législation, société révolutionnaire de Sens à la Convention, 6 prairial an III.

the poverty of citizens with the honourable title of *sans-culottes*. We mean by the word *sans-culotte* only a good patriot, a friend of liberty.[1]

This was certainly the definition that would have most appealed to the artisans and shopkeepers who formed the cadres of the revolutionary movement. A *sans-culotte*, we often read, may have a comfortable income provided that it is the recompense of hard work. Property is sacred, so long as it is not excessive. Surplus wealth produces luxury and idleness, and these lead to depravity.

Thus the approach of the revolutionary to the problem of labour is moral rather than social. Every man should engage in some form of useful work, not only because the State needs all hands, but because idleness is evil. The *sans-culottes* were particularly severe on those who did their work badly and without enthusiasm. The public executioner of the Orne Department was sent before the revolutionary tribunal for having consistently neglected his duties, and, far from keeping his guillotine clean, having allowed it to get into such a filthy condition of rust and dirt that when he was carrying out a public execution in Alençon, it took three attempts to sever the victim's head from his body.[2] A bad workman was a counter-revolutionary in the making, and so was a worker who went on strike or who attempted to leave his workshop; the pressing needs of war production further accentuated the hostility felt by the average revolutionary to all forms of collective labour agitation.

As his name implies, the *sans-culotte* is also distinguishable by his dress. He eschews all the frivolous trappings of the *ancien régime*: powdered wig, scent, silk breeches, silk stockings, bows, buckle shoes, flowered waistcoats, lorgnettes, silver-topped canes, and other such foppish fineries.[3] He wears his own hair long, has a simple coat and cotton trousers. Then there is the vexed question of the mous-

[1] *Arch. com. Brie-Comte-Robert.* Société populaire, 2me registre, séance du 20 germinal an II.
[2] *Arch. nat.* D III 194. Comité de Législation, Alençon, tribunal criminel du Département de l'Orne au Comité de Législation, 5 nivôse an II.
[3] Speaking at the *société populaire* of Tarbes, Monestier du Puy-de-Dôme introduced the members of the club to his colleague Isabeau in the following words: 'Vois, tournes tes regards sur cette société . . . tu ne trouveras pas beaucoup de ces têtes artistement coiffées, pas beaucoup des grandes cravates de trois colliers, pas beaucoup des petites bougles [sic] de gilets cours d'habits pinces, pas beaucoup d'eaux de rose des parfums . . ., des figures mitonnées, en un mot pas beaucoup des *messieurs*, pas beaucoup de muscadins. Notre langage ressemble en tout à notre costume' (*Arch. Hautes-Pyrénées* L. 1186 bis. Société populaire de Tarbes, 21 prairial an II).

tache. Opinions differ strongly as to whether the moustache is or is not a revolutionary emblem. On the whole, the balance would appear to favour this adjunct when worn *à la gauloise*, that is in the Vercingetorix manner. However, opinion was not unanimous, and country people tended to think of the *'hommes à moustache'* from Paris and the other big cities as bandits, on account of their fearsome appearance,[1] and in the capital itself the long, shaggy moustaches favoured by the officers and soldiers of the civilian *armée révolutionnaire*— as also by General Hanriot and his personal staff—ended by identifying their bearers in the eyes of the general public as partisans of Hébert and the *Père Duchesne*.[2] Beards were definitely proscribed. The Committee of Public Safety allowed the Anabaptists of Alsace and Franche-Comté to retain theirs, but, locally, revolutionary authorities tried to invoke the decree prohibiting all external signs of religious *cultes* as applying to the beards of Anabaptists, rabbis, and Orthodox Jews. Was not a beard, they argued, a *'signe extérieur du culte'* and *'un reste des préjugés gothiques'*? In many places local committees obliged their wearers to remove these *'marques du fanatisme'*.[3]

Simplicity in dress and manner, a proper married status, regular attendance at the local *société populaire*, the execution of guard duties whenever required, and the undertaking of useful productive work were not enough. No man could be a good revolutionary without virtue, and a great deal of the time of *sociétés populaires* is taken up denouncing members who have misbehaved in one way or another. Thus we find Romme, subsequently one of the 'martyrs of Prairial', after delivering a formidable peroration on the standard theme of republican virtue and royalist vice, sending before the revolutionary tribunal an inhabitant of Agen, a revolutionary

[1] For instance, *Arch. nat.* F7 4774 26 d 4 (Louvet-Dubois, affaire de Thieux, Seine-et-Marne) concerning 'un détachmente de l'armée révolutionnaire commandé par un chef à qui l'on donne dans les campagnes le nom du *Général Moustache*'.

[2] *Arch. nat.* F7* 2496 (registre du comité de surveillance de la Section de l'Homme-armé, séance du 27 ventôse an II), 'Le comité arreête que le nommé François Carterait . . . se disant brigadier de la gendarmerie seroit conduit à la Conciergerie parce qu'il se disoit porteur d'ordre de couper les moustaches aux canonniers et autres personnes, en conséquence nous paroissant très suspect dans la circonstance critique où nous nous trouvons' (a reference to the arrest of the *hébertiste* leaders three days prevoiusly).

[3] For instances of this kind at Montbéliard, see my article 'Les Débuts de la déchristianisation à Dieppe', *Annales historiques de la Révolution française* (1956), pp. 191–209.

official, for having attempted to gain the favours of the wife of a prisoner by promising to obtain her husband's release. Such a man, thundered Romme, was a counter-revolutionary, for vice was counter-revolutionary.[1] In most clubs one side of the hall was reserved for women, and often only married couples were allowed to sit together. Women were excluded from some clubs altogether, and the efforts of politically-minded citizenesses to form clubs of their own were eyed with disfavour: the *société républicaine des deux sexes*, known derisively by the Paris *sans-culottes* as the *société hermaphrodite*, was suppressed. A ruthless war was waged on prostitutes, who were held to be counter-revolutionary: the revolutionary authorities particularly attempted to drive them from the garrison towns. The results of this preoccupation with public virtue were strongly resented by such ardent revolutionaries as the soldiers of the so-called *armée révolutionnaire* on their arrival in Lyon.[2]

Obscene literature was hunted down in the book-stores of the Palais-Royal.[3] Betting games, carnivals, fancy dress, billiards, and cards were unsuitable activities for revolutionaries. Betting deprived fathers of the wherewithal to feed little mouths,[4] carnivals and masked balls might permit counter-revolutionaries to escape in disguise, and it was both immoral and unlawful for a man to dress as a woman or a woman as a man.[5] Billiards, besides using up precious candles in a time when grease was needed for war manufacturers, kept revolutionaries away from the clubs in the evening,

[1] *Arch. Lot-et-Garonne*, 2me registre de la société d'Agen, 8 messidor an II.

[2] The attacks made on prostitution by revolutionary authorities were not based only on moral and military considerations. *Sans-culotte* opinion was inclined to assimilate prostitutes to the other hangers-on of the *ancien régime*. It was inevitable that *sans-culotte* opinion should eye with such disfavour a group so patently illustrating all the vices of the *ancien régime*, all the faults that were the most hateful to these puritanical shopkeepers.

[3] *Arch. nat.* BB 3 73. Comité de surveillance du département de Paris, 3 pluviôse an II.

[4] *Arch. nat.* D III 177 (23). Comité de Législation, La Charité: société populaire de la Charité-sur-Loire à la Convention, 3me sans-culottide an II: 'Personne n'ignore quels sont les terribles effets de la passion du jeu pousée à l'excès. Le père y oublie sa famille, le magistrat son devoir, le patriote y laisse impunément sonner l'heure de la séance de la société.'

[5] *Arch. Marne*, Registre (non-inventorié) du comité de surveillance de Sainte-Ménehould. 'Séance du 26 pluviôse . . . le comité prend des mesures contre des citoyens qui se disposent à se travestir dans ces jours nommés ci-devant gras. On fera proclamer la loi du 7 aôut 1793'. One exception was, however, encouraged: that of patriotic girls who dressed up as men to enlist: according to revolutionary propaganda several of these covered themselves with glory on the battlefield.

and it was better not to get the reputation of being lukewarm as far as the meetings were concerned.[1] Cards often led to brawls, and, save on the rare revolutionary packs, bore the figures of kings and queens and other feudal symbols.

The revolutionary was allowed one outlet: it was generally accepted that a good *sans-culotte* was entitled to his drink. Wine was necessary for health, it had nutritive qualities and in time of food-shortage could replace all solid foods save bread; it was a warrior's drink and gave force to the arm of the ploughman.[2] In Normandy similar virtues were claimed for cider. The revolutionary, so severe where some other passions were involved, was unexpectedly tolerant of drunkards, and revolutionary tribunals were extremely indulgent when it could be proved that counter-revolutionary utterances had been made under the influence of wine. The *sociétés populaires* did their best to keep noisy drunkards away fron their meetings, but anyone who has consulted many of their minutes gains a very strong impression that much of the noise, disorder, shouting, and quarrelling that so often held up proceedings was due to intoxication. Wine stains, not blood stains, are fairly common on the pages of these minute books, written often in a trembling hand. This is not at all to suggest that the Revolution was a sort of non-stop bacchanalia, but that partial drunkenness was often an impor-tant component in a certain type of revolutionary excitability, particularly in meetings or committees. In 1793–4, the urban population was consistently under-nourished and the *sans-culottes* often drank a great deal of wine of the lowest quality—the *vin de Choisy* was notorious for its high chemical content—on an almost empty stomach. The *aubergistes* and the *limonadiers* whose establish-ments were situated on the great highways played a particularly important part in the political life of the provinces, transmitting the news, ideas, and propaganda brought to them by the soldiers who passed through on the way to the armies on the frontiers.

Civic balls and dances, often in former churches, were given official encouragement, to celebrate great events such as the re-capture of Toulon. Civic banquets were another feature of the

---

[1] *Arch. Haute-Saône* 361 L I. Société populaire de Gray, 21 frimaire an II. 'Un membre a demandé que la société fît une pétition à la municipalité pour défendre toute espéce de danse jusqu'à la paix et pour faire fermer les cabarets à 10 heures du soir.' This was an example of war-time rather than of specifically revolutionary puritanism.

[2] *Arch. Savoie* L. 1770. District de Chambéry, séance du 4 frimaire an II.

revolutionary's collective leisure. France being very short of food, and food being rationed, these were often rather dreary affairs, consisting of many speeches and patriotic songs and only one course—the *plat-républicain*. These banquets were also intended as a substitute for the old religious feast-days, revolutionary symbolism taking the place of Christian.[1]

The revolutionaries were optimists; they were convinced that they were in the process of creating not only a new form of society, but also a new revolutionary man, virtuous, serious, patriotic. Hence, in the revolutionary régime, the cult of youth and the idolization of children, seen as the guarantors of the future. Much time was given, in *sociétés populaires*, to the interminable delegations of little citizens and citizenesses, led by their school-teachers, reciting the Declaration of the Rights of Man and singing patriotic songs. There are a number of instances of small children appearing as witnesses before the revolutionary tribunals and the *comités de surveillance*. At the same time, little mercy was shown towards 'uncivic' children: when two little girls of eight and nine admitted to having pencilled a black moustache on the bust of Marat that stood in the foyer of the theatre at le Havre, the rather sensible Norman revolutionaries took the matter very much to heart.[2] There are plenty of cases of children of fourteen and fifteen being guillotined, particularly in Lyon and Marseille. This, of course, should be attributed to normal eighteenth-century judicial standards which treated children in their teens as responsible adults. Revolutionary justice was indeed more humane in this respect that the judicial system of the *ancien régime*.

In most respects, of course, revolutionary France was a young

[1] These banquets were sometimes rendered more light-hearted by such incidents as that which occurred when sixty citizens and their families of the Section du Bonconseil, in Paris, sat down to table at the *Panier-Fleuri*: no sooner had the plates been served than the guests perceived with horror that each plate bore a feudal emblem: the publican was called for and was asked to remove the offending plates, but this he refused to do, adding that if the citizens were so ticklish in their republican sentiments, they could eat off the table without plates. This they proceeded to do, but not without first smashing 180 of the offending plates, which they later refused to pay for (*Arch. nat.* F7 4774 80 d5, Pottier). A *pâtissier* of the Section des Amis de la Patrie, in order to satisfy popular demand for the *gâteau des rois*, the traditional Epiphany cake dear to all French families, in Nivôse an II, hit upon the simple solution of calling his cakes *gâteaux Marat*, and both his customers and revolutionary orthodoxy were satisfied (*Arch. nat.* F7 4669 d3, Dennevers).

[2] *Arch. Havre* D 2 38. Conseil général de la commune.

THE REVOLUTIONARY MENTALITY IN FRANCE

man's country. It provided new opportunities for the young and looked to the future with unqualified optimism. The ardent patriotism of youth was common to all the revolutionaries. A measure of generosity towards individual foreigners in France, including prisoners of war, was combined with an intense nationalist hatred for all foreign enemies, or supposed enemies. Cosmopolitanism was a crime. Revolutionary centralization, and the attempt to suppress regional differences, especially in language—Jean-Bon-Saint-André and his colleagues complain frequently of the way in which the Breton peasants cling to their 'Gothic jargon'—go along with this.

In their desire to break with the past the revolutionaries also turned their attention to manners. Bowing and scraping and the kissing of hands were branded as decadent, while the *club national* of Bordeaux prohibited clapping, as a form of applause worthy only of slaves. 'Expressions of joy and agreement', decreed a resolution of this club, 'should henceforth be made through the medium of the virile and republican word *bravo*.'[1] A club in the Indre denounced 'the custom of saluting one another with a great sweep of the hat' and recommended a curt sign with the hand.[2]

This preoccupation with a complete break with the past received its most absurd expression in the wave of 'debaptizations' that swept France in the autumn and winter of 1793. Place names were the first to suffer, to be followed by Christian names drawn from the Saints' calendar. After France had become at least nominally peopled with Anacharsises, William Tells, Marats, Gracchi, the more ardent revolutionaries, particularly those of the Midi, fell back on the names of useful plants, trees, fruit, and even fish. The list of the members of the *société populaire* of Perpignan reads like a seedsman's catalogue: *Absinthe* Jalabert, *Haricot* Vidal, *Endive* Pagès, *Érable* Fabre. An inhabitant of Lyon named Février took the first name of *Janvier*.[3]

[1] *Arch. Gironde* II L 27. Club national de Bordeaux, séance du 6 brumaire an II.

[2] *Arch. Indre* L. 1581. Société populaire de Châteauroux, séance du 22 brumaire an II.

[3] *Arch. Pyrénées-orientales* L. 1454, société populaire de Perpignan. A Parisian, Jean-François Lyon, took the name of *Aristide Lille*: 'le nom de Lyon lui inspirait trop d'horreur' (*Arch. nat.* F7 4774 27 d5). One should add that much *sans-culotte* opinion treated with suspicion this particular type of extravagance, which, it was felt, tended to make the new régime appear ridiculous. It was also suggested that many of those who were so anxious to change their names were

In the countryside, a certain peasant common sense and inertia acted as a check on the more fantastic forms of revolutionary enthusiasm. Orders were given for the destruction everywhere of wayside crosses: but many rural revolutionaries, anxious not to antagonize their fellows, invoked shortage of labour and the expense of the operation to delay carrying out this and similar orders. By delaying tactics and by the force of rural inertia many village municipalities went through the Terror with the external aspects of rural life largely unchanged. The true *sans-culotte* was essentially a town-dweller.

He seems to have had scant respect for learning and the arts. At Auch, a member 'proposes that no man of letters of this town be received in this club for three years, but that *sans-culottes* be admitted at once', and the club decided that 'those who have received a careful education be excluded'.[1] It should not be inferred from resolutions of this sort that the revolutionaries were resolutely philistine: what they were trying to do at Auch was to exclude from revolutionary office-holding, which was one of the perquisites derived from membership of a club, all those who had enjoyed privileges in the course of the *ancien régime*, and what greater privilege than education?

Any one who reads for the first time the minutes of local revolutionary clubs and other bodies will be surprised by the almost complete absence of political discussion and by the credulity displayed in accepting the official version of important political changes. Clubs which had subscribed to the *Père Duchesne* and whose members even copied the pungent Parisian slang of which its able demagogic journalist was a master, the moment he had fallen accepted without a murmur the official account representing Hébert as a counter-revolutionary agent of foreign powers, and lost

---

in fact people who had something to hide. As in any revolutionary movement, some of those who were the most anxious to prove their revolutionary zeal by exaggerated professions of faith and by ostentatious gestures had a political or criminal past that did not bear too close a scrutiny. There was much foundation for the current suspicion of the more modest *sans-culottes* towards those who *affectaient des principes exagérés*, along with *bonnet rouge*, pipe, moustache, sabre, and all the other paraphernalia of the perfect revolutionary.

[1] *Arch. Gers* L. 694. Registre de la société populaire d'Auch. cf. *Arch. Isère* L. 936, société populaire de Bourgoin, 27 thermidor an II. 'Les hommes qui savoient lire, écrire et avoient de l'esprit étoient fort dangereux à la république' (a remark attributed to Sadet).

not a day in sending congratulatory addresses to the Convention and to the Committees thanking them for their vigilance in saving the Republic from him. Events such as the execution of Danton or the 9 thermidor are accepted with the same unquestioning trust, when they receive a mention at all. In a great many minutes the major political events in Paris are passed over in complete silence.

This apparent political supineness was probably not due to fear, to time-serving orthodoxy, or to the desire to be on the right side: plenty of clubs admitted candidly, after the execution of Hébert, that they had been taken in by the *Père Duchesne*, whom they had believed to be a genuine revolutionary patriot. The revolutionaries were extremely naïve politically, they had an almost religious trust in their representatives and in the Convention. Their readiness to believe in even the most fantastic constructions of Fouquier-Tinville's judicial imagination is to some extent explicable by the long series of myths and popular legends about 'famine pacts' and 'foreign plots'. From 1789 onwards, the average revolutionary lived in an almost physical fear of a counter-revolutionary *coup*: moreover, plots and conspiracies were not merely figments of popular imagination and of official propaganda, there *were* plots, there *was* collusion between ultra- and counter-revolutionaries.

Of course, one would hardly expect to find voices of dissent in such public assemblies as the *sociétés populaires*, whatever individual revolutionaries may have thought in their heart of hearts. It would be naïve indeed to expect open discussion of the major political issues of the period in every urban or rural club. But such discussions were impossible primarily because of lack of information. When local revolutionaries were engaged in discussing people or questions that they knew well, they were quite capable of expressing most unorthodox views and of attacking with the greatest bitterness their own local representatives. What was lacking was political discussion on national issues and on the day-to-day Paris scene. And, when all is said and done, most revolutionaries in the provinces were far more interested in concrete problems concerning the food shortage, hoarding, rising prices, and a depreciating currency, than in political events in the capital. Everyday life in small provincial towns during the Terror was far less dramatic than is often imagined, and the realities of life were the queues and the black market rather than the guillotine and the *trompette guerrière*. Local societies showed much more interest in projects for improving communications and for obtaining contracts for local industries than in political discussion, and if they successively celebrated the *Fête de la Raison* and then that of the Supreme Being, if at one time they took in and applauded the *Père Duchesne* and later devoted themselves to somewhat academic discussions on the evils of atheism, if they voted congratulatory addresses to Robespierre and to Collot d'Herbois on their escape from an assassin's bullets and, a few weeks later, were congratulating the Committees on having nipped in the bud the appalling plots of the former, neither official pressure nor open threats ever prevented them from discussing the forbidden and especially dangerous subject of food supplies, so that the only way in the end to ensure that this explosive matter was not dragged into the open was to close the clubs.

Nor were the revolutionaries cowards and time-servers: there were of course a certain proportion of these, especially among those who had been most vociferous and who had made themselves the most conspicuous in taking revolutionary names and in other eccentricities of that type.[1] But, during the period between 1795 and 1816, many of the better-known revolutionaries, both from

[1] One of the most conspicuous and successful of these professional revolutionaries, who took part in the revolutionary movement for the material advantages that they could get out of it, was the self-styled patriot Palloy, a wealthy architect with a large house at Sceaux, who hit upon publicizing himself by doing a brisk trade in stones of the Bastille, which he supplied, for payment, to any *société* in France. Palloy never missed an occasion to blow his own patriotic trumpet, and when he was not peddling Bastille reproductions, he was composing odes and patriotic hymns suitable to every revolutionary occasion. At Sceaux he entirely controlled the local *société*, which he used as an instrument for his own publicity. One is not surprised to find him, at later stages of his career, composing laudatory odes to the Emperor and welcoming Louis XVIII to Sceaux with an adulatory poem.

There were many Palloys in the provinces, but it was above all in the army that one finds some of the most unscrupulous career revolutionaries. The personal dossiers of many high-ranking officers who gained promotion under Bouchotte and who were particularly flamboyant in the display of revolutionary enthusiasm are often most revealing as to the strength of the convictions so loudly—and profitably—expressed. We may thus see former commanders of *armées révolutionnaires*, men who took an active part in the *sociétés populaires* of fortress towns and who did not allow themselves to be outdone by anyone when it was a question of making revolutionary resolutions, humbly and respectfully presenting their claims to a *croix de Saint-Louis* when the time came, in 1814 or 1815, to emphasize their undying respect for the dynasty. The former soldiers of the *ancien régime*, who, as a group, gained more from the Revolution than almost anybody else, were often the first to betray it and to adjust themselves to each régime that followed.

Paris and the provinces, were to be ruined economically, and a few thousand were to be imprisoned, shot, or deported for the fidelity with which they were prepared to defend, in time of adversity, the political and moral standards that they had so zealously preached in their brief period of power.

Of course, such revolutionaries as have been considered in this article only represented a tiny minority, just as the *sociétés populaires* themselves accounted for less than 5 per cent of the population of many of the localities in which they existed; and it was their small numbers that were to accentuate their isolation from the mass of the people and greatly to facilitate the task of Fouché's police in the years of repression. Even at its height, however, the revolutionary movement suffered from indifference and public inertia. This was especially true of the rural communities, where the activities of both *comités de surveillance* and clubs were largely seasonal: both might thrive in the autumn and winter months, but the spring sowings put an end to the collective political activities of such rural *sans-culottes* as there were: there are constant references to rural *sociétés* being closed down for lack of attendance, the whole population being engaged in field work. Even in the big urban *sociétés* there recurs a constant and anxious complaint: attendance is slipping dangerously, members are not turning up to meetings, it becomes more and more difficult to form a quorum large enough to carry on business, many 'brothers' only come when there is a *scrutin épuratoire* and once they have obtained a clean bill of revolutionary health, they go off with their *certificat de civisme* in their pocket and are seen no more. Despite threats of permanent expulsion against those who absented themselves from more than three sessions running, the leaders of these *sociétés* were already losing the uphill fight against absenteeism in the spring and summer months of 1794, long before the rigours of the year III, when even the most enthusiastic *sans-culottes* did not feel inclined to sit about in freezing conditions such as had not been experienced since 1709. This decline in political interest and growth of public indifference can be dated from the months of March and April 1794, when, with the fall of the *hébertistes*, the clubs both in Paris and in the provinces found themselves reduced more and more to a passive and congratulatory role: as there was nothing more of interest to talk about, people naturally stopped coming. But even at the height of the revolutionary movement, clubs containing a total membership of five or six hundred very rarely saw more than a hundred and fifty or two hundred at any one session.[1]

The greatest threat, then, to the existence of that artificial, collective man, the *parfait sans-culotte révolutionnaire*, came rather from human nature than from the efforts of the enemies of the Revolution. The *sans-culottes* set too high a standard, their revolutionary man was too perfect to be true, and if from the purely human point of view there existed what might be called a revolutionary temperament, a factor quite as important in explaining the general comportment of the average *sans-culotte* as any political affiliations, such a temperament could not resist the pressure of time, boredom, fatigue, and laziness. To understand the small minority that remained faithful to their former ideals, one is driven to seek the key to their surprising steadfastness in character and in temperament rather than in social and political background. The general mass of *sans-culottes*, on the other hand, fell away without more than a murmur and disappeared once more into the political limbo of the years 1795–1815.

It may be objected that the purely impressionist portrait I have attempted to give of the average, rather than of the perfect, revolutionary, is as much a caricature as the prints and cartoons of London and Verona. I do not think, however, that to suggest that revolutionaries took themselves very seriously, that they were lacking in irony and flippancy, that they were often unimaginative, prejudiced, and ignorant, is unfair. If the average revolutionary did not belong to any clearly defined sociological category, he did in fact have both the virtues and the limitations of the small tradesman: economically a reactionary fighting against industrial concentration, he was puritanical and even priggish, extremely independent, unimaginative, and prejudiced, an anti-feminist and often a busybody: he was hard-working, a good family man and generally honest. Despite all the efforts of Thermidorian propaganda, the tribunals of the year III were seldom able to substantiate charges of theft and peculation against men who had articles of great value passing continuously through their hands.

The revolutionaries, in short, were enthusiasts; their sincerity was patent, if naïve, and, in some cases, was to be dearly paid for;

---

[1] For attendance figures over a period of a year in an urban club, see my article 'Politique et subsistances en l'an III: l'exemple du Havre', *Annales de Normandie* (1955), pp. 135–59.

and just as there is a revolutionary temperament as distinct from an authoritarian temperament, so among historians there will inevitably be those who feel an instinctive sympathy for these enthusiastic, if sometimes misguided, workers in the vineyards of the Revolution, and those who on the contrary will dismiss them as trouble-makers, hooligans, or time-serving followers of a party line.

My portrait of the revolutionary is incomplete in many respects. The whole problem of terrorism, for example, needs separate treatment. I have deliberately limited myself to illustrating some of the more personal traits of the revolutionary mentality, without embarking on a discussion of their rather vague economic aspirations, of the attitude of the *sans-culottes* towards the clergy and towards Catholicism, towards strikes and wage-claims, towards charity and pauperism, of their vague gropings at theories of popular sovereignty. This is only an interim report but I hope that it will correct some illusions and help to give actuality to a group of people that has only recently come into the categories of serious history.

Revolution and Counter-Revolution
1789-1816

8 The Beginning of the Revolutionary Crisis in Paris[1]

'No', says Professor Godechot, in the first word of the first sentence of the book, 'the Fall of the Bastille was not a flash of lightning in a clear sky.' The author returns lovingly to his 'cyclical', 'Atlantic' thesis, previously developed in his textbook, *Les Révolutions*, and even enlarges upon it, by introducing two 'cycles of violence' common to the whole of Europe: 1515 to 1660, and 1770 to 1800. In his anxiety to fit the Fall of the Bastille into his 'Eur-American' frame, he is driven to inflate the most ordinary grain riot into a sedition and to blow up some traditionalist window-breaking and clubbing into a mounting revolutionary ferment, embracing most of Western Europe and extending from the mid-seventies to the outbreak of the French Revolution and, of course, beyond. It is not an entirely convincing thesis: nor need it detain us long. For one thing, for any given two decades of the eighteenth century, it would be possible, in France at least, to tot up quite an impressive score, by counting up examples of popular violence. At almost any time, contemporaries will tend to think of the period in which they are living as a particularly violent one. Equally, in his anxiety to produce an impressive balance-sheet of riot and disorder, with the figures rising sharply in the appropriate decades, the author fails to distinguish between traditionalist, predictable, semi-permissible, and generally harmless forms of disorder, and the much rarer 'sedition'. There was nothing revolutionary, nor even potentially dangerous, about the recurrent French market riot or rural *arrêt* of grain convoys—there was often a degree of tacit complicity between the rioters and the local magistrates; and such ancient forms of disorder were confined within the bounds of unwritten rules that both sides observed. Nor can the Gordon Riots be described as revolutionary, and they were certainly not directed towards *une plus grande justice sociale*. Even the 'flour war' of May 1775 followed a predictable pattern, fanning

[1] Review of Jacques Godechot, *La Prise de la Bastille: Trente journées qui ont fait la France* (Paris, 1965).

145

out of the traditional centres of riot—grain ports, locks, river valleys. The only novel thing about it was its extent: it spread to three provinces.

The author is being wise after the event. The French repressive authorities were probably nearer the truth when, in the early eighties, and with the example of the Gordon Riots before their eyes, they could congratulate themselves on the discipline and orderliness of the Parisians and on the general *douceur des moeurs* of a society both civilized to a degree never before achieved and well policed. The author would say that they were unable to read the signs and portents, only too apparent to him and to his colleague, Professor Palmer, from their observatories in Toulouse and Princeton, on both sides of the Atlantic; but they were merely judging from what *they* saw and from what they knew, of long experience, of the inhabitants of Paris. The *lieutenant de police* and his subordinates knew what they were about, and they devoted to their study of the habits of the common people a clinical enjoyment that did not exclude an odd sort of friendliness, compassion, and humour. Had they a mind to it, they could have become chroniclers as perceptive, as well-informed as Vidocq, one of their nineteenth-century successors (who had, over Lenoir, the added advantage of having done his field-work on both sides, first as a criminal, secondly as Prefect of Police). They were, in fact, so confident, that they kept their repressive forces down to a minimum. July 1789 caught them unawares, because it confronted them with an entirely unprecedented situation; far from developing out of a chain of events occurring over the previous twenty years in foreign cities, 14 July was quite unlike anything that had ever happened before. It was unique; and the causes of its uniqueness are revealed in the author's own account. They were specific to France, and, to some extent, to Paris.

But Professor Godechot will not have it so. We are asked to make at least a formal obeisance to his collection of revolutions, and to do the Atlantic Tour with him first—it is an all-inclusive trip, taking in Boston (one of the capitals of the west), London, Geneva, and Amsterdam—a roundabout route to Paris, which we eventually reach, bedraggled, rather dusty, and confused.

Once there, however, it is very good going indeed, and we soon make up the time lost on so much sight-seeing. Professor Godechot's account is exceedingly valuable, and, once it gets down to details, very readable too. Yet, of all historical events, the Fall of the Bastille might, at first sight, appear to have been completely worked out, both as history and drama. After Durieu, Braesch, Chauvet, and Rudé, could there be anything more to be said? Clearly yes, and a great deal more, for the author has not only gone over the ground already covered, with minute care, discovering, both in the Archives Nationales and in the French war records at Vincennes, much new evidence, particularly regarding the organization of police powers, troop movements, and the maintenance of public order within the city. Concentrating largely on the problems facing the public authorities, in their relations with a population many elements of which were still as picaresque as they had been at the time of *Gil Blas*, early in the century, the author has pursued his inquiries in sectors which, however obvious, appear to have been largely neglected by previous historians for this over-familiar *iournée*. The central issue, as he sees it, is the control of the police powers. How did a government long organized for prevention and, eventually, for repression, manage to lose the initiative? It is, of course, a central issue, for revolutions can be said to begin, physically, when the police troops dismount from their horses and begin to fraternize with a rebellious crowd.

For, as Tocqueville so frequently reminds us, the old royal government owed its effectiveness as much to terror, or to the threat of terror, as to reverence, deference, loyalty, and awe. It was, so far as the common people were concerned, a military government. The King of France kept up his colossal army not only to give his gentlemen employment suitable to their honour and rank, not only to meet the exigencies of a disastrous and unnatural alliance, but also as a police force for use at home. The Suisses had been brought in at the time of the revolt of the Camisards, early in the century; the Flour War of May 1775 had been successfully terminated, without undue bloodshed, by a combination of Suisses and Gardes Françaises. Throughout the century, the poacher, the *faux-saunier*, the smuggler was more likely to be brought before the *prévôt de la maréchaussée*, or before the Intendant himself, than before the ordinary civil courts. For a large section of the rural population, the reality of the King's government would be represented by men at arms, mounted police, military courts, garrisons, billetting; and for the townsman, government, in its mystery and secretiveness, would be embodied in the men in black, bearing white sticks, going about their business discreetly and, generally at night, the *porteurs d'ordres*: 'Monsieur, J'ai l'honneur de vous faire part d'un ordre, de la part du Roi, à votre nom'. After the visit of these exquisitely polite officials there would be one inhabitant less in the quarter. In all probability, nothing more might be heard of him for years.

Nothing could be left to chance, and a government that was deeply suspicious of most of the King's subjects—especially the poorer ones (and these would account for 80 per cent of the population) and that was in the habit of considering every imaginable problem (even disease, epidemics, and natural disasters) exclusively from the angle of public order, sought to be minutely informed about every detail of life. The key word, in the language of that government, is *la police*—policing, rather than police, not so much a body of men, as a form of administration, invasive, endlessly inquisitive, vigilantly interventionist, occasionally repressive. Virtually every human activity, including reproduction, formed the subject of information for the benefit of the Government and was subjected to one form or other of police control. There was a *police des filles*, a *police des garnis*, a *police des moeurs*, a *police des enfants*, a *police des nourrices*, a *police des marchés*, a *police des grains*, a *police des vins*, a *police des liqueurs*, a *police de la voierie*, a *police des chevaux*, a *police des apothicaires*, a *police des boulangers*, a *police de la boucherie*, a *police des abattoirs*, a *police des imprimés*, a *police des spectacles*, a *police des journaux*, a *police de la religion prétendue réformée*—as well as the usual civil, criminal, military, and prison varieties. The overriding need was to be informed; information could economize on repression, and repression was expensive and, sometimes, dangerous. It was certainly the *most*—if not the *best*—informed government in eighteenth-century Europe; and there was probably no other so confident, thanks to its omniscience, in its powers to deal with any imaginable form of scandal or disorder, private or public (it did not make a clear distinction between the two; a young man who abducted the daughter of a *commandant de place* was considered as much an enemy to public order as a blasphemer or a highwayman; gambling, *la dissolution des moeurs*, or a novel such as *Les Liaisons dangereuses* were as dissolvant of good government as Jean-Jacques). In this respect, the old Government was as much a victim of its insatiable curiosity, of its voracity for information, much of it trivial, as of its consequent over-confidence.

Indeed, the most surprising fact that emerges from the author's admirable chapter on the police was the numerical weakness of the instruments of repression available to the Government, especially as far as Paris was concerned—and Paris was the only place that really mattered. The *guet* was a tiny force—120 men by day, 180 by night; the *maréchaussée* amounted to only 410 horsemen for the whole Paris region, with only seventeen in the city itself; the main onus would fall then on the Gardes Françaises, 3,600 men, many of whom were married and were thus semi-civilians (the author might have added that these police troops were also deeply and irretrievably involved, as procurers and protection men, in the prostitution trade, and had, in the ten years before the Revolution, been steadily moving over the narrow border separating law enforcement from complicity in crime). There were a further 1,500 troops—*gardes du corps*, hussars, foreign mercenaries—in Versailles. Altogether, this would amount to a total repressive force of about 6,800 men, available from within one to five hours' marching distance of Paris—one armed man to a hundred Parisians, if we take the population of the Capital as between 650,000 and 750,000 —about 300 permanently on hand in the city itself. Of course, there were vast reserves of troops in the garrison towns, but it would take at least four days to bring them in from the nearest of these (Amiens, Lille, Cambrai, Valenciennes), and as much as a fortnight to get them from the military towns of the eastern frontier (Metz, Strasbourg, Toul, Bar-le-Duc, etc.). This is a very different situation from Mercier's optimistic assessment when, in 1782, he demonstrated the impossibility of a major disorder on the scale of the Gordon Riots occurring in Paris. As far as numbers were concerned, Mercier was probably right; but he did not take the time factor into his calculation. A delay of five to fifteen days might be fatal. Also he did not reckon with the possibliity of the troops themselves proving unreliable; they had shown themselves entirely reliable in May 1775, indeed, the Gardes Françaises were still reliable as late as April 1789. Mercier, like the lieutenant and the police authorities, was counting too much on the docility of the inhabitants of a city in which there had not been a major disturbance for over twenty years. They had every reason to believe, too, that they knew the Parisian through and through, could call the bluff on his insolent, but harmless, *gouaille*—the eighteenth-century equivalent of the sort of safety valve provided, particularly under an autocratic regime, by the carping, vulgar, and equally harmless, irreverence of the *Canard énchâiné*—could count on his inherent servility, go along with a certain amount of noisy fractiousness, and always be one step ahead of any unusual rowdiness on his part. Mercier was convinced that a posse of men-at-arms could send the Parisians shrinking back into their courtyards, alleys, and workshops, the first time at least; but that a repetition of methods of force might have a contrary effect. The lieutenant was presumably of the same opinion, since he relied on so small a force to hold down a population of three-quarters of a million. This was in any case the last time that France would actually be short of police. Every subsequent government, possibly learning from the lesson of July 1789, has, on the contrary, had at its disposal enormous forces of repression, to such an extent that, on a number of occasions, the régime has often found itself at the disposal of the police, not the police at the disposal of the régime.

Force, in any case, was not the only check. Indeed, in this respect, the authorities responsible for public order showed a certain sophistication, particularly in their efforts to avoid a spectacular display of force. There is a well-known passage in Mercier that describes Louis XV walking unconcerned amidst a mere handful of *gardes du corps*, through a seething crowd of lawyers' clerks, to the Palais to deliver the *coup de grâce* to the Paris Parlement in 1771. All foreign visitors were amazed by the accessibility of the King to all his subjects; Young describes the crowds of ragged villains that were able to approach Louis XVI in the corridors of Versailles. The king, like his 'good people', was *bon enfant*, and, despite Louis XIV, something of the spirit of Henri IV had survived. During Lent, Louis XV came to Paris, in procession, prostrating himself, and washing his feet in public. Occasional familiarity of this kind flattered the Parisian and gave him a proprietary sense towards a monarch who thus showed himself in 'his' capital. Certainly, neither Louis XV nor his unfortunate successor was in the least afraid of Paris and its inhabitants.

At a lower level the policy seems to have been to combine a display of mildness—and thus of self-confidence—with a strict control over the likeliest instruments of violence. In Paris, neither the *guet* nor the *maréchaussée* carried fire-arms; they were armed only with sabres. A series of police ordinances made it an offence to carry pistols, knives, daggers, or any weapon small enough to be concealed in clothing. Gunsmiths' shops were strictly controlled, while *marchands de cannes* were forbidden to sell sword-sticks. The usual weapon for a brawl was a heavy club—what later became known, among the Lyonnais, as a *juge de paix*—and the usual result of one would be a broken head.

At the same time, the authorities kept a minute watch on the lodging-houses, every traveller being considered a potential regicide, a murderer on the run up from the provinces, or the agent of a foreign power. Prostitutes were carefully tabulated by the *police des garnis*; the main concern of the repressive authorities was to identify those who let them rooms, by the hour or by the night, and at what price, so as to exercise over them the blackmail of arrest, the *souteneurs* being, very rightly, considered as a valuable source of information, as well as of profit, and, when properly handled, the most effective allies of the criminal police. Prostitution could be allowed to exist—indeed, from the police point of view, it was necessary that it should exist—as long as it was known about; lists of *filles de joie* were kept up-to-date week by week. The Palais-Royal, because it was the one spot in Paris in which the well-to-do inhabitants of the western districts might meet up with the artisans and shopkeepers of the poor quarters of the north and east and where both had immediate access to the class of prostitution or gambling that would best suit their pockets, was likewise the object of constant surveillance. It was an obvious trouble spot, an equally obvious source of information and rumour. In the summer of 1789, under the very eyes of the police, it became the principal centre of sedition. Arthur Young wondered at the impunity enjoyed by its orators and its print shops. The police appear to have confined themselves to the role of informants; perhaps, with their own careers to consider, they preferred to let matters take their course and to wait upon the events. Certainly, many *inspecteurs*—including the majority of the *police des garnis*—later found employment with the revolutionary authorities, to whom they supplied as much inaccurate information as they had done, so zealously, to the old government.

Certain categories of casual or itinerant labour were equally a matter of concern to the police, whether because they were thought to be professionally brutal and violent, or because they were recognizable 'foreigners'—dark, hairy men, with strange accents—Auvergnats, Savoyards, Limousins—men of the brutish sort, savages among the civil Parisians, and the pre-ordained scapegoats for any unusual trouble. But laundrywomen, *brocheuses,* *revendeuses,* *crieuses de fruit,* discharged soldiers (especially former cavalrymen), sailors, coal-heavers, river-workers, bargees, the wild *flotteurs* from the forests of the Morvan, were singled out as specially prone to violence; the lawless inhabitants of the faubourg Saint-Marceau—*chiffonniers,* *décrotteurs,* *tondeurs de chien,* tanners (a stinking, revolting, sanguinary trade) *savetiers,* unskilled journeymen, foundrymen—were allowed a considerable degree of licence to administer their own rough justice, to an audience packing the windows and shouting their approval, so long as they confined their turbulence to their own, peripheral, quarter; it was when they showed signs of coming out of it, of marching on the centre, that the authorities became alarmed. It was the same during the Revolution; when the inhabitants of the two sections, des Sans-culottes and Finistère, crossed the river, there would be trouble for the central government; several *journées* were decided, one way or another, when they moved over from the left bank. It was likewise assumed that horsedealers and *brocanteurs* were the allies of thieves and fences and locksmiths, the potential allies of house-breakers; and, if the police wanted to pick a man up, the big *foire aux chevaux,* in the same faubourg, would be the first place they would look. Equally suspect were those in the transport trades—especially carters—that crowded in the inns on the edge of Paris; Gentilly, Ivry, Montrouge—centres of every imaginable source of law evasion. It was as if the main concern of the police was to check movement, to stop people from moving from one place to another—they were particularly officious in rounding up unemployed girls and having them sent back to their villages in Normandy, the Île-de-France, Burgundy, the east and the north-east, the principal sources of supply of female labour—or, at least, to control their movement by a series of paper checks, internal passports, and so on, that gave an extremely active *portrait parlé* of their holders: name, age, place of birth, residence, trade, height, colour of eyes, shape of nose, *le visage marqué de la petite vérole,* nicknames—so many aids to identification. For, above all, people must be prevented from disappearing from view, they must not be allowed to *prendre la couleur du paysage.*

A similar obsession is reflected in the ferocious series of orders prohibiting the *travestis,* and attempting to limit the number of carnivals and other occasions for dressing up. People were not to be allowed to dress as men when they were women, for the same reason that they were not to be permitted to cross, undetected, from one province to another. In a city in which it was possible, in a matter of thirty seconds, for a man dressed from head to foot in black to disappear down one of twenty or thirty alleys leading off the *quais*— the chosen domain of the old-clothes' merchants—thence to emerge a parrot green (Mercier has such a scene, with the customer dancing awkwardly on one leg as he endeavours to pull on a pair of plum-coloured breeches before the arrival of the *guet*), the task of the police cannot have been easy. It was all very well to insist that the *forts de la Halle* display their official insignia, and that each trade walk in its traditional uniform: such insistence was as likely as not to increase the confusion, simply by increasing the opportunities for disguise. The *fripiers** were themselves subjected to a rigorous supervision, as a 'dangerous' trade; but in the poorer quarters they were so numerous that a depleted police could not possibly keep check on their changing stocks. A deserter could quickly convert himself into a civilian and disappear in the jungle of the Cité or the Gravilliers, as long as he had a single friend—preferably a girl—and did not have to fall back on a *logeur*. And there are endless references —in novels and plays—to the prevalence, in Paris, of armies of false *abbés*, very convincing *chanoines* and monks, the favourite operational kit of confidence tricksters, blackmailers, seducers, kidnappers of girls, and the better sort of burglars. It was, it seems, even possible to obtain the sober clothes and the white sticks of the dreaded *porteurs d'ordres*; Mercier witnessed a false one being caught out in the act of attempting to arrest a real one.

Every night patrol of the *guet* would bring in its dejected, ragged, and shivering group of runaway children—ranging from 9 to 15 and often coming from as far away as Reims, Soissons, Chartres or Alençon and, more often, from Versailles, Saint-Germain, Belleville, Saint-Denis, Marly, Fontenay-aux-Roses, Antony, Sceaux, Montreuil, Vincennes, Passy, Auteuil, on the periphery of the Capital—discovered sleeping on the *quais* among the wood piles or wine barrels, under the arcades of the markets, crouched on pavements warmed by the baker's furnace; but these would be only a fraction of the unhappy boys and girls who left their homes for good or who stole out at night from their laddered rests, in the *soupentes* of brutal *patrons*. Again, it was not so much a matter of protecting families, as of preventing the armies of crime from obtaining new recruits. Ultimately, the intervention of the police would not amount to much, at least in the warrens of central Paris —a city as much designed for escape, for hiding, as Lyon with its network of *traboules*, cutting through houses and avoiding the dangerous nudity of the open street.

Gipsies were relentlessly harried. Pedlars—those who came to the town from the countryside to sell rabbit-skins, those who brought the countryman the almanacks, broadsheets, and popular prints of the town—were likewise subjected to minute regulations; the purpose of their *patentes* was to enable the authorities to keep a check on their movements, rather than to bring in money (though it could also restrict their numbers, another way of achieving the same end).

The police were reassured, felt that they could face up to a situation predictably localized, so long as they knew where people were to be found, at work or at leisure. They knew, for instance, that on Sunday or Monday evenings (often on both) there would be a stream of drunken journeymen, on their way back from the *guinguettes** of Issy and Suresnes to their homes in the faubourg Saint-Marceau. Their route was predictable, their drinking habits were regular. Disorder was likewise governed by the Saints' calendar, by the recurrence of the great feast-days—whether those of the patron of each parish, or those of each trade—and by the great annual fairs. The police were forearmed. Hence, too, the advantage of single markets: the Halles—the *forts* of which, a closed and proud community, were mostly Picards—the horse market, the river port of la Grenouillère, the slaughter-house, the corn market, the wine market, the fish market, the tanneries; of specialized centres: quai de l'Horloge, quai des Orfèvres, rue des Regrattiers, faubourg Saint-Antoine, les Gobelins, le Gros Caillou, Montfaucon, the Palais-Royal, conveniently centralizing crime, information, and vice—and as it turned out, sedition—each trade in its quarter, each man on his storey (the apprentice on the seventh, the master on the fourth, the *bourgeois* on the first), the *bateaux-lavoirs* on the Seine, wood in Charenton, the laundry-women in Vaugirard and Grenelle, the soldiers in the École Militaire, the Auvergnats and the Limousins in the crowded streets around the Grêve.

The difficulty was that people were not going to stand still, merely to oblige the police and make their task easier. A population could not be 'frozen' administratively, despite a multitude of passports, *patentes*, metal badges (*Afficheur*, *Allumeur*, *Crocheteur*, *Portefaix*, and so on for a score of outdoor trades and occupations), with name and number to be worn at all times, barriers, and so on. A considerable labour force left Paris every summer for the harvest fields of the Brie and the Pays de France; and there was no guarantee that people would stay in one trade or in one quarter; a small shopkeeper or a skilled craftsman was no doubt the prisoner of his clientele, of his neighbours who owed him money, of his shop, workshop, and equipment, and of the particular needs of the area in which he worked. But this was not the case with unskilled labour, and the lower one went down the scale, the greater would be the incentive to keep on the move. It is not uncommon to find a journeyman change the parish of his place of sleep—such as it was four or five times in the year; at a certain level of poverty, one could not afford to stay put; there were no ties, only debts, no movables, other than what might go into a large-sized handkerchief. And, as unemployment grew more widespread, there would be a greater tendency to double or triple employment, in different parts of the city. The author calculates that of the army of domestic servants that constituted 16 per cent of the population of Paris—the largest single occupational unit—as much as 87 per cent had been born out of Paris. And domestics, though they were most numerous in the new quarters of the west and in the *noble faubourg*, were to be found everywhere, roaming the city, carrying out errands, trading in information and gossip, and frequently changing their livery.

The Paris population had become potentially more 'dangerous', both as a result of the enormous extension of the building, food, and clothing trades of the 1770s, and of the recession of the late 1780s, following the Eden Treaty with England. The author shows that, in 1789, some half-a-million people—two-thirds of the population—were on the borderline of want or below it, and were in need of relief; the inhabitants of the parishes of Saint-Marcel and Saint-Jacques-du-Haut-Pas were the worst hit—at least, it was in these overcrowded quarters that the greatest amount of relief was distributed. There was also a permanent hospital population—composed of the old, the infirm, the very sick, the mad, foundlings, etc.—of 14,000. The occupational cut-down gave, as in every eighteenth-century city, a dangerous preponderance to domestics—16 per cent in Paris, 12 per cent in Toulouse—and the course of the

Revolution was to prove that no class could be more literally egalitarian, and more savage in its pursuit of vengeance, than former coachmen, cooks, footmen. The revolutionary committee of the Section du Bonnet Rouge, perhaps Fouquier's most effective provider, was entirely composed of such people, and they knew what they were about. A great many of his *dénonciatrices* were ex-lady's maids who took a cheerful joy in denouncing *milady*. The tailoring trades accounted for 15 per cent; and what more archetypal terrorist than a shoemaker? Unskilled and casual labour made up a further 13 per cent; the dangerous army of food and drink—the *marchands de vin* were the first to respond to the call of sedition, later they often became the natural spokesman of militancy in their quarters—11 per cent.

Perhaps even more alarming is the 11 per cent of *oisifs*—either unemployed, unemployable, or unwilling to be employed, containing no doubt an incalculable army of spongers, hangers-on, *badauds*; people who got up late, spent their day walking about the city—the boulevards in the morning, the markets in the afternoon, the Palais-Royal in the evening—'taking the air', watching, listening, dawdling, hanging about the posting houses, climbing in on weddings, funerals, baptisms, when they were large enough, in the prospect of a free meal (Mercier's *promeneurs* dressed constantly in formal black, so as to be prepared for anything that might turn up). Such people would gape at a burning house, watch eagerly on the edge of a brawl; they were constantly available to the provincial, newly arrived, ready to fill him with their Parisian lore. A drink and a free meal might recruit them to any cause. They were, in fact, more dangerous than the professional criminals, between the police and whom there existed all manner of links and tacit understandings. There is no greater threat to established order than the nameless man who lives alone in a garret, receives no mail, has no friends and no occupation, no fixed hours, and no reason to be in one place rather than another. The events of July 1789 were exactly what such people had been waiting for for years. They probably account for a host of unidentifiable *meneurs*. Excitement for a time filled their days; the summer of 1789 was a golden one for the *badaud*; and fledgling provincials poured into the city.

This, then, is the background to Professor Godechot's slow build-up of crisis: an authority over-confident and self-satisfied, the lower echelons of which, after being reproved for having displayed too much repressive zeal, notably in April 1789, were no longer willing to commit themselves to decisive action that might result in bloodshed and consequent blame—this was particularly the case of some of the high-ranking officers of the Invalides; a repressive arm too small, too scattered, and, in the last resort, no longer reliable—even some of the mercenaries mutinied at the critical moment; a population on the borderline of extreme want, containing a high proportion of 'dangerous' trades and of the idle, batallions of resourceful, knowledgeable servants—not cap-in-hand retainers, but so many vengeful *Jacques*; a population that was young, without roots in Paris; a general loss of deference, following scandal in high places. The rest is familiar, though the author has added some telling details. He shows, for instance that it was a very close thing indeed, that there was something like a race between the repressive authorities and the future revolutionaries; the first troop movements towards Paris were ordered on 23 June, the day of the *séance royale*; three days later, on the 26th, the Government began calling in massively the great garrisons of the east; most of these would be expected to arrive in Paris between 12 and 16 July. By the 16th something like a quarter of the French Army—most of the cavalry, household troops, and foreign regiments—would have been in, or just outside, Paris. These movements were widely known—they could hardly be concealed, for so many Parisians were themselves from the north and east, had relatives there, who wrote to them from Lille, Amiens, Arras, Reims, Châlons, Charleville, Givet, from Vesoul, Chaumont, Nancy, Metz, and Bar-le-Duc, or who met *pays* from these places who had come to Paris on business. (In his analysis of the local origins of the *vainqueurs de la Bastille*, the author shows that the Departments most heavily represented, apart from Paris itself, which accounted for about a quarter of them, were the Nord, Somme, Aisne, Oise, and Ardennes; then, the Côte-d'Or, Haute-Sâone, Marne, Haute-Marne, Moselle, and Bas-Rhin—a fair enough representation of the origins of the population of Paris at the time, still very much a 'North of the Loire' city, if one were to add the Norman departments, the Yonne, and the Eure-et-Loir. The Moselle and the Bas-Rhin, however, are unrepresentative, and the percentage of *vainqueurs* from there can be explained by the number of former soldiers in their ranks, whose military skill had brought them to the forefront, with the formation of the national guard.) The Government was beaten to the post;

A SECOND IDENTITY

during the night of 12–13 July Paris was largely given over to criminal elements; on the 13th the middle-class *milice* was in control. The *14 juillet* was won by Frenchmen from the north and the east. In this respect, it was quite unlike the *10 août*, which saw Bretons and Marseillais fighting side by side with Parisians. It was not the victory of a nation. But, of course, it had national and international consequences.

This is the most complete and most intelligent account of how the Revolution began in Paris, of how a government lost control of the situation, marched behind events, and thereby ceased to govern. So it is, of course, an exciting story; nor, thanks to the immense diligence of the author in running down every possible clue, is it an entirely familiar one. In such a situation, the vanquished are probably more interesting than the *vainqueurs*. We all know, more or less, how and why the Bastille fell, what happened to its defenders and to its prisoners—one of them, a mad Englishman, after a few hours' triumphant liberty, had to be sent to Charenton; another, a mad Frenchman, managed to live it up for five days, before being similarly disposed of. What Professor Godechot has to tell is how the day was lost by the Government. It is a less familiar story than how the day was won, and certainly a more profitable one to present rulers and future ex-rulers.

9 The Bells of Anjou[1]

As an example of just what an English historian can achieve when writing about France Professor John McManners's *French Ecclesiastical Society under the Ancien Régime* must rank with Douglas Johnson's biography of Guizot; like that work it has qualities of serenity, detachment, compassion, and understanding that it would have been hard perhaps for a Frenchman to command. Here certainly is a case when it can be said that certain aspects at least of the national history of a country can best be handled by a foreigner.

Guizot was a Protestant, a fact that, sometimes unconsciously, has governed the attitudes of generations of French historians of every tendency. The definitive history of Vichy and the Occupation will probably also have to be tackled from outside, and on Professor McManners's own subject the contributions of French local or national historians have all been strongly marked by prejudice on the burning question of clericalism or anti-clericalism. Works on the provincial clergy before and during the Revolution by members of the priesthood, with possibly the sole exception of those of the late Canon Sol on the Quercy, have tended to be primarily chronicles of martyrology—some of them have even been entitled *Histoire des Persécutions* . . .—in which the revolutionaries are depicted as monsters, men of blood, pillagers, and enemies of God. Even in the books of leading historians of the Revolution, like Mathiez and Lefebvre, non-juror priests are writen off only too readily as bad Frenchmen, *mauvais patriotes*, enemies of the people, counter-revolutionaries, who sided with the enemy of their country and raised the standard of revolt, thus putting themselves outside the national community and beyond reach of human sympathy.

Such neo-Jacobin historians are as ready with their collective condemnations of groups and categories as were, in 1793 and in the year II, the members of the revolutionary government and the judges of revolutionary tribunals and military commissions; the *prêtres*

---

[1] Review of John McManners, *French Ecclesiastical Society under the Ancien Régime: A Study of Angers in the Eighteenth Century* (Manchester, 1961).

réfractaires tend to escape identity, emerging in their works only as faceless pariahs, good at best for deportation; if they were hunted down, guillotined, shot, massacred, drowned, they had what was coming to them. And among French Catholic historians the war between Constitutional Church and non-juror Church has by no means ceased; the apostles of compromise, the middle-of-the-road men who tried to go along with the Revolution, have seen their motives impugned as much by the historians of the Church as by the faithful of their own times; and it is only recently that the *prêtres constitutionnels* have found at least a measure of support and understanding from the leading ecclesiastical historian of the revolutionary period, Monseigneur Leflon.

Professor McManners's work deals only indirectly with the Revolution; in one of those telling metaphors of which he has the secret, the author writes: 'We can review the revolutionary events externally only as if they were unmotivated facts, like rain falling on the just and the unjust. . . '. Yet, though he is concerned more with the drowned than with the drowners—for a number of his canons, his monks, and his priests, chiefly the older and weaker ones, were to be the victims of Carrier's *baptêmes républicains* in the winter waters of a Loire in flood—he does not condemn out of hand the terrorists; he shows impatience only with Choudieu, for whom he reserves one of his rare condemnations, describing him on several occasions as a 'bilious anti-clerical'. His account of the split between the Church and revolutionary France is serene, intelligent, and sad.

The Revolution is merely the epilogue—often a tragic one—to an account of a settled society, the members of which planned ahead for years (in 1780 they had worked out that the next time a certain procession would fall on 1 May would be in 1815) and could reasonably expect to die in the place, or at least in the province, in which they had been born. A canon of Angers would almost certainly spend the rest of his life in the town; 'his office . . . was a dignified *cul de sac* in the ecclesiastical hierarchy' and it was the same with the lower clergy, with the nuns and the monks. It is a very static, very conservative provincial society and provincial culture, very far away indeed from the Palais-Royal, closer to the Plantagenets than to Diderot or Voltaire. It is far more concerned with the justification of present status and privilege by reference to the past, by laborious and erudite appeals to local custom, by minute research in local records than with the wicked things that were being written in Paris.

Angers was still largely a medieval town in the Age of Enlightenment, though many of its buildings were literally crumbling (the author has much to say about holes in roofs, overflowing gutters, towers noisily subsiding into disused moats) and its enormous monastic establishments gave indifferent cover to a lonely handful of individuals lost in the echoing emptiness of damp, decaying, vaulted halls. The place had become too big for the society it was designed to house and the disparity was so obvious, so visible, the waste of space was so evident that people of a practical turn of mind could not fail to see certain fundamental questions written on the ground. The fabric certainly was still there; the bishop, the canons, the chapter, and the monastic houses owned most of the town and all the best land surrounding it, and authority was almost entirely theocratic; unlike Tours, it had no civil representative of the central government there to contest the economic, spiritual, and administrative authority of bishop and chapter. Every inhabitant worked in some way for the Church; the cathedral offered employment to a multiplicity of trades. In this sense, Angers was untypical of French urban society in the late eighteenth century; its entire economic life was bound up with the ecclesiastical hierarchies; its immense provincial pride was derived primarily from its reputation, still unchallenged at least in Angevin eyes as a centre of orthodox theological learning and a training-ground for ecclesiastical scholarship. It was very far not only from Paris but also even from Nantes, Bordeaux, le Havre, Lille, Marseille, and Rouen.

Professor McManners deserves gratitude, then, for insisting so much in his introduction on the particularities of both Angers and the Anjou as well as on the endless diversity and the vivacity of French provincial life everywhere, on the eve of the Revolution. This is a fact that so singularly escaped the generally perceptive observation of Arthur Young, though it may be said in his defence that much of this life was so subterranean, so somnolent, so carefully hidden away behind shuttered window or priory wall, so inbred and institutional, that an English traveller looking at the empty streets might well have taken the tolling bells as the only evidence of human activity.

Angers is certainly a special case; but no town is quite like any other; each province has preserved administrative institutions, a culture, decaying academies and a patriotism that are unique. So Professor McManners is quite right to warn his readers that his conclusions must not be applied on the national level. This is the right order of things; only by working on the local level, on provincial or municipal records, can we obtain any advance in our knowledge of French society in the years before the cataclysm. Professor McManners of course is not a pioneer in this sense; there have appeared recently valuable studies of urban society in Rouen and Orléans, of the provincial nobility in and around Toulouse, of the peasantry of the Sarthe and Lower Burgundy. But the present book has qualities that are absent from these useful and important works of research.

For one thing, Professor McManners does not belong to that steely school of French historians who have apparently adopted as their battle emblem a remark much favoured by Georges Lefebvre at his worst (that is in his pseudo-scientific moments): 'pour faire de l'histoire, il faut savoir compter'. Here at least is a study of French society in the late eighteenth century that does *not* have statistical tables, graphs, and maps with a complicated range of shadings from sepia to deep mourning, with arrows and figures like telephone wires on every other page. The author makes no bones about it: 'the picture that can be given', he writes, 'is an impressionistic, not a statistical one', and elsewhere he makes the brave assertion that 'social history is primarily a history of persons'. This warm, human, gently humorous book is indeed a far cry from Lefebvre's grimly statistical Orléans, as spiky and as heartless as a drawing by Bernard Buffet, with its regiments of taxation rolls, its lists of tradesmen, office-holders, its roll call of *bourgeois*, *grands*, and *petits*, as exciting as a telephone directory: so many hat-makers, so many basket-makers, so many cutters, so many *marchands*, so many *négociants*—whatever may differentiate these last two categories.

Professor McManners's people are not the flat, playing-card figures of sociology and of the historians of social structures—the knave of hearts representing a prince of the blood, *apanagiste*, with 100,000 livres of income; the ten of diamonds, a provincial *hobereau* with ten *métairies*; the eight of clubs, a city merchant and municipal office-holder; the king of spades, a *shogun* milking a province.

Nor are they the conventional chessmen of some parliamentary history, members of 'interest groups', operated like automata in response to strings and wires pulled by great dukes and by city merchants. His churchmen have three dimensions. They are not great men, historical figures, portrait-length, with their hands on the bauble. They are not of one piece, and they are as contradictory, as fallible, as unpredictable as the average, neither saintly, though there is one saint, nor wholly bad, though there are some indolent, pleasure-loving people. They are rather ordinary, often narrow, unimaginative provincials, incapable of seeing far beyond chapter wall or the vineyard surrounding a country presbytery. Even the bishop is generally of the local higher nobility, though unlike the other characters in the book he seems often to have adopted as a golden rule of conduct that the farther away he was from Angers, the better. There are also one or two quite fantastic individuals, like the amazing megalomaniac Robin, whose frequent incursions into the narrative add an element of comedy to this study of a lost world: Robin is never very far away, and one finds oneself waiting for his next act of unpardonable impudence, for his next outburst of odd cantankerousness.

Professor McManners, then, is more concerned with individuals than with groups. Much of his material is derived from the personal records, letters, and accounts of individual churchmen; and from a selection of potted biographies he draws wider inferences that concern the contesting groups existing within the First Estate. The author is both a moralist—though a very indulgent one—and a portraitist; it is in his character sketches and in his interpretation of motives that we can see him at his most perceptive. But his book is not just a chronicle of oddities; the author uses individual cases to illustrate tendencies that he considers to be general. Here again he goes about things in the right order. It is interesting and instructive to see how he does it. For instance, this is what he has to say about the last of the *ancien régime* bishops of Angers, Mgr de Lorry:

Debts drove him in the end to fulfil the residence qualification, and eighteen years spent in minor bishoprics had developed in him a sort of shrewd evasiveness. . . . These consecrated noblemen brought to their task both the vices and the virtues of their race; a few were immoral, many were luxurious and non-resident, a few were deeply pious, most were decent and dignified, and a number of them showed remarkable administrative ability.

There is on de Lorry himself the gentle epitaph: 'Thanks to birth and favour he had proceeded with easy assurance into high office which he did not deserve. With the same aristocratic dignity, he left it when his hour had struck . . .'. This is all we want to know about de Lorry, and more than we can ever expect to know from either the Palais-Royal literary caricature of the profligate, libertine bishop *à la Rohan* or from a general study of the social origins of the episcopate. Professor McManners makes a shrewd judgement on the man and on his caste.

There is, too, an amazing passage on the life of a nun, a calling the inner secrets of which had of course much exercised the salacious imagination of writers from Diderot to Restif. That, however, is not the author's angle of vision; he is not writing anti-clerical propaganda; nor is he concerned to titillate the reader's curiosity on the subject of the most closed of feminine institutions. He attempts to project himself into the mind of an elderly nun who after years as a Carmelite prepares for death; we can see her cell; we know of her daily activities; the objectives behind them are hinted at, made convincing. It is an extraordinary feat of historical imagination.

Professor McManners is not ignorant of economic facts. Some may reproach him with not having provided statistical tables to illustrate the wealth of the church in this theocratic town and with not having sought to assess the total amount of church property that changed hands as a result of the Revolution; he tells us what sort of people bought it, for how much and what they did with it, and that is enough. There is no compelling necessity for a history-book to be an inventory of stock. In any case, the economic inducements of a clerical career are adequately and often strikingly illustrated —both in human and income terms—once more from personal examples. By using Brossier's account books, he is able to assess the expenses of a canon in the middle of the 1760s. There is the passage about a dean, the son of a magistrate of the Présidial— for the *noblesse de robe* had its connections with the plums of the Church too—'who followed the normal course of an elder son who sought ordination, and made over his inheritance of lands and feudal dues to his younger brother in return for a yearly pension of 1,200 l.'.

He has much more to say on the speculative nature of pluralities, on the standards of living of individual canons and *curés*, information that is less statistical than relative, in that it shows primarily just how comfortable might be the condition of an idle and insolent canon, just how wretched that of an underpaid and overworked parish priest, debarred even from saying Mass in any of the finer churches or chapels of the city; and this is what matters, for it was along these seams of material discontent and injured pride—and a churchman is as much concerned with status as anyone else, since nearly all his sacerdotal acts are themselves symbols of a hierarchy —that the First Estate was finally split. In consequence some of the characters in this book went over to the Revolution, married, and fought in the republican armies—though they were a minority.

He never neglects inducements that are inexplicable in terms purely of financial interest. Having worked so long on ecclesiastical records, on the endless and complicated litigation of provincial France in the late eighteenth century, he is constantly aware of the enormous pull of vanity and status among both clerics and laymen. 'In a provincial town', he observes, 'churches were the chief public places where men could make display of their rank'; later it would be the *garde nationale*, the *fête civique*; one way or another there would still be processions which illustrated visually the place each man occupied—or thought he should occupy—in a small, closed society. We are given any number of examples of slightly ridiculous incidents involving pushing and shoving, even the exchange of blows, among churchmen, for the possession of a stall or for the use of an altar. Like the *frères*, the canons and *curés* seem to have been quick to take up the cudgels, whether for orthodoxy or for the right to hold a censer. They were muscular enough.

It was not only a question of vanity. Behind these quarrels over precedence there would often be disputes over property or over the levy of some ecclesiastical due; but a lot of it was just a matter of collective pride. The clergy in this respect set a bad example to the rest of the population; there were searing rows between the corporation of wig-makers and that of candlemakers about which should come first in the Corpus Christi procession. Indeed, what makes this account so deeply tragic is that men so often involved in petty disputes over bells or a stall should have to face a few years later terrible issues of conscience, make agonizing choices involving the fundamentals of their beliefs, should even have thrust upon them martyrdom or the gnawing unhappiness of exile; a canon weeps when he sees Canterbury Cathedral, for it reminds him of his own great church. They were such ordinary men, caught up by cruel times.

Professor McManners is above all a human historian, and he achieves his greatest success when describing the characters, foibles, hopes, and fears of this group of obscure clergymen, a society that he describes as mellow and unprogressive, which 'like the city of Ys of Breton legend the seas had covered . . .', a society which the author has rescued from oblivion, brought back to a second life. Such is his success that one nearly always has the impression that he is speaking of people whom he has known personally, as his teachers in a theological college or as his comrades when preparing for ordination. But in spite of his modest disclaimers this book is also what its main title promises. It is a contribution to the general history of French society during the last years of *l'ancien gouvernement*, as it was to be called, with a tinge of nostalgia, by the Prefects of the First Empire. At last one can understand, in human rather than theological terms, just what it meant to be a Jansenist, what *richérisme** was about, why the Jesuits were so unpopular, why some bishops sought allies among the lower clergy in order to combat stiff-necked canons ('a bishop, more particularly an idle one, must have allies'), and why the Church had to fight so hard all the time to defend its material wherewithal against the claims of royal fiscality and seigneurial interference ('it was impossible to relax, so that every minor issue must be fought').

One learns also how the claims of the lower clergy to run their own church differed from the arrangements made by the revolutionary government under the Civil Constitution of the Clergy, why there should have been anti-clericalism especially among the patrician class even in a town like Angers, what the Oratoriens and the Ursulines were teaching their pupils, why the monks made such a poor showing during the Revolution and why the nuns such a good one. Ecclesiastical institutions, the cumbersome administration of the Church of France, are minutely described in their workings at the level of diocese and parish. There are frequent references to the Church's administration of charity, especially in the important and tragic matter of foundlings, and to what happened to so many charitable institutions as a result of the Revolution—an extremely brutal chapter of social history and one that remains largely still to be explored. Nor does the author neglect the role of ecclesiastical foundations in the care of young girls and the redemption of fallen women.

We are reminded too of the development of anti-clericalism as a weapon of the revolutionary *bourgeoisie*, when in September 1790 as the result of a serious grain shortage and a sudden rise in the price of bread, the violent, lawless *perreyeurs*, workers in the slate quarries, invade the town and are driven back only after more than sixty of them had been slain by the middle-class national guard. The rioters, it was suggested by the municipal authorities, had been incited to revolt by members of the clergy, who had ordered the tocsin to be rung. This was not the first, nor the last, time that the *possédants* would attempt to use anti-clericalism as a weapon of social conservation.

The final assessment of this admirable book can best be made by the author himself, in words that reflect both his common sense and his artistry. 'Sloth, narrow-mindedness, institutionalism, pettiness, and not startling vices, were the temptations which beset the religious of Angers.'

And of this lost clerical world, he concludes:

If there were magic peals and haunting choirs there were also battles over bell-ropes and tumults in vestries. But this angular, prickly complex of mingled good and petty evil formed a natural community and a spiritual abiding place. It may have saved some souls; it certainly inspired many loyalties. With all its injustices and rivalries, it had the essential quality of homeliness—it drew its children back again when their years of exile were over. Anjou had always been like that—

> Malheureux l'an, le mois, l'heure et le poinct,
> ....
> Quand pour venir icy j'abandonnay la France!
> La France et mon Anjou.

10 The *Enragés*[1]

Just as it is perhaps unwise to base the title of a book on a question, it would certainly be unfair to judge the book on the answer. For it is almost immediately apparent that, whatever they were, the *enragés* were *not* socialists: and Dr. Rose's *The Enragés: Socialists of the French Revolution?* is very good value indeed at £1, not because of his answer, but because he seeks to define the *enragés* by applying to them a whole series of other tests.

The *enragés*, a name they were given by their enemies, who were many and powerful, were a group both tiny and weak. Some historians have limited them to three only; the most commonly agreed total—and one for which the present author opts—is five. A few have put it higher; it is very much a matter of taste, according to whether one is to restrict membership to Paris or to extend it to include an unspecified number of provincial 'wild men' of similar temperament. Dr Rose's members are Jacques Roux, a priest from the Angoumois who became the juror *vicaire* of Saint-Nicolas-des-Champs in the Gravilliers district of Paris; Jean-François Varlet, who was Paris-born: Théophile Leclerc, of planter stock, born in the Forez and often described, because of his political activities there, as 'Leclerc de Lyon'; Pauline Léon, the daughter of a Paris *chocolatier*; and Claire Lacombe, an actress from Pamiers.

The *enragés* are no doubt unique in the history of left-wing extremist splinter groups in that they cannot be defined in terms of an exclusive ideological content; nor can their identity be established by the purity of the doctrine that they preached. Despite the fact that one of Roux's biographers, Maurice Dommanget, should have published his *Jacques Roux, le curé rouge*, with the Éditions Spartacus—a publishing venture at one time associated with one of the many independent Marxist *groupiscules*—nothing less like the Spartacists than this disparate group of revolutionary individualists could be imagined. They had in common, it is true, political failure, and Jacques Roux met a violent death. They have too certain

[1] Review of R. B. Rose, *The Enragés: Socialists of the French Revolution?* (Melbourne, London, 1966).

168

historians in common; for it is their very lack of success that has inspired the interest displayed in both groups by Dommanget and by Guérin. To most, failure is not a particularly significant—or endearing—touchstone; but allowances must be made for Trotsky-ites and adherents of the P.S.U.[1]

Even in their crude political aspirations and methods, the *enragés* are indistinguishable from the general run of *sans-culotte* militants and even from many of the Cordelier leaders; the only thing that distinguishes them from the so-called *hébertistes* is their timing (they got in first, but this did them more harm than good), as well as the sincerity and the lack of ambition of at least one of their number. For while Hébert attempted to *use* the people to help him into a position of power, Roux, who was one of the most sympathetic personalities revealed by the Revolution, voiced popular grievances in their own right, because he thought that something should be done about them, because, as a priest in one of the poorest quarters of Paris, he was utterly shocked by what he saw—people starving, blanketless, in crowded attics; unemployed journeymen and jobless builders' apprentices with large families, deprived of relief; the wretchedness of the very old and the infirm, of pensioners and of mothers of large families, of women in the former luxury trades, of governesses and seamstresses, of former organists and the prole-tariat of ecclesiastical society—*chaisières*, *suisses*, and so on—all categories for whom the Revolution had not only done nothing but had actually undone the little that had been done for them by the old government.

Roux was the sort of person who gravitated to the extreme left as a result of *une capacité de s'indigner*—according to Alain, one of the marks of the breed. He was one of those rare people who took equality literally and who believed that at least it should mean a full stomach for all. He was constantly harping on this dangerous theme; dangerous, because most of his parishioners—and people in the class beneath the *sans-culottes* all over Paris—saw it that way too, thought that the Revolution should mean enough food for all. Roux was not a socialist or a communist or anything of that sort; he

---

[1] This was written before the recent student unrest in France. It is, perhaps, appropriate that the more extravagant and gratuitously violent of the militant minority pressure groups at the University of Nanterre should have taken to themselves the title of *les enragés*, a compliment no doubt to Varlet.

expressed no views on property or on the *loi agraire*; it is doubtful if he even thought about such things. But he became indignant when he saw that many were starving in the middle of a revolution, while a few were obtaining all the basic daily needs of life. This made him angry, and so he demanded immediate, tangible remedies, in the language of his parishioners. What was worse, when he came to the bar of the Convention or of the Commune, he did not come alone; he spoke for and with the inhabitants of a couple of Sections who were so devoted to him that even a year after he had committed suicide in a *robespierriste* gaol, they were being pulled in for publicly recalling the memory of the 'Good Priest'. His followers were Auvergnat water-carriers, Savoyard chimney-sweeps, market porters, builders' apprentices (of whom there were many in the Gravilliers), journeymen carpenters, coal heavers, river workers, categories that had no stake in the Revolution and that hardly impinged on the so-called 'popular movement', that of the *sans-culotte* militants. They were not householders; they remained, even in 1793–4, as sub-citizens with military service as their only 'right', and with no one other than Roux to speak up for them.

That was why Roux was a dangerous man who had to go; he was not even a demagogue who could be bought off, and the *hébertistes*, who were and could be, loathed him for it. He was in their way and as long as he could write and speak they were made to look rather fraudulent. So they co-operated with a revolutionary government (which they were seeking to replace) to destroy Roux; every argument—especially the lowest—was used against him: that he was a priest, that he had never formally abjured the priesthood nor publicly renounced Christianity—he went on preaching in the summer of 1793—that he was unmarried, that he lived with a *gouvernante*, that he had quarrelled with Marat (after sheltering him), that he had been denounced by Marat a few days before his assassination—and Marat's 'widow' was induced to come forward and denounce the impostor who had the impudence to claim Marat's succession (Roux really was a friend of the people, but in small letters). Robespierre and his colleagues could not stand a person who was really in contact with the common people, who knew what they wanted (which was not Virtue or Supreme Beings), and who was constantly coming up with inconvenient truths.

Robespierre did not like to be reminded of food; he probably thought eating an immoral activity, or at least rather an indecent one; anyone who suggested that the Revolution was about food ('vulgar groceries') had not got the Message. The Revolution was about higher things—Virtue, and so on. Robespierre loved the People dearly, and knew what was good for them; there had been no mention of food in the history of Sparta. He simply could not stand men like Roux; and when, with the enthusiastic help of Hébert and the Commune, he had hounded Roux to suicide and had then discovered, to his fury, that even without their spokesman the lower orders continued to complain about the lack of food, the bad quality of bread, the unfairness of a rationing system that still left the best bits to the rich, he made food a forbidden subject altogether. People were not to talk about it; there was no food crisis, he said; those who referred to one would create one; if they did talk about food, they were making trouble and were, even if they did not know it, counter-revolutionaries. Two months after Roux's suicide, fifteen journeymen and apprentices from the Section des Lombards were arrested by Robespierre's police because they had publicly raised the question of the meat ration—a taboo subject—an action that was a posthumous testimony to Roux's own effectiveness as a popular spokesman.

Roux is interesting and very endearing because he is the only personality who went into the Revolution without the intention of gaining anything. He did achieve a few modest successes, was elected to the Commune, even seems to have been particularly horrible to the unfortunate Louis XVI in the last weeks of his life—saying, according to the legend, that there was really no point, given his position, in the former King having his teeth seen to (though this seems out of keeping). He started a paper, wrote a number of pamphlets; but these were not thought of as vehicles of his ambitions, in order to bring him to power on a tidal wave of popular indignation. Roux wanted the Convention to do something about starvation, poverty, food shortage, the unequal distribution of the necessities of life; and when the Convention failed to respond, he denounced it.

That is about all there is to him; he was not a *doctrinaire*, nor the forerunner of any nineteenth- or twentieth-century political creed. He was just an unusually good priest. Nor was he a member of a group. There was no group. Roux, Varlet, and Leclerc had only this in common: that they were rather awkward charlies, odd men out, excluded from the 'respectable' forms of revolutionary agitation, and making more direct a popular appeal than any of the 'ins', including the members of the Commune. But that is all; Roux was certainly irascible, *exalté*, even a bit mystical; but he was not a crackpot. Varlet, on the other hand, was. The authorities were worried about Roux; Varlet they rightly considered as harmless— the sort of professional eccentric that any régime can afford to tolerate—and that some invent. There was something reassuring about the presence each day on the terrace of the Tuileries of this young egomaniac with private means, on his stand, and surrounded by his acolytes dressed, like himself, as super-*sans-culottes*. He became part of the Paris scene, just as, for thirty years, Prince Monolulu was an integral part of the landscape at Hyde Park Corner. The authorities had no need to worry about Varlet; they knew that if they blew, he would fall down. They had something on him—he was of military age and (very naturally) preferred defending the Revolution in Paris rather than on the frontiers or in the Vendée. And, if he got out of hand or a little uppish, a sharp reminder from above or a brief spell in prison would be enough to bring him back to his senses. He always knew when to take a hint. And so he survived the great government purge of 'ultra-revolutionaries' that followed the destruction of the *hébertistes* in the spring of 1794; indeed in May he was vice-president of a purged Section. He only suffered minor harm during the Thermidorian reaction, and even the police of the Empire thought him scarcely worth bothering about. By then he had become one of the things to see in Paris, like the double-bearded policeman of the Porte Saint-Martin in the 1930s. If he had not had a private income, he could well have qualified for a small government pension.

Roux was in his forties: Varlet was in his middle twenties: Leclerc in his early twenties. But that was about all the last two had in common, save a rivalry to succeed Marat as journalists. Leclerc came from a comfortable planter background, and he had no real understanding of popular grievances. (As in the case of Varlet, a small income of 5,000 *livres* separated him from the mass of the common people; no great sum, but enough to isolate him.) All that he shared with the people was a taste for violence, and his programme—if it could be called that—added up to little more than incessant and screaming demands for more violence, more terror, more repression against more people, more (better and wheeled) guillotines. In this, of course, he was not alone, being indistinguishable from scores of men of blood, from Vincent downwards: like Vincent, he made it his special concern to call for a vast purge of the Army. But unlike Vincent he did not have an official post. Vincent and Hébert could get heads. Vincent could get *generals* guillotined: the only heads that Leclerc got were those already booked by other people. For instance, he screamed and yelled for the execution of the Général-Comte Custine, but so did Vincent. Leclerc was like a boastful, but not very good, gun who was always claiming other people's grouse. Like Varlet—but like so many other young men who used the Revolution as a form of self-expression—he much enjoyed himself and was filled with self-conceit. He probably thought that the Revolution had been specially contrived to give him an opportunity to play a role (which he did, briefly, in March, 1793, and again on the *31 mai*); but, enjoying no support from any of the organized pressure groups—Jacobins, Cordeliers, Commune, Ministry of War, Sections—he had to make do with obscure third-line institutions with little, even potential, nuisance value—Société des Femmes Révolutionnaires, and to a limited extent Société des Défenseurs de la République. Furthermore, to base a political career in 1793–4 on feminine support and on women's rights was a form of political suicide. Still, he was rather fortunate, after having called for the death of so many people, to have survived himself. He even got a wife out of the Revolution.

Roux and Varlet had no apparent connection with the two women who are genarally included in the group: Pauline Léon and Claire Lacombe. Leclerc went to bed with Pauline and seems to have married her. For that matter, the *hébertiste* Mazuel went to bed with Claire, but this, for some reason, has never got him into the group. It is not clear what Pauline and Claire had in common, other than that they were both women, in their twenties and attractive. This would hardly bring them together—on the contrary. Both too were feminists, of the most tiresome kind. They were busybodies who, while most women were concerned with keeping their children in food and clothing and with standing in queues, tried to induce the authorities to make the wearing of the cockade compulsory. No wonder they made themselves odious to the *dames de la Halle* who

173

did not like being told what was good for them by two girls of 23 and 25, both of whom had had a comfortable childhood and neither of whom had children. Though Dr. Rose is very gentlemanly about it, there seems to be some evidence that one form of revolutionary militancy displayed by the two *amazones* was to have slept with a number of the younger and better-looking extremists. In any case, just as Leclerc got a wife out of the Revolution (and then got out of the Revolution), Pauline abandoned militancy with her marriage. Claire eventually went back to the stage. In this she had something common with Varlet, for as an actress she seems to have been poor. But this again can hardly be taken as indicating the existence of a group. Failure or semi-failure must always represent the largest of the negative confraternities. It is too big to be meaningful; it is only in very exceptional circumstances, such as those of June 1940 in France, that the half-baked, the dunces, the crackpots, the egomaniacs, are able momentarily to combine and turn the tables on the clever, the competent, the *diplômés*, to form Vichy.[1] And Vichy was not governed only by imbeciles; there was Laval. In the year II there were plenty of competent people available.

Roux was sincere and probably a bit mad. Varlet seems to have been more than a bit mad and was able to keep himself, for long periods on end, in an almost hysterical state of excitement. But his 'madness' did not make him blind to the red lights winking ahead, and his sincerity had a habit of going into cold storage at the crucial moment. Leclerc was ambitious and, after May 1793, ineffective. His sincerity was rather *par éclipse*; it went on and off, like a lighthouse well regulated to the political barometer. As for the women, no doubt they can be credited with the sort of sincerity that goes with militant feminism, when militancy takes the form of dressing up or undressing in public, posturing, declaiming, and, between times, going to bed with *frères-ès-révolution*. Unlike the market women and the housewives, it is hard to see what these two rather spoilt girls had to be indignant about.

Ultimately, the *enragé* group is one of many historical myths, invented in this instance by a combination of 'government men' and rivals in violence. All they had in common, as Dr. Rose very neatly

---

[1] The Vichy régime has been variously described as the *république flottante*, owing to the preponderance of naval officers among Darlan's Prefects and Sub-Prefects, and the *république des recalés*, owing to the large numbers of people who had ploughed the *baccalauréat* or the *licence* in the entourage of the Marshal.

puts it, was 'a common misfortune, not a common political programme'. For their programme—more economic Terror, more
political repression, a wider purge of the Army and the civil
service—was that of Vincent and Hébert. And Roux at least was
less concerned with terror than with social justice. The only thing
in fact that the five had in common was to have fallen foul of the
Jacobin dictatorship in the winter of 1793 and the spring of 1794—
a fate that they shared with a mass of ultra-revolutionaries up and
down the country who, like them, after preaching the virtues of
repression suddenly discovered that Terror could be used against
themselves and that it is a game best played by Governments.

Why then all the fuss? Dr. Rose does much to provide an answer.
The *enragés*, like the equally over-inflated *babouvistes*, have given
to various nineteenth- and twentieth-century revolutionaries the sort
of historical genealogy that they felt in need of. Marx and Engels
began the process in 1845; Michelet, in 1853, treated them as a
coherent party; by 1870, they were even safely in *Larousse*. In the
early 1920s Dommanget re-exhumed them; in 1930 they were the
object of a detailed study by Jakov Zakher, a Leningrad historian
who disappeared in 1934 to re-emerge in 1956 and resume his
chair and publish a new version of his book just before his death.
Since 1958, a Leipzig historian, Walter Markov, has made a minute
investigation of the pre-revolutionary career of Roux and has added
yet another adjective to the over-fed dictionary of revolutionary
labels—*jacquesroutins* (partisans of Jacques Roux), so that, along
with the almost yearly colloquium on *babouvisme*, we may soon
expect an international gathering devoted to *jacquesroutisme*.

The present author has attempted to cut the *enragés* down to
size. But even he tends at times to make too great claims for them—
a tendency natural enough, for if he had not, there would be some
danger of his subject, like the *peau de chagrin*, shrivelling up,
eventually to disappear altogether from view or to fall apart into
five separate chunks. As it is, most of his conclusions are cautious
and negative, even when he tries to squeeze something positive out
of this disparate group. We learn what the *enragés* were *not*, rather
than what they were; for they did not amount to very much and,
save for Roux, too little is known about them, probably because
there is little to know. It is something of an achievement to have got
ninety-four pages of text and a book of 102 pages out of this quin-
quicycle. This is certainly as much as they deserve. Dr. Rose has

given the definitive account of them, and after digging them up has turned them upside down, emptying their pockets and their heads —not much in either—and has then reburied them with a decent reverence but without fuss. This should be their last resting place; for it is difficult to see what could be found about them or said about them that the author has not already found and said. This is a very thorough, informative, and eminently sensible study—and a model, too, of how to make really effective use of five very different case histories—of a small group of *exaltés* and crackpots, saints and thrusters, who, in their various ways, made a brief impact on the Revolution.

11 The Comte d'Antraigues and the Counter-Revolutionary Mentality[1]

Probably the best hope of a success of the Counter-Revolution within France was in 1790; and the most likely place for it to succeed was in the south-east, where there existed a hard core of popular royalism, bitter religious divisions that polarized and made more extreme political alignments at both ends of the spectrum. Mlle Chaumié stresses the anti-protestantism of ultra-royalism, an anti-protestantism that was based on years of close and hated coexistence and sometimes, as in the case of d'Antraigues himself, even of Protestant ancestry. D'Antraigues hated Protestantism, but admired the rebellious independence and extreme provincialism of the Cevenol Protestants, as effective adversaries of Court despotism and centralized tyranny. There existed also a proud but impoverished gentry, bitterly suspicious of the court nobility, and of what they called 'ministerial despotism', a terrain admirably suited to prolonged resistance, even of small groups, in the fastnesses of gorge, mountain, and chestnut forest, in what had always been the traditional bandit country and became, in the early years of the Directory, the favourite stamping ground of organized bands of highwaymen, deserters, and outlaws.

In the second year of the Revolution—as indeed in the sixth, the seventh, and the eighth, or again in 1815—the stronghold of ultra-royalism would be the Vivarais (the wilder and least accessible areas of the Ardèche) together with scattered but well-placed and often communicating islets of royalist violence and extremism in the Vaucluse; in the Gard, where popular ultra-royalism fed on the grievances of Catholic artisan and wage-earner against their Protestant patrician employers; in parts of the Bouches-du-Rhône and the Var, with pockets of sympathy extending to the Toulouse region and, beyond, to the Pyrenees, where both Catalan and Basque peasantry, after the first enthusiasm for the Revolution, began to look to Charles IV as the natural defender of Church and

[1] Review of Jacqueline Chaumié, *Le Réseau d'Antraigues et la Contre-Révolution 1791–1793* (Paris, 1965).

177

King. Seen from the latitude of the popular royalism of the south-east and of the Midi as a whole, the most likely champion of the faith, of provincialism and decentralization, and of the rights and privileges of the faithful southern nobility would by 1790 be the King of Spain, not the Emperor.

Hence the importance, at least in 1790 and 1791, of winning over the Court of Madrid. D'Antraigues was not the only royalist agent to attempt to set himself up as the principal informant of the Spanish Government, though as a southerner he was probably the first to realize that the only effective help for a counter-revolutionary movement in France at this early date would have to come from Spain. Most of the secrets of the extremely devious policy of the Court itself were communicated to Charles IV, who was appealed to in the name of the Family Compact as the cousin of the French King. Accordingly the historian concerned with the realities of the Counter-Revolution needs to go to Madrid and to Simancas in search of clues.

The author of the present work is the only historian to have done so to date. She is a former pupil of Georges Lefebvre and a *conservateur* at the Archives Nationales, who edited the secret correspondence between the Courts of France and Spain in the early years of the Revolution. In her latest book she is concerned with d'Antraigues's notes to Las Casas from the beginning of the Revolution up to the King's death; a further volume will take the reports up to the execution of Marie-Antoinette.

Like her subject, who constantly insisted that the only effective help for the Counter-Revolution could come from Spain, Mlle Chaumié has concentrated entirely on the link-up between d'Antraigues and his small group of ultra-royalists, all but one (a Norman) like himself from the south-east, and sharing his hostility to the Protestant *bourgeoisie* of that area and his deep suspicion of Vienna. Owing to the light that it throws above all on d'Antraigues's strange personality, this book is certainly the most original and penetrating study of the Counter-Revolution to have appeared since the subject first began to attract the interest of historians after the Second Restoration; Mlle Chaumié, who shares Lefebvre's concern for individuals and for personal motivations, as well as for the study of social structures, has succeeded in re-creating, in their contemporary terms, the prejudices and the assumptions of those aristocratic anarchists from the south-east of whom d'Antraigues was the most typical member. Her book comes in a series entitled *Histoires des Mentalités* and there could hardly be a more suitable commentary on her whole approach to the history of the Counter-Revolution. For the real subject of this book is d'Antraigues himself, though as much as two-thirds of the text is devoted to long extracts from the inaccurate, wildly coloured, and often useless information which the secret agents supplied, at great cost to the Spanish Government, to Las Casas.

D'Antraigues, as a *mystificateur* who may even have believed in his own myths, is a marvellous and most engaging subject; Mlle Chaumié is much more concerned with the man who wrote the reports than with the reports themselves, a sense of priorities that previous historians, exclusively concerned to estimate the value of the information provided by d'Antraigues and to identify his sources, have generally lacked. The only interest of the reports is the light that they throw on his personality, aims, and prejudices; and d'Antraigues is both an admirable and an easy subject for study: admirable because it would be impossible to discover a more typical case. Here is Counter-Revolutionary Man in person; he *is* the Counter-Revolution and Mlle Chaumié does not have to invent him, she merely has to describe him, or, better still, let him describe himself, which he is only too ready to do. He is an easy subject because, like most people of his caste or class, and of his area, once he had made up his mind he did not easily change it, living and dying with his prejudices. His philosophy of life was both simple and unyielding; and nothing that happened during the Revolution caused him to alter in any way ideas and attitudes that he had already clearly elaborated at the time of the *révolte nobiliaire*. There could be no greater enemy of compromise; indeed he spent the more effective part of his life combating all forms of compromise between the monarchy and the new régime. At times he was even ready, or at least he said he was, for such things are difficult to prove, to ally himself with Jacobins, in order to frustrate the schemes of the Court party, of the middle-of-the-road royalists and of the loathed Breteuil, the Bad Baron of d'Antraigues's Tales of Mystery & Imagination. There is in fact no better example, in the life and attitudes of an individual, of that *politique du pire* that has so often characterized the extremes of French politics since the Revolution. Mlle Chaumié describes him as an extremist of the most violent kind.

Conspirators are seldom dull. There is something very engaging about the unsinkable Comte d'Antraigues who, when one scheme after another curls up underneath him, always has a ready explanation for their failure and ten other better ones to propose. The reader is constantly surprised by the optimism of a man so consistently unsuccessful; but then he was a dedicated conspirator who had lost all sense of proportion and most of reality and who was usually, in his Swiss exile, about as misinformed as those he misinformed. This is probably the case with most secret agents, but d'Antraigues was particularly prone to this occupational risk; he was an individualist, perpetually conducting a one-man conspiracy, the Counter-Revolution was to be his, and his alone; he alone held the secret of ultimate success; the King of Spain must on no account listen to information coming from any other source. While his informants in Paris supplied the Count with the sort of information that he would have liked to hear, he did exactly the same when writing to Las Casas; much of the information came in fact straight out of the head of Lemaître or Despomelles, and some of the rest was probably invented by d'Antraigues, whose object was not so much to inform the Spanish Government as to hector it.

He believed above all in plots and counter-plots, because he was lacking in any direct political experience and because he was bitterly suspicious of those who, like Ministers—evil personnified —were not; because, too, he was an aristocrat who had no perception whatever of popular grievances or popular attitudes. The only role offered to the common people in his scheme of things was to be a passive object that could be bought by evil men and made to do anything for gain. He thought that everything could be explained purely in terms of plots, of personal intrigues, of secret encounters in secret committees, of sudden and inexplicable realignments. Neither d'Antraigues nor his Paris agents ever bother to explain anything, they merely state. D'Antraigues was even to claim, though as usual without giving a shred of evidence, that he had placed his men within the Paris *comités révolutionnaires* (one would really have to discover an institution in which he did not have an agent). Born later, he might have made a fortune writing for the *Série Noire*; or, more probably, he would have become involved in some such piece of right-wing infantilism as the Cagoule. Certainly he would have fallen for anything that involved dressing up. In fact, the only element lacking in his panoply of the perfect conspirator is the

Beautiful Spy; his agents apparently rely exclusively on masculine sources.

Honour was his guiding light; but it did not prevent him from enjoying every minute of his life as a secret agent. Codes, secret inks, passwords, nicknames, the language of numbers—all were greedily used to transmit his generally worthless information. One feels that d'Antraigues was more concerned with the means of transmitting his reports than with the reports themselves. Here was really a vocation, an artistic talent; for he loved intrigue, loved to think of himself as the secret informant of kings and emperors; he at least was convinced that the fate of Europe might hang on any one of his notes. Without the Revolution, he would probably have remained a small provincial nobleman, blown up with pride of birth, nourished on a terrible goulash of political theory and historical myth—Vercingetorix, Louis IX, Louis XII, Rousseau, the *champ de mai*, the Fronde—wasting out his days at Villeneuve-de-Berg. It is doubtful if he would ever have amounted to very much, other than as a conversationalist and as a pamphleteer—he was an extremely able polemicist—had not the Revolution given him an opportunity to give full rein to his romanticism, his anarchical violence and his aristocratic pride.

He was naïve, in the way that extremists tend to be, and manically suspicious, also, in the way that they tend to be. He even seems to have managed his own death well; he was probably assassinated by his servant, on the orders of an unknown party.

He might be described as a *babouviste de droite*, for, when all is said and done, there is not much to distinguish an ultra-royalist fanatic from a *conjuré de l'Egalité*. 'Il y a', writes Mlle Chaumié, in one of her most perceptive passages, 'une parenté de tempérament qui les unit. Les ultras des deux bords se rejoignent par leur haine en quelque sorte viscérale de tout esprit libéral. Ce réflexe se retrouve d'ailleurs tout le long de notre histoire.' We can well believe that d'Antraigues may have had a genuine liking for some of the Jacobin leaders, though it is perhaps too much to go the whole way with Mlle Chaumié when she asserts that he actually came to agreements with some of them—an argument that brings us back to the assertions made by Fouquier-Tinville and Saint-Just when accusing the *hébertistes*: 'les deux extrêmes se rejoignent, qui dit ultra-révolutionnaire, dit contre-révolutionnaire'.

D'Antraigues belongs to an historical family, the later reincarnations of which can be traced through the *chevaliers de la Foi*, through the royalist *gardes du corps* and small gentry, such as Froment, of the *verdets** and the *miquelets** and the other murder gangs in the Duc d'Angoulême's Kingdom of the South, through the Ministers of Charles X—all southerners—through the ranks of the hopelessly faithful, living in a moth-eaten Central European court in exile, through royalist *boulangistes*, early Gaullist paladins, a few early Vichyssois, too, up to the present time. The latest appearance on earth of the recurrent d'Antraigues, in his Fifteenth Coming, would be one of those young officers, younger sons of an impoverished provincial gentry, from the Massif Central or the Toulouse area, who planned, with an aristocratic incompetence reminiscent of the methods of the *comte-conspirateur*, to assassinate General de Gaulle when he visited the École Militaire; he too had forfeited the loyalty of his *féaux*, by sacrificing their honour.

So we must retain d'Antraigues, if only because he is, in himself, a temperament, a movement, an historical phenomenon, but reject his information. Indeed, it is difficult to understand why so many reputable historians should have devoted so much research and ingenuity in their efforts to identify d'Antraigues's alleged informants within the Committee of Public Safety, within a score or so of problematical secret committees, and within the Directory; like Our Man in Havana, probably he did not have any. We have only his word for it, and d'Antraigues evidently included lying among the noble virtues; but if he did, they must have been placed there by the republican authorities themselves, for the information that they supplied was so trite and so inaccurate that it could only harm the counter-revolutionary cause if acted upon. Nor were those who passed on the information—Despomelles, Lemaître, and so on—any more impressive; they were a silly, seedy lot, who, like d'Antraigues himself, living in his closed mind in the Cloud-cuckoo-land of exile, relied more on their imagination than on observation. Although they were in Paris they seem to have been quite incapable of seeing what was going on under their noses, or even of describing what little they did see. They even got the 10 *août* all wrong, although one of them was supposed to have been there. They sent their master the sort of news that he wanted to hear, and he sent Las Casas only the sort of news that he wanted the Spaniards to hear; like the psychological warfare colonels in Indo-China who later became the first victims of their own brainwashing, both d'Antraigues and his agents suffered from a mental process known as 'l'intoxication'. They had such little regard for truth, they were so anxious for things to turn out the way they wanted them or expected them to, that they let their imagination get the better of them. Lemaître further stimulated his own by copious drinking. D'Antraigues was a man of some literary talent and considerable invention, but he wore blinkers and could see only straight ahead.

Mlle Chaumié's book is essential reading for a fuller understanding of the counter-revolutionary (and for that matter, of the revolutionary) mentality. It is a magnificent addition to the 'impressionistic' school of the history of human beings and political and personal mentalities.

12 Our Man in Berne[1]

Dr. Harvey Mitchell and Mr. W. R. Fryer have written books concerned with the same subject: British relations with the French Counter-Revolution, British plans for the political solution to be imposed upon an erring, republican France (and on the French people) during the period from the outbreak of war to the end of the Directory. Both centre primarily on the personal influence of a single man, William Wickham, British Consul-General in Berne, the confidential agent of Grenville, head of the Secret Service in Western Europe and entrusted by the British Government with the task of organizing relations with the various rival groups of French Royalists and of directing the efforts of the Counter-Revolution towards aims that coincided with the interests of British policy.

Not only is Wickham the central figure in both books, but his unpublished papers also form the basis—and, indeed, the pretext— for Mr. Fryer's *Republic or Restoration in France 1794–7*, most of which consists of a closely knit analysis of Wickham's dispatches to Grenville and of his correspondence with his various agents in France and with those of the exiled French Court. In *The Underground War against Revolutionary France* Dr. Mitchell has likewise drawn considerably on Wickham's published correspondence and on that, mostly unpublished, of Drake, Wickham's counterpart in Genoa; though unlike Mr. Fryer he has extended the range of his sources to include the reports on elections and on public opinion supplied by local authorities to the Directory and to the Ministry of Police, as well as diplomatic papers from Paris and London; his bibliography is also far more extensive. Mr. Fryer has chosen, as his rather complicated title implies, a subject more specific, referring almost exclusively to the efforts of a single, albeit a highly important, agent of Wickham, the former *constituant*, d'André, to

---

[1] Review of Harvey Mitchell, *The Underground War against Revolutionary France: The Missions of William Wickham, 1794–1800* (Oxford, 1965); and W. R. Fryer, *Republic or Restoration in France, 1794–7: The Politics of French Royalism, with particular reference to the activities of A. B. J. d'André* (Manchester, 1965).

organize royalist opposition in France along lines agreeable to the British Government.

Both works are devoted to the complicated, highly specialized, and necessarily obscure history of intrigue, espionage, plot and counter-plot, secret rendezvous and ample distribution of Secret Service funds. A host of people pass briefly through each narrative, but they are little more than names, and neither work has much to tell us about the state of mind of ultra-royalism and the assumptions of the counter-revolutionary militant. This is because both historians are concerned—as indeed Wickham was—with purely political solutions, adopted at the highest level, imposed from above, through the intervention of narrow political élites, without reference to popular opinion. Wickham had a positively Burkean distaste for *la canaille*; he took a missionary zeal to his task of bringing retribution on a presumptuous and seditious French populace. D'André, for his part, had helped to organize and had applauded the Massacre of the Champ de Mars and his political philosophy might be contained in one of his own observations to his English protector and friend: 'puisque la nation n'est rien, if faut la négliger et s'attacher à ceux qui la gouvernent . . .'.

We are dealing then with high statecraft, and neither Wickham nor d'André appears to have had any inkling, even, of the strength within France of popular royalism which, in the famine conditions of 1795 and 1796, offered a much better platform for the royalist cause and for effective counter-revolutionary violence than the evanescent intrigues of ill-informed conspirators and corrupt double agents. Dr. Mitchell refers obliquely to the regional distribution of royalist pockets, rightly insisting, in this respect, on the importance of the southern Departments, and he has some interesting things to say about the distribution of the Institut, a royalist cover organization, over some sixty Departments. Mr. Fryer has no time at all for such provincial matters, not allowing himself to be deflected for one instant from his *tête à tête à deux voix* between his twin heroes (for he treats them as such) and, apart from a brief but highly intelligent discussion of British war aims in France, he steadfastly refuses to be drawn beyond the narrow frame of his sub-title.

Here then are two political histories, confined to the activities of the British Secret Service in France between 1794 and 1800 and its relations with a narrow range of selected French agents. They have more to say about British aims than about French reactions to them and they are far more informative about Wickham than about any of his agents. The Counter-Revolution emerges in both accounts as a type of intellectual exercise, a complicated chess game, played according to the obscure and, to the layman, meaningless rules of the professional secret agent. After studying both accounts the reader is not much the wiser about the aims of the Counter-Revolution, though, through a welter of misinformation, over-optimism, procrastination, incompetence, and misunderstanding— the occupational diseases of movements directed by refugees from abroad, financed by a foreign government and out of touch with internal opinion or even with the realities of internal politics—he does at least come away with a pretty good idea of why Wickham failed so utterly in everything that he undertook. As Mr. Fryer observes, near the end of his long-winded account of d'André's mission, there was 'something rather splendid' about failure on such a grand scale; the British taxpayer might not have thought so, but he was not consulted. Both Wickham and d'André seem positively to have basked in the rays of disaster and to have thrived on setback. Wickham at least emerges as a living personality, and in Mr. Fryer's book even the colourless, ineffectual, hopeless d'André acquires some life.

It is unfortunate for Dr. Mitchell and for Mr. Fryer that they should have published studies on an almost identical subject simultaneously. Not only have they thus been unable to profit from each other's findings; they also lay themselves open to a comparative estimate of their works. Dr. Mitchell's book draws on French as well as English sources, and covers the whole story from start to finish. His is the definitive account of Wickham's missions; he is also aware of the complexities of French political regionalism, and occasionally his account strays from Paris and Berne to the ultra-royalist fortresses of the South and to their hoped-for conquests in Lyon, the Franche-Comté, the Forez, the Languedoc, the Vivarais, and parts of Alsace. Though it is unattractively written, though the author chooses to translate all quotations and is often uncertain about the spelling of place- and proper-names, and though he brings on a bewildering number of characters with the barest introduction, his is by all counts the better book.

Mr. Fryer writes rather more agreeably, but he is inclined to pomposity, is longwinded, and has a taste for the statement of the obvious: he has the merit of quoting in the original French. But historians should be careful not to rely exclusively on a single source of evidence; Mr. Fryer has constructed a whole book—and one that is longer than Dr. Mitchell's far more comprehensive account—on a minute analysis of d'André's correspondence with Wickham. There is not really enough here to go on, Mr. Fryer spreading d'André thinly over a very large slice, with the result that there are far too many phrases such as: 'How far d'André was involved in this is not clear. It seems almost certain that he knew of it and took some part in it . . .', or 'it is indeed quite as possible that d'André received [an idea] from others, as that he originated it'. With so much uncertainty, so much obscurity, the reader begins to wonder whether d'André is worth so much trouble and whether he had anything like the importance either he himself or his faithful biographer attributes to him. Yet Mr. Fryer has to admit that the intervention of his hero did not amount to very much and that most of his schemes were built on a void. We come away with the feeling that he has allowed his new material—discovered with legitimate excitement no doubt—to dictate to him a subject and that he has blown up into a whole book what might have better made the material for an article. Ultimately, Mr. Fryer is pursuing a subject that is only just there, and one of his remarks concerning d'André's activities might be taken as a commentary on the whole subject of the poor man's Grand Design: 'probably it would have made no difference in the outcome'. Quite clearly it did not.

Both authors are out to prove that Wickham was important, and important he undoubtedly and unfortunately was. Mr. Fryer attempts to foist d'André upon us as well: Wickham thought he was important, convinced Grenville that he was, paid out to him huge sums of Secret Service money, so, says the author, we must take Wickham's word for it. His importance is not at all convincing, but there is no doubt about his expense. Wickham, of course, *was* important because he had the full confidence of the British Government—or at least of Grenville, who was concerned with this sort of thing—and because he was able to persuade Whitehall that he was the right person to be 'Our Man in Berne' (a position that he managed to hold for six costly years), that he knew all about France, could talk the Pretender into anything, and could conjure up, at his bidding, vast insurrections or great sweeping victories at the polls in various parts of France. There is no doubt about his enthusiasm; Wickham certainly derived more enjoyment from his activities than we do reading about them. He must have loved every minute of his Secret Missions; they were a change from the Aliens' Office, and he was one of those Englishmen who liked living abroad.

After leaving Oxford, he had taken a law degree at Geneva, and had married a Swiss girl. Switzerland was a pleasant enough background until it was overrun by the French, when Wickham had reluctantly to pack up shop and return to the Island Home (he was later employed as Chief Secretary to Ireland); his job was exciting without being particularly dangerous, and it was infinitely satisfying to his *amour propre*. For here was young Wickham, the mentor of his schoolfellow, Grenville, proposing one blueprint after another for the immediate overthrow of the French Directory; here he was lecturing Louis XVIII and his brother, the Duc de Vauguyon and de Saint-Priest, on the benefits of clemency and the merits of constitutionalism, laying down the law to the fine flower of the French nobility; here he was foisting on the British and on the much less enthusiastic ultra-royalists, who, with their experience of the stables, knew a non-starter when they saw one, the well-intentioned but ineffectual d'André, the right sort of moderate, middle-of-the-road *feuillant*, that is to say a born loser. Of course, dealing with such impossible people as the French *émigrés*, with their attachment to the *politique du pire*, Wickham must have had his trying moments, too, and he certainly displayed a limitless fund of patience. Even so, he seems to have had a marvellous time; and, whatever they may have thought of him, Louis XVIII and his brother had to listen to him, for he supplied the money, and could cut it off if he felt he was not getting a return.

It is unfortunate that the two historians should have made so little of Wickham as a person. He was certainly unimaginative and over-sanguine; he was violently prejudiced, conducting his own private war against the people of France as a whole; he was a leading member of the belligerent faction within the British Government; he made endless muddles and miscalculations; but he was not the rather dull, colourless fellow that emerges, in sepia tones, in the present works. Although they are quite unalike as people, Wickham has some of the more engaging traits of that impossible rascal, the

Comte d'Antraigues: the same buoyancy in adversity—Wickham is like a cork on the murky, troubled waters of Counter-Revolution—the same divorce from reality, the same steadfast refusal to be discouraged, as one Grand Design—the expression is Wickham's own and has been adopted, apparently without any intended irony, by Mr. Fryer—after another flops, with a slight whimper, as one project after another is quietly but decently interred, without fuss, as one agent after another fails, goes over, rats, panics, leaves with the cash, or gets caught.

There is no general rising in the Midi, Lyon does not come over, though Wickham has Précy's word as a gentleman that it will next time, the garrison fails to take over Strasbourg and Huningen—there has been a slight mishap—the elections for once go fine, royalism is about to win legally, but the Directory, instead of allowing itself to be voted out of existence, repudiates them, much to the surprise and consternation of Wickham. Pichegru, Wickham decides (after, it is true, some hesitation and misgiving), is to be our man, he will bring over his army with him, but the Directory takes his army away, and we are left with Pichegru; the royalists in Paris arm to arm, they will infiltrate the *garde nationale*, so as to prepare for a military take-over, but the Directory moves first, calls in the Army and arrests the leading royalists in their homes; the Prince de Carency ('a voluptuary, an adventurer and a swindler', states Dr. Mitchell, appetizingly), the son of the Duc de Vauguyon, turns out to be a double agent and gives the show away to the Ministry of Police; the Instituts spread, but they are an open secret, the police let them disseminate in order to acquire complete lists of royalist adherents in the Departments; wonders are to be expected of the *constitutionnels*, but then it turns out that, like d'André, they are incapable of movement and sit and wait till the Directory's police clear them up, and that the only effective royalists are the ultras, the wild and violent men, who, says Wickham, are to be avoided at all costs. Wickham never says die and, in Mr. Fryer's account, he even acquires a Rin-Tin-Tin stature. 'Could Wickham . . . rise to this occasion?', he queries, after yet another Grand Design had, as expected, come a cropper; 'he could and did'.

In 1798, when the dust has scarcely settled over the ruins left by Fructidor, here is Wickham confidently going ahead with schemes to gain control of the Army, to overthrow the Directory, this time by engineering an alliance between the royalists and the

Jacobins. He reports home that the commanders of Bordeaux, Toulouse, Sélestat, Huningen, Besançon, and Strasbourg have promised to surrender their fortresses, that the second-in-command at Belfort can be counted on, that there are 300 officers in Paris itself ready to participate in the *coup*, that a provisional government headed by Royer-Collard and others is about to be established, pending the arrival of Louis. 'The cost of the entire operation', writes Dr. Mitchell, 'would come to 1,000,000 livres or about £40,000.' Cheap at the price.

When he returned home, Dr. Mitchell states, 'the French remembered him long afterwards as their most dangerous foreign adversary on the continent; the police records amply testify to his "Machiavellian cunning and largesse" '. There could be no disputing the latter, but the modern reader is not convinced of the former; the French have at all times overestimated the intelligence of our Secret Service. Nor is it really surprising that Wickham got away with it at home. After all, he knew about France, he was an expert on French affairs, there was no parliamentary check on his information, nor on the cash at his disposal. The real mystery about Wickham is whether he himself believed all the rubbish that he passed on to the British Government. As he seems to have been an honest man, it is probable that he did.

Is this then all the Counter-Revolution amounted to? All these comings and goings, secret rendezvous in Swiss inns, a 'brilliant scheme' to take over the Republic's postal services and use them for the dissemination of information and royalist propaganda ('nothing was to come of this daring proposal', comments, with melancholy, Mr Fryer), the proliferation of cover organizations, agencies, institutes, *sociétés*, the recruitment of agents, the purchase of Army commanders, generals, colonels, and whatnot, a multifarious band of persons unknown or scarcely known? There is an air of unreality about the whole business; it is like a children's game, with its codes, its nicknames—d'André, rather suitably, is often referred to as *Baptiste*—a shadowy never-never land of mystification and graft. D'André was honest, but hopelessly oversanguine, the Micawber of the Counter-Revolution; most of the others were madcaps or scoundrels or both. Immense sums were exchanged, to no apparent effect. Wickham paid out, asked for more, got it, handed on masses of information, most of it useless, out of date or obtainable in the gazettes, or totally inaccurate, and recommended to the British Government policies and persons that had no backing within France. He did not realize, until it was too late, that the Army, as a whole, would not tolerate a Restoration in any form; embarked on an ideological crusade against republican France, he vainly sought *l'interlocateur valable* with whom Britain could discuss a solution satisfactory to British interests, and all he could find was a d'André. *A chacun son Bao Dai.*

One of Dr. Mitchell's chapters is entitled: 'An Exercise in Futility', another 'Too Little and Too Late' (though presumably this does not refer to cash), one of Mr. Fryer's, 'The Illusion of Success'. There we have it; we are in the Hall of Mirrors at Madame Tussaud's. But there is more to it than that, for the two present works are a striking illustration of what happens when a government allows its foreign policy to be dictated to it by an irresponsible, ideologically committed, misinformed, and misinforming Secret Service, without reference to the aspirations of the majority of the inhabitants of the country concerned. Wickham failed largely because he thought of the common people as *la canaille*, *banditti*, 'Jacobin rascals'; and Mr. Fryer—for Dr. Mitchell is at least aware of the existence of a popular republicanism—has failed to give a comprehensive account even of this limited aspect of the Counter-Revolution, because he too is concerned only with the gentlemen and because the disenfranchised have no place in his select book. Both books should be compulsory reading for secret service candidates in Britain and the United States. In this respect, at least, the career of William Wickham would not have been a total failure. It has a certain educational value.

13 The White Terror[1]

Dr. D. P. Resnick has, in *The White Terror and the Political Reaction after Waterloo*, an excellent subject, exciting and almost untouched, for the last general work on the second White Terror in the south of France was written nearly ninety years ago.[2] He had also, to guide him, a considerable volume of recent work, in French and in English—Dr. Tilly's intelligent study of the Vendée came out in the same series as the present book—on popular loyalism, counter-revolutionary violence, and the mentality of the White terrorist.[3] Yet, despite the advantage of being the first in the field— or so he claims—and with plenty of examples of how to handle a subject related to the history of popular mentalities, the author has made a poor job of his assignment; his book reveals a startling lack of historical perspective, and its coverage both in space and in time is altogether insufficient.

A flurried look at four Departments (the Var, the Bouches-du-Rhône, the Haute-Garonne, and the Gard) is unlikely to reveal either the complexity or the extent of a series of movements that included as many more Departments in the south and south-centre, and that spread up the valley of the Rhône. In his journey from Toulouse to Nîmes, the author leapfrogs over the Tarn and the Hérault (both Departments, however, in which the number of political arrests for the period July 1815–June 1816, was, according to the author's own calculations, exceptionally high: 105 for the Tarn, 135 for the Hérault) and, save for a brief and unoriginal account of the lynching of Brune in Avignon, he has failed to extend his inquiry even to the Vaucluse, one of the most fanatical centres of both White Terrors, and, with the Gard, perhaps the principal recruiting ground for White terrorism all over the south-east.[4]

[1] Review of Daniel Philip Resnick, *The White Terror and Political Reaction after Waterloo* (Cambridge, Mass., and London, 1966).

[2] E. Daudet, *Histoire des conspirations royalistes dans le Midi* (Paris, 1881).

[3] See above, p. 111, 'The Counter-Revolt'.

[4] See Gwynne Lewis, 'La Terreur blanche dans le département du Gard (1815–1817)'. Unpublished D.Phil. thesis.

Furthermore, as one of the most consistent features of these movements—as of the Terror of the year II—was the 'invasion' of one Department, or of one District or *arrondissement*, by the White terrorists (or, in 1793, by the *apôtres civiques*), *verdets*, national guards, and others, of its neighbour, any attempt to study the White Terror in a purely departmental context is likely to result in greatly underestimating its true extent and incidence, as well as in a failure to appreciate its ability to hit, suddenly and unexpectedly, in localities widely scattered, with the murder gangs, their crimes committed, disappearing almost without a trace over a welcoming border. The murderers were not the only ones to take advantage of departmental regionalism; after the first wave of violence, large numbers of Protestants—several thousand in the Gard—fled their Department of origin, sometimes taking their dead with them, or burying them first in their fields or by the roadside, as though having one person murdered among one's relatives was something to be concealed, since it might invite a repeat performance (as indeed it often did); most of these took refuge in the Protestant valleys of the neighbouring Department of the Lozère, but some went as far as the Ardèche and Lyon, while a few wealthy patricians made their way to Paris.

Equally, any study of White terrorism that does not take into account such ultra-royalist centres as Lyon and Arles must necessarily be so incomplete as to be, in national, and even regional, terms, meaningless. There seems to be no rhyme or reason about Dr. Resnick's choice of Departments, nor about his omission of others. The Var, the Bouches-du-Rhône, and the Gard are adjoining; yet while he establishes connections between murders in Marseille and Aubagne and massacres in Toulon (as in 1795, the Marseillais assassins moved into the former Jacobin strongholds of the Var, marking their passage with the scattered corpses of countrymen in the villages along their route), he does not suggest that there may have been any between the White Terror in the Bouches-du-Rhône and the Gard. Yet, judging from what happened in 1795–6, there quite certainly would have been; in the prison massacres of the year III in Marseille there are frequent references to the presence of Nîmois among the killers of the 'Compagnie du Soleil'; the Nîmois also 'invaded' the Vaucluse, in the course of their operations in the same year, while, in 1815, the *verdets* from Beaucaire appear to have been reinforced from Tarascon. Ultra-royalism had its traditional strongholds in the south-east, drawing on them when it was a matter of sending the *sabreurs*, the *égorgeurs*, and the strong-arm men against localities where it was weak.

After this hurried excursion south, the author settles down in Paris. The rest of the book is concerned with a somewhat different topic: the efforts of the Ultras to organize, all over France, a judicial terror to be directed against the widest possible categories of people, and those of the Government, on the contrary, to limit this repression to a minimum of persons mentioned by name. Dr. Resnick gives a clear account of the organization of the *cours prévôtales*,* offering interesting details about the number of their victims. His figures for the incidence of the purely political judicial repression, though derived from government sources, are likely to be accurate. Their main interest is to bring out very sharply the unequal weight of repression from one area to another (the Map of Terror had shown similar variations in 1793–4, and again in 1795–6). The areas of particularly severe judicial repression emerge, rather dramatically, as two principal regional blocks: first, the four Departments of the Aude, the Tarn, the Hérault, and the Gard (but not, surprisingly, the Haute-Garonne, an old centre of neo-Jacobinism, based on Destrem and his circle of friends); secondly, the group of Departments centred on the Isère: the Ain, the Jura (which, under the Empire, had been the principal recruiting ground for Malet's supporters), the Doubs, and the Drôme, where the severity of repression can be attributed, as in the Isère itself, to the ramifications of the Didier Conspiracy in Grenoble (Stendhal was to claim, with some exaggeration, that the ultra-royalist terror in Grenoble at this time was far more ferocious than that of the year II; he had, however, experienced the second and could hardly recall the first). Finally there were a few isolated pockets of heavy repression: the two adjoining Departments of the Eure and the Seine-Inférieure, the Charente-Inférieure and the Ille-et-Vilaine.

So the author's figures provide some useful pointers; but as they are not then related to actual names (he has at no stage examined the personal *dossiers* either of the leading White terrorists or of their more illustrious victims, though, for Ramel and Lagarde notably, these exist in the Archives Administratives de la Guerre in Vincennes) it is difficult to appreciate what exactly they may represent in historical terms. It is certain, for instance, that many of those arrested at the height of the White Terror figured on police lists that had been drawn up during the previous proscriptions of 1795, 1796, 1799–1800, 1810, 1812–13, some of them had been *abonnés* of Babeuf or of Bazin, or of both, others correspondents of Malet and Destrem. It is in the nature of the police to hit at the same people over and over again, and, at all periods, the French police in particular has tended to think first of all its old customers. The police authorities were not likely to lose sight of them, as many of the lists printed in 1795 and 1796 of *les hommes à surveiller* were handed down from one generation of police to the next, to form the basis of each new 'purge'. In the meantime, entirely new categories had been added, so that the lists supplied to Decazes contain a very mixed bag including ageing terrorists—mostly well beyond the age of political militancy, one would have thought—former *babouvistes*, republicans of the Malet vintage, leading officials of the Empire, English Protestant observers, Italian and Polish refugees, together with entirely new categories of popular suspects: boiler-men, printers and compositors, foundrymen, students, that suggest the shape of things to come. One needs then to find out who these people were (Dr. Resnick refers to some who were arrested in the Haute-Garonne as 'having committed excesses during the Revolution') and what had happened to them between 1790 and 1815. The author does not tell us.

He claims, in his introduction, that French nineteenth-century historians, with their own axes to grind, have tended to inflate the gravity of the White Terror in the south, if only as a means of condoning the Terror of 1793–4.

Of course no one would suggest that the two Terrors were in any way comparable in point of numbers; even so, Dr. Resnick, far too prone to rely exclusively on official sources, certainly under-estimates the number of people murdered, even in the Gard; he has no figures at all for the Vaucluse, and for the Bouches-du-Rhône he provides an estimate only for Marseille, but, as in 1795–7, there were murders in such places as Lambesc, Aubagne, Auriol. It takes an historian of the experience and flair of Professor Rudé to give an effective count of the dead; and, at a time when authorities at all levels had an obvious interest in concealing deaths—especially from the Allies, some of whom were displaying a tiresome concern for their Protestant brethren in the south—even to the extent of failing to register deaths in the *état-civil*, of frightening relatives into non-compliance with the law, and of forbidding funerals by daylight, government statistics cannot be taken as presenting anything like a complete count of the victims of ultra-royalist savagery.

At times Dr. Resnick appears to imply that the Protestants of the south—and their friends in Scotland, Wales, and England—were blowing up a series of minor incidents into a nineteenth-century Saint Bartholomew's Day, in the interest of the Protestant cause. Why they should do so it is hard to see; the Protestants of the Gard were presumably not out to get themselves assassinated in order to embarrass the Duke of Wellington (one has yet to discover an instance of a racial or religious minority deliberately having itself massacred as a means of promoting sympathy abroad). On the contrary, the Protestant community in general, and particularly that of the Gard ('that disgusting Department', as a harassed Restoration Prefect called it), from old experience had acted at all times—though perhaps not in 1790—with great caution and restraint, with an eye not to giving any pretext to vengeance. In this area, their principal concern would be to keep out of notice. Many more people were murdered than Dr. Resnick suggests; but the survivors were often embarrassed by the compromising solicitude of English observers, sent to see what had happened, and by the campaign on their behalf undertaken by the *Morning Chronicle*.

Having not gone into the history of the previous Terrors, the author often fails to understand the nature of that of 1815 which, at least in its anarchcial form, was inspired to a great extent by thoughts of vengeance; and vengeance must always refer backwards. He shows no sign of having read anything outside his immediate area of study; and he is, historically, both ignorant and innocent, with no notion of the assumptions and methods of the French police—and these survive when régimes do not—or of the ways of French judges and magistrates. There is a reference to 'the liberal writer of Protestant family, Benjamin Constant'; and we learn that Fouché 'had a political past that extended to the early days of the Revolution'—a masterpiece of discretion that would have appealed to the organizer of the Lyon massacres of 1793. And he displays his candour when stating that the Minister of War, the Duc de Feltre, 'wished to make it clear that he did not consider the provost courts at all similar to the Revolutionary tribunals'. He has made it clear to Dr. Resnick! But the major weakness of the book is a total lack of historical background; the White Terror of 1815 cannot be studied in isolation.

Even in this slim book, however, there are a number of clues that would be well worth following up. For how familiar it all is! The geography of violence, killing, and anarchy, the dangerous but inevitable partnership of dearth and Terror (the author manages to get right through 1816 without a single reference to the acute food crisis of that year—a dearth that produced the usual forms of popular disorder and that added a new, anti-popular, element to the judicial and military repression), the murderous literalness of words and the foolhardiness of those who uttered them (*Vive l'Empereur, Merde pour le Roi, Qui va là? Républicain*), the continuity of Terror, surviving lustily on a repetitive diet of vengeance, by decade and by generation, the traditional calendar of murder and massacre, the week-end killing, the saint's day bloodbath (Ramel was murdered, suitably enough, on 15 August, Lagarde was shot on a Sunday, after vespers).

Indeed, as Dr. Gwynne Lewis has shown in his articles in French and English on events in the Gard, some of the murderers of 1815 were those of 1791 and, possibly, of 1795 too; and, in those long-remembering communities, with their spreading family relationships, one murder could be expected to raise up as many as fifteen avengers. According to a *commissaire du Directoire*, in the year IV, about a quarter of the population of the Bouches-du-Rhône could claim a victim to be avenged, whether White or Blue. In towns like Avignon and Nîmes, the murderers all lived in one street or one quarter, their victims in another; in the former city the Carreterie, the republican stronghold, would again and again be the principal objective of White murder gangs. And, in more favourable circumstances, the artisan population might emerge from there, to beat up or kill the Whites. Certainly there had been any number of return matches between the two by 1815. Equally, there is nothing more like a *cour prévôtale* of 1815–16 than that of the old *prévôt de la maréchaussée*; and their repressive zeal was directed against much the same categories of habitual law-breakers: the smuggler (especially in the Nord and the Ardennes), the rural bandit, the occasional *taxateur*, the pillager of grain, those who destroyed forests, those who set fire to crops and to mills.

Like the previous White Terror of 1795–7, that of 1815 had two quite distinct and even opposing aspects: the apparently anarchical violence of the murder gangs of the south, and the government-directed, judicial Terror, operating principally through the ordinary courts, and directed as much against the common people, as an instrument of social repression, as against certain political categories: in the year III, former office-holders under the Terror in the year XVIII of Louis XVIII, former office-holders under the Empire. The anarchical form of Terror—particularly the southern variety—actually encouraged law-breaking; the *verdets*, like the *compagnies* twenty years earlier, recruited readily among deserters, smugglers, poachers, rural bandits, *mauvais esprits* (a category that the author translates as 'bad spirits'), servants, ex-soldiers, porters, former seamen, procurers, innkeepers, professional killers, Negroes. The organizers—*chevaliers de la Foi* or former *gardes du Roi*—could not afford to be over-fastidious, but they seem even to have shown a positive preference for the man with a violent past. This Terror was also directed against property and property-owners (especially purchasers of Church lands), tax collectors, married priests, and even generals. It may have been anarchical, but it was hardly spontaneous, being carefully planned, and aimed as much at the representatives of the Paris government as at those who had served the previous régimes.

In Toulouse, for instance, General Ramel was murdered, after minute planning on the part of the local leaders of the *verdets*, not because he was unpopular or because he was suspected of bonapartist sympathies—he was in fact completely loyal to the new régime—but because he was inconvenient; his existence prevented the *verdets* from enjoying the monopoly of force and of thus being able to terrorize at will the Toulousains (the *verdets* were, at least in this area, only a military minority). Similar calculations inspired the attempt on the life of General Lagarde in Nîmes; the presence of a *commandant de place* loyal to the Government, respectful of the law, and, above all, determined to see that the Protestants should enjoy the freedom of worship guaranteed to them by the *Charte*, was intolerable to those who had decided to use murder, not merely to satisfy a craving for vengeance (this was after all something of a luxury, to be offered as an extra inducement to the potential recruit) but to further a political programme the purpose of which was to seize all the positions of power on the spot. Murder was in fact much the most effective weapon of ultra-royalism in this part of the world; it removed altogether those who were the most determinedly inconvenient and frightened many others into resignation or even into complicity. It was also the most obvious weapon to hand, since it could be used with almost complete impunity, at least in the south. Those who shot Ramel and Lagarde never had to suffer for it; the unsuccessful assassin of the latter was even formally acquitted!

There could be no more dramatic way of demonstrating the inability of the central Government to protect life and property, even to raise taxes, and the omnipotence of the secret government— a very open secret—of the south, of the Duc d'Angoulême's *royaume du Midi*. Southern terrorism relied for its striking force on the local *gardes nationales*—some of these even had two sets of uniforms, official and unofficial, to represent their alleged and their real functions, the one for parades, the other for killings—and for its impunity, once the killings had achieved their purpose, on local *juges de paix* and local jurors, equally defiant of central authority, equally subservient, when not openly sympathetic, to local bullies and to those who hired them. It proved quite impossible to convict self-admitted White murderers in the Gard and the Bouches-du-Rhône any time between 1795 and 1797, or between 1815 and 1819, in spite of elaborate efforts on the part of the higher authorities (*agents nationaux, commissaires du Directoire*, some but by no means all prefects and sub-prefects) to secure the appointment of reliable jurors among well-to-do property holders. The only hope, if the murderers could ever be found at all—a rare occurrence, as they were generally given ample warning of impending arrest, often by the magistrates who had signed the warrants—was to have them tried in another Department, preferably right out of the area, for the judges of the Bouches-du-Rhône would as likely as not acquit the assassins sent to them from the Gard, and vice versa.

Certainly the most alarming aspect of this recurrence of political violence in the south-east is the degree of complicity in crime on the part of respectable and honourable people who, in normal circumstances, would have regarded murderers with horror and who, when faced with a highwayman, would have sought help from the police or the *gendarmerie*, but who, under the impact of the politics of vengeance, thought nothing of paying brutal, but simple, men to kill their political and religious opponents, fêting them, playing on their conceit, congratulating them on their *coup de main*, calling them by their nicknames, filling them with drink, before and after, letting them go to bed with their servants, after. The poacher, the deserter, the bandit, and the corner boy must have thought that the world had turned upside-down when they found themselves invited to the local *château*, vigorously patted on the back by the squire, in the presence of his womenfolk, and told that he was a fine fellow *qui n'avait pas froid aux yeux*.

Perhaps, too, there was a natural link between the gentleman *frondeur* of the south and the poor man who lived by daring; both admired physical prowess, both could look back to long, happy years of marauding and violence, both, too, had lost much by a revolution that had put the emphasis increasingly on middle-class values. The Comte d'Antraigues, who admitted to a sneaking admiration for the 'Jacobin rascals', because he thought that they were bold and determined ruffians who would stop at nothing to achieve their ends, would, in a context other than exile (with its necessary paraphernalia of codes, secret inks, plots and counter-plots, assassination attempts organized from afar) have made an admirable gang-leader, at the head of his own tenants and retainers, in the badlands of the old Vivarais, burning the houses and farms of purchasers of *bien nationaux*, and carrying out his cherished ambition to become 'the Marat of the Counter-Revolution'. And there were plenty of gentleman like d'Antraigues in this lawless part of the world.

But d'Antraigues and his kind represent an essentially rural pheno-menon, in an area notoriously backward, with few communications and only scattered hamlets. What is much more alarming is to dis-cover that some of the great figures of early nineteenth-century France, while perhaps not directly involved in the murder gangs (but their hangers-on, their bailiffs, their *intendants*, their servants, even their confessors, often were), knew of their existence and were informed in advance of their impending operations in such places as Toulouse or Nîmes. A man like Villèle was clearly able to live with this sort of thing and to profit from violence when it was used to political effect. It is equally alarming, though much less sur-prising, to learn that, in the case of the two unfortunate generals, the police authorities were hand in glove with the murderers; in-deed, one of the assassins of Ramel was the son of the *commissaire principal de police* of Toulouse. Urban killing not only enjoyed a wide degree of permissibility, but it was also given the most official and effective of protections.

The government Terror, on the other hand, was directed as much against smugglers, murderers, rural outlaws, beggars, and vagrants as against political suspects. As in 1795, the central Government and its agents in the Departments did their utmost— but their utmost was not very much—to bring to book the political assassins as well. On both occasions, the contrast between the anarchical terror of the south-east and the Rhône valley, and government repression, via the courts and military commissions, is dramatically striking. The Government had its own reputation to keep up, though in the year III it may not have been much of one; it could not merely resign its functions and hand over whole areas of France to the politics of vengeance. For this was what was at stake, in 1795 as in 1815: whose law was to run? Whose arm was to be felt? The White terrorist of the years III–VII, like that of 1815, employs the rural shotgun, the Mediterranean stiletto (that could be used for eating too), the woodman's axe, the pitchfork, the scythe, the sabre, the sword-stick, the dagger, even the *gros bâton*; in this part of the world, despite decades and decades of police regulations, almost every man is armed, has to hand something that will stab (*saigner* or *suriner*, along with *couper en morceaux*, are the expressions most in favour in this sunny land). The Thermidorian Terror employs the guillotine and the firing squad, the government Terror of 1815–16 the firing squad and the gallows ('another alteration', notes the author, on the subject of the *cours prévôtales*, 'was the specification that those convicted of crimes calling for capital punishment die by hanging rather than by the guillotine, instrument of the Revolution . . .').

So much for what is known (at least by the historian who is prepared to read back in time and to explore the records of local courts, as well as those of the Ministry of Justice), and for what can be guessed—for, in the uncharted zones of the history of crime, a good deal of guessing is essential (at least by anyone who has read *Les Chauffeurs du Nord* and similar blood-and-thunder literature).

But how much more is suggested by Dr. Resnick's subject! How, for instance, does the Gard, with sixty-five people, three of them women, condemned to death for murder, parricide, wife-slaying, husband-poisoning, robbery and murder, banditry and murder between 1793 and 1830, compare with other Departments in the south-east? (Dr. Resnick claims that crimes of violence were rare in the Gard.)[1] How many more got away scot-free, owing to the enormous difficulty, in this part of the world, of getting juries to convict for murder? One can be pretty sure at least of one thing: that out of a total of twenty-three persons condemned and executed in Nîmes for murder between 1815 and 1830, none had been a *verdet*; six, on the other hand, were poor Protestant villagers, who had shot and killed a few *verdets* who had come to them with threats and force.[2] Certainly, the acceptance of violence in the Gard cannot be measured numerically in terms of convictions. It is the people who got away and those that helped them that matter, and one would therefore need to count up acquittals as well (at least forty known murderers were acquitted by the tribunal of Aix or succeeded in having their cases removed, on appeal, to another court, between 1795 and 1798; indeed, only eight were convicted).

What then was the explanation of this apparently almost visceral ferocity of the southerners (and of the Lyonnais) and of this general acceptance of murder, political or private, as a social convention? Parisian observers, appalled by what they saw going on, whether in 1795 or in 1815, put it down to the climate, to *la chaleur du tempérament*, to the verbal intemperance of the ancestors of Marius and César (visitors from the north have always made the mistake of taking what these mighty fabulists say literally), to family traditions that made of vengeance a fraternal or filial obligation for the survivor, to a long tradition of administrative anarchy (it was called 'liberty' down here), to the existence, in and around Marseille, a city with its multiplicity of *îles*, frequently described as an assassin's paradise, of a cosmopolitan riff-raff composed of the scourings of the Mediterranean shores, to a crime wave that had begun, in 1788, as housebreaking and pilfering and that had, under the impetus of the Revolution, extended to violence and murder and had continued almost unabated ever since, to the economic decline of the southern Departments, and to the existence, at least in certain of them, of easily identifiable hate figures: mamelukes and Corsicans in Mar-

[1] See *Liste des condamnés à mort (à Nîmes) 1791–1884, par un ancien magistrat* (Nîmes, 1884). During this period, seventy-nine persons were condemned to death by the Gard criminal court for murder or attempted murder, murder with robbery, banditry, poisoning, etc.

[2] ibid. They were peasants from the village of Arpaillargues.

seille, Protestants in the Gard, the hated and very isolated *mathe-vons* in Lyon; finally, to the habit, so general in these parts, of carrying arms.

The authorities of Marseille at least had their own explanations to offer; in 1795 they were to claim that the prison massacres were the work of 'strangers', who had come especially to the Second City, no doubt on orders, to carry out their killings (they even identified some of them as Lyonnais, Nîmois, and Catalans) and in 1815, as Dr. Resnick shows, the city authorities, when asked about the massacre of the mamelukes, once more fell back on an argument that had done yeoman service in many places in the course of the Revolution (Parisian observers were willing to state that those who had taken part in the September Massacres were people 'who did not have the accent of the Parisis', and the authorities of the Vaucluse claimed that a series of murders perpetrated in the neighbourhood of Avignon in 1795 was the work of a gang from Montpellier). Southerners seem to have accepted the fact of violence among themselves; but they did not like to have it publicized up in Paris. In any case, any undue violence, as apart from a family vendetta or a wayside killing, must be the work of strangers. Whatever the explanation, the figures are there for the finding; and there still remains the problem presented by the rural killer, known to all, the pride and terror of his village, *le champion*. For he is a leading figure in the year III; and anyone who would take the trouble to move away from Dr. Resnick's narrow highroad in order to plunge into an arid, aromatic, stony, and pitiless country-side, would no doubt meet up with him again.

It is easier to understand why the Nord should have been, for a time, such a bandits' terrain: smuggling kept a sizable army of crime constantly afoot or mounted (the foot smuggler, says Vidocq, was a Fleming, the mounted one a Walloon),[1] and skilled in forays with the *douaniers*. From smuggling it was an easy stage to banditry; and the smugglers had at their disposal an elaborate network of inns and friendly houses, both in cities such as Lille and in small towns like Béthune and Doullens; these were run by retired smugglers who were also receivers. The smugglers' network was available to the *chauffeurs*, who could thus sleep near their jobs and lie low in the city when the jobs were done. If the worst came to

[1] Vidocq, *Les chauffeurs du Nord* (Paris, 1845).

the worst, the frontier was near and could be easily crossed. Similar networks existed on the other side, both before and after Belgian Independence. Violence in the Nord both between 1795 and 1798 and in 1815–17 was criminal rather than political (though the *chauffeurs* of the year IV claimed to torture their wealthy farmer victims in the name of Christ and King), it could draw on a long tradition of lawbreaking; and, on both occasions, could readily recruit among a mass of deserters or discharged soldiers. It was no doubt much the same in the Moselle.

The principal merit of this small book is at least to have raised some of these questions in the minds of the reader. There can, of course, be no satisfactory answer to them until the relationship between Terror and crime, between political vengeance and private vengeance has been more thoroughly explored, and until the social composition of the *compagnies*, the gangs, the *verdets*, the *miquelets*, and the *chauffeurs* has been the object of research in the records of the criminal courts. The White Terror of 1815–16 was not a flash in the pan; it had deep roots in an unhappy, recent past and in regions where, for at least a generation, political issues had been habitually solved by violence.

Aspects of French History and Society
1815–1968

14 Prefects of the Restoration[1]

It is not easy to write administrative history attractively; and subjects such as appointment, promotion, retirement, salaries, pensions, living expenses do not generally promote a mood of levity. One of Dr. Richardson's most significant achievements in *The French Prefectoral Corps 1814–1830* is to have marshalled an army of five or six hundred names (and what names! the Narbonne-Lara and the Narbonne-Pelet, the de Quatrebarbes, the Saporta-Montsallier, the Jégou du Laz, the Du Puy-Montbrun, the Levezou de Vézins, the Tournon-Simiane, the Aucapitaine, the Villiers du Terrage), to have kept this multitude throughout under firm control, marching them up and down, dismissing them, recalling them, and yet, at the end of it, not to have tried our patience in the least with this Restoration equivalent of the *Bottin administratif* (the *Bottin*, of course, like the *Chaix*, has its devotees, but they are of a special kind). For this is no mere chronicle of names and the author's prefects emerge, not always with their reputations unscathed, as individuals, as well as members of a *corps*, the cohesion of which was based on shared assumptions and on a common sense of service (and, in most cases, on a common social origin).

The secret is that Dr. Richardson likes his subjects and has indeed, in the time spent with them, acquired something of the language (he refers, at one stage, to the '*sans-culotte* prefects' of the previous régime) and attitudes of people who combined insolence with honour, honesty with independence, courage with incompetence, stupidity with generosity and family pride with compassion. For an historian who has to deal almost exclusively with noblemen, it is just as well to feel at home with La Varende and Michel de Saint-Pierre and to show both enjoyment and skill in the exploration of the Grand Armorial.

It would be a poor qualification for the historian embarking on popular movements to start with the feeling that the common people smell; and it is impossible to appreciate the qualities and weaknesses of the prefectoral corps of the Restoration without

[1] Review of Nicholas Richardson, *The French Prefectoral Corps 1814–1830* (London, 1968).

understanding and, at least to some extent, sympathizing with, the old French nobility. Dr. Richardson writes as though he knew these people; and it is evident that he has talked, to good purpose, to many of their descendants, themselves not so very far removed, in mentality and assumptions, from a generation that had reached manhood on the far side of the Revolution and that seems so oddly unsuited to the nineteenth century (they did, in fact, succeed quite effectively, for fifteen years, in keeping the nineteenth century at bay!).

The prefects are, one suspects, a pretext; what Dr. Richardson is really concerned with is to explore the noble mentality, to rediscover the realm of ling and fern, of *manoir*, marsh, and woodland, so dear to Hylas de Fierdrap, and to penetrate deeply into an ancient and close-knit provincial nobility. Whether this was what he intended at the start, or whether he discovered his true subject in the course of research, only he could tell us. It does not really matter, for much of the best history has been written in this way, almost by accident. One can be reasonably sure that Dr. Richardson would not have tackled those exceedingly unattractive, efficient, and featureless bureaucrats, the Napoleonic prefects, far more effective no doubt than his own people, but with about as much personality as M. Pompidou. This book is about a caste in its last, and almost unique, period of power and political influence: it is, in fact, an introduction to the study of a ruling élite that, for a few years at least—and these were certainly not the unhappiest ones in French history—combined pride with power and that, almost ever since, has had to make do with pride without power. It is to be hoped that, after the prefects, the author will tackle the Restoration nobility as a whole, for he is clearly the right man for the job.

Nothing could bring out more strikingly the contrast between the bureaucratic anonymity and the administrative tyranny of the Empire—the most repellent period of modern French history—and the easy-going liberalism of the Restoration, than a study of the prefectoral corps; for perhaps the only advantage of the Hundred Days was to have made inevitable a clean sweep of the Napoleonic prefects, and after the Second Restoration only two, in fact, survived, and these simply because they were so completely faceless.

The prefects of the Empire were professional administrators, those of the Bourbons were amateurs, with a variety of careers and experiences behind them, and few of them became prefects by vocation; it was, in almost all instances, a second or third choice. A number had served in the various Allied armies, others had set up in business in England or America, many of them were aware of the advantages of parliamentary government, and had been spared the iron school of autocracy offered by Napoleonic France (a man was more likely to learn the merits of liberalism in emigration than in France). Napoleon's prefects were young, thrusting, vigorous, ambitious, and unquestioning. Those of the Bourbons had mostly seen better days; in 1815 their average age was 42, and by the end of the two reigns it was over 50; often they were not particularly vigorous, and, as they had to manage elections, they were forced to count with local opinion and consider regional pressure groups; a Napoleonic prefect might move from Niort to Geneva, from Geneva to Rome, from Rome to Brussels, from Brussels to Aix-la-Chapelle, from Aix to Cologne, from Cologne to Rouen, and still deal with the same problems, in the same stilted, administrative language, according to the same formulas. Ney had become a Marshal of France at 36; the best the Restoration could offer was the Prince de Hohenlohe, Marshal at 62, whose military experience had been gained entirely in the Austrian service.

The Restoration was an elderly régime in a country in which two-thirds of the population were under 40, and so it was divorced irreparably from *les enfants du siècle*, from all the Julien Sorels of provincial France; it appealed back to the ancient values of honour and service, and was constantly preoccupied with the past. The prefects, like everyone else remotely connected with the Faubourg, read Scott (they had, in any case, plenty of time in places like Digne or Gap); the Restoration Government founded the École des Chartes. Napoleon had had no use for any history, other than his own. The Napoleonic prefects—*préfets à poigne*—were appointed largely on administrative merit and on subservience; those of the Restoration claimed their posts as a right, quoting their family trees. It was, after all, a position for which no formal training was required, though many of the younger members reached the corps via the *auditoriat*; and there was little choice for those who were too old to return to the Army, as for those who had once been employed in the *parlements* (very many Restoration prefects had been officers in the old royal army, a few had been *parlementaires*).

Dr. Richardson does not deal with the actual day-to-day work of his prefects—this is not in his brief—but, from what he says of them, it is easy to guess that they were less efficient than their predecessors, though any comparison would be difficult, so different was their task. Napoleon's prefects had primarily to keep a population at war, obtain men and money, put down sedition and prevent any expression of public opinion. Their successors were largely concerned with electoral management; there was less territory to administer, and less administration in what was left. It would be interesting to see how the two régimes respectively faced the food crises of 1812 and 1816. One would guess that, in their attitude to the poor (who were seen by their predecessors as primarily idle), the Restoration prefects would have been more compassionate than the bureaucrats of the previous régime. For they had the aristocratic virtues of paternalism and charity.

The author guides us patiently through the massive three-stage movement of personnel following the First Restoration, the Hundred Days (when Carnot brought back a few of the old dechristianizing *représentants-en-mission* of the year II, such as Roux and Mallarmé, the former even being sent back to the Aisne) and the Second Restoration, following through with an exhaustive analysis of the promotions, demotions, transfers, dismissals, and appointments made by each of the Restoration Ministers of the Interior. It is not an attractive, nor an easy, assignment, but it is done smoothly and painlessly.

There is an interesting section on appointments and on the working of the various lobbies; relatives, school friends, comrades of *promotions*, companions of exile. Here, thirty years before *Numa Roumestan*, sixty before *Bel Ami*, 100 or so before Jerphanion and Jallez, is that familiar phenomenon, *la montée à Paris* (that the author rather felicitously describes as the myth of the big city, made fashionable by Restif, and later developed by *Fantomas*!). With a reduced Court, and no longer in Versailles, and no more *gagistes*, ambitions could only be satisfied and services rewarded through *la fonctionomanie*. Candidates might write up from their provinces, but to achieve anything they were better advised to come up in person and do their round of visits—an operation not nearly so burdensome, however, as under the Second Empire or the Third Republic, for, as the author reminds us, the Faubourg Saint-Germain was a very small place; and though there is a formidable number of names in the book, most of them were either related or connected by past obligations or experience. Dr. Richard-son, with his truly formidable knowledge of family relationships and professional connections—and with some thousand *dossiers* ranged unobtrusively in the background—shows how it was done, how a *place* could be won, and, how, with a change in the Ministry, it could be lost.

He also discusses the relative scale of appointments available. One prefecture, in spite of the surviving uniformity of Napoleonic cen-tralization, was not just like any other. The plums were, of course, the big cities, in the populous Departments: after Paris, Lyon, Marseille, Bordeaux, Toulouse (rather surprisingly, the author does not mention Lille and Rouen in the top rank, though they must also have been much sought after), for these offered more prestige and a larger expense account (they must, on the other hand, have entailed more actual work and many more worries). In the same category, though for different reasons, was the Seine-et-Oise, with its concentration of royal châteaux. At the other end of the scale would be the horrors of Privas, or Digne, or Mende, the bore-dom of Guéret (Jouhandeau's hateful little town) or of Château-roux; and the cost of living in these holes would also be higher. It was a fearful threat to brandish against an undisciplined prefect to hint that he might end up in the Lozère or the Basses-Alpes.

Most people wanted prefectures near Paris, and these were valued accordingly; even Laon jumped a class. All sought to be near their homes and estates, but this was seldom permitted; they might, if lucky, get as near as a neighbouring Department. There were also special cases; no one wanted the Gard (it was rather like being made Secretary for Ireland), no one who did not have a military background could be sent to Corsica (and no one, surely, *wanted* Corsica?), those sent to the Haut- or Bas-Rhin needed to know German, it was unwise to send a Protestant to the Midi, though there was one in the Lozère—a reasonable choice (the author does not tell us how many there were in the Corps).

There were other special attractions: the possession of a palace, in the shape of a former Hôtel de l'Intendance, plus garden, as in Besançon, Bordeaux, and Troyes; or the presence of a large garrison, important for a prefect with many daughters. The prefects made what they could of the places to which they were sent; some took up history, some antiquities, some became attached and did not want to leave, some organized balls and concerts, of one it was said that he was 'un homme qui s'écoute manger', and, on another occasion, that he 'ne passe son temps qu'à table, au jeu, ou au lit. Jamais il ne se lève qu'à midi et souvent plus tard'; he was a man whose nobility could be traced back to the fifteenth century. How much time most of them put in and what sort of work they did the present study, concerned only with the composition of the Corps, does not tell us.

As might have been expected, the sub-prefects, more often local men, were more deeply embedded in provincial politics and lasted longer than their superiors. In Falaise one lasted from 1801 to 1830, in Mamers (later in the century the fief of the Caillaux dynasty), from 1802 to 1830; in Château-Salins, the sub-prefect remained from 1814 to 1848. The sub-prefect of Saint-Claude had previously been mayor (in succession to his father and his grandfather); there was a sub-prefect in the Basses-Pyrénées who had been in various administrative posts in the Department ever since 1795 without a break. The sub-prefect of Bastia, we are told, 'suffered from the lively enmities aroused by the murders his own and his wife's family had allegedly perpetrated'.

The *sub-prefecture* is the important unit of local influence; and the sub-prefect tended to be a long-established *notable*, often of an ancient military family that had, for generations, given the monarchy officers of lower rank. He was accordingly more difficult to deal with than a prefect, as he could bring into play *pairs*, local deputies, bishops, and relatives of Ministers. It was strongly felt that, in the Gard, sub-prefects should not be recruited locally; but, it seems, it was not possible to do anything about it. One or two Restoration prefects, dismissed by the July Monarchy, entrenched themselves as sub-prefects in their home areas. As a study of local families, Dr. Richardson's book will serve as an essential introduction to any detailed analysis of provincial society and politics during the early nineteenth century.

His concluding chapter is both brilliant and sad. For this was the last occasion in French history on which the *ban* and *arrière-ban* of the old nobility occupied positions of authority in the French state. July 1830 sent them back, horrified, to their *manoirs*, whence, politically, they never re-emerged, save to enjoy the brief vengeance of *la France rurale* in 1871. They are to be found again, in force, in the ranks of the Papal Zouaves of 1860, and in the Affiliated Volunteers of the West of 1870. Many of their descendants have since found their way to Saint-Cyr, Saint-Maixent, and Saumur. There can be few examples in modern history of a collective political suicide quite on this scale. Yet, judging from the present book, most of them, in office, had been honest administrators, doing their best to further a policy of clemency and reconciliation.

The trouble, of course, was that they conceived their service as a personal form of duty to Louis XVIII and Charles X; they were too honourable and, ultimately, too disinterested (though, when matters of personal loyalty had not been at stake, many of them had proved quite capable of holding out for more rewards and favours than were their due) to serve a usurper.

There is about Dr. Richardson's book an autumnal quality, suitably reminiscent of the melancholy landscape of *Dominique* in a west from which many of these men came and to which they returned to enjoy many years of damp decay, tortured by the ocean wind that brought rain and rheumatism. Something certainly was lost when these people went home: a sense of honour however much vaunted—and honour has since been made the excuse for so much indescribable nonsense—a certain impulsiveness, a capacity to answer back. These men were not *préfets à poigne*, because *préfets à poigne*, when all is said and done, are nothing better than lackeys, blindly subservient to an omnipotent and impersonal state.

This is an attractive book. It is also a model of research. The author has looked far and wide for his material, gutting the enormous provincial *annuaires de noblesse*, and using with great intelligence the personal dossiers existing in the Archives Nationales and in the Archives Administratives de la Guerre. Only those who have worked on similar material, involving some hundreds of personal case histories, can appreciate what this means in terms of patience, staying power, organization, and flair. The danger would have been the creation of a gigantic, formless, repetitive chronicle of names; this the author has avoided, by rigid economy and by carefully planning the sequence of his chapters. His account is entirely coherent, and, thanks to his style and to his remarkable ability to use literary allusions, it is most enjoyable to read. It is consoling to be so pleasantly reminded that history, backed with all the guarantees of research, can be so elegant and so readable.

15 Douglas Johnson's *Guizot*[1]

Guizot was 6 when his father was guillotined as a federalist and died four years after the establishment of the Third Republic; but 'Aspects of French History, 1787–1874' still gives little indication of the range of subjects covered by his latest biographer. For Douglas Johnson's is the best general account to date, either in French or in any other language, of the workings of the political system of the July Monarchy. Nor is it without reason that Mr. Johnson acknowledges his debt to Charles Pouthas, for this is a work in the best Pouthas tradition: straightforward, unpretentious, good history, the result of exhaustive research, written with a vaguely Gallic elegance, and giving proof of that solidity and rugged common sense that one associates with the French Protestant. It is as if some of Guizot's own qualities had communicated themselves to the author, who is, however, not blind to his subject's more obvious failings. His book is anything but a hagiography, and it is doubtful whether the reader will come away with any greater liking for this rigid man, though he will certainly end up by respecting him.

Guizot is something of a pretext and one suspects that Mr. Johnson may have been even more attracted by the many general themes that he develops with such insight, honesty, and sympathy, than by the man who, if he did not attain the feline nine, could at least claim to have had five lives, all of them long, and whose portraits and caricatures constitute the sole ornament—other than a portrait of the formidable Madame Guizot *mère*—of a text as unadorned and as sober as a *temple réformé*. To write of Guizot is to write of French Protestantism, and this the author does with a sympathy, with an understanding, and with a sense of fairness that, in one degree or another, are lacking in the works of such recent specialists of French Protestant history as Daniel Robert, Émile Léonard, or Poland. But Guizot was also an historian, though perhaps not a very good one (he generalized), a political theorist, though, it must

[1] Review of Douglas Johnson, *Guizot: Aspects of French History, 1787–1874* (Toronto and London, 1963).

be admitted, rather a woolly one, an educationalist and, like some educationalists, monumentally dull and sometimes plain silly, and, as a practical politician, especially in his attitude to social reforms, one of the most consciously conservative, even reactionary statesmen of nineteenth-century Europe. At least, however, his conservatism was reasoned, for there was never a more unemotional man in his public attitudes.

Mr. Johnson endeavours to keep track of Guizot through his multifarious and generally successive lives, and these offer the principal subjects for those aspects of French history that give his book such an unusually wide range of interest. There are, for instance, quite original chapters on the dismal state of university and *lycée* education during the tyranny of Bonaparte, on the highly ambitious and liberal educational reforms of the Restoration, and on the whole, bitter, everlasting, and insoluble problem of the schools with relation to Church and State.

Guizot was writing and lecturing in a period which saw the foundation of the École des Chartes and the beginnings of the great French school of historical research; here again there is a lead-in for the author to discuss more generally Restoration and mid-nineteenth-century ideas about the importance of history, historical method, and research; nor does he make any excessive claims for an historian who tended to make generalizations about behaviour and about the desires and fears of a hypothetical individual (he was, in this respect, a tepid, unenthusiastic, reasonable version of Carlyle). But Guizot was aware of class, both in history—he has earned the praise of the leading historian of the English Revolution in this respect—and, of course, in the alarming Paris of his own period of power, like his contemporary Tocqueville, he was concerned with social structures.

Mr Johnson even pursues him into theology, for this formidable man was concerned to give the Église Réformée a corps of doctrine, and emerged, rather as one might expect from a person so prone to general ideas and general systems, as the arch-enemy of the Independents and of Protestant democracy, thereby creating a split within the church that has lasted to this day. Guizot was *un homme sérieux*, a French Gladstone, not a vulgar trifler like Thiers. He is not a sympathetic figure; but his enemies, so unaccountably bitter and unfair, are even less so, and the farther one progresses through this long, closely written book, the more one becomes irritated, then disgusted by the puny, paltry, visceral demagogic appeals of his many opponents—moderates, neo-Jacobins, Bonapartists, rabid nationalists, Catholic obscurantists, chauvinistic hack journalists and cartoonists of hate. Guizot was rather lucky in his enemies, for they bring out, by comparison, his own reasonableness, his good sense, his intolerance and incomprehension of stupidity, his contempt for ostentatious patriotism and romantic polonomania, his refusal to participate in the collective myths of his compatriots. Their tricks are so low, their calumnies so absurd, that there is certainly some danger of accepting Guizot's own assessment of himself and of forgetting his insensitivity to the bitterest problems of the 1830s and 1840s in France, those of misery and pauperism; Guizot, like other Calvinists before and since, regarded poverty as the manifest proof of moral failings.

There is little to remind one in this book, which is concerned more with government than with the governed, that Guizot's rule coincided with the development of Vaugirard and Grenelle, two of the plague spots of the July Monarchy. One can understand why he should have been so intensely loathed by the working classes. But it is difficult not to feel some sympathy for a statesman who was so properly contemptuous of national hysteria and who spoke of patriots in much the same tone as that other eminently sensible politician, Walpole. Guizot had most of the Protestant virtues as well; he was a cosmopolitan, with an international education and, at all times, with one foot outside France, and he was interested in serious matters at a time when so many of his compatriots were giving themselves over to a cheap, chauvinistic Napoleonic cult or were following with intense excitement the 'glories' of the campaign in Algeria (to the conquest of which Guizot remained opposed).

It would be hard to exaggerate the debts that France owes to her Protestants, who have nearly always been on the right side in the moral and intellectual civil war that has divided Frenchmen for the past 170 years; and Guizot is a typical enough representative of an intelligent, cultivated, and generally liberal *famille spirituelle* that included such varied personalities as Louis Rossel the *communard*, André Gide, André Siegfried, Roger Martin du Gard, Marc Bernard, the present director of the French archives and the present occupant of the quai d'Orsay. During the *Affaire*, the Protestants were *dreyfusard* almost to a man; few if any Protestants could have been found in the various fascist or near-fascist *Ligues*, during the Occupation they were *anti-vichyssois* and contributed considerably to the Resistance movement, and, in recent years, individual *pasteurs* have taken a leading part in the campaign against the Algerian War.

Guizot's period in power coincides with one of the most violent decades in modern French history. The political system of the July Monarchy, the product of violence, was itself constantly threatened by violence, whether in the form of one of more than eighty attempts on the life of the indestructible King of the French—for this was the golden age of Infernal Machines, rigged up in the backyards of the rue Saint-Charles and hidden under beds until their emergence in a twisted tangle of barrels, through a window of the boulevard du Temple, on one of those monotonously unsuccessful *jours H*—or again in that of an appeal to the predatory, almost biological violence of the new urban population, but recently arrived from the countryside, unassimilated, insecure, hated and feared alike by the *bourgeois* and by the long-established artisan or shopkeeper, a pariah race, physically identifiable, living apart in their barrack-like quarters, heralded from afar by the pungent smell of excrement. Mr. Johnson is more aware than any recent historian of France of the terrible tradition of violence that has been the inner rot of French political 'attitudinizing' since the Revolution; he insists on the constant threat of violence, as a means of overthrowing a Government that was secure in the Chambers, by appealing to those—and he says that they were becoming more and more numerous in the 1830s and 1840s, the July Revolution having shown that power was there for the taking—who were at all times ready and eager to come out into the street, from artist's garret or engineman's cellar, to start the shooting. He finds no words strong enough to condemn the readiness shown by political leaders opposed to Guizot, men quite as moderate as himself, when driven frantic by deprivation of office, to have recourse to this ever-present, ever-mobilized army of crime, desperation, misery, rage, and spleen (a word much favoured by Baudelaire), in order to bring down a ministry that they thought had lasted too long. He is even more severe in his condemnation of those intellectuals, pamphleteers, artists, for whom violence served as a pep pill, as a substitute for talent, hard work, concentration, coherent ideas, imagination, and as an escape from the boredom of everyday life.

This was the age of Lacenaire, the *poète-assassin*, of a theatre-going public that idolized Frédéric Lemaître, of a Baudelaire giving vent to his splenetic rage against a materialistic ruling class, in the evocation of corpses buzzing with the teeming life of decomposition. And how right the author is to emphasize the futility of a tradition that has continued almost unbroken, from Hébert to Maurras, or even to Jean Genêt, with his horrible evocation of Barcelona corner boys, his idealization of the dreadful *soeurs* Papin, true revolutionists, apparently, because they murdered, in incredibly brutal circumstances, their middle-class master and mistress—a form, no doubt, of political engagement?

In the 1840s the most criminal of all, in this concert of violence, in this daily incitation to murder, were those who, because they believed that Frenchmen were becoming fat and flabby, were losing sight of grandeur, were living only for *dinde truffée* and *suprême de volaille* (surely a more desirable aim in life than erecting barricades or massacring Arabs?), called for war as a means of effecting a moral regeneration. Daumier returns again and again, lovingly, to the groaning table of the rich, he harps on the theme of the *ventre législatif*, in an effort to persuade his audience that the July Monarchy was a régime of the fat (at least one is safer in the hands of the heavy eaters than in those of a dyspeptic Robespierre or a vegetarian Himmler) and to bring out the hordes of the underfed; Daumier is one of the most persistent heralds of hate. Guizot had to contend not only with that Café de Commerce strategist, Thiers ('Je ne suis pas un grand soldat comme Thiers'), but with people like Lamartine, who became a revolutionary out of boredom, and who enjoyed every minute of blood, balcony, and barricade.

There was something extremely doubtful, almost obscene, about the Paris revolutionary—almost a profession—of the 1830s and 1840s, and Mr. Johnson is certainly right to hint at his proximity to the criminal world. He belonged to a dangerous, peripheral class, situated uneasily somewhere between the *petit bourgeois*, the *intellectuel raté*, and the man of the people—the nineteenth-century equivalent of those alarming inhabitants of the fringe of Paris at the time of the first Revolution, carters of Montrouge, horse-dealers and itinerant pedlars of Gentilly and Ivry, rivermen of Charenton, laundry-women of Vaugirard and Issy. It is possible, of course, that Guizot himself may have deliberately exaggerated the potentialities of this army of violence in order to frighten the Paris middle class into continued acquiescence in his interminable tenure of office; he certainly made what he could of the threat from the *classes dangereuses*. But at least he did not appeal to such doubtful and dangerous allies; and, in this all-important respect, he was a much greater man than any of his contemporaries, for the aim of both his foreign and his domestic policy was to attempt to break out of this insane circle of violence, revenge, and historical memory in order to ensure for the property-owners the peace and the security that they so much desired.

A few months after his overthrow the literature of violence was to have at last its long-hoped-for red dawn; the June Days were the most appalling bloodbath of the century. Among the *fédérés* there were many who were merely artists in violence; and the four days of slaughter cannot be interpreted solely in class terms. This was what Lamartine and his kind had—perhaps unconsciously—been working for during the previous ten years. Was there, after all, any Paris or Lyon barricade, in the nineteenth century, that brought any permanent advantages to the French working class? Did the *canuts** get anything at all out of their revolt? And did the *communards* achieve anything other than a romantic tradition? The cycle of violence has merely cluttered up the present with commemorative ceremonies, red banners, and with a martyrology that has been of little practical service to the French working-class movement; living syndicalists are more valuable than shot *fédérés*, their dying gaze facing steadily backwards, to the glories of the year II. Guizot was the first to condemn the effort to find a justification for violence in the present by the evocation of the revolutionary violence of 1793.

It is not possible to list all the other qualities of this wise book. Writing of a Cevenol who became something of a Norman, the author, who lived and worked outside Paris away from the Archives Nationales, repeatedly insists on the diversity of French political life, on the persistence of regional ties, on the danger of generalization on a national scale. He is aware too of the complexities of the French grain trade, of the recurrent psychosis of the fear of dearth. And who else could have written of Guizot's most unscrupulous and demagogic rival: 'In Thiers there were unplumbed depths of shallowness'? It is nice to find an historian who can write like Oscar Wilde. Observations such as 'The Revolution gave historians [of the 1820s and 1830s] a sense of time', 'A divided society appeals to history' (and the French are still doing so) may seem obvious, but they are in fact examples of historical perception.

But perhaps Mr. Johnson's greatest quality is one that he shares with another recent English historian of France, Professor J. McManners:[1] the capacity to write French history in French terms, from within. He does not write down to the French, nor lecture to them on their foolish ways; at the same time, his angle of vision is not entirely a French one. He tries to understand why Guizot should have been so unpopular in his own country, and his conclusions are honourable to the statesman, revealing as a judgement on French opinion at its silliest, and, above all, a tremendous tribute to an historian who is English, who knows France so well, and who can write so well of a man who said of himself: 'Je vis aussi en Angleterre. C'est beaucoup d'avoir deux vies et presque deux patries.' One is tempted to think that the same could be said of Mr. Johnson, so long has he lived with his subject, so lovingly is he able to evoke the Val Richer where the old man lived out his long years of retirement, among the gentle pastures of Lower Normandy. Guizot may have got a better historian than the man himself deserved; but his whole life is so very much an illustration of the difficulties standing in the way of Anglo-French understanding, of the mutual mental blockages that so often cut the wire of cross-Channel intellectual exchanges, that the subject has been well worth the talent of an English historian of such knowledge, sympathy, and wisdom.

[1] See pp. 159–67 above, 'The Bells of Anjou'.

16 The Women of the Commune[1]

Books written about women by men can never be entirely satisfying; they will be patronizing and irritatingly protective, or they
will be pornographic or at least written for the interest of the *voyeur*,
or equally they will be openly contemptuous and hostile. In the
first category we can place all those man-written histories of the
secrets of the alcove, a speciality much favoured by several generations of French historians and that forms one of the gilt-edged
stocks in trade of the publishing houses of the boulevard Saint-
Germain. This is, of course, also history written for men about
women whose sole function in life was the satisfaction of the sexual
desires of the great and the famous. Such a concentration on the
history of the courtesan is an interesting revelation of the male-
imposed standards of a certain French middle-class society. But
such writers as Restif and Cleland are in a class above this; Restif
in particular really does have a lot to say about one of the largest
female wage-earning groups, prostitutes; but again, the assumptions of these writers are masculine ones; Fanny writes gaily enough
about herself, but it is not so much her voice that we hear as that
of her creator and, in spite of all the terrible things that happen to
her at various times, she usually miraculously escapes pregnancy.

Cleland was writing for a male public. Restif did his best to cross
over, he was a marvellous and insistent observer of the other half of
society, but his impetus is not that of the disinterested sociologist;
his first glance is for the foot, whence his eye travels upward. His
account of the *dames du Palais-Royal* is calculated to titillate; it
must have served as a useful guide for country gentlemen up in the
Capital.[2] In Restif's observations there is little place for the girl
who has not fallen or who is not about to fall. The virtuous working
girl (probably a rare species in any case), the *bourgeoise* spinster
(much commoner in that class), the *bigote* of the upper middle class

---

[1] Review of Édith Thomas, *Les Pétroleuses* (Paris, 1963).
[2] *Les Parisiennes ou XL Caractères généraux* . . . (4 vols., Neufchâtel, 1787)
and *Le Palais-Royal* (IIIme Partie).

are not worth bothering about, for they are not interesting, they have nothing to offer a masculine reading public. And one feels that Restif would have had little time for the *militante*, for one of those committed citizenesses of the Société des Femmes Révolutionnaires. He was not as cruel as Laclos, who, through Valmont, dwells so lovingly on the sicgc and fall of *la présidente*; but he liked to keep his women subjects in their place—that is, primarily, in bed, or, at worst, in the kitchen, in the shop, or in the steaming heat of a laundry boat. He had no time for those who discoursed in clubs or coffee houses, if they were not of the same social standing of his own fabricated Marquise.

Most nineteenth- and even twentieth-century French historians, when dealing with such *militantes* as Théroigne de Méricourt or Claire Lacombe, or with an international adventuress such as Etta Palm van Aelders, tried to play down their political importance and even to put in doubt the sincerity of their commitment, by writing them off as the mistresses of one or other of the male revolutionary celebrities. Claire, for instance, is hardly allowed a life of her own at all, she is merely the mistress of Varlet, maybe of Momoro too. Théroigne was certainly that of many; but it was not her most original occupation. It has never been suggested, for instance, that these women, in their very sexual freedom, were striking out for women's rights and were asserting the right of their sex to choose their own companions. While it is very generally admitted that a great many *sans-culottes* had chosen the path of free love rather than marriage, a *militante* who did not imitate Hébert's former nun and set herself up *bourgeoisement* through the proper channels of civil marriage, would be dismissed as 'une femme légère'. Much was made at the time, and more has been made since, of the fact that the Fête de la Raison should have been presided over by an actress; it would then follow that the fête itself was little better than a blasphemous orgy—the side-chapels occupied by drunken men and women celebrating the new divinity in a manner suitably appreciative[1]—and that it could not be taken seriously. Théroigne and Claire are loose women, out for a good time and plenty of excitement; their commitment to the revolutionary cause can only be read in terms of their current lovers whose political

---

[1] See, for instance, the comments of Mercier, in *Le Nouveau Paris* (Paris, 1797).

colour they will temporarily take on. Claire is at once an *enragée* because she may have been associated with Varlet, and an *hébertiste*, because she may have slept with Momoro. By a similar system of measurement, Théroigne could be considered as having, at one time or another, espoused pretty well all the colours of the political spectrum. Once it is suggested that they moved from bed to bed at the same tempo as an increasingly precipitant political stampede of the revolutionary Gadarene, then they can be written off as light-headed creatures, suitable subjects for books by Lenôtre, Cabanès, Robiquet, and others of the *petite histoire* school.

It is not quite the same thing with the upper-class ladies on the other side. Royalist literature and some Hachette historians of the present century reserve a deferential place for the gallant ladies— eighteenth-century *Jehannes*—who, in the west, lead out their *manants* in defence of Christ and King (we are not, however, shown them presiding over the torture and massacre of republican prisoners). This is a form of militancy to be condoned, for these are great ladies, with a natural right to leadership, a right as self-evident as the inclination of their *manants* to come out, cap in hand, and to die for Christ, for King and for Madame la Marquise. No one would ever presume to suggest that there was anything indecent about these bloody-minded women presuming to meddle in military affairs; this type of *amazone* is all right, and there is no praise too great for the devoted *comtesse* who somehow manages to carry on in the absence of her husband, an *émigré* with the *armée des Princes*, or for the *châtelaine* who hides refractory priests and the secret emissaries of Pitt. In this case, a discreet veil is thrown over their private lives; such heroines could only be pure. They would not be likely to sleep with their gamekeepers it is true; but to suggest, for instance, that the Marquise de la Rochejacquelein could ever have been unfaithful to the Marquis would be as impious as to claim that Jehanne had consorted with more than her Voices.

Most writers—even those sympathetic to the Revolution—have denied the female lower orders any claim to political militancy at all. The market woman and the fishwife from the faubourg Poissonnière can only be motivated by jealousy and hatred—by that inverted cascade of jealousy to which Restif refers: that felt by the *lingère* for the *boutiquière*, by the *boutiquière* for the *marchande*, by the *marchande* for the *négotiante*, by the *négotiante* for the *avocate*, and by the *avocate* for the *présidente*. The violence of the *femmes du peuple* is almost biological; they are furies, scarcely recognizable as human beings, all claws out, urging the men on in their axe-work. They probably were, in fact, both more resentful and more blood-thirsty than the men, but they did not go into the Revolution merely for the pleasure of seeing the princesse de Lamballe cut up and her components—the expression used is *la fressure**—promenaded half across Paris, for display in inn after inn, though this spectacle must have been infinitely pleasing to many a poor woman, as a dramatically visual example of the mighty being pulled down from their high seats and thrown into the gutter. (Restif insists, with his usual perceptiveness, that women would be more subject to envy than men, more appreciative, therefore, of any primitive form of turning the world upside-down.)[1]

Women—especially mothers, with an average family of six children[2] (but there are some *sans-culottes* with as many as fifteen or twenty)—had more admissible motives for revolutionary commitment, because they would always be the first to feel the pinch of want and to be aware of hoarding and under-the-counter transactions. The bread riots are their particular contribution. But even historians as sensitive to popular motivations as George Rudé and Albert Soboul will hardly allow them a more positive role; there was, they point out, no female *sans-culotte* movement in its own right, and they rightly insist on the strongly anti-feminist bias of the *sans-culotte* movement itself. The *sans-culottes*, who showed some concern for the fate of natural children, do not seem to have been moved by that of unmarried mothers, and, when they were employers, were as much given to seducing their poor servant-girls —from Brittany, Normandy, and the east—as were their social superiors.[3]

Certainly it was not a woman's revolution. Even so, we do not yet know the whole story; there has, for instance, been no comprehensive study of female labour during the revolutionary period. Yet we know that, in wage agitation, the *fileuses* of the government cotton mills of the year II were among the most enterprising and

---

[1] *Les Nuits de Paris.*
[2] On the size of the families of the poor in an urban community in the late eighteenth century, see Olwen Hufton, *Bayeux in the Late Eighteenth Century.*
[3] See my *Problems of French Popular History*, Part Three.

the most insistent in putting their case to the Commune, even succeeding in lobbying Hébert and in getting their case taken up by that professional putter-of-wrongs-right, the Père Duchesne, who, both as a demagogue and as one of the ablest journalists of hate before Rochefort and Maurras, was well aware of the importance of fishing for feminine support and knew what untapped sources of screaming violence there were to be found in the garrets and the *cours des miracles* of the rue Saint-Denis. Fifty years later, Eugène Sue reserved all his most hideously cruel roles for women;[1] revolutionary Paris too cannot have been lacking in nightmare characters like la Chouette. The very abundant, class-inspired Thermidorian literature devoted to the former terrorist cadres has its *buveuses* as well as its *buveurs de sang*; there are plenty of references to the presence in the galleries of popular clubs of dishevelled harpies who acted as a sort of Greek choir, calling stridently for more Terror; and *dénonciatrices* were certainly more numerous than *dénonciateurs*; they might even be said to have constituted a primarily feminine vocation, like the sister one of *corbeau*—or writer of anonymous letters, a specialist who came very much into her own during the Revolution. Fouquier-Tinville received a colossal daily female fan mail and his favourite witnesses were *concierges* and *portières*.

The best that women could expect then from the Revolution would be a place on a float, in one of the recurrent revolutionary jamborees, in the role of Innocence or Motherhood, alongside Wisdom. But let there be no mistake about it: Innocence would eventually have to lead to Motherhood; the vestals were not to be kept permanently in blue. And if there were any decline in morals during the Revolution, as so many middle-class and royalist writers have asserted (though without a shred of evidence), it would have been a decline exclusively to the advantage of men. Certainly some of the more vigorous ultra-revolutionists, the wild men of the provinces in the course of the anarchical winter of 1793, used their enormous powers of repression to requisition local girls—not only *filles d'auberge*, but even the carefully kept daughters of the rich; they would have been foolish to have missed the opportunity of a lifetime.[2] And there is plenty of evidence that, higher up still, some of the *représentants en mission*, the satraps of Terror, progressed through the countryside in their open cabriolets, with horses and

[1] *Les Mystères de Paris*, ed. Jean-Louis Bory (Paris, 1963).
[2] See my *Les Armées révolutionnaires*, vol. 2 (Paris-La Haye, 1963).

outriders and a clatter of cavalry, flags in the wind, the embodiment of the Sovereign People escorted by an army of beplumed women that they had picked up *en route*. Nantais inquiring about imprisoned relatives had to pass through several roomfuls of such persons, before reaching the great Carrier himself. It was not surprising that some contemporaries, and most Thermidorians, spoke of the *représentants* of the year II as pashas and oriental satraps.

By 1793, prostitutes had become politically suspect, as attached to their former clientele of the old ruling class; they were also rightly accused of affording recruits an easy berth, far from the battlefield, in the (relative) safety of a hospital. But one suspects that their main sin in the eyes of the revolutionary militant was that they sought to lead an independent existence. Certainly, popular leaders were convinced that there was no more counter-revolutionary a class in the Republic—other than hairdressers—but they were probably wrong about this. Prostitutes were girls of the people, recruited from such wretched employments as laundress or domestic—some of them too were former slaves, *les dames du Palais-Royal* representing a wide range of colour—and they were drawn from pretty well every province north of the Loire.[1] Most of them were country girls who had but recently been assimilated into the population of the Capital. One would suspect that had *la Paysanne* lived longer, after having been perverted by evil men from the top ranks of society instead of being edifyingly killed off at an early age to give a moral ending to an otherwise happily pornographic story, she would have thrown herself with enthusiasm into the revolutionary movement, if only to avenge herself on those who had brought about her ruin.[2] As we will see, prostitution was wholly on the side of the Commune eighty-five years later.

This, then, is merely to state some of the problems. So far as France is concerned, the Women's Revolution still awaits its historian. And it will probably take a woman to write it, though there are dangers, too, in women writing up their own history. Vera Figner, one feels, gives rather a prudish, high-minded account of Russian terrorism; she is such a prissy bore. Were they then all so utterly

---

[1] In 1795, they were, in fact, drawn from only half a dozen Departments in the north-east, the east, the Paris region, and Burgundy. Few came from the west. See my *Problems of French Popular History*, loc. cit.

[2] Restif, *La Paysanne Pervertie*.

noble, so pure as all that? And Paz Ferrer writes of her murdered
father as if he had been quite inhumanly perfect—a marvellous
parent, a friend to mankind, a great scholar, the leading education-
ist of his day; it is too much. There are hints of this too, at times,
in Mlle Édith Thomas's latest book, *Les Pétroleuses*. It is not
altogether by chance that she should previously have written (at
the behest of the French Communist Party) a life of the well-known
female partisan leader, Joan of Arc, and, reading through her indignant and sometimes strident feminism, it is not difficult to perceive the outlines of a founder member of the Union des Femmes
Françaises—a pig-tailed, heavily shod Front organization that has
condemned the pill and that the present authoress left, along with
the Party, some years ago. Mlle Thomas was also an authentic
heroine of the Resistance. These are no doubt good qualifications
to write about Louise Michel and the dedicated, infuriating, noble,
brave, and sometimes merely bored women of the Paris Commune;
the author thinks so, and says as much in her preface. But they can
be dangerous too, and at times the masculine reader at least will
become impatient with some of the sillier antics of these *militantes*,
will find himself out of sympathy with many of their more flamboyant posturings, and with the reverent, unsparing seriousness
with which Mlle Thomas analyses, in great detail, the quite excruci-
ating 'social' and 'educational' novels of Marcelle Tinayre, *La Marguerite* and *Un Rêve de femme*.

Marguerite is brave, selfless, dedicated, unsparing, and quite
exasperating. Will she ever shut up? Will she ever stop preaching?
Will she ever come off the barricade of Rights for Women? Does
she ever take a day off from the Struggle? Must even sex be enlisted in the Fight against Selfish Man? She must certainly have
lost many potential well-wishers to women's rights by her bossiness
and her impossible rectitude. Louise Michel is of a similar stamp,
and even more forbidding. But at least she is not just an intellectual
prig in revolt against a conventional, provincial, middle-class background (Marguerite is from the Allier); Louise came to feminism
by the hard, stony road of illegitimacy, being the natural daughter
of a small nobleman and of a domestic servant; there is more
warmth in her, but also a great deal of pedantry and a limitless
capacity to annoy and to educate. During the siege, she spends her
time, when out of the firing line, reading Baudelaire to the *fédérés*
or playing the harmonium in a ruined Protestant chapel; and, on

the long journey to Cayenne, she insists on embarrassing a perfectly well-meaning naval officer by playing the pauperess and going about the deck without shoes (the captain supplies her with pair after pair, which she persists in giving away to 'those in greater need'); there is a very good French word for this sort of person. Louise also displays a tendency towards self-dramatization common to most of this group of militant amazons, a tendency that takes the everyday form of dressing up, *à la George Sand*, in male attire—possibly the inevitable first step towards a militancy that must first of all seek to establish a visible equality with man, as well as to demonstrate a capacity to undertake that most masculine of all occupations, killing, and to display the so-called male virtues—physical courage, brutality, and so on—a tendency that, thanks to the exceptional circumstances of the Commune, takes the rarer form of parading in uniforms of fantastic design, covered with pistols and pouches.

But Louise is a warm-hearted, generous, and indignant woman—one of Vallès's *coeurs vaillants*. The Commune also attracted to Paris half the *désoeuvrées* of Europe, in search of excitement, in the hope, too, of recovering from yet another messy love affair or to indulge in that peculiarly loathsome form of tourism: watching and dabbling in other people's civil wars, while, of course, holding on to a safe passport. There is the illegitimate daughter of a Russian general who gets no end of fun out of the Commune, parading in a parakeet uniform, firing off her pistols, killing Versaillais, preaching in clubs, sleeping with one *communard* leader after another, eventually to return home by train, satiated and happy, to marry a guards officer of her own class. She is quite exceptionally nasty—a female pre-Hemingway who derives sexual stimulus from the smell of battle. But there are a number of others almost as bad: the inevitable Poles, romantic, ostentatious, silly, quick to identify the cause of the Commune with their own particular case histories as social misfits or with the professional woes of their country, and dividing their time between bed, barricade, and political rostrum. Far from being women of the people, they are the daughters of Heine's professional Polish heroes, of Krapulinski and Eskrokiewicz, and they carry into the Commune the arrogance of the *szląchta* class, its impossible courage and its delight in posturing. Thus Paulina Mekarska (Paule Minck), whose father had been an aide-de-camp in the 1830 Insurrection and whose mother was a French noblewoman, takes up her revolutionary activities with much the same attitude as people of her kind might have had to the organizing of charity bazaars; she preaches, and she preaches *down*, and her uniform is the most fantastic of them all. There are a number of other noble ladies of this kind, including one extravagant Italian, the granddaughter of a female victim of the Neapolitan counter-revolution and a representative of hereditary revolutionary élitism. Mlle Thomas is too inclined to take these women at their own estimate of themselves; they are picture-postcard heroines all right, but they are equally certainly not revolutionists. Indeed, it is difficult to decide just what they were fighting for: an independent Poland—free only for the *szląchta*—or freedom to live with whom they pleased and to change their men as many times as they liked. It is doubtful whether they felt any sympathy for the economic and social grievances of the general mass of French women who threw themselves into the defence of the Commune with such courage and ferocity.

Even so, despite some rather starry-eyed passages on the subject of Louise Michel and Andrée Léo—the daughter of a Cherbourg naval officer—Mlle Thomas has written a pioneering work in the history of women. It will be of particular interest to those who are concerned with the history of the French Revolution, for she has done for her *communardes* what still remains to be done for the women of revolutionary France. It is true that her task has been made much easier by the existence of more than one thousand *dossiers* of courts-martial cases, the reports of which illuminate the social origins, age, marital status, professions, and motivations of many of the accused. The Commune had the advantage of being defeated, so that we can learn a great deal about those who took part in it; it would be difficult to do the same for the women of 1793–5. Even so, there are a number of hints in the present work that might be taken up with profit; for if, in the eighty years following the Revolution, the pattern of male employment had changed almost beyond recognition—one would look mostly in vain for *sans-culottes* among the ranks of the *communards*—women representing an economically repressed and retarded class still offer much the same occupational structures as in 1793. The vast majority of Mlle Thomas's rank and file are the proletariat of the clothing trades—seamstresses, dressmakers, finishers, cutters, and so on—together with a liberal sprinkling of the even more wretched and disinherited army of washerwomen, *repasseuses, ouvrières en linge*. Already by the time Restif was writing, the *bateau-lavoir* on the Seine, which throughout the eighteenth and nineteenth centuries was to be one of the most characteristic features of the Paris landscape, to the great joy of generations of painters and tourists, had produced something of factory conditions, these floating slums being academies of violence, vice, and crime, and conditioning a collective, pariah mentality; it was the easiest of steps, from one of these hulks, ashore and upstairs, to prostitution.

Equally, already in 1789, there was a second army of laundry-women encamped on the outskirts of Paris in the uneasy suburbs of Vaugirard, Issy, Gentilly, Montrouge, at all times ready to respond to the call of violence and to march into the precincts to watch the houses of the rich burn down. In the Commune, too, the *faubouriennes* from the south and eastern fringes are among the most ardent recruits to the armies of feminine intransigence, constituting the handful of identifiable *pétroleuses*. There is, in this respect at least, a continuity from the Revolution to 1871; and if there existed a detailed study of female participation in the June Days of 1848, it would almost certainly reveal these same elements: those who worked with needle and thimble, scissors and flat-iron, those who sweated in the fetid prisons of laundries, semi-naked and ardent, those who coughed up their lungs in damp basements and dark *arrière-cours*.

Nor is one surprised to discover among the *militantes* one or two women publicans—*aubergistes, limonadières, marchandes de vin*, and so on—natural leaders of opinion and purveyors of news and rumour, predestined officers to a movement that had its roots deep in the *quartier*, the *arrondissement* ('Ils n'entreront pas, citoyen . . . si chacun défend bien son quartier', a *fédéré* explains to Vallès, who comments bitterly: 'C'est ce qui va nous tuer, cette idée! Quartier par quartier! . . . La Sociale reculera!'),[1] and often the first to serve themselves and to stoke up the fires of revolutionary violence on their own stocks. The parallel is made all the more striking by the fact that, among the rather disparate group of the committed, there is an elderly drunkard nicknamed la mère Duchesne—a direct and

[1] Jules Vallès, *L'Insurgé* (vol. 3 of *Jacques Vingtras*).

no doubt deliberate call-back to revolutionary imagery (the Commune also had its newspaper, the *Père Duchesne*, its battalion of 'les enfants du Père Duchesne'). Though Mlle Thomas displays at all times a commendable energy in defending her women from Versaillais imputations regarding their morals and their private lives, she is quite ready to admit that among the *cantinières*, and even among the *amazones*, temperance was not one of the banners behind which the women of the Commune were ready to march; feminism still had a long way to go, in 1871, before finding expression in *L'Assommoir*.

Though she is inclined to write off the claim made by a military judge that, of some 1,200 women arrested after *la Semaine Sanglante* (there were as many raped and bayoneted to death during the week itself), 240 of them had been prostitutes of a sufficiently professional status to have their *fiches* with the police—an argument likely to find favour with the *bourgeois* thesis that one of the reasons for the destruction of so many public buildings by women would be to destroy such evidence—Mlle Thomas agrees that, in the III*me arrondissement* at least, the prostitutes flocked eagerly to the Commune, taking a militant part in the clubs and in the women's battalions, drawn to the movement by the possibility of rehabilitation and re-employment (the Commune was to set up special schools for this purpose). Their active participation is further suggested by the provincial origins of most of the women who appeared before courts-martial and who later received prison sentences or were deported.

A few—a very few—*communardes* quite definitely came from the *bas-fonds*, from Sue's *tapis franc*; such, for instance, was the Belgian *chiffonnière*,* Marie Wolff, who had behind her a long police record for theft and vagrancy. But these are very exceptional cases, and the armies of the Commune, so far as women were concerned, were seldom those of professional crime, though they might be those of occasional crime, of the sort of petty crime induced by want in a mother of a large family.

More revealing is the average age of the *militantes*. These were women who had experienced long years of every sort of misery and humiliation; most of them had been born in the 1830s or 1840s and were old enough to have grown-up children at the time of the Commune; some of them had certainly experienced the June Days and what followed. Of those deported, most were aged from 35 to

51, with the heaviest concentration between 40 and 45. Only some of the intellectuals of middle-class origin—especially the foreigners —were in their twenties. The *communardes* of 40 and over belonged to a defeated generation; and they knew what French *bourgeois* society meant, and did not like it.

The author, however, and this is one of her greatest merits, does not confine herself to the analysis of social structure; she is too alive and warm-hearted to associate with that *maison de redressement* school of history. Her women, however irritating they may be at times, are entirely real people, and she never loses sight of the individual case history. Thus we find in the group a number of *dénonciatrices*; whom do they denounce? Mainly the police—seen as the informers of the Versaillais—their wives and daughters. There is no doubt at all about the popular loathing for *M. le commissaire*, and for all he stood for, in marked contrast to the situation in 1793, when the *commissaire de police* had been an elected official, one of the people in fact, and with a ready ear for popular grievances. They denounced, of course, hoarders, wholesalers, and speculators; above all, they denounced parish priests and their *vicaires*, and we are left in little doubt about feminine approval of, and participation in, the massacre of the rue Haxo, when a number of clergy, gendarmes, and others were shot by a squad which seems to have contained some women soldiers.

One can measure from such incidents the progress of popular anticlericalism since the Revolution; in 1793 there were very few women—and most of them had been publicans, such as the celebrated Mère Duchesne of Vermenton[1]—who had taken part in active dechristianization, while the Paris prostitutes, according to the police reports, still carried crosses around their necks, the *sans-culottes* tending, on the contrary, to despise their womenfolk for allowing themselves to remain under the influence of 'ces vieux druides'. In 1871, the female working class of Paris emerges as enthusiastically anticlerical, and most of the spokeswomen of the movement are also militant atheists. Probably they were as much concerned with clerical condemnation of free love and of the unmarried mother as with the Church as a pillar of Versaillais order. Vallès quotes the case of a woman of 30 who had taken part in the execution of the hostages, during the *Semaine Sanglante*:

[1] *Les Armées révolutionnaires*, vol. 2.

elle n'a pas d'idées sur la *Sociale*, celle-là non plus; mais sa soeur a été la maîtresse d'un vicaire prêtre, puis, enceinte, a quitté les siens en volant leurs épargnes. 'Voilà pourquoi je suis descendue en voyant de ma croisée les soutanes.'[1]

In this respect, it is interesting to note how many of these women had been seduced, at some stage of their careers, either by priests or by their employers and how many too had been abandoned as children, to experience the appalling cruelty of the very ill-named *bonnes soeurs*, always the object of the particular hatred of the women of the common people of Paris, in charitable institutions. Probably more revolutionary vocations were born of illegitimacy, seduction, the totally unequal standards governing masculine, as opposed to feminine, misconduct, than of want, misery, and the rigours of *bourgeois* society.

This revolt against male-imposed standards of behaviour imposed on the Commune a female popular front, extending from the provincial noblewoman to the rag-and-bone woman of the faubourgs, the common programme of which was free love; most of the *militantes* had come from broken homes, many of them, after an unsuccessful experience of marriage, had abandoned their husbands and set themselves up *en ménage* with the men of their choice. After his death in 1885 it was his *compagne*, Séverine, who finished and published Jules Vallès's *L'Insurgé*. A few may have been merely promiscuous; but sexual freedom was the commonest theme, giving to the whole movement an anarchical character that greatly embarrassed such masculine conformists as Rossel and Dąbrowski and that explains—without excusing—the abominable ferocity shown by the Versaillais, particularly by naval officers, towards the women of the Commune or towards any woman of the people whose eyes were incapable of concealing the hatred felt by the women of Belleville for the enemies of their class. Many were raped during *la Semaine Sanglante*, before being shot or bayoneted to death.

Of course, the lower down one goes the more purely economic and social grievances become apparent. There were many *communardes* who were not in the movement just out of anticlericalism or as a gesture in favour of sexual equality, and who did know what *la Sociale* was about. Mlle Thomas, who is well versed in the history of the French Revolution, is fully aware of the importance of female participation in riots and disorders arising out of food

[1] op. cit.

shortage—and, as Vallès reminds us, the Commune had been born out of those twin enemies of the common people, *la disette* (dearth) and *le froid*. In this respect too there is a continuity between the women-led hunger riots of 1795 and the attacks on food shops during the Commune. There is also a common hatred of the baker —Vallès himself was happy to set fire to a baker's shop during the last days of the Commune and he describes with some satisfaction the execution of a baker, in the Latin Quarter, as a suspected spy— and the wholesalers, and a common belief in the existence of vast hoarded stocks and in clandestine transactions involving the export of supplies to the Prussians. We still hear the old tales of *la disette factice* in 1871, and the women of the Commune, like Hébert's clientele among the fishwives and the market women, knew what it was to queue, at four or five in the morning, with the thermometer at thirty below, outside the baker's or the insolent butcher's (who reserves his choicest morsels for his wealthy customers). 'Des femmes partout,' writes Vallès of a demonstration in January 1871, when cold and shortage are at their worst, 'grand signe! Quand les femmes s'en mêlent, quand la ménagère pousse son homme, quand elle arrache le drapeau noir, qui flotte sur la marmite, pour le planter entre deux pavés, c'est que le soleil se lèvera sur une ville en révolte.' And, like the female readers of the *Père Duchesne*, the Bellevilloises, whose blind violence was at times to alarm even Vallès, insist that the best cure for shortage is to shoot a few grocers and to string up a few hoarders.

On the popular level at least, then, there were many points of contact and even a certain continuity between the attitudes and assumptions of the female *petit peuple* of the Paris of the Revolution and the aims and activities of the more committed and conscious *militantes* of 1848 and of 1871. There is, however, one important sector of female employment which appears to represent a complete break in the revolutionary traditions of the two periods; for the most surprising thing, perhaps, that emerges from this original study is the absence—total, or so it would appear—of the enormous army of domestic servants from the ranks of the committed in 1871. In this respect, the position is the reverse of that of 1793–4, when milady's maid proved such an effective and enthusiastic instrument of the revolutionary committees of the Paris Sections, denouncing her former mistress, her master, her master's family, and taking such an evident satisfaction in the humiliation and ruin of the old ruling class; there is probably nothing more ferocious than a Servants' Republic, and the faubourg Saint-Germain in particular had experienced to the full the vicious ferocity of domestics' rule, when it had been subjected to a committee composed of coachmen, cooks, valets, dancing masters, piano teachers, fencing masters, and language teachers, who themselves drew on an enormous fund of information supplied to them by the female proletariat of below stairs.

Perhaps in 1871 the well-to-do *bourgeois*—for these were the only ones who could afford to leave the beleaguered and fuelless city—took their servants away with them to Saint-Cloud or to their country seats. Perhaps, too, by 1871 one could already witness that transformation, completed by the turn of the century, and noted by Mirbeau in his admirable *Journal d'une femme de chambre*, by which the kitchen and the scullery became the most vociferous auxiliaries of the extreme Right, especially in its most violent and brutal manifestations. Célestine is, of course, anti-Semitic, though she has been well treated by a Jewish family (her anti-Semitism is that too of many of the *Communards* of popular origin), she is therefore *antidreyfusard*, she is for the Army and against the Republic, and, though she despises most of her mistresses (and manages to get her own back on several), and is well aware of the corruption and filth of the social order (she has frequently been employed in order to seduce the son of the house in order to keep him at home and out of the clutches of the grasping *gourgandines**) she is at no time a revolutionary; she accepts her place below stairs—preferring it at least to the alternatives of factory employment or the street—and she is even something of a snob, taking her standards, as it were at one remove, from a gentleman's gentleman, her favourite lover, who claims to be well thought of in the ducal world and boasts about his entrées to Jockey Club and paddock, rather as the bruisers that were the Marquess of Queensberry's chosen drinking companions may have boasted about their high-born patron. By 1900, *la valetaille* and *la piétaille*, the stable lads and the tipsters, are 100 per cent Action Française. So far as one can gather, at least in the absence of any information to the contrary, during the Commune too the maids were on the sides of their mistresses and of M. Thiers, not on that of the seamstress, the laundry-woman, and those borderliners of domesticity, the unhappy governesses, so many of whom may be found militating, with the schoolteachers, in the ranks of the *communardes*. Pride being such a great provider of revolutionary vocations, it may be that the governesses had suffered more than those who considered it to be their natural place in the world to be below stairs. Certainly, a seduced governess was more likely to become a revolutionary than a seduced parlour-maid.

Les Pétroleuses, then, is a highly important contribution to the history of the Paris Commune, in one of its obscurest corners. Mlle Thomas has filled in what had previously only been hinted at, in man-written accounts such as those of Lissagaray, Vuillaume, Lefrançais, and she has added depth and carefully planned detail to the always perceptive Vallès. There are few questions that she has left unanswered, though after reading *L'Insurgé* in particular, one wonders whether, among the *militantes*, those in an advanced stage of tuberculosis were as numerous as in the ranks of so many of the pathetic and obscure heroes of Vallès; whether, in fact, there might not also be some connection between their sexuality, their violence, and their romanticism, and that terrible disease of the poor. Were in fact the *tubardes** as numerous as the livid-faced *tubards*, so many of whom were to cough up their lungs in London, Brussels, Cayenne, and Lausanne?

But the present work is also an invitation to assess feminine assumptions in feminine terms. In a period such as the French Revolution, when women are, to a large extent, mute on the subject of their own particular grievances, these being filtered through man-written petitions when we hear them at all, these assumptions are not easy to come by; but, by concentrating on female types of employment, by scrutinizing the judicial records for traces of feminine categories of crime, some such progress could be made in our understanding of *ces coeurs vaillants* and of *ces mégères**—the ancestresses of the heroines and female villains of Sue, Vallès, and Mlle Thomas—and who may be assumed to have made their own particular contribution to the Great French Revolution.

17 Charles Braibant and the Third Republic[1]

Personal or family reminiscences are always difficult things to handle, if one is to avoid the triple dangers of whimsicality, false modesty, and self-mocking archness. There has been only one *Diary of a Nobody*, and Henri Queffelec, in his *Journal d'un salaud*, has written the one possible classic on the subject of the professional sponger. M. Braibant is not a nobody; he has been a public figure of some eminence as a regional novelist, as an active Director of the French Archives, as a crusader for 'Son et Lumière', 'le Quart d'Heure de Culture', and other visual or extra-scholastic aids designed to increase the familiarity of the French general public with their own and other people's history; he was also, during the inter-war years, a moving spirit in Les Amitiés Internationales, one of a number of bodies created in the interest of world peace and European reconciliation. Much, however, of the present volume—there is a second to follow, covering the period of M. Braibant's administration of the Archives Nationales—is taken up with the author's family history; and, let us face it, other people's families are liable to be extremely boring to the general reader, however fascinating our own ineffable 'Tonton Jacques' or 'Auntie Ethel' may appear within the closed circuit of tribal mythology. And so it is with M. Braibant's forebears, safe under their glass wreaths in their native Ardennes; we become a little impatient with the episodes of his father's legal career or with the uncertain health of young Charles himself; even more impatient with the author's tendencies, unfortunately so common among his compatriots, to attribute traits of character to mysterious, regional-biological influences.

There are, however, every now and then, in this rambling, chatty, pleasingly naïve *voyage à travers le siècle*, flashes of historical insight that pull the reader up, reviving his attention. For instance, writing of his Lutheran grandfather, who had been a *fédéré* in the

[1] Review of Charles Braibant, *Un bourgeois sous trois républiques* (Paris, 1961).

237

June Days, the author has the following bit of information to offer: 'Il s'établit pour vivre marchand de vin au village de La Chapelle, 36, rue des Poissonniers, cet embranchement de la route de Picardie que prolongeait *intra muros* la rue du Faubourg Poissonnière. . . .' M. Braibant's ancestors came in that way; he himself was born in a commune east of Paris; the *Lillots*,* the Picards, the Artésiens still tend to huddle under the protective shadows of the Gare du Nord and the Église de la Trinité, just as the Bretons stick to the XIV*me*. The great highways of an ancient, rural, provincial France still push deep into the liver-shaped Capital; the rue de Flandres carries its own meaning. During the July Monarchy and the Second Empire Paris still retained its colonies of Rhineland artisans, of poor Prussians, the latter, like the Auvergnats, looking to *la limonade* for a living.

Again, referring once more to his grandparents, at a later date in their career, M. Braibant once more opens a wider perspective of failure, Micawberism, and emigration: 'Ne réussissant pas à Paris, le couple partit pour le Brésil de dom Pedro, mirage de tant de Français de ce temps-là . . .'. We are all too prone to accept well-established clichés that *les Français sont casaniers*,* forgetting that Brazil has in fact never ceased to draw French immigrants, along with Positivism; that Jules Supervielle, and many poor Basques before and after him, have found their way to Uruguay; and that there are still innumerable family ties between Saint-Jean-Pied-de-Port and Montevideo, just as *la grande famille*, the French Protestant community, is criss-crossed by marriage links with Geneva, the Canton de Vaud, Torre Pellice, and Edinburgh; Louis Rossel, the military leader of the Commune, was the son of a Cevenol *pasteur* and of a Scotswoman, herself the daughter of a dominie. Argentina and Chile have been for over a century the Micawber-lands of the Gapençais and of the poor mountaineers of the Briançonnais; generations of Dauphinois have emigrated to South America, and Georges Arnaud, leaving France after the terrible experience of having been accused of murdering his parents, was not the only Frenchman in recent years to have tried his luck in Venezuela.

We are grateful to M. Braibant for other general comments that reach out beyond the anecdotal. When he states, for instance, that 'les Canadiens [the French Canadians] sont, je crois, les gens qui attachent le plus de prix aux documents relatifs à leurs origines', one can almost hear the groans of assent from the harassed archivists of the *section généalogique* of the Archives Nationales, and one is reminded of the slightly insane, but harmless, ancestral pride of one's own 'Acadien' friends. It is salutary, too, to have recalled the persistence of popular anti-semitism in the small garrison towns of eastern France; the family tailor in Bar-le-Duc was one of a number of Ashkenazim tradesmen in a town 'où, comme dans toutes les villes de l'Est, on ne les aimait pas'. It is also flattering that M. Braibant, who on more than one occasion expresses his admiration for the administrative competence of the July Monarchy and for the reforming zeal of Guizot (especially in the author's own particular field of public records), admits to a lingering admiration for the English Tory, and likes us, too ('J'adore les Anglais, je l'avoue à ma honte . . .').

In so far as there is any central theme in his darting narrative, it is his own increasing awareness, following a brief adolescent enthusiasm—provoked by *Le Petit Journal*—for colonial conquest, of the nagging, delirious, mean chauvinism of *concierge*, intellectual, army officer, *petit bourgeois*, and shopkeeper, in a mounting crescendo of hysteria during the years following the Franco-Prussian War to the present day. What adds dignity and purpose to this memorial of an old-fashioned liberal is his constant condemnation of national myths and his early perception of the dangers to France of colonial adventures. 'Si je regarde derrière moi notre demi-siècle,' he writes of France since Dreyfus, 'je vois un cimetière de chimères nationalistes conçues par de soi-disant réalistes.' It is good too to hear a Frenchman diagnose the inner sickness of post-war France: 'le chauvinisme négatif . . . un immobilisme obstiné et aveugle qui consiste, pour une nation, à se cramponner contre toute raison à une situation avantageuse qui n'est plus en rapport avec ses moyens . . .'. Better still, 'le brissotisme peint en blanc de Chateaubriand et de Maurras', as a description of the mental aberrations of part of the French traditionalist Right, of the maladies of a Barrès. He has no time for either popular polonophilia or for the Walter Scott romanticism of the neo-paladins, from the French gentlemen who fought in the Carlist Wars to the last, dreadful madness of a Bougret de la Tocnaye, brought up in one of those damp, mouldering manor-houses of western France described by Hervé Bazin, in a windowless world of Napoleoniana, Jeanne-d'Arquerie, Lyautisme, and Mermoz-erie, a Chamber of

Horrors of French nationalism: the busts of Bonaparte crowding each other out on the marble tops of commodes, the death-masks lurking sulkily in dark corners, against mauve flowered wallpaper, plaster casts of Réal de la Sarte's constipated *Jehanne*, her face drawn in agonized incandescent anglophobia, presiding over the mad, *chouan* dinner party.

We can feel grateful to the sane, homely M. Braibant for insisting on the unostentatious, rather drab virtues of the July Monarchy, and for rescuing from oblivion or, more often, calumny the men of peace who, at one time or another, have had the thankless task of clearing up: such statesmen as Rouvier, Joseph Caillaux, Aristide Briand. The author is not afraid of blowing his own trumpet, he does it lustily and rather often, but the sound that comes out of it is pleasant to the ear. Though he certainly exaggerates the influence of his beloved Amitiés Internationales, one can only sympathize with its aims, designed as it was to combat the many-faced figure of French chauvinism: the universalism of the intellectual, the neo-medievalism of the officer class, the carping *poujadisme* of the shopkeeper, *l'esprit cocardier* of the popular novelist. It is easy to understand why this crusader for common sense and for international understanding should have been one of the first victims of the Fifth Republic.

M. Braibant would have been well advised to forget Jean-Jacques when embarking on his own recollections. On the other hand, he strikes a familiar note when he emphasizes the close connection between sexuality and the spirit of conquest; in early adolescence he pictures himself following the Tonkin war through the lurid pages of *Le Petit Journal*, in his tree-top retreat at the bottom of the garden: here is young Charles Braibant, clad in topee and white leggings, pushing inland at the head of his *fusiliers-marins*, burning villages, reducing the native population to his despotic rule, in order to satisfy the wilder fantasies of his sexual reveries: '. . . Je violais garçons et filles, je les obligeais, sous la menace du revolver, à s'entre-caresser sous mes yeux . . .'. We may wonder how many military vocations were determined, at an early age, by similar fantasies, and be amazed at the temerity of parents in leaving within reach of prep-school boys numbers of the *Illustrated London News* devoted to the Zulu War, copies of *Jock of the Bushveld* and the recollections of travellers among unclothed peoples. There is probably a Loti lurking in many soldiers and explorers and one can appreciate why the Auxies should have been tempted by the promise of drink and Irish girls, although, as it turned out, even if they had gallons of the former, the latter were not to be forthcoming. There is an increasing need for historians to examine the connections between war and sex, between Revolution and patterns of personal behaviour; by recalling the tree-top dreams of an adolescent, M. Braibant has, once more, through the channel of family recollections, opened a window on to a wider perspective.

There are many other gleanings to be made in this meandering chronicle of family history, personal recollections, disquisitions on French administration and hankerings after the happiest of the Republics—that which was done to death in a hole-and-corner manner in Bordeaux in 1940. M. Braibant is particularly interesting on the subject of the radical antimilitarism of the Algiers *pieds noirs*, many of whom had been victims of the younger Bonaparte, whom they further suspected of wishing to form an Arab kingdom. There are, especially, some fascinating pages on that extraordinary episode, the Commune d'Alger of 1870–1 and on the subsequent emergence of *Cagayous*,[1] in his stronghold of Bab-el-Oued. On the purely technical side, the historian will find much to interest him in the author's description of the organization of the French naval records and *bibliothèques des ports*. Certainly no one could accuse him of false modesty and there are plenty of hints, in this volume, of what to expect from the next, when M. Braibant will be dealing with his period as Directeur des Archives de France, a post in which he achieved much publicity for the institution he headed, and reaped, for one of the most starved and neglected sectors of the French civil service (how many prefects in the past have expelled the *archives départementales* from the *dépôts* built for them, in order to make room for the police or the C.R.S.?), considerable material benefits, in terms of new buildings, more pay for the archivist, and a greater public awareness.

---

[1] *Cagayous* was the Algiers equivalent of Lyon's *Gnafron*. Boastful, a great consumer of *pernod*, and with plenty of time on his hands, he was a lower-middle-class philosopher of the poorer quarters of European Algiers. Like the inhabitants of these, he expressed himself in a dialect based on a mixture of French, Spanish, Italian, and Maltese, together with numerous, though unacknowledged borrowings from Arabic, that was clearly much appreciated by his readers, but that is largely incomprehensible to anyone not *au fait* with the language of the *pieds noirs*. Le *Journal de Cagayous*, a weekly comic, prospered most during the period 1900–14.

18 Indignant Patriot[1]

Georges Hippolyte Darien was born in Paris, 46 rue du Bac, on 6 April 1862 (his real name was Adrien). His parents, who had a small haberdashery shop in this strongly Catholic quarter, were French Protestants; but, his mother having died when Darien was still a child, his father married a militant Catholic. Having completed his schooling at the Lycée Charlemagne, Darien joined the French artillery as a 19-year-old volunteer, probably to get away from his stepmother, whom he loathed. Within a year, after a steady pile-up of charges—dumb insolence, answering back, arguing, quoting military regulations, 'not going through the proper channels', and so on—he was court-martialled and condemned to be transferred to a penal battalion in South Tunisia, where he served, under appalling conditions, for the next five years.

On his release in March 1886, he broke with his family, and took an attic room in the rue de l'Odéon. His first book, *Biribi*, based on his experiences in Tunisia, was written the same year, though it was not published till 1890. *Bas les coeurs!*, a novel about the Franco-Prussian War and the Commune as seen from the comfortable security of Versailles, probably based on childhood memories, appeared in the previous year. His next book, *Le Voleur*, was written in 1896 and published in 1897; during the interval, Darien had lived for long periods in London and in Brussels. It has been suggested, on strong evidence, that during this time he earned a regular income from burglaries committed mostly in Belgium and in France, but also in Holland, Switzerland, and the German Empire; and that Randal, the hero of *Le Voleur*, was himself. He certainly acquired a professional knowledge of the organization of international crime in the 1890s. In 1900 he wrote *La Belle France*, a bitterly violent pamphlet. His last novel in French, *L'Épaulette*— a second blast at the Army—appeared in 1901. He also wrote a

[1] Review of re-issued novels by Georges Darien, *Le Voleur* (Paris, 1955), *Bas les coeurs!* (Paris, 1957), *La Belle France* (Paris, 1965), and *Biribi* (Paris, 1966).

novel, in a sort of English, that was published in London in 1900; its subject concerned the efforts of a family of German Jews from Bremen to set themselves up in business in the East End. After 1901 his writing stopped altogether, save for a few articles, written in 1903 and 1904, for an ephemeral anarchist paper. After writing *Le Voleur*, Darien discovered *Progress and Poverty*; he remained for the rest of his life an enthusiastic Georgist. Nothing more is known about him. He died in Paris, in complete obscurity, in August 1921.

Darien was above all an individualist with an iron Protestant independence, not unlike that of his fellow Calvinist, Louis Rossel (like Rossel, he was an embittered patriot). He was awkward, angry, intolerable, and unyielding. In a generation thick with polemicists he stands out far ahead of all the other *grands exaspérés*, thanks to the sheer vigour, the deadly accuracy, and the literary elegance of his denunciations of contemporary French society. He was also that unusual being—a Frenchman who liked, and who understood, the English. His knowledge of the criminal underworld was obtained if not at first-hand—as it possibly was—then at least from those in the trade, especially from fences. He is the author of the most effective indictment of the French colonial army written in the nineteenth century; and one of his greatest merits is the lucidity with which he analysed the roots of French chauvinism. Like most French protesters of the last century and of this, he tended to interpret politics and social history in terms of the sombre plots of the police; anarchism, with which he at one time flirted, is written off as one of the 'accessoires de la maison Vidocq'. *Le mouchard* is a leading character in all his novels. The authors with whom he has most in common are Jules Vallès, Julien Blanc, and Jean Genêt; but it is difficult to compare a man who was so ruggedly and so constantly and uncomfortably independent with anyone else.

Darien is a poor novelist. His books are shapeless, repetitive, and long-winded; and most of his characters are crude, grimacing clowns—mere receptacles for the author's set pieces: the Deputy, the Minister, the Banker, the Officer, the Doctor, the Lawyer. *Le Voleur* is an allegory as naïve and as far-fetched as *Les Mystères*; it is liberally sprinkled with fortuitous encounters that bring together, in suitably dramatic conditions, the principal characters;

everyone is paraded back at least twice; no one is allowed to step out of the narrative quietly; nothing can be left to chance. The Abbé Lamargelle is right out of Dumas *père*; Roger *la Honte* and Canonnier out of Sue. The only person in the least bit credible—but how he talks, how he moans, how he rages—is Randal. *Le Voleur* is a *roman des moeurs*. *Bas les coeurs!*, from the literary point of view, is a good deal better, and much more readable; but this too is a political novel. The characters are monsters, but they are possible monsters; there is one saint, but he has human proportions and a sense of humour. *Biribi* is a very superior piece of journalism; there is no doubt about it being drawn from life, but it is hard going to get through so many pages of hate, rage, suffering, despair, and dreams of vengeance. Darien's masterpiece is not a novel at all, but a pamphlet: *La Belle France* never lets up for a moment; the intensity of exasperation is sustained throughout, as the author tears off the bandages and joyfully applies vinegar to the wounds.

For Darien's vengeful aphorisms are dazzling fireworks of words in the night sky. They make their point with cruel eloquence. They might form an anthology of gallophobe sayings, a late nineteenth-century *Anti-Gallia* directed primarily against the awful French *bourgeoisie* of the so-called *belle époque*, who were quite as sordid, as depraved, as selfish, as sententious, and as horrid as Darien—and the great Steinlen, a Darien in line—portray them. *La Belle France* was published in 1900, the beginning of *moderne style*, but still the high tide of the *maison Larousse* (see in *Larousse*, under *Maison*), so familiar to generations of English schoolboys brought up on illustrated French textbooks—the middle-class house, with its towers and turrets, weathercock, gothic outside pipes, *oeil de boeuf*, the French Primer house, the French Primer bandstand in the regimented park, the French Primer *mairie*, fake Henri IV, that fearful, self-confident architecture of pretentious sham, stuffy interiors, gothic lavatories with flowered bowls, no bathrooms, maids' bedrooms in the fake Louis XIII-windowed attics, with no wash-basins and no lights, and no locks on the doors, so that the Old or the Young—or both—Master could get in:

toutes les antiques saletés empilées les unes sur les autres, se coudoyant, se bousculant, s'éborgnant, les arceaux, les clochetons, les gargouilles, les tours, les tourelles, les poutres, les poutrelles, les balcons, les clochers, les minarets, les dômes, les créneaux et les machicoulis, les reconstitutions, les reproductions, les abominations, les copies, la gélatine, le nougat et le fromage mou, les palais, les lupanars, les églises, les tavernes, et les goêles présentent . . . toute l'horreur de leur écoeurante et niaise banalité.

The effectiveness of Darien as a polemical writer owes as much to his talent as an observer as to the acidity of a style hewn out of exasperation. Darien knows what he hates, he has lived with his *bourgeois*, and, with him, we can hear them talking, giving forth the sort of moralizing *lapalissades* that one associates with *messieurs décorés*, *pères de famille*, and *inspecteurs d'académie*, as if every affluent parent, every citizen of girth and means had adopted, as his form of everyday communication, the rumbling periods of a Speech Day discourse. What better secret of success, what more infallible recipe for the French middle classes in the 1880s, than the advice given to Randal by his father: 'Avec de l'économie et en faisant son droit, on peut aujourd'hui arriver à tout.' We can hear too his uncle, when he clinches an argument: 'Le Code est formel.' Or when he observes, ponderously: 'La caserne est une bonne école. Le service militaire obligatoire a beaucoup fait pour accroître les rapports des hommes entre eux.' It is the sort of thing that Topaze would have written on the walls of his schoolrooms, and of a kind with phrases like *L'Instruction fait la Grandeur des Nations* that one may still read on the outside of the municipal buildings of Saint-Denis.

Public morality is given private illustration; Randal is rewarded by his mother for having shut the front door in the face of an aged tramp, after telling him: 'Allez donc travailler, fainéant, vous ferez mieux'—an episode which elicits from the good lady the comment: 'C'est très bien, mon enfant. Le travail est le seul remède à la misère et empêche bien des mauvaises actions.' It was the least one could expect of those airless rooms, cluttered with marble-topped tables, marble wall brackets, tasselled curtains, and Fichet Safes, rooms that smelt of avidity, a hopeless world in which children were encouraged to imitate the horrible little sneaks and prigs of the Comtesse de Ségur's dreadful tales and in which servants were dismissed without a reference. Darien returns to it constantly, with a sort of loving repulsion. One of his parents' friends has gone bankrupt. Randal is no longer to play with his children, his father refuses to speak to the man, and, at meals, the little boy picks up bits of their conversation: 'Des détournements considérables'—

'une cocotte'—'la ruine et le déshonneur'—'sinon plus'—'des habitudes de taverne et de bouge sans nom, des fréquentations abjectes'—the bare bones of a *bourgeois* Rake's Progress, as banal and as insipid as a hero of Paul Bourget. But there is better to come. The uncle wishes to inquire about a burglary, committed in a neighbouring house (that of his daughter's fiancé—of course the engagement has to be called off): 'J'ai été à la Préfecture, où je connais quelqu'un, c'est toujours utile d'avoir des relations dans cette maison-là.' The police tell him all he wants to know. And he displays the anti-feminism characteristic of his class, country, religion (for he was nominally a Catholic), and period; Randal asks him what his daughter thinks about the broken engagement, he replies: 'Elle n'a rien à penser. Je suis son père, je pense pour elle.'

Only at one stage removed from these middle-class *dictons* is the advice given by Paternoster, a *notaire* struck off the list for fraud and established in London as an international fence, when he tells the two professional burglars, referring to the French middle class: 'Il leur faut des fonds d'Etat. . . . Voilà pourquoi je me tue à vous dire de faire, autant que possible, vos coups en France! Voilà un bon pays! La Rente ou les Chemins de Fer. Excellent pays pour les voleurs! La peur y a discipliné les capitaux.' When they return to London with their haul, which includes a considerable amount of stock, he puts aside the more speculative Belgian 'industrials'. 'Je garde la Rente, les chemins de fer et le Suez'—the Holy Trinity of the provincial middle class. The final judgement comes from the philosophical Abbé Lamargelle: 'La France n'est ni religieuse, ni athée, ni révolutionnaire, ni militaire, ni même bourgeoise. Elle est en actions.' Already at the time of writing, many of these were in Russian bonds. If only for this glossary, this *Petit Simonin* of of the Third Republic, Darien has richly earned his exhumation by the wise saws and sayings of the middle class of the lush years the publisher Pauvert. And it is suitable that Jean-François Revel, the author of *En France*, should have chosen to write the preface to the 1965 edition of *La Belle France*. The two books have much in common, though Darien's is the better, the more forceful, and the more virulent.

But Darien has something that is totally lacking in other tigers of letters: a sense of humour that is always biting and, on occasions, even light-hearted. The descriptions of the burglaries are quite hilarious, partly because the situation itself is very funny—the breaking-in, the splintering crack of wood, the niceties of *vol avec effraction*, a safe opened *à la césarienne*, that is from its side, the discovery and forcing of hidden drawers in a genuine Louis XVI desk, the joyful removal of the miser's pile, robbery followed by a meal in the dining-room, with the dirty plates and glasses left on the table ('je fais un sale métier', observes Randal, of one such meal, at the expense of a provincial former colleague of Paternoster, absent on a pilgrimage to Lourdes, 'mais au moins je le fais sale- ment'). There is a heady joy in breaking into an empty house, in taking one's time to do the thing properly, room by room, smelling out the money and *Rentes*—Darien claims that the experienced professional can *smell* absence, as well as presence, in a room, can tell how long it is since the owners have left—tearing into the calculating, suspicious, ineffectually preserved intimacy of some mean tyrant. It is exactly the sort of situation that makes the work of that other pillager—the research historian—so enjoyable.

All this is described in the sharp language of the profession. Thus, of a Jewish confidence-trickster—Darien reserves his less exalted criminal roles for Jews—who will not put his hand to burg- lary, Roger remarks: 'C'est dommage qu'il ne veuille pas travailler à la dure.' The same specialist, while operating in the study of a Brussels businessman, on a tiny safe, expresses his disgust at having to work on such shoddy material: 'c'est attristant de s'attaquer à une boîte belge aussi ridicule quand on a travaillé dans les Fichet', a superb piece of French professional chauvinism and an example of Darien's eagerness to ridicule the inhabitants of the neighbouring kingdom. In the course of a burglary carried out in an hotel, on the spur of the moment, more or less for the love of the thing, Canonnier tells Randal: 'va dans la chambre et mets le secrétaire à la question'. It is, of course, as easy to be funny about burglaries as about funerals (Merlin in *Bas les coeurs!* is asked what one of these was like; he replies: 'Un enterrement comme les autres: beaucoup moins de morts que de vivants'); but Darien can, at times, be funny about his own wretched poverty; thus, at the beginning of *Biribi*, when his step-mother is, as always, leaving the sentence unfinished, at the evocation of the word 'Protestants' ('les Protestants, tu sais, ils ne sont pas comme nous . . .'—as much as to imply that Protestants are not really French), he observes with sour humour: 'Je suis protestant en effet, mais je crois que, pour le moment, ce sont mes vêtements qui protestent.' This is a change from the litany of bitterness in Vallès or in Bloy and even from Darien's usual grinding vocabulary. Such oases are, it is true, rather rare in the stony desert of his indignation. The desolate landscape of Southern Tunisia seems too often to have invaded his prose, as well it might, after five years spent in the French equivalent of a glasshouse (with the Corsicans in the role of the Liverpool Irish).

Fortunately he is not constantly blinded by indignation. Though he generally sees contemporary France through a red haze of rage, his vision is none the less acute and many of his remarks about middle-class society are penetratingly apt; Darien is an historian's novelist. Nothing could be more effectively illustrative of the spy mania of 1870 than the incident involving a blind man with blue glasses and a white stick, beaten up as he gets off the train at Versailles. The whole of *Bas les coeurs!* is excellent reportage, on the theme of the effects of war, defeat, foreign occupation, and civil war on a closed, self-satisfied, selfish, and cringingly cowardly middle-class provincial society. Where better to depict the French *bourgeoisie* at its worst than in the Versailles of M. Thiers? It is very well done indeed—all the better for a sort of contained rage, Darien for once succeeding in disciplining his indignation and in keeping it from boiling over all over the text. First of all, the cadre: Versailles, the dead, the utterly dead, capital, its long sad avenues reflecting, at their distant ends, a hopeless sunset, silent, shuttered houses, miserable, spiritless, clipped, drilled trees. The small boy realizes something extraordinary has happened when he sees people out in the street at ten at night; it is the outbreak of war. The war begins in an atmosphere of insane optimism, with all the amateur strategists of the Café de Commerce variety—the *professeur de lycée*, the coal merchant, the grocer—winning the war over the green baize cloth. But the child notices that the soldiers—poor peasants from the neighbouring Beauce or Breton-speaking farm-hands—as they march to the station, are drunk and surly and in no hurry to get there; every now and then they break rank and sit down on the pavements. There are flowers in their rifles, but also bottles sticking out of their haversacks. A young officer, having tripped on an apple that has rolled from a market stall, knocks out the old peasant responsible for the store ('Je m'excuse, mon officier, je m'excuse'), with his silver-topped cane; the silver is all bloody.

The Empire disappears discreetly, surreptitiously; the Republic is proclaimed, from the balcony of the Préfecture de Seine-et-Oise, by the perennial professional anticlerical *arriviste*, Vilain. The Prussian officers are very correct; they pay on the dot and are much appreciated by the shop-keepers, particularly by the grocer-strategist, as well as by the boy's father, who makes a handsome profit from supplying the Prussian artillery with wooden supports for their cannon, engaged in the bombardment of Paris. A prosti-tute—'une horizontale de basse classe'—has her hair cut off because she is seen coming out of one of the Prussian barracks, in the Écuries; but an upper-class lady ends up in bed with her wounded Prussian officer—it is all part of her nursing duties and the war effort. There are—as in all his books—Jewish profiteers. In this case they are so-called refugees from Alsace who do a brisk trade in furniture stolen from the ruined houses of Saint-Cloud; the boy is ticked off by his father for calling them Jews; 'on les appelle des Israëlites' (his father shares the profits, as they use his workshops as a depot). There are references to the activities of *francs-tireurs*, and the boy's grandfather, the acting mayor of a neighbouring village—he succeeds in getting the mayor deported to Germany—denounces one of them to the Prussians, who have him shot. Hos-tages are held in the village church; there is a Prussian officer seated at the organ, playing waltzes. The population turns out to cheer M. Thiers on the avenue de la Reine, every time the little man drives by. When the *communard* prisoners are brought in, the Ver-saillais again line the avenue; the women hit out at the *communardes* with their umbrellas. The little boy is impressed by the serenity and the dignified bearing of these women, some of whom are dressed in silks, others like working women. It is a horrible story about horrible people; Darien tells it with gusto.

Le Voleur is good social history. The burglars obtain their infor-mation either from an ex-*notaire* (a profession in which there are often more 'ex' than acting) who maintains a regular correspondence with his former colleagues about their clients' movements, or from family priests. Ida, the fashionable abortionist, has a solid upper-class clientele in Paris ('j'ai un si joli salon; on se croirait chez un dentiste américain'); it is a safe profession—'il n'y a guère à craindre que les dénonciations des médecins'—highly profitable. She de-scribes the French urban middle class of the 1890s as 'la bourgeoisie avorteuse'; on the other hand, working-class girls are not given the same opportunities; for one thing, in a country obsessed with the problem of manpower, they risk being denounced to the police as soon as they are visibly pregnant; but they are also generally unwilling to get rid of their unborn children. Here Darien is on one of his favourite themes, for, in one sense at least, he is a true revolutionary, in that his politics do not stop at the kitchen sink. His greatest originality, as a social novelist, is to have emphasized the wretched condition of women—of all classes (indeed, upper-class women are the least free of all)—in nineteenth-century France. This he attributes to the joint influence of Catholicism and the *Code*. Even the so-called honour of a deceived husband is worth more than the life of an adulteress; the ridiculous Mouratet, having been tipped off, shoots his wife and her lover dead, in their box at a masked ball; the bodies are hustled out under a tarpaulin by scene-shifters; the *commissaire* is used to this kind of situation: 'Ah, Monsieur, les cocus assassins!' he explains to Randal; they are part of his daily bread.

With the exception of *Biribi*, in which there are no women at all, the novels teem with tyrannized daughters and wives, while Darien's favourite candidate for the Avenger—for the Criminal-Hero who will eventually turn the tables on *bourgeois* society—is the emancipated female, Ida, the abortionist, Margot, the ex-servant and enormously successful *cocotte*, Hélène, Canonnier's daughter. His concern for the subjection of women in Catholic countries, while adding fuel to his Protestant convictions and to his Anglophilia, made him an excellent observer of the marriage policies of the French middle class.

Darien puts his finger, too, on one of the principal causes of the attachment of the French *bourgeoisie* to the Army: 'la bourgeoisie trouve . . . dans le corps des officiers, le pivot solide, sinon gratuit, autour duquel ses filles, pénétrées de grandeur, peuvent faire tourner leurs ambitions'. On the subject of prostitution, he distinguishes between *la cocotte*—the natural ally of burglars, as she tips them off and as she preys on middle-class society, the ruin of which she will eventually bring about—and the ordinary prostitute, the *mauvais lieu* being represented for what it was in the Third Republic—a stronghold of reaction, militarism, clericalism, and chauvinism. Like the daughters of the less affluent middle class, whose best hope would be to catch a *polytechnicien*, or at least a *cyrard*—even a *lieutenant de gendarmerie* or a *capitaine de l'Intendance* would do at a pinch—Madame Irma and her kind could not very well have got along without an institution that provided her with her most numerous, most regular, and least demanding clientele.

In France there was an ancient tie-up between military service and the brothel; the *bleus*,* as soon as they had drawn their pay and pinned on their favours, head *en masse* for the *gros numéro*; Courteline's heroes have nowhere else to go in the evenings of Bar-le-Duc; and, in the 1900s, *revanchard* patriotism burns nowhere more fiercely. Both in race and garb, the brothel population was admirably representative of the French Empire as a whole— Antillaises, Tonkinoises, Sénégalaises, Gabonaises, Malgaches, Tahitiennes, Libanaises, Berbères being much in demand, among both military and civilian connoisseurs (it made colonialism worth while and also provided an object lesson in France's lack of racialism), in their various stages of national undress. But a sure favourite was the girl—and it did not matter whether she was a Bretonne or from Pézenas—who, as her only article of clothing, wore the big, black Alsatian bow in her hair.[1] If officers and soldiers, despite the *mise-en-carte*, every now and then caught the pox, the prostitute caught patriotism. It was a reasonable enough exchange.

Darien also saw in the brothel the secret meeting ground between anticlericalism and the Church (a favourite theme, in view of the fact that a number of the establishments were to be found virtually in cathedral closes); the brothel was a guarantee of *bourgeois* morality, preserving the economically valuable virginity of daughters. He was sometimes a poor prophet, for he believed that the *bourgeois* Republic would collapse, that the France of *la belle France* would disappear, once Frenchwomen obtained the rights that he assumed they had possessed in the eighteenth century, and that the signal for the longed-for social revolution would be a vast female uprising against a society built for the satisfaction of masculine

[1] During the period 1944–5, when sections of the B.L.A. were stationed in the Lille–Roubaix–Tourcoing area, soldiers who contracted venereal diseases were asked to describe, for the benefit of the R.A.M.C. records, the physical appearance and clothing of the women—in this part of the world generally *serveuses montantes*, that is girls who worked behind the bar, but who would, for an inducement, work upstairs as well—they had slept with. One of the commonest replies was: 'She had no clothing, but was wearing a *croix de lorraine* round her neck.'

selfishness, greed, lust and vanity. Like so many of the rebels of his time, he was obsessed by the example of the Commune; his revolution too was to be led by a Louise Michel or a Sévérine. He could not predict a *bourgeois* Republic *without* brothels and *with* women voters, nor a working-class régime that would retain the double standard. He was as wrong about women as he was about the revolutionary potentialities of a war that he ardently hoped for; but at least, unlike the bearded brethren, the doctors of Marx, the theorists of Revolution, who invoked *les grands principes* and beat their wives or lived off their *compagnes*, Darien carried his protest into his own private life.

Having experienced the colonial army at close quarters, and from the worst possible end, Darien had little hope of the future military prospects of his country, delivered over to the inept leadership of colonial generals. He was convinced that France would lose the coming war, and that out of defeat would result revolution, followed by a great wave of popular patriotism. Darien was not an anti-militarist, he denounced the French Army because he thought it was rotten, inefficient, poorly led, and corrupted through and through.

Darien had plenty of occasions to observe, at close quarters, the full horrors of London poverty in the 1890s. London was the base from which, for a number of years, Randal operated as an international house-breaker. His market was the Common one—plus Switzerland—but, like those who oppose it today, he was wise enough never to involve England in his European transactions, other than as a clearing house. He had a hearty respect for the English criminal law and knew enough about the Victorian prison system— which he considered the most brutal in Europe—not to be tempted to experience it at first hand. It was not only that; England had been good to him, had left him alone, had allowed him the comfortable detachment and anonymity that constitute the particular enjoyment of being a foreigner with means. Here he was in a place where there appeared to be no *mouchards*. There were Jews, of course; but no Corsicans and few Catholics. He clearly lived very comfortably, in Soho and in St John's Wood, well looked after by Annie, his 50-year-old housekeeper, who had been dismissed without out a reference by a clergyman and who eked out a wretched existence cutting out the photographs of celebrated actresses and sticking them to the bodies of swans or other graceful beasts. He received visits from an international menagerie of *affranchies*—Irish girls, Russian ladies, Ida, *broussailles*, Scottish red-heads (he was himself sandy and prided himself, when travelling in France, on being taken for an Englishman). He even gets place-names right. He clearly knew a lot about the London underworld, was fascinated by the city, watched with secret admiration the huge army of crime, and believed, much as Brecht must have done, that one day the London 'mob' would make the *septembriseurs* look like lambs.

It is a very cosmopolitan London—no longer recognizable to us —made up of anarchist refugees, international crooks, cross-Channel *cocottes*, music-hall artists, German artisans, Jewish tailors and small businessmen, Central European chess-players—a London in which Europe began at Fenchurch Street, Blackfriars, Cannon Street, and Charing Cross, which it was possible to reach, three times a day and once a night, without a passport, from both Brussels and Paris and in which it was possible to change in any bank (stolen) French, Belgian, and Swiss silver francs.

Not that, when all is said and done, Darien was really anti-French, despite the bitterness of his polemics and the grimacing, denunciatory stream of his prose. The enemies at home are always the worst and it takes a Frenchman to write with effective virulence about France. Yet, in the end, excessive indignation and ceaseless denigration can be dangerous paths to follow; there is the example of Rochefort, that of Bloy, that of Céline. Ultimately, Darien was an unsatisfied patriot. His France was a concept too perfect to survive in the political jungle of the late nineteenth century; in much of his indignation there is a strong element of personal disenchantment.

Darien hated and despised weakness. The result is that, politically, he is both inept and rather sinister. His politics were those of hate. What he hated most was *bourgeois* parliamentarianism. The deputies are referred to as 'les coquins mis en carte par le suffrage universel'; the villain of *Le Voleur* is Courbassol, the Minister; the parliamentary system is 'la gargouille parlementaire', 'la galette populaire', 'une dégoûtante farce'. The socialists are no better; one is described as 'un raté fielleux qui laisse apercevoir, entre ses dents jaunes, une âme à la Fouquier-Tinville'; all are 'pisse-froids de la casuistique révolutionnaire, qui préconisent l'enrégimentation'. He cannot forgive socialism the crime of internationalism; a nationalist socialism, could it exist, would be another matter, 'car tout n'est pas mauvais, mes chers frères, dans l'idée nationaliste'. He sips anarchism, but comes away disappointed and more embittered than ever; his anarchists too are vegetarians, milk-drinkers, theorists; they have no blood in their veins. One of them has a shrill voice, none of them is virile. His socialists are misshapen, have bad breath and thick glasses. The Third Republic has given France over to Jews and foreigners; at a reception at Mouratet's Randal notices a Belgian poet, a Croat pianist, half a Russian, a shoal of Jews, Italians. The French themselves have become 'southernized'; they are dark, deformed and ugly; they have lost all national physiognomy, such as they had still possessed in the eighteenth century, when they were blond and healthy; there is no uglier race in Europe.

While Darien ridicules his compatriots for their attachment to historical myths and their preoccupation with historical charades— when it is not the Pucelle or Bayard, then it is the sashed *représentant en mission* or Bonaparte—he feeds on a most extraordinary hotch-potch of historical nonsense, derived primarily from Henry George and partly from his own readings of Protestant history. He makes the extraordinary assertion that the French Revolution was the work of Catholic internationalism, concerned permanently to weaken France and make it subservient to Rome. His historical thinking is similar to that of the Comte d'Antraigues or the Comte de Paris: the Revolution destroyed the ancient French liberties, communalism and provincialism, imposed centralization, and spoliated the ancient nobility, for the benefit of an unworthy, grasping, and cowardly middle class. Only Turgot and the *physiocrates* had had the right idea, but they came too late; the decline of France had begun with the Wars of Religion and had been completed by the Edict of Nantes. Only Protestantism could have produced an independent, strong, and healthy nationalism. The absurd French railway network, radiating out from Paris, was constructed in order to facilitate the work of the police, as it forced every traveller through Paris, the termini of which were easy to watch. He rants against Christianity as the religion of the weak and the resigned.

And like so many revolutionaries of his period, he looks forward eagerly to the advent of war, equating war and revolution, as

Guizot and his neo-Jacobin opponents had done fifty years earlier.

He was convinced that *bourgeois* France would so mismanage military operations that the people would turn their arms on their officers—the sort of fantasy one would expect from the ex-soldier of *Biribi*—massacre them, overthrow the *bourgeois* parliamentary state, form a people's army, and fight a revolutionary war of liberation against the *bourgeoise* of other countries. Who then here was the neo-Jacobin? Yet he was aware of the strength of the repressive machinery of the *bourgeois* republic; he is indeed obsessed by the memory of the June Days and of the Commune; after the Red Terror and the White Terror, he writes, there will come the Tricolor Terror, when the French middle class will make the workers' blood run once more in the streets of Paris. Darien reckoned without Poincaré and Clemenceau; and he should have known better than to have claimed that armies offered the best conditions for revolutionary ferment and activism. It is the sort of nonsense that Queslier talked. Yet, in Darien's five years in Tunisia, there had been only two or three feeble revolts, easily dealt with. He reckoned too without the nationalism of the French working class, as patriotic, when it came to the day, as himself. A similar surfeit of indignation had *boulangisme*; Darien denounced the anti-semitism and produced anti-protestantism displayed by the *anti-dreyfusards*, yet so much of what he wrote could have been taken up and used by Drumont. The politics of indignation may lead in most unexpected directions.

19 Communism and the French Intellectuals[1]

This is an intellectual's book about intellectuals. Caute is an historian of concepts and he finds it difficult to accept that political leaders may at times act in response to motivations that are not entirely the result of intellectual choice. In reading his account of the Parti Communiste Français in its relations with a narrow group of French intellectuals, and of chosen intellectuals with the Party, one is at times reminded of such historians as Talmon and Franco Venturi. Just as Talmon would insist that Robespierre, in his every act—and there were some thousands of them—as a member of a wartime emergency coalition, was consciously translating into the field of political realizations the general principles of the *contrat social*, so the present author establishes, for our understanding of the day-to-day policies of a large parliamentary party, five 'principles of utility' to which he refers, with repetitious insistence, throughout his book. These are defined on page 35, though Caute constantly refuses to make them all-embracing: 'there is no suggestion', he comments, 'that the Party has ever formulated its policies in this way, or acted *consciously* on the basis of such a scheme . . .'. The principles do, in fact, come out of Caute's head, and not from any central brain-machine situated in the rue de Châteaudun.

Yet, despite this initial qualification, the author clings with unrelenting rigour to this conceptual framework throughout the remaining 380 pages of his book. The resulting style is often Germanic in its humourless ponderousness; there are constant echoes of Strangelove, more rarely of Alice. Thus, on p. 79, there are references to 'eulogies of the Soviet Union (fourth principle of utility)' taking precedence over 'agitation through front organizations and professional bodies (third principle)', and, on p. 115, we are told: 'Indeed, this, the third principle of utility, deserves to be named the Vaillant-Couturier principle, in honour of its greatest

[1] Review of David Caute, *Communism and the French Intellectuals 1914–60* (London, 1964).

256

exponent'. On p. 132, Communist intellectuals who, 'acting on the fourth principle of utility, rose to combat Koestler, put up a poor performance...' We hear of the first principle on p. 149, of the third on p. 150, of the fourth on p. 151; on p. 157, there is a bumper sentence with references to fourth, second, and fifth. On p. 169, we are back to the fourth principle and, on p. 189, to the first; on p. 220, the first and second are in harmony, on p. 233, the third principle is in difficulties. On p. 252, the second and fourth combine, but on p. 267, they are clashing, as they are once more on p. 311. On p. 317, there is 'a bold affirmation of the ultimate supremacy of the fourth principle of utility', while on p. 331, we learn that 'the fourth principle of utility mutilated the second and the fifth'. On p. 334, the fifth is abandoned to the fourth, and on the next page we have the summing up of a chapter: 'Put in other words, the second, and most important, principle of utility was violated by the fourth in the supposed interests of the fifth'. Alice's letter to the fish then recedes, and, on p. 345, we are back to the first principle. By this time, the conscientious reader, in his attempts to follow the signposts, will have thumbed page 35 almost to pulp; he will also have decided that the Party leaders, whether they were rogues or fools, were certainly the most ponderous bores, and that there is a certain affinity between them and Caute. One could only wish that the author had paid more attention to his own misgivings over his method, when he observes, with uncharacteristic reserve: 'even so, too Machiavellian an explanation might be misleading'. This would certainly be the most telling epitaph on a book the approach of which is consistently schematic and at most times anti-human.

This too is perhaps the most serious weakness in an historian who avowedly sets out to describe—and to explain—why various individuals become politically committed, when confronted, often brutally, with specific political situations. Caute is the first to admit that on the road to *engagement*, theoretical Marxism has played only a minimal part, in France at least. French communist and progressive intellectuals have seldom been very strong on their doctrine—perhaps this is why they are such easy people to communicate with—and have indeed often been criticized by dialecticians of a more rigorous discipline. Though Caute makes little enough allowance for human frailties such as pride or envy, or even for enthusiasm and generosity, he is generally prepared to admit that the *choc électrique* that has driven each successive generation of French intellectuals into the fold of cell and *colloque* has nearly always been the result of a political event and of the personal awareness that it aroused: the horror of the 1914–18 War, the massacres in Morocco following the Rif, the awareness of the realities of French colonialism in Algeria or the Antilles, the Spanish Civil War, the activities of the fascist leagues, the Front Populaire, the experience of the dangers and the hopes of the Resistance period, gratitude to the Red Army for having saved France from Hitlerism, German rearmament, the subservience of successive Fourth Republic Governments to their American masters, the introduction into France of American standards and fashions, the formation of NATO, the presence in France of former Nazi generals. Indeed, what emerges most clearly from this rather bodiless Debrett of intellectuals is that those who were most concerned with theoretical perfection and who argued the most fiercely about the revealed purity of doctrine were the future schismatics— those who, later, making a virtue of their doctrinal orthodoxy, became the most systematic and passionate anti-communists (their insistence on the gospel sometimes taking them deep into the various aberrations of French fascism). Yet the author is often prepared to welcome, if not with bouquet and red carpet, at least with the adjective 'distinguished', those who, for one reason or another, have left the Party or who have moved away, with the maximum of publicity, from its various Front organizations.

His insensitiveness to the human incentives to commitment spring from a vision that almost totally excludes all phenomena not directly connected with the highly particular world of cell and C.N.E. It is rather as if one were to write a history of the French Revolution without ever mentioning the fact—the ever-present and dangerous fact—of Counter-Revolution. At times one has the impression, when reading Caute, that anti-fascism was something that the Party manipulators invented in order to bamboozle unwary intellectuals into commitment and into enrolment in a Front organization; he implies as much when he insists on the organizing abilities of Willi Münzenberg. It is the same later when he deals with political and intellectual anti-Americanism. Anti-fascism grew out of a real and visible threat; anti-Americanism, as well as tapping the hidden depths of anti-Anglo-Saxon prejudice in the dark corners of the French *petit bourgeois*, arose from the increasing conviction that the United States were preparing to embark Europe in a war of aggression against the Soviet Union. Neither sentiment was the exclusive invention of the P.C.F. But, if one is to omit the *camelots du roi* and the *jeunesses patriotes*, and if one does not constantly have in mind Raymond Cartier, *Paris-Match*, and America's tame Frenchmen (there are not many intellectuals among them, it is true), it is impossible to understand the strength of what might so often be described as a 'protest vote', which has been one of the principal sources of strength of the P.C.F., particularly among the teaching profession, since the Liberation. This is one danger that arises from too exclusive a concern with the love-hate relationship between Party and intellectuals. Both were subjected to pressures from without.

A more serious limitation is Caute's lack of experience of French life. The author was born in 1936, so he has never experienced the Front Populaire and the ambiance of intellectual and moral civil war that reigned from the mid-thirties to the War; he seems unaware of the wider emotions of commitment. In this austere and rather élitist account of intellectual attitudes there is little place for fraternity. The *lendemains qui chantent* merely give out a hollow sound, the revolutionary poetry of Aragon and Éluard (there is no mention of Blaise Cendrars, perhaps because he was Swiss) are made to appear faintly ridiculous—perhaps this is deliberate, as many of them are presented very oddly in English translation ('Bring down the cops, comrades, bring down the cops . . .')— Caute is evidently incapable of appreciating the depth of hatred that a Frenchman may feel for the police,[1] while Party attitudes— always or nearly always—appear as coldly calculated and uniquely inspired by one of the famous Principles of Utility, as immutable as the *code civil*. The author has not walked arm-in-arm with fraternity, in the great *14 juillets* of the mid- and late thirties and mid-forties; and, having read of the period from the seclusion of American or English libraries, he has no awareness of the *Grande Espérance* or the Front Populaire. This was when Georges Lefebvre was lecturing to spell-bound audiences on *Quatre-vingt-neuf* and when the Revolution was 150 years old. The France of the mid-thirties seemed a very young country, with immense possibilities, both the student and the wage-earner were beginning to discover the Mediterranean, paid holidays were spreading the vacation habit widely down the social scale, to reach the saule-grass wildernesses of H.L.M. and to

[1] This was written in 1964.

A SECOND IDENTITY

join the Porte des Lilas to the sea. Perhaps the most typical memorial of this period was Léo Lagrange's Ministère des Sports et des Loisirs.

The author has little conception of the strength of loyalty to a generation, to the friends of the Cité Universitaire, to *la bande*, to the warmth of personal feeling that so often resides in the key-word: *les copains*. This is not merely a code word by which members of a secret society may recognize one another, it also designates a reality: that of common experience, often of common provincial origin—for so many young men and young women, from the Centre and from the Midi, were to discover in the Party a shelter from the selfish loneliness of Paris and the merits of a Strangers' Club—and of loyalty to friends and to shared enthusiasms. Party members—and intellectuals perhaps more than any others, for they tend to be more romantic—are far more likely to be influenced by group loyalties than by theoretical considerations.

For the P.C.F., like the French Reformed Church, has been described as *la famille*; and this is particularly apt when applied to intellectuals who, in so many cases, have come to the Party, *en rupture de ban*, as a reaction against an Action Française father, or out of a sense of guilt derived from a wealthy background (Aragon is the son of a Third Republic Prefect of Police). For the intellectual, who does not enjoy the easy solidarity of the factory and the neighbourliness of the H.L.M. at the Porte de Montreuil, the Party can become *la famille* in every sense; and to be excluded from it is indeed to be driven into a wilderness. The P.C.F. is easier to join than to leave; and most of those who joined it in the thirties at least have stayed. The generation that followed, and that entered the Party at the first flush of the revolutionary dawn of Liberation France, proved more fickle, more given to gestures of revolt. Many of those who have stayed, have done so *faute de mieux*. Undoubtedly, the single most important factor in intellectual commitment to the Party is patriotism, a fierce and historically conscious neo-Jacobinism that defends French values against the incursions of *franglais*. For those who are concerned to preserve the political and cultural independence of their country the French alternatives are neither particularly attractive nor, above all, in the least effective. Others stay, because they are encased in a nexus of personal relationships. The Party is not so much a doctrine as a way of life, with, at all seasons, its collective festivals that recur with the same regularity as the great religious feast-days: *le Mur*, the assassination of Jaurès, the birthday of Thorez, the *fête de l'Huma*, 14 July (which, in recent years, the Party has been almost alone in celebrating), and so on. It would be interesting to inquire how many Party marriages have originated at the Mur des Fédérés. No wonder it is difficult to leave all this behind. But the author is necessarily more concerned with disenchantment than with fidelity, with noise than with silence, with those who leave, with the maximum of clatter: letters to *Combat*, articles in *Preuves*, joining the P.S.U., press conferences organized by *L'Express*, than with those who stay inside. And there is no place in his chronicle either for those who leave without a fuss —simply by failing to renew their subscription—and those—the most numerous group of all who, without ever actually entering the Party, regularly vote communist at each municipal or national election, in order to register their protest against subservience to America (under the Fourth Republic) or governmental neglect of French education (under the Fifth).

On the other hand, it is equally difficult to subscribe to the author's view that 'motives such as majority-conformism, physical fear, the desire for security or the prospect of immediate financial advancement . . . can largely be ruled out from the start'. Certainly, both during the Front Populaire and in the three or four years that followed Liberation, there would be a positive material inducement for both schoolteachers and, even more, for research workers, especially in scientific subjects, anthropology, and sociology, to join the Party. For some years, the Centre National de la Recherche Scientifique was largely dominated by Party adherents, who were able to make their influence felt through the *syndicat des chercheurs*; in this particular instance, the taking out of a Party card would be a form of social insurance, for it would enable the *chercheur* to enjoy the full support of an efficient and vociferous lobby in the event of his research grant not being renewed, for one reason or another (including those of incompetence or sloth). Even Gaullist educational authorities are extremely unwilling to lay themselves open to the charge of having victimized a teacher or research worker for his political affiliations. Some calculation of this kind, however vaguely formulated, may account for the undoubted attraction exercised by the Party over the intellectually second-rate in this field.

Party intellectuals have not often been discriminated against as far as University appointments are concerned. If there are, in fact, few enough Party members in this profession, this is due primarily to the poor quality of P.C.F. scholarship in so many fields, and to the active encouragement so often given by the Party to the second-rate, in a systematic effort to abase excellence and independence (the employment of the hatchet-man Poperen, now in the P.S.U., to execute Soboul, is a good example of this premium on mediocrity). If there are so few P.C.F. university professors, the Party largely has itself to blame, for having attempted to dragoon young *agré-gatifs* or even *agrégés* into political activities remote from their specialist interests. It is hardly surprising that so many of the post-war *agrégés* have left—bitterly frustrated—a Party that showed such little imagination for its utilization of their skills. The Party can, however, offer its intellectuals compensations, not only in terms of security, but those perhaps more persuasive, of pride and self-satisfaction. A not so very great geographer can be blown up into the dimensions of a *maître*, with an international reputation, with his books translated into ten or more languages. The P.C.F. meal ticket is, in this respect, a more attractive one than that offered by the cultural services of the American Embassy. As Caute so rightly reminds us, the French Party has at all times been much given to mutual admiration, often offering a positive en-couragement to artistic sterility and lack of imagination; it was human enough for André Stil to have seen himself as a worthy successor of Balzac, when so many Party organs had described him as such. One can recall at least one rock-bottom Party historian whose commitment began on the golden day when, on his arrival at the Warsaw Central Station, he was given the chance to inspect a company of soldiers lined up in his honour, to the accompaniment of the *Marseillaise* and the Dąbrowski March.

Nor should fear—even physical fear—be entirely excluded; for, while many joined the Party (or voted for it) during the second half of the forties, from the conviction (reasonable enough at the time) that the United States were preparing for war, there were others, less numerous, who took out their Party cards as a guarantee of personal—as well as professional—security. While the Prague coup of February 1948 undoubtedly shocked many intellectuals out of the Party, it equally panicked an unspecified number in. The Red Army seemed much nearer to Paris after that; and Party funds received large donations from unexpected sources.

These are only a few of the personal motivations of intellectual commitment. There are certainly others that must necessarily escape the historian, if they do not always escape the novelist or sociologist. Yet, if we are to have any understanding at all of the dilemma facing French intellectuals during the last thirty years, we have at least to make an effort to perceive them. Caute's major failure is that he does not do so. This lack of impressionism—and impressionism can only be effective when it is backed by a wealth of experience and observation—casts over the whole book a pall of gloom and lifelessness which is seldom relieved by the author's rather creaking attempts at humour. The author's solution is to become increasingly schematic, and this, at times, leads him into judgements that simple common sense would have preserved him from; he suggests, for instance, that the publication of Albert Soboul's thesis in 1958 bore some unspecified relationship to destalinization—the implication no doubt being that, if it had appeared in, say, 1952, the general argument would have been different, and no doubt less hostile to Robespierre. Caute is so obsessed with the interrelation of events in the Soviet Union, changes in the Party line, and the shifting attitudes of the P.C.F. towards French intellectuals, that he tends to interpret everything in terms of 'orders from Moscow', a thesis as crude as the old, old 'oeil de Moscou' of Tardieu's reactionary régime.

There are other similar cases of the author being caught out by his constant desire to relate the particular to the general and to fit his whole scheme of things into the narrow, arbitrary, and artificial frame of his beloved Principles of Utility. It is also, of course, easy enough to score off such consummate mental gymnasts as Aragon or Garaudy, but Caute takes such a positive, wearisome glee in this process, that, at times, one suspects that there is in his own approach to the subject a powerful element of personal disenchantment. He wants his intellectuals to be as Olympian as himself, in a sort of perpetual prize-giving, distributing here praise, there blame; and he fails to understand that, for a Sartre, and for many other partially committed intellectuals, their attitude would be conditioned primarily by their sense of priorities. At a period when the major threat to French political and cultural freedom came from the United States, it would have been rather ludicrous to insist that intellectuals should constantly balance their attacks on America with an equal quota of attacks on the Soviet Union. Because many would not indulge in this enjoyable, *New Statesman*-like game of moral superiority and intellectual self-righteousness it does not necessarily follow that they were being either hypocritical or silly, or that they were blind to certain aspects of Soviet life.

This is, on the whole, an impartial book, and also a tragic one, for the author is above all concerned for truth and intellectual freedom; yet so many of his judgements are loaded, and, like so many before him who have written about communism and communists, he cannot resist the temptation to play the game of *Tu en es un autre*. We are everlastingly being reminded of the mistakes, the crimes, the vacillations, the lies, the contradictions of Soviet policy. French intellectuals—not only the communists, but presumably the Cardinal Archbishop of Paris, pretty well every reputable writer in the country, nearly all the newspapers, with the exception of the *Populaire* and *L'Aurore*, and the whole of the immense crowd that assembled spontaneously, and in outrage, late at night, when the news of the execution of the Rosenbergs reached Paris, on the place de la Concorde, to shout their horror—the American Embassy had to be protected by tanks—are upbraided for having made such a fuss about ritual murder in New York, while not making an equal protest about some political injustice being committed at that moment on the other side. Yet this indignation was genuine and, in fact, owed little to Party propaganda; it sprung primarily from a deep disappointment in American democracy, on the part of people who had wanted to believe in the merits of American democracy. It was the *Americans*, after all, who electrocuted that unfortunate couple. Caute, with his eyes riveted on the rue Lepeletier and the carrefour de Châteaudun, tends at such times to lose his sense of proportion. The Party was not as omniscient, nor as omnipresent, nor nearly as powerful, as he would have us believe. Anti-Americanism among French intellectuals did not need any encouragement from Party propaganda, the Americans themselves supplied most of the material necessary for its growth. The fact that such statesmen as Édouard Herriot, such newspapers as *Le Monde*, vigorously and courageously fought German rearmament does not mean that they were influenced by *L'Humanité*; they were merely being good Frenchmen. So too on many occasions were the Party intellectuals themselves.

It is nevertheless a considerable and valuable achievement to have revived the Bronze Age of the pre-Thorez Party; the author is particularly good on the twenties; indeed, there seems to be some mysterious affinity between Party weakness and Caute strength. He writes the most perceptively of the Party in decline, especially when it reaches rock bottom in 1929. As its fortunes revive, the author's style becomes increasingly staccato, with more and more personages crowding into the narrative, while his tones take on a rather querulous note. He is thin on the Front Populaire, and rather dull on the Resistance; his post-Liberation chapters have the same massively scissors-and-paste effects as Alexander Werth's laborious compendium of press cuttings. The reader comes away with the impression that he has heard all this before—and, if he has lived in France, he *has*, for the author, in absence of documentary material, is obliged to lean heavily on the press, on reviews, and, subsidiarily, on novels. The result of such a heroic undertaking is not un-expected. After having submitted himself to some thousand leaders from *L'Huma*, to some hundreds of articles from *Les Lettres françaises*, and *La Pensée*, and having ploughed through, with self-flagellating energy, the thousand-plus pages of didactic sheer-good-ness and utter-badness of Aragon's demagogic *Les Communistes*, having read the novels of André Stil, something of the turgid, humourless, and totally devitalized style of French communist writing has seeped into the author himself. Caute certainly does not improve matters with his constant habit of giving the barest synopsis of a novel to illustrate some point in his argument, with the result that both *La Conspiration* and *Le Silence de la mer*, which really are good books, are reduced to a few lines of *X meets Y* formulas. His opening chapters and his conclusion, when he is able to escape from the mass of potted examples and quotes, read well and succeed in presenting an over-all picture. But the middle—and the middle goes on for most of the book—almost always tends to sag under the enormous weight of names, quotations, and brief incursions into Soviet history, with the result that the author, despite a great sound of whirring and flapping, often fails to get his crenellated narrative off the ground at all. There is both too much and too little in this massive apparatus; too much bald fact, too many reminders of what was happening at any given time in the Soviet Union—too little warmth and perception. It tells us, on the whole fairly, what happened in a limited, and therefore artificial field. But it is not the whole story; the subject should have been fitted into a wider frame, to allow the author to consider influences which come outside the narrow margin of the confessional in which intellectual and hierarch pursue their whispering dialogue, beyond the strident, theological arguments between Old Believers and New Schismatics. 'A plague on *all* your houses' is one's tempted reaction, after coming away from so many hours of *normalien* disputation. The trouble is, of course, that Caute clearly has had no sort of personal contact with the people he is writing about, with the result that we are presented with a ghostly gallery of bodiless, but extraordinarily loquacious, minds, in a never-ending celestial *colloque*, in the rarefied *huis clos* of a marathon debate; the people, the faces, the crowds in the street, the human appetites have been left out altogether; so that we come away, irritated by so much wrangling, and vaguely puzzled as to what it was all about.

20 Revolutionary Situations in France 1789–1968

French history has been dominated by the violence of Government, ever since the suppression of the great provincial revolts and peasant risings of the seventeenth century and that of the Camisard rising early in the eighteenth. Every succeeding French régime since that of Louis XIV has been based on force (some more than others). Every French Government, in a greater or lesser degree, has been a police régime. In every French Government in modern times the key Ministry has been that of the Interior (or that of Police). France, then, constitutes the ideal 'model' for the study of 'revolutionary situations', if only because there have been so many of them, because Government and opposition have so often confronted in crude terms of force, and because one 'revolutionary situation', however ultimately unsuccessful, will eventually create another. It becomes a tradition, a habit, an almost respectable reference back to an accepted past. It has often been said—and rightly—that Paris *sent le poudre*, with each Quarter harking back to its hour of heroism and barricade. And what failed on previous occasions may be so improved on as to succeed on another occasion. Failed revolutions, 'revolutionary situations' that have gone wrong, that have gone off half cock, and have been followed by systematic repression and political reaction do not, unfortunately, carry their own lessons. The failure is forgotten, the exhilaration of the first moment of revolt is commemorated and cherished, the martyrs of each failed revolution are remembered (and failed revolutions have the advantage over successful ones in putting out a larger crop of martyrs) and idealized, the cult of anniversaries stimulates vengeance and clothes violence—often empty violence—in the prestigious clothes of history. In 1948 it would have seemed that the unfortunate weight of history had been shed and that the people of France could at last escape from the fruitless and obscene cycle of violence and barricade, blind destruction and chance death. Twenty years later, a 'revolutionary situation' suddenly emerged, after ten years of Gaullist paternalism and political anaesthesia and exclusive concern for the material comforts of an unquestioning and vulgar pursuit of the new car, the TV, holidays in more and more exotic surroundings, early marriage, a family of manageable size, and the youthful climb up the technocratic ladder, as people, on the road to material success and managerial position, moved further and further out of the city, to live in pseudo-rural 'neighbourhood' estates: riding, swimming-pool, tennis, park, children's playground, patio, whisky, invitations to young married colleagues in the same income group, a limited infidelity (in the same income group), talk of the next car and the next holiday, rapid trips abroad for the firm (discreet infidelity, limited to the Common Market zone), masculinity and violence expressed in terms of horsepower and speed of driving. What strikes one most about the technocracy of the Fifth Republic is its excessive vulgarity: the vulgarity of the close-cropped young executive who, via *Réalités*, has put himself through an express course in fashionable historical interpretations, the vulgarity of his wife, who has mugged up *paella* and *cous-cous*. It is the France of *Les Stances à Sophie* and *Week-End*, of *franglais* and *manpowerisation*.

The May Revolution was an appeal back to a fraternal past, an attempt to recreate Paris neighbourliness in terms of the Quarter and with the memory of the barricades of August 1944 (and of the earlier ones). At first, in the almost universal hatred of the police, it drew on a sufficient consensus to create a revolutionary situation and to keep it going (in order to keep it going), though, even at the start, it had to have recourse to professional strong-arm groups and to semi-gangsters, who later proved an embarrassment. At first, too, before the full effects of the disruption of the public services could be felt, middle-class parents could feel proud of the heroic exploits of their children in the face of the C.R.S.; the consensus was sufficient too to bring in the younger workers, normally completely out of sympathy with student theorists of revolution (Mao, Fidel, and 'Che' are middle-class icons, teen-age pin-ups, it is doubtful if they were ever normally seen in car factories), to split the French working class generationally, and, out of a social climate that had for some time been dormant, produce a general strike of revolutionary implications. At the beginning, there was *accident*, aided by the activities of a tiny group of militants. But, at this stage, the revolutionary situation showed signs of careful *organization*.

Everyone had played according to the rules: Charles X had gone, Louis-Philippe had gone, Thiers had gone. De Gaulle—an historian if ever there was one—would go. But he didn't.

So much for the appeal to precedent. Then there was *theory*, mostly empty, nihilistic, and inappropriate, as if a revolution can ever be an end in itself, as if one can ever live on the barricades or in a theatre, as if comfort, sleep, meals, work, routine, leisure can eternally be sacrificed for talk and 'activism', as if Fidel spent his whole political career conquering Cuba, even if he continues to dress as he did. As if one can become a revolutionary overnight. without study, without preparation; as if a revolution can be created by setting a light to the petrol tank of a car, a belief shared by Cairo crowds. 'Impossibilism' became an end in itself, as it had so often before in the intransigent history of France; and there were once again allusions to the purifying effects of terrorism, to the dreadful beauty of Terror.

And so we have the 'Group of March' and the 'May Revolution' to add to a clutter of dates of days and months. The lesson of the failure has been lost, and only the near-success remembered. The 'activists' are training for the next round, the working class bought off, the Government forewarned. There will be no *accidental* revolutionary situation in the near future. But, in the events of the five weeks of May–June, there is much for the historian to ponder on; and he will need to rethink his more distant revolutionary history in terms of accident, organization (especially in the techniques of riot), militancy, and activism, of violence as an end in itself, of destruction and of failure both social and academic.

So much work has been concentrated, over the last 170 years, on the long-term causes of the first French Revolution that the time has perhaps come to redress the balance and to examine the more immediate, possibly accidental, physical causes of the advent of a revolutionary crisis. For any theory derived from a view of the 'inevitability' of revolutions is likely to be misleading as an historical interpretation, and, above all, dangerous as a 'model' for future action. There have been many attempts to 'anatomize Revolutions' and to establish a 'standard revolutionary situation' so all-embracing that it will fit any case, at any time, anywhere, so that the student-terrorist of the windy University of Essex can feel himself fully prepared once he has doffed the full kit of the *guerillero* in the

Cuban jungle. The search for an 'anatomy of revolution' is inherent in most Marxist thinking (though Marxist thought, in this respect, can generally be re-adjusted, with the benefit of hindsight and a re-examination of the Sacred Books, to make allowance for the failure of a potentially revolutionary situation to develop and to explain, in the light of the Iron Laws, why things went wrong when, on a prior analysis, they had appeared to be coming along nicely). And Marxist thought, in recent years, has been able to adjust itself to revolutionary situations that excluded the participation of the industrial working class, military defeat, and mutinies, while assuring that of the mass of the peasantry in a primarily rural, undeveloped economy.

At the other extreme, the search for a 'model', in an effort to predict the advent of a revolutionary situation, and thus to face up to it, either with suitable legislation and social palliatives, or with sufficient repressive force to prevent it from developing, has been the constant preoccupation of American academics in the employment of the C.I.A. With the various brands of Marxists, it is a matter of proving the superiority of one's own particular theology; and with American academics, to improve the techniques of prevention. Thus in the U.S. both history and sociology have been enlisted in the service of the police and of the forces of repression, in an attempt to categorize, to regiment 'revolutionary situations' into a limited series of 'models' allowing for any situation predictable at least in terms of the past.

Similar, though perhaps less blatant, considerations have governed much of the work on revolutionary history undertaken by American historians in the last twenty years. In his anxiety to establish the existence of a chain or 'cycle' of revolutionary crises for 1760 to 1800, Professor Palmer has undoubtedly been motivated by cold-war assumptions. He is, first of all, anxious to play down both the unique importance and the 'Frenchness' of the revolutionary crisis in France, to the advantage of the preceding American revolution, thus placing the French Revolution in a corset of 'inevitability' almost as narrow as that postulated as dogma by the various Marxist schools; events in Paris in June–July 1789 had to respond to hidden suboceanic currents, spreading out from Boston, and including, in a general revolutionary (or *quasi*-revolutionary) seismograph the revolutionary earthquake zone of Euro-America. The waves of his 'Atlantic Revolution' lap the frozen shores of

Trondhjem, the warmer shores of Smyrna, while this North-Atlantic Gulf Stream spreads even up the Vistula to Warsaw. So, we are told, whether they knew it or not, those who took up arms in July 1789 were acting as units in an historical chain-gang, bound and manacled to what had gone before: Jefferson and Franklin, Wilkes and Liberty, even poor mad Lord George Gordon, Geneva, Amsterdam, and Brabant—people and events of which they were no doubt unaware—it does not matter; bound and manacled too to what was to follow: Babeuf and Buonarroti, on their bicycle made for two, Amsterdamer, Swiss, Piedmontese, Hungarian, Austrian, Polish, and Greek Jacobins, and Jacobin clubs in the Balkans and the Near East, in Edinburgh, Leeds, Sheffield, Dublin, and Bergen. His cycle too is adjustable to failure; when a revolutionary situation does not develop, as it should have done according to the dictates of his cyclical machine, it is dismissed as a *quasi*-revolution. A more recent historian has described the year 1795 as that of England's *abortive* revolution. The Dean of the Faculty of Arts of Princeton makes, one suspects, the same sort of mistake as the young Régis Debray who believed that the Cuban island 'model' could be applied to the Bolivian uplands. Neither makes much allowance for the particularities of national conditions and for the elements of accident. And Professor Palmer, like Professor Talmon before him, makes enormous claims for theory in the inception of a revolutionary crisis. His approach is political and constitutional, much is made of the magic word 'democracy'; there is no room, in his elegant scheme of things, for thirst, hunger, drought, envy, social resentment, boredom, hatred, malice, distress, failure, poverty, hope, panic, and fear.

Others, Brinton, Arendt, Caute, Stone, have likewise tried each to establish his, or her, own machine of revolutionary situations, no doubt to their own satisfaction, but hardly to the enlightenment of previous crises, though of course so wide is their scope, so comprehensive and, above all, self-evident are most of their premises, that they may, somewhere or another, some time or another, score a bull's-eye in the future. Brinton makes much of militant minorities, and of single parties, bending the most disunited to his commanding will; Caute favours military defeat; Stone constructs six types of revolutionary situation, uses strange words for what historians call social resentment, makes the point that revolutions can only succeed by violence, and the further one that repression works best when it knows what it is looking for. And for those who are shocked by the expression 'revolutionary situation', he tells us that American scientists have proposed to substitute that of 'internal war'. And Stone follows Brinton in proposing as an iron law the progress from Constitutionalism to Girondism, from there to the Revolutionary Government, followed by Reaction, anarchy, near-civil war, and a military dictatorship. They are both following in the path of Alison, the nineteenth-century English historian of the Revolution who was so convinced that it took four years to progress from Constitutionalism to Terror that he went to Paris in 1834 in order to see his theory proved and witness the sudden emergence of the second year II; he did, it is true, get his Terror, but it was that of the Government, at the expense of the working class of Lyon. All this makes our history easier, and gives great satisfaction to the American reading public (possibly the most unimaginative, certainly the most ignorant in the world), convinced that it now has the key to any great and violent sedition, past, present, or future. So they can either rest in peace, or order their machine-gun-proof front doors and steel shutters. Yet 'revolutionary situations' have arisen in the absence of military defeat (1789 was one), without a wide consensus between the classes (in 1968, this followed the development of a revolutionary situation, it did not create it), and revolutionary situations have arisen even when the repressive authorities knew only too well whom they were looking for (as in 1789); on this occasion, they had lost the will to repress. And many of Dr. Caute's learned arguments boil down to this: revolutionary situations succeed when they have force on their side and when the revolutionaries have the will to use it (the *communards* had force on their side in March 1871, but they did not have the will to use it; and when they had the will—and the discipline—to use force, the Versaillais had had time to recover, and had assembled more force —a lesson that was not lost on Lenin), revolutionary situations fail when the Government retains the use of force. It is rather like saying that, in a battle, the stronger side will win. Or that, to keep the people down, you need a reliable police and a well-armed, well-paid, contented army. Thiers knew that.

Ernest Labrousse has proposed a rather more sophisticated formula for the genesis of a revolutionary situation. Such a situation, he observes, will arise when the vast majority of the inhabitants of a country are united in a total rejection of existing society and of the reigning order of things. It is a good formula, because it emphasizes the importance of purely negative polarizations in bringing together, briefly, people of widely different origin, status, temperament, and wealth. A revolutionary situation is, by its nature, brief; it must either develop into rapid success or collapse. In July '89, it was created in forty-eight hours, in March 1871 in twelve, in May '68 it dragged on for five weeks. In the initial stage, a single hate figure is the most effective of all sparks. In July '89 it was provided by Breteuil, in July 1830 by Guizot, in June 1848 by Cavaignac, in March 1871 by Thiers, in May '68 by the C.R.S. But even such a formula will only cover the actual genesis of a crisis. If a revolutionary situation is prolonged, other fears will arise to divide the ranks of the potential revolutionaries, to devour the moderates (this year, as the crisis dragged on, the Maoists and other young philosophers of neo-terrorism came more and more to the fore), and to frighten to the side of repression those who are alarmed by the spectacle of prolonged and senseless violence, disorder, and damage to property (July 1789 was so successful because it was accomplished, along with the total demolition of the Bastille, which belonged to the State, without the smashing of a single householder's windows).

Ultimately, every revolutionary situation is unique and unprecedented. If it were not so, few would ever ripen, for repressive authorities have always known their job better than historians, have indeed themselves always been the best historians at least of habitual and predictable sedition. Few historians love the police and the magistrates. But they would be foolish to underestimate them. Here then is the difference between a habitual sedition, a market riot, week-end rowdiness, feast-day drunkenness, the Sunday and the Monday brawl, the harvest stabbings, the wedding or baptism rural killings, anti-fiscal arson, the masked assault and robbery of Carnival, the coal-heavers', the tanners', the river-workers' punch up, the rag-and-bone man's predilection for brutal murder, the well-known dangers of a certain quarter, the anarchy of a laundry-boat, the criminality of a horse-market, the violence and sexuality of the Halles, the Christmas Day anti-Protestant or anti-Jewish man-hunt, the annual violence of anniversaries and thanksgivings, the Monday market riot, the rent-day suicide, year-in year-out infanticide, covered by the complicity of a whole community of the very poor, the known habits and location of abortion the ancient ties between theft, receiving, prostitution, the old-clothes' trade and informing, the post-dance fight, the wine-shop 1 a.m. eruption, the inter-village fracas, the dawn duel, the 4 a.m. suicide, the 2 a.m. wife-slaying, the Breton versus Picard clubbing, the knife-drawing of sailors, the sword-drawing of the Gardes Françaises in defence of their regimental honour, the drinking bouts between butcher's apprentices and stonemasons, the eating bouts between Upper and Lower Normans, the antipathy of Rouennais for Havrais, the lack of deference and boastfulness of barbers' apprentices—all matters that the eighteenth-century police of Paris, or of Lyon, or of Marseille, had at their finger-tips, had encountered again and again, would encounter again and again, could always face up to, generally with a minimum of force and ostentation—the difference between all these and a revolutionary situation which by definition, at least the first time it occurs (and there is seldom a second round of play, for the police are ready for the return match), is both unprecedented and mysterious.

For in any such situation, even 1789, and despite all the minute analysis of short-term and long-term causes, despite the *rudéfication* of the Crowd, of the rioter, there still remains a *zone d'ombre* of impenetrable mystery. All is not explained, even when all has apparently been explained, the Mob rehabilitated, its components dressed in the respectable clothes of their respective trades, provided with families, shops, and apprentices, an address, character references, trade, occupational or subsistence motivations (if it is not about bread, which, predictably, it usually is, then it must be about wine, or transport costs, or wages, or recruitment). There is always an explanation for the presence of anybody. The wine-merchants and publicans are up in arms over the *barrières*, the builders' labourers have been unemployed since the winter of 1788, the textile workers for two years, the totally unemployed and the seasonal labourers are threatened with imminent expulsion from the city, girls who cannot justify their means of existence and have no fixed address are about to be sent back to their villages (a supreme humiliation, as they have been writing home to impress their parents, sisters, and school-friends with the success they have met in the metropolis), the runaway children are being rounded up in ever larger numbers nightly, the soldiers are in arrear of pay and have their feet under the table in the homes of local artisans, into whose families they have married and whose grievances they share, individual members of the Gardes Françaises are living off the earnings of prostitution. Everyone can give a good account of himself, his place in a sedition that is becoming a revolution can be explained.

And yet this is not the whole story. Wine-merchants and publicans have always been law-breakers, Limousin builders' labourers have always lived on the verge of starvation, the clothing trades have long been overcrowded, seasonal labourers are always being sent home, country girls are always falling, children are always running away from cruel parents, soldiers are seldom in pay, generally marry into their own condition and supplement their income as best they can, neither boredom nor social resentment nor envy waits upon the calendar, the sponger sponges throughout the year, though the summer is a hard time for him every year, the university student becomes increasingly discontented with society as the summer months approach, while some always work hard and others do not, some people are always on the verge of starvation, some trade or other is always going through a bad patch, Kings of France nearly always have brothers and cousins, it is just part of their bad luck, it is often very cold in the winter and very hot in May, fear constantly stalks in the countryside, especially during summer nights, yearly lit up by arson. No riot has ever been completely spontaneous, while, at almost any period, at any time of the year, one trade or another will be conscious of specific grievances, so that counting heads and establishing their occupations will suggest little more than that grave-diggers or shoemakers are almost continuously in a state of agitation. Nor has anyone yet heard of a law-abiding wine merchant or of a virtuous soldier.

Yet, to take July 1789 (or May 1968), the situation was quite unprecedented, it had no parallel in the turbulent, violent history of sixteenth-century Paris (though the massacre of Saint Bartholomew's Day had, in fact, gone on for nearly a week, the killers had extended from professional Croat or Albanian slaughterers to ordinary Parisians), of the Ligue (a Parisian form of popular anarchism), or of seventeenth-century *frondeur* Paris. In the eighteenth century, save for the pro-Jansenist riots in the parish of Saint-Médard (the poorest quarter of the city, an area much given to excess of mysticism and, during the Revolution, of popular violence, an area too long habituated to the spectacle of violent, dismembered, death, thanks to the presence of the Schools of Anatomy) and the occasional *parlementaire* fracas in front of the statue of Henry IV, the population had been orderly and disciplined.

There existed, of course, 'dangerous classes', 'dangerous quarters', 'dangerous months', and 'dangerous days' as indeed in any other eighteenth-century city. But the Paris of Restif and of Mercier was in fact much less 'dangerous' than that of Sue and Balzac. The police did not need to be told to keep a wary eye on the river-workers and their women, on pedlars and all those on the move, on locksmiths, gunsmiths, ironmongers, blacksmiths, on laundresses and seamstresses and fruit sellers, on scrap merchants and old-clothes merchants, on wine merchants, publicans, *logeurs*, and prostitutes. They knew that the inhabitants of the faubourg Saint-Marceau were more violence-prone than any other, and they tended to keep out of that quarter altogether. They were aware too that Paris was surrounded by a circle of anarchical *communes*, neither town nor village, clusters of turbulent carters' inns, of hutments, of cardboard dwellings and even tents, in which dwelt an uncharted, moving population, neither townsman nor villager, but that most alarming of all species, the *faubourien*, that camped, like the Turks outside Vienna, within sight of the golden domes. These were the temporary resting places, the night spots of itinerant crime, and of those who walked, rode, and wandered for their living, of those who did not possess passports and could not be identified. They possessed no priests, no churches, no parishes and lived apart from the normal community. If ever envy, hatred, and violence were to march on the centre of the city and on the affluent quarters of the west, they would recruit their ragged armies from Saint-Marceau, from Saint-Denis, and from the disease-ridden, pestilential places on the fringe. By the end of the century, Paris was surrounded by a bannerless multitude that no doubt dreamt of anarchy, rape, pillage, and arson, and that awaited, with the patience of the utterly brutal, the signal to move, keeping up the fires of hope on the adulterated, fiery wine of the Paris region. This, at least, was what the police would expect; for things in fact appear to have turned out very differently.

There was little that the repressive authorities did not know about the location of potential violence and crime. Paris was an ordered and predictable city; the hired killer had his place in society, even if he did not actually put up a brass plate or a trade sign. One would know where to go for a professional job of this kind; and one could even take one's choice of methods of dispatch: there were those who stabbed silently, those who strangled, those who suffocated, those who battered with blunt instruments, those who drowned, those who pushed out of windows, those who used poison, those who cost a lot and those who did it almost for nothing. They did not figure in the trade almanacs, but they were always perfectly easy to find; they went to their regular cafés, boasted of their prowess, and consorted with women who flattered their brutality. They were brought in every now and then and sent to the galleys.

Paris was then, despite its size, a reassuring city in the eyes of the police. It contained dangerous elements, but it was easy to keep them in check; and it housed an army of violence, while a second encamped on its fringe. The habitually violent, like the habitually criminal, do not normally constitute a threat to the established order, of which they form a semi-recognized part. Like the police, they have a stake in society. We do not expect to find such people in the armies of revolution and in the ranks of the revolutionists. They are below, or at least outside, the bounds of social resentment; and their conservatism does not readily accept new institutions, unfamiliar authorities, and judges with unknown faces. As far as can be ascertained, few such people participated actively in the revolutionary movement at any stage, though after 1795 quite a lot of them took to the woods in the ranks of counter-revolutionary bands.

It is occasional violence that poses the problem both in contemporary terms and, above all, to the historian. Crime no doubt had its part in the events of June–July 1789, though it seems to have been circumscribed to one glorious night of pillage and rampage; and it was certainly not a student who stabbed a policeman through the heart in the course of the May riots of this year. But there was no faceless Paris underworld *à la Taine*, ready to respond to the call of some unknown Super-Criminal, of some Pied Piper of Saint-Marceau.

There remain, then, several principal problems to the mystery of the breakdown of government—for it is a mystery—and of that very, very fine line that separates a sedition from a revolutionary crisis: that of leadership, of organization, of marching orders, of a hidden élite of militancy, and—who knows?—of financial stimulus, for if a revolutionary situation cannot be bought, be contrived to order, it can certainly be helped on, maintained, encouraged, once it is under way; that of the role of boredom, of an uneasy conscience (for so many militants can be shown to have been able to afford the luxury of full-time militancy, so many of them having been of middle-class origin); that of failure, academic or social, in the genesis of a revolutionary mentality; that of unprecedented violence, of popular savagery; and finally, perhaps the most elusive, the element of accident in the development of a situation resulting in the inability of a government to carry out the primary task of government, that is to maintain order and to keep control over the weapons of repression, army, police, etc.

The problem of leadership must, unfortunately, for ever remain a mystery, at least in the June -July 1789 context (for there is abundant evidence of the predominant part played by militant minorities at the inception of the May crisis). Yet there are plenty of traces of a plan, the soldiers and N.C.O.s of the Gardes Françaises were steadily worked upon in the three weeks before 12 July, those who took up arms knew where to look for them and what to do with them; there were points of assembly, people came to the Palais-Royal both for news, for orders, for encouragement, and even for payment. People did not just march anywhere, they went to the place de Grêve, the ancient, traditional centre of popular government, they went to the Invalides, attacked the *barrières* and lynched certain officials, concentrated on the Bastille. In any riot, once it is under way, and however chaotically it begins, there is a man or a woman who stands out, pointing the way, holding an emblem, shouting a slogan. No one can identify him or her afterwards, but he or she will be remembered both by participants and onlookers. We must not discount *all* police evidence on the subject of leadership and organization, simply because it is police evidence and because the police nearly always have a thesis to prove.

The element of accident is all-important, as every succeeding revolutionary crisis in France has illustrated. The commonest cause of a riot accidentally developing into a revolutionary situation is either the over-use or the under-use of the repressive powers of Government. Force is a delicate weapon needing a very fine element of calculation in its use. The old royal authorities were well aware of this and always endeavoured to make their force as unobtrusive as possible. To deploy a regiment, to call in troops from the frontier was likely to indicate panic and would stimulate popular fears; it was also a back-handed compliment, and therefore an encouragement to the potential rioter, generally a conceited man, as well as an outraged one, and especially subject to indirect flattery of this kind if he sees himself as a full-time student revolutionist. Generally it was safer to wait upon events and, if repression were needed, to use it at night, against a small number of selected individuals. In the morning they had gone, and so had those who had arrested them. Visible force was always dangerous; it might intimidate, but equally it might make people desperate or, worse, foolhardy (especially if they had a female audience to egg them on to prove their masculinity) and when people are foolhardy, then there will be deaths, and then *anything* may happen; the spectacle of a corpse in the streets—or even of a wounded man or woman or, worse, a child, in a pool of blood—is the most fearful and convincing indictment of a régime. Also it is dangerous to identify a régime that is supposed to be mysterious, that relies on awe, mystery, and deference, with a group of soldiers (especially foreign ones, and native ones may not be reliable) or police. Hatred of the police, if not of the *gendarmerie*, is an ancient tradition in France; and the first victims of popular vengeance, at the outset of any revolutionary crisis, have been police and informers.

On the other hand, hesitation, vacillation, the delay in the use of force may simply give riot the time to organize, to move into the vacuum, assume responsibility for order, and administer its own form of terror, through direct democracy, public denunciation, and voting with a show of hands—the favourite political technique both of the *sans-culottes* and of the militants of May '68. In 1789 we have all these phenomena: too much, too visible force, then a withdrawal of force, then a threat of force that failed to materialize, finally the spectacle of the joyful impunity of riot. In July 1830 a few civilian dead brought down Charles X. In February 1848 Guizot and Louis-Philippe were overthrown in the most accidental of revolutions, though it was one that bored intellectuals like Baudelaire had been longing for for years, the greatest crime of the July Monarchy being that it was commonplace and very ordinary, and the crime of Guizot being that he had stayed in power for too long (only eight years, as compared to de Gaulle's ten). In March 1871 the Government itself deliberately provoked a revolutionary situation in order the better to repress it (much the same had happened in June 1848). In both cases repression was used on a colossal scale, and to great effect. In May 1968 the Government, by deploying too much force too brutally, created a revolutionary situation out of a students' demonstration in its inception no different from hundreds of previous students' demonstrations; and the students, in an effort to create a revolution by prolonging a revolutionary situation, and by challenging violence with violence (often of a sophisticated and well-organized kind that at first took the police by surprise, then increased their brutality), produced an effective counter-revolution, and opened the way to Reaction and to the permitted violence of Committees of Civic Action. Violence, as most of the history of France demonstrates, in the last 170 years, ultimately serves the purposes of Government. Many of the *vainqueurs de la Bastille* were shot down on the Champ de Mars, the victors of July 1830 were killed in December 1832, those of February 1848 were killed in June. After the experiment in popular rule and 'direct democracy', Thermidor. After the risings of Germinal and Prairial year III, thirty-five years of repression. After 9–11 May, 31 May. After March 1871, May 1871. Revolutionary situations do not create themselves, nor can they be sustained by the creation of more revolutionary situations; nor do they spring, fully armed, out of theory, nor do they respond to the dictates of a 'model'. Revolutionary situations are accidents, and opportunities, not ends in themselves. To suggest the contrary is to open the dangerous paths of adventurism. And revolutionaries need to do their home-work, they may even have to take examinations; Robespierre was a scholarship boy; Billaud Varenne went to a good school; it took Carnot twenty years to become a revolutionary; Robespierre marinated in over ten years of genteel poverty and social resentment in a small provincial town. By the time they became revolutionaries, most of the leaders were in their late thirties or their forties. Saint-Just was an exception, though one can see why he should have become the idol of generation after generation of *maîtres d'internat*. Vallès must often have dreamed of being a member of a Committee of Public Safety at 26. Perhaps I too am falling into the trap of historical prediction and pattern. But, in France at least, the evience does seem to suggest that violence as an end in itself generally redounds to the advantage of Government, even if the Government is a new one. And it would be hard, in historical terms, to point to an instance of a revolutionary situation arising simply by people talking about it.

In all this, there is finally the imponderable element of temperament, personality, youth, generational conflict (generational monopolism, the erection of an age group into a privileged class, the Terror of the Young against the Old constitutes perhaps the most alarming of all Terrors, even more alarming than that so ardently preached, by the steely Saint-Just, of Virtue against Vice, though Saint-Just was working for much the same thing—only the Young were entirely pure and Virtue could only be ensured by the extermination of most of those over 25), personal and social alienation, social resentment, violence as an outlet to boredom and frustration, an uneasy upper-middle-class conscience, left-wing élitism, the contempt for the past, for the common people, for scholarship, for knowledge, arrogance, conceit, and 'impossibilism'. Most of the nineteenth-century French revolutions or revolutionary outbursts were revolts against boredom and complacency, while violence was ardently stimulated by intellectuals in search of ideas and inspiration. M. de Lamartine was not the only person who became a revolutionary *pour se désennuyer*. And in May 1968 predominantly middle-class students, from the west of Paris, revolted against the complacency, the vulgarity, the conformity, and the lack of freedom of a paternalistic régime; their more militant, more theoretical leaders, self-styled *enragés*, misread the past, showing contempt for free discussion, and applying the sub-tropical experience of the present to the tarmac of the boulevard Saint-Michel. Great revolutions spring from a multitude of long-term causes; revolutionary situations can arise out of a misunderstanding, or may be sparked off by professional riot techniques. Their roots are more difficult to perceive because more accidental and faster-developing. Their results, when a revolutionary situation is enjoyed merely for its own sake, are likely to be a reinforcement of authority, with the rallying to the régime of a frightened *bourgeoisie*, of young professional couples, and of those over 30.

21 'L'Argot Ecclésiastique'[1]

Any closed society is likely to produce its own, often barbarous, inbred horseplay, its tribalistic initiation ceremonies, and, above all, its own semi-secret language. When the brutal *bizutage** of Saint-Louis, Saint-Cyr, Grignon, or Agro is safely a thing of the past, still to be evoked with sentimental nostalgia, something of the secret languages of adolescence is liable to persist, if only as a sign of recognition and mutual esteem—like a masonic handshake—and perhaps too in an effort to remain young and to combat obesity and family responsibilities. *Normaliens* will still speak of *caïmans*, of *archicubes* and of *thurnes*, when among themselves, or in the presence of the uninitiated, even if they are Ministers of State or *professeurs aux Hautes Études*; a *saumurois* of 80 will greet a surviving member of his *promotion* in the vigorous language of the young men in white gloves and heavy swords who go to bed, not alone and with their spurs on, and who, like Courteline's monocled dragoons, spend noisy evenings *chez Madame Irma*. The President of the French Republic tends, it is said, in private conversation still to relapse into the vocabulary of the pre-1914 *cyrard*.

The *séminaire* and the *presbytère* are no exception; priests, in their world somewhat apart, have to rely on one another for company, for encouragement and for assistance, much more than any professional body or trade group. There is a feeling of red-faced fraternity, of knowledge and experience shared—and denied to others—about any social occasion at which *curés* and *vicaires* come together; and it would be hard to equal the almost schoolboy gaiety of those lunches or dinners to which neighbouring priests invite one another. In the Hôtel de la Croix Blanche at Avignon everything is on a somewhat monumental scale, even the pepper-pots and the plates; its clientele consists largely of *ces Messieurs*. It is not, of course, a fantasy of advertisers that so many *digestifs* (as so many patent medicines designed to relieve indigestion) should carry the names—and often the portraits—of thickset Gallican priests, their faces reassuringly rubicund above their old-fashioned white-edged

[1] Review of Jean Follain, *Petit glossaire de l'argot ecclésiastique* (Paris, 1966).

bands; in the present glossary, the second phrase is *l'ami du clergé*, the bottle of calvados as it circulates among those in charge of souls in the lush pastures of Lower and Upper Normandy: 'Confrère, passez-moi l'Ami du Clergé'. This, like many others, is something of a private joke, *L'Ami du Clergé* being a newspaper addressed almost exclusively to the rural priesthood. And whether that most recent addition to the language of drink—*garçon, un kir!*—is in use among the Burgundian lower clergy, as well as among the general public, there is no doubt about the clerical origin of the drink itself (its inventor would be too old to qualify for the title *Ogino*, used, we are told, to designate those very rare canons nominated since the Council). In a country like rural France, where eating brings men together, *la mine couperosée* is a good image to put out; a vegetarian priest who drank water or *lolo* would make little headway among the *maqueux de Neufchâtel*. This is not to subscribe to the vulgar demagogy of *Clochermerle* or *Don Camillo* —both what French critics have described as *romans putains*. The very value of the present collection is that it represents exclusively the language in use among priests themselves.

It is a language which displays a healthy irreverence and an ability to speak of everyday priestly functions—'Grandeurs et Servitudes du Sacerdoce'—in most non-mystical terms. Irreverence towards the higher ranks—*les violets, le harem, le homard, le protozoaire*, for respectively the bishops, diocesan administration, a Cardinal (M. Follain claims to have heard a Cardinal's chauffeur explain to a young chaplain: 'J'attends mon homard')—and irreverence, mixed this time with some dislike, towards those who normally bar the way to these mighty personages; *le roquet*, for instance, designates the secretary and private chaplain of a bishop. (Outside the church it is, of course, used to describe any small dog with a loud bark.) It is reassuring to learn that priests describe as *entrer en piste* their passage from the sacristy to the altar, that *biner* is the verb used to indicate the celebration of two masses in one day, *triner* for three—there is also *binard* and *trinard*, people either to be pitied, or to be disliked for working overtime—that *faire la moisson* is used to describe a period in which a priest has a heavy load of funerals and masses for the dead. Perhaps the best of all is *extrêmiser* (to administer extreme unction). *Sucer le bonbon* is to kiss a bishop's ring. *Antibiotique* is apparently a recent (episcopal) addition to the language on the part of Mgr. Richaud: 'Savez-vous ce que chez nous gens d'église on dit des coadjuteurs: ce sont nos *antibiotiques*, ils nous prolongent.' *Entrer dans la marine*, like *l'ami du clergé*, is regional. *Le huitième sacrement* is the collection.

The French clergy clearly have much in common both with the Army and with medical students and doctors. There is a pleasantly innocent, boyish quality in the irreverence of their metaphors; we even find an old English favourite to describe a certain type of shovel hat, long since condemned, blown away by the wind of change from Rome: *la T.S.F.* Nothing could be farther removed from the carping anticlericalism of *La Calotte* or from the vulgar winks and nudges of *Le Canard* ('On sait, hein? On est au courant, hein? On connait les curetons?') with its insistence on the perfectly innocent *mon gouvernement*, *une carabasen*, both words, the latter Breton, but in general ecclesiastical usage to indicate the elderly servant of a priest. This is the language of people who are matter-of-fact about their functions and happy in their vocation and who live in close harmony with their colleagues; it is gently irreverent, never iconoclastic or displeasing; it would not have displeased Saint Vincent de Paul, whose language, one is told, 'ne manquait pas de verdeur'. It has a distinctly Gallican flavour, an ecclesiastical *bouquet de France*. M. Follain's little dictionary, which has a violet cover and is beautifully printed, carries an air of conviction, even though—and this is hardly surprising—it does not bear an *imprimatur*. It may shock the convert; it will certainly not shock the French clergy, many of whom could have greatly added to the collection. As it is, it is a welcome addition to *Le Petit Simonin* and other similar works on *argots*, *la langue verte*, and so on. The *argot* of this particular milieu might be described as *la langue violette*. M. Follain's work should be read with a kir, a benedictine, or a calvados.

Blood and Soil

22 The Memoirs of Marie Besnard[1]

Famous murder trials light up the years and give a more precise sense of period than the reigns of monarchs or the terms of office of Presidents. The year 1937, as well as being that of the *Expo* which brought Paris the doubtful gift of the Palais de Chaillot, was that of the *affaire* Weidmann, the young German who came to France, succeeded in obtaining a job as a guide to the German Pavilion, murdered five or six people, and was the last person to be publicly executed in France. The Occupation will long be associated with the trial of Georges Arnaud, accused of the murder of his father and his mother, found battered to death in a wing of their château in the south-west; it was also the foundation of the reputation of Maître Floriot as the most redoubtable counsel at the Paris Bar. The immediate post-war era, the period of the Provisional Government, belongs incontestably to the extravagant Dr. Petiot, though his activities with his private gas chamber and human-burning central heating system date to the more favourable circumstances of the Occupation; wars offer undreamt-of opportunities to mass-murderers, both on the State and on private-enterprise levels.

The Fourth Republic should go without doubt to Marie Besnard—though her final trial took place under the Fifth—*la bonne dame de Loudun*, the lady in black, accused of having poisoned by arsenic eleven, then, more modestly, five of her relatives, among them her husband, her parents, her in-laws, and various aunts and cousins, including an old lady in her ninety-second year, who, Marie not unreasonably suggested, might be taken to have died of old age. There have, it is true, been other *causes célèbres*, and other miscarriages of justice. Dr. Petiot himself claimed to have killed twenty-seven people, which puts him *hors concours*; the Dominici affair made possibly more of a stir, especially in England, in view of the eminence of the principal victim and the horror of Elizabeth

[1] Review of Marie Besnard, *The Trial of Marie Besnard*, translated by Denise Folliot (London, 1963).

Drummond's death; and at one time it was seen by the deputies of the Basses-Alpes as a threat to the Department's tourist industry. The case of Madame Chevalier aroused perhaps almost as much attention, and more sympathy—but not for the victim, who was Mayor and Deputy of Orleans and Under-Secretary of State for Health; Madame Chevalier, who had shot her husband, was acquitted. And there have been plenty of other examples of the over-eagerness displayed both by the French police and by French *juges d'instruction* and *procureurs-généraux* to secure a conviction in a murder case, at no matter what cost (including the physical and mental torture of the accused and recourse to prison informers, in an effort to produce the much-prized *aveu*). The most notorious of these was the trial of Marguerite Marty before the Perpignan *tribunal criminel*. It was largely thanks to the campaign conducted in the press by Georges Arnaud, who had himself been through the same terrible ordeal, that a retrial was eventually allowed, resulting in Mlle Marty's acquittal.

Marie Besnard stands out, however, among these pygmies, for one reason because her case went on for such an extraordinarily long time—her first trial was in 1952, her last in 1961; her imprisonment lasted from 1949 to her release on bail in 1954—for another, because so many alleged victims were involved, and, perhaps most of all, because at each of her successive trials the experts, eminent professors, pathologists, chemists, were made to look bigger fools. It was the clash of experts that caught the public fancy and there was an element, too, of macabre comedy in the journeyings to and fro across France of intestines, livers, stomach linings, gall-bladders, kidneys, bile-ducts, all finally inextricably mixed up in one another's jars—and even these multiplied, twelve left, thirteen returned—in the repeated exhumations and reburials (at the third trial there was even a scale model of Loudun cemetery, a piece of gross extravagance as Marie Besnard saw it, costing as it did 4,500 NF). There was general satisfaction at the discomfiture of the ineffable Dr. Beroud and of his unfortunate assistant, M. Médaille. It was unwise, too, to have chosen the first experts from Marseille —a place which, quite unjustly, suffers from having Fernandel as its best-known citizen and which has been only too successful in selling its own Cannebière image of itself as a manufacture for improbable stories and *galéjades*.

THE MEMOIRS OF MARIE BESNARD

At her first trial Madame Besnard had already been prejudged by an extremely hostile press campaign. Her guilt was taken for granted; on her first appearance in court, at Poitiers, she was hissed and booed, while her extremely able and devoted counsel, the late Maître Gautrat and Maître Hayot, were greeted with cries of *les Parisiens à la porte*, so strong was the current of Poitevin opinion against her. Even her appearance went against her; the fact that, like so many French peasant women, she habitually wore black—and, goodness knows, she had enough people to mourn to keep her in black for a lifetime—was taken as a sign of hypocrisy, as were her frequent references to her Dear Departed, and the cross that she wore, some felt with undue ostentation. She was short-sighted, wore large and rather thick glasses, which gave her eyes a fishy expression—*l'air glauque, le regard sournois*. She wrote with green ink. And it looked very much as if she had had an affair with a German prisoner of war who had been employed by her as a farm-hand; it was to be another ten years before official Franco-German friendship fully flowered.

In her introduction to *The Trial of Marie Besnard* Sybille Bedford suggests that such a miscarriage of justice as this long-drawn-out affair could not have occurred in England, where suspects cannot be held in prison indefinitely while the prosecution rakes up more material against them, subjecting them at the same time to every form of mental torture, and where, in murder cases, matters are conducted far more expeditiously. This may well be so; on the other hand, it was partly the very length of her affair that eventually saved the *dame en noir*. One has an uneasy feeling that, in England, and with more efficient experts—Sir Bernard Spilsbury would not have got himself into the sort of position in which the unfortunate Dr. Beroud was to find himself—she might in fact have been condemned the first time, and then hanged; and then someone else would have had to write her trial. It is unwise to use the case to score points off French justice, as compared to our own.

Here then is Marie Besnard's own account of her tribulations, told in simple, direct language, illuminated now and then by an engaging dry humour and by a considerable degree of peasant slyness, and illustrated at frequent intervals by the sort of agricultural and animal metaphors that the (former) leader of the Soviet Government favours in his public declarations, an account that has been very adequately translated in that it preserves much of the original simplicity and crispness. Marie does not believe in beating about the bush, she is crude, direct, unsentimental; with a considerable amount of rural shrewdness, she is not an educated woman, never having got beyond the *certificat d'études primaires*, and her choice of reading would be the horoscope page in *Confidences* or *Nous Deux*. She has certainly never heard of Balzac or even of her near neighbour, Hervé Bazin. In her desire to preserve the earthy, rural vigour of the original, the translator has, however, at times, misdirected her aim (for instance, 'I had decided to make a clean breast of it' is not the same thing as 'J'avais décidé de tirer la chose au clair'; and one is a bit doubtful whether 'the young man who had made her "jump the gun"' is quite the right expression for a certain situation unfortunate for girls). One can also be grateful to the translator for having resisted the prevailing mode of translating everything; the *procureur général* remains the *procureur général*, we are not served up with such horrors as 'procurator fiscal' or 'process-server'. And the governors and directresses of prisons are given the titles their *pensionnaires* reserve for them: *Monsieur chef, Madame chef*.

It is a horrible story, about horrible people (the only pleasant characters in the book are the barristers, two or three very enlightened and human prison governors and directresses, a Salvation Army official, a bishop, and some of Marie's fellow-prisoners—all of them, incidentally, townsmen and townswomen), in a horrible little market-town, the centre of a very rich farming district. The inhabitants of Loudun live off the *rentes* of their land, the *notaires* abound there. Animal health takes precedence over human health; and Marie realizes there must be something up when her sister-in-law, who lives opposite, stops feeding her chickens and rabbits (there was indeed, for she at the time was hanging from the banisters). One is reminded of *The House with Green Shutters*, of *Eugénie Grandet*, of some of Maupassant's short stories, of Hervé Bazin's account of his own dreadful childhood, a little farther to the north, in the damp, fanatical Craonnais, and, perhaps, most of all, of a remarkable film by Clouzot, one of those jewels that appeared on the dunghill that was Vichy, *Le Corbeau*, the picture of a small, inbred, airless community in the grip of a writer of anonymous letters—itself essentially a rural and feminine occupation.

Suitably enough, Marie's principal accuser, Madame Pintou, is the postmistress—a person well placed for the acquisition and diffusion of nasty gossip. But she is by no means the only *oiseau noir* in the place. Madame Besnard's other enemies, with the exception of the eccentric Massip, are mostly persons that she or her husband, Léon, had given help to, in one way or another. It is possible, of course, that *la bonne dame* may not have been particularly tactful in the manner in which she administered charity; one does not have the impression that she often did something for nothing and one can be quite sure that she would not let services rendered remain unremembered. But clearly her principal fault, in the eyes of these people, was her wealth; even more, that she apparently got richer and richer as the years went by, and that the one person to profit from each successive death, so many of which occurred in her own comfortable house, was herself. For, in her book, people are always dying, the priest and Maître Demeule, the *notaire*—this is the order Marie puts them in her book, though, in fact, it should be Maître Demeule, the *notaire*, and the priest—are always hurrying to her house, sometimes just in time, sometimes not. Marie is always sending for her mourning, on several occasions two or three days in advance (local gossip, for what it is worth, would have it that she was also in the habit of ordering the coffins in advance too, even as much as a month ahead). One way or another, we are never far from the death-bed, plates of cold soup, *pots de chambre*, vomit, death rattles, funeral dinners—both hot and cold—are the accessories of this pretty tale; more often than not, there is someone dying in the big bed upstairs, under the enormous, red, feathered quilt.

What is it all about? Money, *rentes viagères*, land, wills, houses, farms, furniture. Marie Besnard was—and, happily, is—a wealthy woman; just how wealthy, it is hard to tell. She admits to an annual income of some 400,000 francs, but this could mean anything, as it is not stated whether they are old or new ones. She admits too to owning three farms, with as many *métayers*; and there is an unspecified number of houses, including the local inn, at Loudun, and in the neighbourhood. She now has a house at Châtellerault as well, and has had her Loudun home completely redecorated since her release. Clearly she was well set up; the frequent visits of Maître Demeule—for whom there is always a bottle of Marie's best —are not merely social. Madame Besnard is constantly buying more land, *pour arrondir son bien*, she has plenty of livestock; one imagines that there would be wads of notes hidden among the sheets and linen, and a *bas de laine* of *napoléons*; there is a full larder and a groaning table; she herself was never happier than when feeding her animals, her husband, the German farm-hand and the successive ageing crones in the seventies, eighties, or nineties who, at one time or another, are declining upstairs or down.

She was clearly an excellent *ménagère*, her meringues were appreciated far and wide, and it was probably her talents as a cook that laid her open to the suggestion that she had helped her husband, her parents, her in-laws, and so on, on their way to Loudun cemetery. One would imagine that she herself was *une bonne fourchette*, and that she never lost any sleep over anything other than livestock, land, and money. Yet she is not just a hard, acquisitive peasant woman, the personification of that sordid cupidity, that brimming stinginess that the Prefects of 1812 attribute so justly to the big farmers who profit by the general calamity to make fortunes out of famine. Certainly, like most farmers, she made money during the Occupation, and she was never short of food. Yet she loves her animals, loves harvest work and the smell of the fields; in prison she was happy when she could work in the kitchen. She liked work, scrubbing, cooking, tidying up.

This is a peasant story all right, and so it is about avarice. Peasants —especially rich ones—are not nice people. French peasants are nastier than most, those from the west of France are possibly the nastiest of all, as well as being superstitious, bigoted, reactionary, and brutish. The ancestors of Marie Besnard might have fought for *Christ et Roi*, in the murderous peasant bands of Charette. Their descendants are concerned with more mundane nastinesses. For it would be difficult to imagine a more unpleasant place than Loudun, with everyone watching everyone else, the flicker of a curtain drawn aside, of a shutter suddenly banged, a woman neighbour, prying on her door-step, who suddenly disappears inside, as if in the presence of a leper, as Marie drives up (the Besnards have an old Peugeot) on her first return from prison, the endless, inane, nagging gossip at the local inn, ricks catching fire, cattle poisoned, a wing of the manor house burnt (Marie does not have much to say about this, but her neighbours do), petty affronts, accusations of theft, two young drunks shouting insults outside Marie's bedroom window. There are those who speak, and those who do not, *ceux qu'on salue, ceux qu'on ne salue pas,* those you look through and those you recognize—a constantly changing pattern of social exchanges, of visits and return visits, an existence governed by elaborate, mysterious, ancient, unspoken rules. Nothing is ever for nothing; everything has to be paid for, equalled out, so that there will be no ill feelings. Human relationships are on a strictly give-and-take basis. Léon's aunt dies; here is the scene described by Marie: 'We went to sprinkle holy water [Marie's most regular form of manual exercise]. As we left Léon said to his mother: "I did the right thing, I presume she did too." "What do you mean by that?" "Did she remember me?" "No, she's left everything to your sister and myself."

"Right, then I shan't go to the funeral" '—and they don't. After this, there is a period of no talking with the in-laws, 'saying no more than good morning . . . as we passed them . . .' and there is still a trace of resentment at the time of the old man's death: 'we were invited to the funeral dinner, a cold meal . . .'. The Besnards do not speak to Léon's sister, who lives in the house opposite. It is the same with friends: Léon and Marie become very friendly with a retired couple: 'they liked good wine, they liked drinking coffee, they got them at our house. We liked good cakes (Marie has a sweet tooth) and every Sunday, when they came to tea, they would get a fine cake from Leuroux, the best pastrycook in Loudun, and bring it with them . . .' The Besnards rent some land to Marie's cousins, the rent is three quintals; 'as we didn't need it, they used to send us a goose every year at Christmas and we were quits'.

This is the iron law, the only code that counts, save possibly one other, that is even stronger: family solidarity. Marie too accepts the common law, and, speaking of one of the prosecution witnesses, makes the following very revealing statement:

Garcin, Madame Pintou's son-in-law, . . . stuck up for her. Now he couldn't do anything else, it was his family. But before, he should have remembered how I helped him all through the war and occupation, sending him parcels of clothes and food . . .

Though, in her account, there is much talk of forgiveness, many references to the 'dear ones' looking down on her and protecting her, Marie is not altogether convincing when she drapes herself in such strenuously Christian attitudes; one can see why her ill-wishers depicted her as hypocritical. She appears indeed more concerned with the forms to be observed at death than attached to her relatives themselves, and so she is particularly outraged at the exhumations, carried out on an almost industrial scale, in Loudun cemetery; her poor Léon is dug up three times, and almost her first visit, after her final release, is to the graveyard. Here she is reassured: 'there were no traces of the damage, the grave was neat, with the chippings tidily arranged between the stone curbs and the five pearl crowns with the crucifix in the middle . . .' The family can then rest in peace. Marie, clearly, is more preoccupied with the dead than with the quick. Her relations with the Almighty are close, personal, friendly; there is no doubt that she has a powerful and watchful ally in God. 'God manages things well', she states, charitably, on the subject of one of the female Judases who had turned against her: 'three days later Pascaline was laid on her back with an attack of sciatica, not able to move . . .'. There is further evidence of divine intervention, this time against her principal enemy, Massip; the *châtelain* had left France for Tangier, after having been fined 1,200,000 francs for insulting General de Gaulle: 'See what queer coincidences there are in life', observes *la bonne Marie* gleefully, 'a coffin arrived, bearing his body to his native land!' Obviously, it does not pay to be on the wrong side. Massip is not the only one. 'Another of those who hunted me, old Toussaint', is not even allowed to have died, he 'croaked', as Marie pleasantly explains to the old boy's grandson, adding: 'Don't bother praying for him, it wouldn't be any use, he's in hell.' It is not really surprising that people found the old girl rather alarming and accused her of having the evil eye.

Like most books concerned with murder, Marie's memoirs are at times extremely funny. Sometimes the humour is unconscious, more rarely we can hear her own cracked, malicious laughter. There is a fine piece about the inmates of the Petite Roquette: 'A large, clean dormitory with twelve white, roomy beds, and I saw at once that there was a much better type of people than in the place I had come from. My companions were abortionists and women who had had abortions. They were educated and talked agreeably. . . . Number Five was for the élite, and I was lucky to be there . . .' When her sister-in-law hangs herself—and again neighbours were quick to point out that she must have been something of a gymnast to have succeeded in tying herself to the banisters—Marie goes with her husband to see the body; it is their first visit to the house on the other side of the street for years: 'My God! when I saw her I thought I'd faint. Even if you haven't much affection for someone, it's terrible to see them hanged.' But she really shared in the fun at the expense of Beroud and Médaille: 'My lawyers proved that they had mixed everything up, muscles and viscera, that they had found an eye in a skeleton. Médaille replied that they had found the eye, but they did not know in which box it had been or whose it was.' It was possibly the straying eye that saved Marie.

Even so, it is mainly with a feeling of relief that we put down this chronicle of petty nastiness, meanness, and delation. Relief for the fact that we live in a predominantly urban community, that we are reasonably safe from croaking gossip and from the attentions of those subterranean beings who write anonymous letters, relief for the fact that the word *dénonciateur* is difficult to translate into English. When all is said and done, one is tempted to exclaim: thank God the English yeomanry is dead and gone, along with stocks and ducking stools, Morris dancing, maypoles, milkmaids, *Tess*, fires burning from the beacons, and the whole nightmare band of rural Walpurgia; we have got a lot to thank the industrial revolution for. There is nowhere in England quite like Loudun; but can we be so sure that there isn't over the border?

23 The Anatomy of a Fascist[1]

Joris van Severen was the son of a well-to-do *notaire* Edmond van Severen, from Wakken, West Flanders, where he was born in July 1894. His mother, a van de Maele, came from Ghent. Both families were *fransquillons*, and Joris and his brothers were given a French education at a Jesuit college in Ghent. While still at school, he became attracted to Flemish nationalism and in the 1900s he had already established close relations with Stijn Streuvels, Modest Huys, and other leading members of the Flemish nationalist intelligentsia; the novelist of peasant Flanders visited Wakken on several occasions. By the outbreak of the First World War, van Severen was already committed, much to his father's disapproval, to the more militant manifestations of the nationalist movement. In 1916 he joined the Belgian Army as a volunteer, was promoted to second lieutenant and was near enough to action to write home about it; but having joined a secret, seditious organization, the Frontbeweging, composed of Flemish members of the Army and designed to combat the predominant influence of French as the language of command, he attracted the notice of the Intelligence section of the General Staff, was downgraded, and, along with other militants, was sent, as a private soldier, first of all to a special depot at Rouen, then to a disciplinary battalion at Parigné-l'Évêque, in the Sarthe. At the end of the war, he was demobilized as a private.

From 1921 to 1929, he was regularly elected as a deputy of the Frontpartij—an extremist Flemish group that had grown out of the clandestine wartime Frontbeweging—for West Flanders, already one of the principal strongholds of the various Flemish movements. In 1929, however, as a result of an electoral manœuvre on the part of his Catholic opponents, he lost his seat. Overnight he became a fierce opponent of parliamentary democracy, denouncing the corruption of parties and the domination of Brussels. In 1931 he formed his own militant armed organization, the Verbond van Dietsche Nationaal-solidaristen (Verdinaso), the senior members of which (*dinasos*) wore uniforms, carried arms, and underwent a

[1] Review of R. Baes, *Joris van Severen, une Âme* (Zulte, 1965).

paramilitary training; there was also a Youth Section. The Verdinaso, as well as aiming at the destruction of the unitary Belgian state and of all existing political parties, also sought to reunite the Flemish provinces of Belgium with the seven northern provinces to form a large Dutch-speaking state (Dietschland-le Pays Thiois), organized on authoritarian and corporatist lines. In this the programme of the Verdinaso was scarcely distinguishable from that of the Vlaamsch Nationaal Verbond (V.N.V.), though the latter at this time still advocated parliamentary tactics—it was represented in the Chamber; later it was to become completely identified with Collaboration. There were also personal rivalries; van Severen, who described himself as the Leider, was too authoritarian to enter even temporary alliances with an organization over which he did not have complete control.

In 1934, without any warning, the Leider completely altered the aim of his paramilitary movement. Now it was no longer a matter of destroying the Belgian state, but rather of creating a Grande Belgique composed not only of Holland and Belgian Flanders, but also the Walloon Provinces ('He generously opened his arms', writes R. Baes, 'to take in the Walloon Provinces') and Luxembourg (and even, it seems, the Dutch Empire and South Africa, for these appear on the huge maps displayed at Verdinaso *landdags*). Dietschland became the Dietsche Rijk. At the same time, branches of the movement were established in Walloon towns and van Severen's bulletin began to appear in (a form of) French. This change of front resulted in a complete break with the V.N.V., whose leaders denounced van Severen as a traitor to the Flemish cause. From about 1936 onwards the Verdinaso began to affect a demonstrative Belgian nationalism, the tricolor flag appearing alongside the emblems of the movement at the *landdags* held periodically in Antwerp, Ghent, Bruges, Malines, and even Brussels; the Leider even laid claim to Egmont and Horn—the occasion for a demonstration in Brussels—and to William the Silent (the present work is dedicated 'à l'ombre de Guillaume le Taciturne, assassiné comme Joris van Severen pour avoir voulu défendre l'intégrité des Pays Bas') and poor de Ligne ('notre cher Prince de Ligne'). At the same time, he professed a deep devotion to the dynasty and to the person of Leopold III.

After 1934 then, the Verdinaso, though undoubtedly fascist in aims, methods, organization, and slogans, could not be described as pro-German. The money seems to have come mainly from Belgian industrialists. In 1939 van Severen publicly adhered to the policy of neutrality, and early in 1940, on the occasion of the first of the invasion scares, he expressed apprehension about German aggressiveness; his followers were told to give their support to the Belgian state, should its existence be threatened. On 10 May 1940 he was arrested at his home in Bruges by the Sûreté Belge, as a result, it seems, of the personal order of the Minister of Justice; in the next few days, several Senators and the leader of the V.N.V. (who had not been arrested) intervened on his behalf with M. Pierlot, the Prime Minister, who gave them reassuring replies. Shortly afterwards, however, with a group of some sixty other suspects—Belgians, Germans, etc.—and on the initiative of a high official of the Belgian Sûreté (the author hints that he was a freemason) he was transferred, by bus, from Bruges to Dunkirk, where the passengers of the bus were handed over to the French Sûreté. They then followed a zig-zag route across northern France, in conditions of increasing chaos, till they reached Abbeville on 19 May. There the group was imprisoned for the night in a cellar under a bandstand, in a small park, where it was guarded by a French infantry unit. During the night the town was heavily bombarded. In the morning of 20 May 1940, some twenty of the prisoners were taken out and shot; these included van Severen and one of his lieutenants, the *dinaso* Jan Rijkoort. Some of the French officers responsible for their execution were tried in Amiens in 1942; but the trial was *in camera* and its findings were not made known.

During the German occupation of Belgium, a number of adherents of the Verdinaso collaborated with the Germans; some of them fought in the Flemish S.S. Legions (Vaderland, Flandria, Langemark), others joined the V.N.V. and the various paramilitary formations of Flemish extremism encouraged by the occupant. Some former *dinasos*, however, took an active part in the Resistance, claiming that they were thus best expressing the doctrines of the dead Leider. Since the war several of van Severen's former adherents have been active in the numerous, extreme-right groups that have continued to pullulate in Belgium up to the present time. The O.S.P. (Organisation du Salut Public), extreme-nationalist and royalist and very anti-'European', is (or was very recently) directed by Louis Guening, an ex-*dinaso*; on the other hand, the

virulently pan-'European' and fascist M.A.C. (Mouvement d'
Action Civique)—the Belgian branch of Jeune Europe and of the
neo-fascist International—had in 1962 as director of its Flemish
section Fred Rassaert, who has written a number of articles defending the memory of van Severen.

The Verdinaso was a movement with a few thousand adherents,
mostly drawn from the middle and lower *bourgeoisie* of the small
towns of West Flanders. It also had some support from Ghent
and Louvain students. Shunned by the Flemish peasantry, thanks
to the influence of the clergy, it had a handful of supporters in
Brussels, and virtually none in the Walloon provinces. Taking a
long view, it was more effective and better organized than Rex,
though van Severen never achieved the spectacular national success
of Degrelle. Professor Jean Stengers has described it as the most
authentically fascist and, militarily, the most threatening of the
various authoritarian organizations that developed in Belgium, on
the model of the French *ligues*, during the anti-parliamentary
hysteria of the 1930s. It seems on the other hand to have been the
object of some suspicion on the part of the Nazis, and though van
Severen frequently expressed his admiration for Mussolini, there
is no certain evidence that he received financial help from the
O.V.R.A.

Since the war the Belgian Government has never made any
effort further to elucidate the circumstances of van Severen's
arrest. A number of accounts have been published in Flemish by
survivors who were eye-witnesses of what they describe as 'Het
Bloed-bad van Abbeville'. An elaborate monument has been
erected to van Severen and his companion in Abbeville cemetery.

It would be sacrilegious to describe this new monument to van
Severen as a mere book. A human hand, it is true, has written it;
humble workmen have printed it, on the purest Flemish paper; it
did not fall from the sky in a shower of golden letters, nor emerge
from a black lake, clutched by a beautiful hand. It was printed by
Vonksteen S.A., Langemark (Belgium) and published by Éditions
Oranje, Zulte (Benelux); it was edited by Staf Vermiere, Rijks-
baan 22, Zulte-aan—Leie (Benelux). The publisher also has an
address in Wilrijk, in the Province of Antwerp (Benelux). There is
no price—how could there be? For this is no ordinary book. R.
Baes is reverently aware of the audacity of her undertaking in thus

rolling away the stone from the entry to the tomb, to reveal the martyred saint, the bullet holes, the embroidered shirt, soiled after ten days' prison wear, the initialled hat, the scented handkerchief. Her intention, she states in the preface, is, whenever possible, to step aside and allow the Master to speak in his own voice, though in the course of the work she frequently intervenes to draw attention to some particular example of goodness, devotion, or heroism. The air trembles with reverence, mysticism and organ music, the complicated harmonies of *carillons*; and we move, soft-footed and hushed, through the stained-glass penumbra, in the best fifteenth-century company—both Breughels are there, van Eyck and Memling too, and noble Flemish knights; at any moment, the Angel of the Annunciation will appear, on the arm of her creator, the Maître de Flémalle. The silence is pregnant; the Master is about to speak. And the Word, whether it comes direct from the Master, or through the recollections of the Disciple—and she must have been a very close one, for there are inventories of his shirts, handkerchiefs, socks, toothbrushes, and toothpaste—is wrapped in obscurity, reaching us in a language faintly recognizable as French. It is very hard going.

But it is well worth the effort, for, all unconsciously, the author has assembled the most convincing and complete account of the emergence of a fascist mentality since Sartre's brilliant short story, *L'Enfance d'un Chef*. It is all that the historian could desire—as complete a dossier as has ever been produced of the fascist mind: the Fascist in action, the Fascist meditating at leisure, the Fascist looking at himself in the glass, the Fascist eating and drinking, the Fascist dressing himself, the Fascist in his garden, among the 'humble flowers' and the 'ancient trees', the Fascist setting his jaws in an authoritarian *rictus*, the Fascist gargling to get rid of the taste of a non-Aryan visitor, the Fascist taking his morning exercises for his physical well-being, placing his arms and head in the position of Christ on the Cross, the Fascist taking his evening dose of Pascal, for his spiritual well-being, the Fascist cleaning his teeth, the Fascist expressing his views on women, the Fascist manicuring his hands, the Fascist acknowledging his debt to the writers of the past, the Fascist putting his people in their place, the Fascist beloved of his men, the Fascist on History, the Fascist on Destiny, the Fascist on Mother, the Fascist on the Blessed Virgin Mary, the Fascist on Ancestral Roots.

It is of no less interest because the fascist in question was markedly unsuccessful as a fascist, quarrelled with most of the other rival fascists, was quite remarkably muddle-headed—at times one feels almost sorry for him, he is such an utter ass, such a woolly bore—until one remembers that other highly successful fascists were utter asses and woolly bores.

There are, of course, many ways to fascism, and many forms of it once one gets there. Briefly, van Severen was a Flemish *maurrassien*—though, of course, without the great literary and polemical talent and culture of Maurras himself. The influence of Maurras was very considerable in Belgium between the wars, especially among the Walloon sections of the extreme right, but van Severen was the most effective exponent of the Frenchman's particular brand of authoritarian nationalism. And, like Maurras, a clerico-fascist, he was bitterly denounced by the clergy of West Flanders when, in 1934, he split with the V.N.V.

But Maurras was not the only influence, far from it; like many of the half-educated van Severen was a receptacle for every type of right-wing thought. He had an unerring flair for the obscure, the bombastic, the violent, the decadent, the studied, and the empty. It could happen, too, such was the voracity of his appetite, that works of some value, literature of some quality, might be shoved down, almost accidentally, between two helpings of gobbled, half-digested trivia, so that in his make-up he constitutes a living, hiccoughing, panting encyclopedia of right-wing thought and literature for the whole period 1900–40. It was amazing what he could take, what he could half-assimilate, chew over.

His favourite sustenance, right up to the end, was a sort of *bouillabaisse* of the French authoritarian right, in literature, the arts, and philosophy [*sic*]; the clerico-fascists, those who loved the Princes of the Church, the purple of Cardinals, and who treated their parish priests like servants, the Blood-and-Soilers, the Ancestral Influencists, the pseudo-peasants, the Back-to-the-Landers, the Super-Patriots-who-Volunteer-as-Common-Soldiers (but who somehow miss their way to the recruiting office), the Cruelty-to-Animals right (French hispanophils), the Cruelty-to-Girls right (much the same thing), the des Esseintes right, the pseudo-medical right, the Flying Superman right, the economic crackpot right, the *à bas les métèques* right: they have all been sent down, not one is left on the plate. Barrès and Péguy are, predictably, the favourites; he moans and groans over the pseudo-peasant ('Ah! Péguy!') and, on his only visit to Paris, the rue de la Sorbonne and the Invalides ('Ah! Napoléon; le grand néfaste!') are the two points of a meditatively reverent, *Ah! Ah!*-ing pilgrimage. He wants to be like Barrès and join up as a common soldier (unlike Barrès, as well as talking about it, he actually *does* it). But, equally, meditating in his garden, or on a retreat at 'Swiss Cottage'—a villa in Ostend belonging to an aunt—he fancies himself as a Flemish Saint-Exupéry, above it all, alone with sky, sun, stars, and Courage, proving himself in hazard (he has at least in common with the French Superman a total confusion of thought, as well as a violent death). He revels in the violence and indignation of poor Bernanos, and communes in the virility and cruelty of Montherlant, a fellow chevalier and a Warrior like himself. His other French masters are Massis, Maritain, Thierry-Maulnier, Bloy, Claudel, Suarès, Bainville, Georges Valois, and Alexis Carrel. But he is closest to Drieu —indeed, in the present book, one is constantly reminded of the effete nastiness of 'Gilles': the same clawing cruelty, the pseudo-aristocratic conceit, the sense of caste, the same physical narcissism. Van Severen, like 'Gilles', scents himself with 'Jicky' (by Guerlain), his shirts, of exquisite cotton, are initialled, his gold cuff-links are initialled too, his suits are dark and cut very severely in a semi-military, semi-monarchical line (he is, after all, a twentieth-century Loyola). But in his most extravagant day-dreams there are also hints of des Esseintes: here is the Leider, seated on heated tiles, being washed and sponged down and dried by semi-naked, coffee-coloured slave boys, who feed him with exotic fruit (this did not get into the programme of the Verdinaso, being reserved only for those admitted into the intimacy of the Crucje van Bourgonje, the Bruges shrine). Like the hero of *À Rebours*, the Flemish knight sleeps on a black, monklike bed in a white, cell-like room; but the sheets are of best Flemish linen, the cell is centrally heated. There is a studied decadence in the gesture of his tapering fingers.

But, for a man who frequently refers to a mystic Celtic Union between Flanders, Wales, Cornwall, and Brittany, who corresponds with the Breton separatists, who, in the words of his Disciple, possess 'une pulpe Celto-germanolatine' (this is going two better than Maurras: van Severen is God, the Son *and* the Holy Ghost), and who in a flash of light reaching him at 'Swiss Cottage' realizes that it is his destiny (or Destiny) to act as a spiritual bridge between Europe and Asia, West and East (inevitably, he makes a bee-line for Tagore), the latinized French are not enough. Van Severen feels a close affinity to Salazar. He dotes on Kipling, considers 'Land of Hope and Glory' the greatest song in the English language, listens, in reverent communion, to the broadcast of the coronation service of George VI, and likes to show off his English to his followers: 'self-control', 'clean' (meaning fascist), 'unclean' (meaning a politician, a democrat, a Bruxellois, a *métèque*, a freemason, a Protestant), 'I'm not in the mood' (not on the Swiss Cottage wavelength in personal communication with one of his political or moral advisers, his personal Brains Trust—a very cosmopolitan affair, since it includes the Virgin Mary—'There are two people I will not hear ill-spoken of, my Mother and the Virgin Mary'—Saint Ignatius, Saint Teresa of Avila, Aquinas, Joan of Arc, Pascal, Memling, a certain Guillaume de Juliers, from whom he claims descent and who also has a carnal relationship with Flanders, and van Eyck's Holy Lamb of God). He also, when 'in the mood', has communications from Ibsen, Nietzsche, and Kierkegaard. No wonder his Jesuit teachers complained of his inattention (the Chronicler adds that he was a lonely, misunderstood boy who shunned the 'cour de recréation').

There are other, more localized, ingredients, especially Streuvels; van Severen began, quite banally, like any other Flemish nationalist. He was influenced too by the Dutch historian, Pieter Geyl, who, in the 1920s, was advocating an historical version of Dietschland. Where he got the idea of the Dietsche Rijk from it would be more difficult to establish; but van Severen, *le médiéval* (as his Disciple calls him—and she adds that he had a medieval face and looked like Memling), may have had it from an ancestor who was present at the Battle of the Spurs. Each brand of fascism contains its built-in myth—Breton *menhirs*, Great Treks, Ukrainian tridents, Sviatopolk; van Severen reached his by following the meandering course of the Zwijn, the great tidal inlet that had connected Bruges to the sea, that had become silted up and had eventually disappeared, as a result of a series of great storms, in the fifteenth century. It was just the right combination of half-eaten history, pseudo-medievalism, legend, and parochialism to produce a West-Flanders fascism.

Van Severen is not interesting as a person; he was a bore and a fool, who had probably been messed up early by a doting mother. But he is interesting as a type, as a *cas témoin*. There is something very satisfying about his literary enthusiasms and cultural pretensions for, at each question put to him, the answer comes out pat; he never lets one down. He is the archetypal Fascist, in his arrogance, in his belief in an élite, and in his contempt for the common people, for 90 per cent of humanity. It is all there. Here is the adored and adoring mother who, unlike the reassuring *notaire*, takes the little ass seriously, and, instead of seeing that he gets on with his homework, encourages him in bouts of disorganized and random reading. Here is Tia, 'la servante au grand coeur', the loyal Flemish retainer, in humble admiration for the Young Gentleman, for the booted Leider, eager to welcome him to the Ancestral Home, deeply grateful for a visit to her gleaming kitchen: she is suitably rewarded, the Leider, 'effondré', his noble fifteenth-century face drawn with grief, personally attends her funeral with a *dinaso* bodyguard in full get-up.

Here is the young subaltern, adored by his men who realize in their brutish, simple way that he is not as others; when he is sent off to a disciplinary camp, after being stripped of his rank, they follow him to the station—he had ordered them not to—weep noisily (in Flemish) on the platform, and run after the train as it pulls out. The Passion has begun: Rouen, the insults, the persecution, the spittle, Walloon spittle too, or that of vulgar *fransquillons* whose French is not as good as his, Parigné-l'Évêque (Sarthe), the first of many Stations of the Cross. It will never let up. There is the Death of Mother. Vile, vulgar bureaucrats, probably from Brussels, have his poplars cut down to make way for a new road: later, he is driven from his house near Bruges; the owner wants it back as he has recently married and has small children. He is uprooted, has to leave the 'humble flowers' and a garden large enough for revolver practice. In his next place, there is no garden at all. 'Swiss Cottage' is sold. The coat of arms of the Dukes of Burgundy, which he hangs over his front door in Bruges, comes crashing down on New Year's Day, 1940; it is an omen. The Flemish clergy spread vile rumours about him, there are suggestions that the boys of his youth brigades wear shorts that are too short (they certainly are very short and very tight-fitting in the photographs). The V.N.V. fail to understand the grandeur of his vision, the significance of the Revelation—the *nieuwe marschrighting*—of 1934 (though in May 1940 their leader intervenes in his favour). Something terrible happens while he is deputy: it is only hinted at, but it seems that while making a speech in the Chamber, he was *laughed* at. Socialists! While in prison in May 1940 the vile gaoler laces his soup with spittle (it has all happened *before*!).

Like the Natural Aristocrat he is, he *vouvoie*'s his Mother and expresses his 'hatred of mediocrity'. The Ideal he pursues is 'invisible aux masses', the world is divided between 'les médiocres et l'élite'; he despises democracy, because it appeals to 'les valeurs basses du peuple'. He holds in horror 'disorder and humanitarianism'. Women are an inferior breed, at best a physical reward for the Returning Warrior. Even then, they had better take care to be properly scrubbed and clean, to keep their traps shut, to be respectful but undemonstrative ('j'ai horreur des femmes qui donnent des baisers en public'). In any case, having carnal relations with Flanders, there would probably not be much left for mere women. There was no female branch of the Movement.

He was a Cold Shower Fascist; his voice was commanding and clipped: once he had spoken, one could only salute and execute a smart about-turn. He wore a uniform, not out of any sense of vanity, but because it was 'la carapace de sa pensée'. He was anti-semitic, speaking of 'le juif Benda'. He thought in Capitals: Order, Discipline, Soul, Tradition, History, Mother (but not Father). He thought in *Gothic* capitals. His programmes—in letters three feet high—are repetitive incantations—*Dietschland en Orde, Dietsche Rijk, Dietsche Rijk, Dietsche Rijk.*

He was a very small man—five foot two or thereabouts. But thanks to all the usual paraphernalia of Fascism—platforms decked in black, covered with emblems, lighting, chin up, the dedicated head, the military stance—thanks to a uniform that included a peaked cap the height of those worn by oyster salesmen on the Paris boulevards—he was able to make himself look taut, severe, brooding, and fateful. Thanks to the mirror exercises, he had acquired the full range of fascist expressions; his smile was reserved for Mother, the Virgin, and, so she says breathlessly, the Author. The photographs of the vast meetings of the Verdinaso are pure fascist: the dark uniforms, boots, belts, legs wide apart, torches, fanatical, staring eyes, the idiot faces, drums and tasselled trumpets, black and yellow flags, the Leider handing a flagged lance to a 13-year-old boy, faces gleaming in the light of torches; this is a fascism as integral as Rex, as the Flemish S.S. Legions, and as the yearly gatherings at Dixmude.

He trained and drilled his gunmen to violence, fed them on hate, persuaded them that they represented an élite, that the rest of the world were *Untermenschen*. He sought to crush Belgian democracy by force. The sheer inanity of the present book should not make us lose sight of what it is about, what its purpose is. Van Severen was not very successful; for that we must thank the common sense of the countrymen that he so despised. The Antwerp docker, the Borinage miner, the Brussels tram-driver, the *cheminot*, Flemish or Walloon, of the C.F.B., the student from U.L.B. (Université Libre de Bruxelles) and Liège were *not* impressed; Bruges should be remembered for Achille van Acker, not for this seedy Knight. That he was ultimately shot by the French was largely accidental. At least it deprived him of the opportunity of giving his full measure as a fascist. R. Baes is attempting to rehabilitate one of the dark figures of pre-war fascism; she is not very successful either; even so, one hopes that this ridiculous book will be widely read outside Belgium, for it would be difficult to find a record more representative in its range of the puerility, the emptiness, the idiocy, and the arrogance of the fascist mind.

[Letters followed from MM. Staf van Velthoven and Guido Eeckels (24 November 1966).]

Appendix: Republic of Vices[1]

This is both less pretentious and more interesting than the authors'
previous volume of their *de luxe* history of the French Revolution
reviewed in this journal on 8 September 1966. It is also much
easier to understand, most of the text this time being in French,
with only an occasional lapse into *Nouvel-Observateur*. Several old
favourites turn up again: 'le *dérapage* des frontières naturelles' (but
not, this time, as a chapter heading), 'désacraliser' gets one mention,
and, in lieu of 'le mental collectif', we have to make do with 'la
précocité du mental par rapport à l'économique'. The authors still
favour standing-up and lying-down metaphors ('La nouvelle
société se couche dans le lit des duchesses et des princes') and, just
in case the reader begins to take things too easily, he is suddenly
faced with a sentence such as: 'plus sérieux est le reproche de
l'inadéquation au réel'. But there are some effective verbal fireworks as well: what an excellent comment, for instance, on the
Thermidorian ruling class is the authors' happy phrase: 'Les
honnêtes gens ne sont pas toujours des gens honnêtes'. There are
fewer sexual interpretations of events; sex, in this volume, is kept
in its place, albeit a large one in a period devoted so ostentatiously
to pleasure: the bed, the salon, the café, the gambling house, the
milliner's shop, the arcade, the boulevard, the street, the park, the
wood.

As a history of French society between 9 thermidor and 18
brumaire, their account is up-to-date, intelligent, and often
extremely perceptive. M. Furet and M. Richet are less concerned
to score points off previous historians—possibly because, for this
neglected period, there are fewer historians to score points off—
and more concerned to get on with their narrative. Hence the
absence of *on* ('on a prétendu', 'on a décrit', 'on a eu tendance à',
etc.). They are excellent on the famine of 1795–6, on the persistence
of banditry in many areas, on the location and spread of the White
Terror, on habits, tastes, pastimes, and everyday life. Their

[1] Review of François Furet and Denis Richet, *La Révolution du 9-Thermidor
au 18-Brumaire* (Paris, 1966).

307

description of the various Jacobin movements outside France is detailed, without being boring or repetitive. The account of Paris society under the Directory is eloquent and, in its description of vice, almost as joyful as those who indulged. There is an interesting section on the triumph of the Rive Droite, the development of the Chaussée d'Antin and the consequent increasing segregation of the Paris poor in the quarters of the north-east, east, and south-east. The authors are perhaps best of all on education, an overriding preoccupation with a régime dominated as much by scholars and great teachers as by speculators, *enrichis*, and generals.

All these themes are brought into dramatic relief by admirably chosen illustrations that give the full impact of the change of tone of a period less concerned with allegoric figures, *la trompette guerrière*, and with propaganda, and more with the pleasures, miseries, and vices of the private individual. Thermidor and the Directory were periods both cruel and selfish; but they were honest at least in their awareness of corruption and in the brutality of their self-analysis. Prints like 'Le Sérail', 'Le Muscadin', 'Le Petit Coblentz'—Isabey's strange, semi-aquatic, figures of conceit and pride of caste, held up by monumental chokers, airing themselves on the Grands Boulevards (*le flirt, la 'bouillotte'*)—are both frank and elegant portrayals of glass-fronted vice and indulgent comments on the social assumptions of a permissive period. When and where, one asks, faced with the slightly drooping ladies of 'Le Sérail', beplumed and with breasts dribbling invitingly over the top of Grecian bodices, their hair in contrived disorder falling into suggestive ringlets, their expressions perhaps slightly jaded but still willing, if not *eager*, can vice have been more attractive, more easily accessible, and cheaper? (It was even available for paper money.) In so many ways, these illustrations suggest, Thermidor and what followed must have represented the revenge both of gilded youth—and *how* he dressed up and paraded!—and of vicious old age, helped on with pretty pink beverages and its gaze magnified by a battery of *faces à main* and spectacles, on the puritanical middle-aged groups—the thirties and forties—who had attempted to set up the Republic of Virtues.

Decaying vice was not the only thing to get back into its own during those years. There is a bizarrely dreamlike print of the returning *émigré*, in tattered coat and breeches holed—*l'habit à la française* though—walking down a poplar-lined, unevenly paved avenue, his nose in the air, his eyelids haughtily lowered, his hand poised on a long, decorative stick, his other hand in his embroidered, heavily patched waistcoat—heading for whatever remains of his estate, the very picture of pride of birth; clearly he at least has learnt nothing. Nor are the illustrations one-sided; plenty show what the period meant, in terms of misery and humiliation, for the common people. Perhaps wretchedness and rags have never been represented in such delicate shades—blues, lilacs, sepias, pinks— as in the generally anonymous aquatints of 1795 onwards. Even the horrors of Cayenne acquire a decorative quality. Grown men carry the mask of vice; but often too they have the faces of choirboys and eighteenth-century cherubs. One of the many merits of this illustrated volume is to remind one of the gulf of taste that separates the Directory from the physically and morally hideous régime that followed the 18 brumaire. The costumes of the Directors are quaint, but decorative; they are not ridiculous and vulgar, like those of the *Sacre*. The Directory could illustrate greed, insolence, gambling, depravity, and misery, tastefully.

The authors are not quite fair on Barère when they write that he was deported, together with Billaud and Collot; Barère was not that sort of person. He got, it is true, as far as Lorient, but he did not get on the boat when it sailed. Nor are they quite fair on Dr. Sydenham, when they call him 'an American historian'. He is English, and has not yet been drained away.

Glossary

bizutage—ragging, particularly of new boys at a *lycée* or in one of the Grandes Écoles. La Borda, the French naval academy at Brest, enjoys a particularly brutal reputation in this respect.

bleu—a recruit.

boîte à bachot—a crammer's, particularly for those who have failed the *baccalauréat* at the first attempt.

brocanteur—a second-hand furniture dealer. Their favourite haunt, until it became fashionable, was the Puces at the Porte de Clignancourt and Saint-Ouen.

brocheuse—a mender of old clothes.

cacique—someone highly placed in the university hierarchy.

cadastre—a land survey.

canut—a silk-worker of the Croix-Rousse in Lyon.

casanier—a stay-at-home.

chiffonnier, -ière—a rag-and-bone merchant. Both male and female were notorious for their brutality.

cours prévôtales—courts-martial set up early in the Restoration to try adherents of the previous régime.

décrotteur—a shoe-shine boy.

exempt—a member of the urban police under the Lieutenant Criminel during the *ancien régime*.

fressure—a butcher's term for offal.

fripier—an old-clothes merchant.

guinguette—an inn on the outskirts of Paris at which it was possible to eat, drink, and dance outside.

Lillot—Parisian slang for an inhabitant of Lille.

mégère—a harpy.

miquelet—a member of a royalist murder gang.

revendeuse—a woman who sells stolen clothes after having altered them to make them unrecognizable.

richérisme—a form of Catholic congregationalism, by which the lower clergy sought to be self-elected rather than appointed by the bishop. Named after the Abbé Richer.

tubard, -e—Parisian slang for a tubercular man, woman.

verdets—a nickname for members of royalist murder gangs, alluding to the green sprigs they wore on their hats or uniforms as a means of identification.

Index

anabaptists, 131
André, d', 187, 190, 191
Angers, 116, **158–67**
Antraigues, Comte d', **176–83**, 200, 254
Aragon, Louis, 259, 260, 262, 265
Archives de la Guerre, *see* Vincennes
Archives de la Police, *see* Paris
Archives Nationales, *see* Paris
Ardèche, Department of, 177, 193
Arnaud, Georges, 238, 287, 288
Auge, le Pays-d', 111
Aulard, Alphonse, 89
Avignon, 192, 197, 203, 282

Baehrel, René, 90
Baes, R., **296–306**
Barrès, Maurice, 301, 302
Bas-Poitou, le, 111
Bastille, vainqueurs de la, *see* Paris
Baudelaire, Charles, 217, 218
Bayeux, 24–5, 48
Bazin, Hervé, 19, 239, 290
Bedford, Sybille, 289
Belleville, 5, 234
Benda, Julien, 305
Benda, Kalman, 103
Béraud, Henri, 10, 18
Bernard, Marc, 18, 216
Berr, Henri, 90
Berteaux, Maurice, 24 n. 1
Besnard, Marie, **287–95**
Blanc, Julien, 19, 243
Bloch, Marc, 85
Bouches-du-Rhône, Department of, 177, 192–5, 197, 199
Braibant, Charles, **236–41**
Braudel, Fernand, 76, 91
Breteuil, Baron de, 179, 273
Brie-Comte-Robert, 54, 129
Brinton, Crane, 271
Brune, Maréchal, 192
Bruxelles, *see* Ixelles

Cadroy (*représentant*), 107, 110

Cagayous, 241 n. 1
Cagoule, la, 180
Caillaux, Joseph, 212, 240
calvados, 283, 284
camelots du Roi, 259
canuts, 9
Cardijn, Cardinal, 27
Carency, Prince de, 189
Caron, Pierre, 14, 73, 78
Carrier, Jean-Baptiste, 160
Cartouche, 109
Caute, David, **256–66**, 271
Céline, Louis-Ferdinand, 253
Cendrars, Blaise, 19, 259
Charenton, 67, 154, 158, 218
Charolais, le, 111
Chaumié, Jacqueline, **176–83**
Chevalier, Louis, iv, xiii, 8, 18, 70, 80, 99
Chiappe, Jean, 54
Choudieu, Pierre, 117, 160
Chouette, la, 225
Cobban, Alfred, 107
comités révolutionnaires, *see* Paris
Coppée, François, 2
correctionelles, *see* Paris
Coty, René, 60
Courteline, Georges, 251, 282
Couthon, Georges, 13, 81
Crouzet, François, 98

Dabit, Eugène, 18
Daladier, Édouard, 21
Danton, Jacques, 96 n. 3, 100 n. 1
Darien, Georges, 242–55
Daumier, Honoré, 218
Déat, Marcel, 22
Degrelle, Léon, 299
Dentz, General, 39
Despomelles, 180, 182
Destrem, Hugues, 194–5
Didier conspiracy, 194
Dominici, *l'affaire*, 287
Dommanget, Maurice, 168, 169, 175
Doriot, Jacques, 54

313